THE · MACDONALD · ENCYCLOPEDIA · OF

Mammals

Luigi Boitani
and Stefania Bartoli

Macdonald

Edited by Sydney Anderson

The publishers would like to thank the following Austra-
lian institutions for their assistance: Adelaide Zoo; the
Cleland Conservation Park, Starling; Victor Harbor's
Urimbissa Fauna Park; Melbourne Zoo; the Sir Colin
Mackenzie Fauna Park, Healesville; the Taronga Zoo,
Sydney; the Western Plains Zoo, Dubbo; the Tidbindilla
Nature Reserve (Australian Capital Territory); the Lone
Pine Koala Sanctuary, Brisbane; and Mr S. J. Cowling
of the Fisheries and Wildlife Division, Melbourne. Our
thanks are also extended to the Rice Creek Biological
Field Station (USA).

A **Macdonald** BOOK

© 1982 Arnoldo Mondadori Editore S.p.A., Milan
© 1983 in the English translation
   Arnoldo Mondadori Editore S.p.A., Milan

Translated by Simon Pleasance

First published in Great Britain in 1986
by Macdonald & Co (Publishers) Ltd
London & Sydney

A member of BPCC plc

British Library Cataloguing in Publication Data

Macdonald encyclopedia of mammals.
   1. Mammals — Dictionaries
   I. Anderson, Sydney
   599'.003'21   QL701.2

   ISBN 0-356-12422-3

Printed and bound in Italy
by Officine Grafiche A. Mondadori Editore, Verona

Macdonald & Co (Publishers) Ltd
Greater London House
Hampstead Road
London NW1 7QX

THE · MACDONALD · ENCYCLOPEDIA · OF

Mammals

CONTENTS

KEY TO SYMBOLS

Habitat   Though many species occupy two or more types of habitat in nature, the usual or preferred habitat of each species is shown by one of the following symbols:

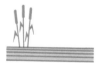

desert

grassland, plain, prairie, steppe, scrub

savanna

evergreen broadleaf woodland

deciduous forest

coniferous forest

tundra and ice

swamp, marshland

tropical or subtropical forest

rivers and lakes, estuaries

seas and oceans

high rocky slopes, upland meadows

Maps indicate approximate distribution of species within their appropriate habitats.

Color of map indicates abundance or rarity of each species, based upon the *Red Data Book* of the International Union for the Conservation of Nature and other current literature, and is shown as follows:

Red: threatened with extinction

White: rare

Yellow: endangered

Green: common or not endangered

Gray: status underdetermined

NOTES ON SPECIES ENTRIES

The scientific, or Latin, name is stated for each species, followed by common or vernacular name(s) most often used.

Classification indicates the order and family of each species and follows the taxonomy usually employed today. Variations in nomenclature are given for clarity in certain cases.

Description generally refers to average-size specimens, except where a range of measurements is given or records of exceptional specimens are noted.

Distribution supplements that shown on the map and applies to the entire species.

Habitat is described for each species in more detail than can be indicated by the symbol.

Behavior covers habits, reproduction, economic importance, or other data on the natural history of each species.

Notes of general interest are sometimes included.

THE VARIETY OF MAMMALS

Mammals are the most diversified of all creatures living on earth today. They range from minute shrews to gigantic whales. The blue whale is the largest living mammal; a species of tiny bat from Thailand is the smallest. In addition, the variety of shapes, coloration, and behavioral patterns of mammals is greater than in most other animal classes. Mammals have colonized every environment. They have mastered the techniques of swimming and burrowing, and have achieved true flight. They live in equatorial and polar regions alike, and feed on whatever food resources are available. There is no doubt that they have taken on a predominant role. Perhaps surprisingly, there are not many mammals—approximately 4,000 species, compared with about 7,500 species of reptiles and amphibians or 8,600 species of birds. Mammals represent a very advanced stage in the long process of animal evolution: the complexity—physiological and behavioral—of an organism such as a mammal is unmatched by that of any other animal. Over relatively short periods of geologic time, when compared with the long periods needed by other animal classes, mammals have assumed widely varied ecological roles, taking over from more ancient forms of animal life.

We ourselves—that is, mankind (*Homo sapiens*)—are also mammals and naturally share with other mammalian families our complex anatomy and physiology, as well as much in our behavioral patterns. And precisely because of his natural affinity with other mammals, man has selected from them those animals which are now his closest companions, such as the domestic dog and cat. A variety of species have taught us about ourselves through observation and scientific experimentation. Man has also destroyed countless fellow mammals under the banner of "sport." And finally, mammals have found themselves burdened with the task of providing man with his major food resources. Human progress has often been at the expense of our fellow mammals. It is thus quite natural that we should have a special regard for these creatures.

Many mammals are not readily seen in the daytime, nor are they easy to observe and study. A number of species are known only from specimens lodged in museum cabinets; we have no knowledge of their lives. Many mammals have only a neutral coloration, and so fail to attract the notice of laymen. The result is that most of us are acquainted only with the striking or sensational species, and it is left to the specialists to fill in the gaps in our information bank. Before we discuss the structure of a mammal and its classification, let us first see how these animals came into being.

THE ORIGIN AND EVOLUTION OF MAMMALS

The origin of the first mammals dates back to evolutionary efforts made by certain reptiles about 250 million years ago. Mammals, like birds, owe their presence on earth to the remarkable range of forms that reptiles displayed for literally

Mammals display a wide versatility, and have adapted to virtually all habitats on land and in the sea.

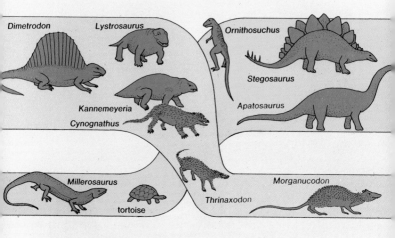

Dimetrodon
Lystrosaurus
Ornithosuchus
Stegosaurus
Kannemeyeria
Apatosaurus
Cynognathus
Millerosaurus
Morganucodon
tortoise
Thrinaxodon

millions of years. The Permian period began 270 to 280 million years ago. It was to last for 45 to 55 million years and was characterized by upheavals in the earth's crust, glaciations, and cold, wet climates. The earth's land was still in the form of two large continents, Laurasia in the Northern Hemisphere (including North America and Eurasia without peninsular India) and Gondwanaland in the Southern Hemisphere (combining South America, Africa, peninsular India, Antarctica, Australia, and New Zealand). During this period there was a proliferation of the most varied forms of insects, and this was possibly to have a decisive effect on the structure of the first mammals. In fact, the Permian period saw the first development of characteristics that later became mammalian. These were in the synapsids, or "mammal-like" reptiles. The most plausible theory today maintains that such small and medium-sized reptiles evolved certain characteristics which enabled them to occupy a new and rich ecological niche, revolving around the exploitation of those new and plentiful insects and of small nocturnal vertebrates, which hid by day from the large predatory reptiles. One of these reptiles evolving in the direction of mammals was *Dimetrodon*. This creature, whose fossil remains are found in Texas, was about 10 feet long and weighed almost 550 pounds. Like other reptiles, it was ectothermic—that is, its body temperature depended on heat absorbed from the surrounding environment. Its activity was thus closely linked with the outside temperature. *Dimetrodon* had an enormous sail-like crest on its back, extending from head to tail. This crest

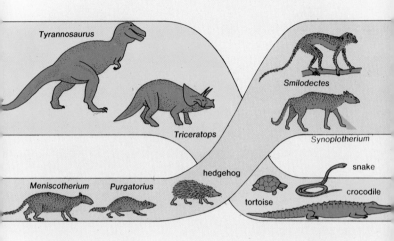

may have enabled it to absorb heat rapidly and thereby raise its own body temperature in a much shorter time than that required by other reptiles. In addition, by means of a mechanism to control its peripheral circulation, *Dimetrodon* might delay dissipation of the heat accumulated. Thus we see the first step toward the evolution of homeothermy, or the ability to maintain a constant body temperature.

Other synapsid reptiles of small and medium size evolved toward forms more closely resembling mammals. Compared with the large carnivorous reptiles, their small size helped them considerably because they could warm themselves up in a shorter time. They, too, fed on insects. There was then a transition from the Synapsida to more specialized forms known as the Therapsida. These advanced mammal-like reptiles, such as *Cynognathus,* a dog-sized predatory carnivore with teeth quite akin to those of true mammals, and the probably herbivorous *Kannemeyeria,* with a beaklike proboscis, appeared in the early part of the Triassic period, some 220 million years ago. Their gait was more mammalian than reptilian. They could move along swiftly on their four legs with their body raised above the ground. But the Triassic was also the period when other reptiles enjoyed an unequaled evolutionary gain. This was the birth of the Age of Dinosaurs. As large dinosaurs multiplied, almost all the synapsids and therapsids disappeared, with the exception of just a few survivors that were gradually evolving toward the first true mammals.

During the Jurassic period, 190 to 136 million years ago, with

Dimetrodon, *a mammal-like reptile, had a large crest on its back, which may have helped the animal to absorb or dissipate heat and thereby partially control its own body temperature.*

Dimetrodon, *a mammal-like reptile, had a large crest on its back, which may have helped the animal to absorb or dissipate heat and thereby partially control its own body temperature.*

the reign of the mighty dinosaurs, early mammals had to be content with crumbs when it came to sharing the earth's resources. Thus they stayed in the form of small nocturnal animals with little ecological significance. The dinosaurs and great flying pterosaurs continued to dominate throughout the Jurassic and the Cretaceous period that followed, 136 to 65 million years ago. But by the mid-Cretaceous, the archaic mammals had split into two distinct groups. These were the marsupials, primitive relatives of today's North American opossum, and the placentals, which in their earliest forms were similar to modern shrews and hedgehogs. Toward the end of the Cretaceous the evolution of mammals got a boost in preparation for that veritable explosion of different forms which marks the following period. The Cretaceous saw the appearance of *Purgatorius*, a very ancient primate that lived in North America and resembled present-day tree shrews.

Some 65 million years ago saw the opening of the Tertiary period. Almost all the large reptiles which had ruled the world for more than 100 million years became extinct. In a relatively short time the earth's fauna underwent radical changes. We do not know why the dinosaurs became extinct; the currently favored hypothesis is based on the notion of far-reaching climatic changes which these specialized reptiles could not long endure. We call the Tertiary the Age of Mammals, for it was they who then dominated while the remaining reptiles were relegated to a secondary role. The well-adapted homeothermic mammals, with their high mobility, more complex brain, and

In (1) reptiles the mandible, or lower jaw, is articulated with the cranium by means of two bones, the quadrate and the articular, whereas in (2) mammals these two small bones have shifted inside the middle ear to form the incus and the stapes (or stirrup bone), which, together with the malleus, direct the vibrations of the tympanum (the eardrum) to the inner ear.

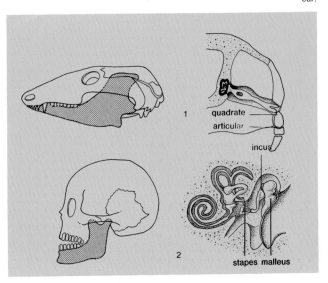

efficient system of rearing their young, had definite advantages when it came to filling the vacancies left by the great reptiles. The Tertiary is divided into seven epochs, corresponding to phases in the evolution of the mammal fauna and marked by different climatic and geologic events.

The first epoch, the Paleocene, lasted from 65 to 53 million years ago, when tropical and temperate climates became widespread and thus prepared the environment for new animal forms. The most primitive ungulates—browsing herbivores—appeared then. These condylarths, such as *Meniscotherium*, became common. They gave rise to a wide variety of hoofed mammals. Other Paleocene mammals remained substantially the same as those of the Cretaceous period; the few innovations included primitive armadillos in South America and the earliest tree-dwelling primates.

From 53 to 37 million years ago the Eocene epoch saw the globe somewhat as it is today. The vast northern and southern land masses had already broken up. North and South America were separated from one another as were Europe, Africa, and Asia; Australia and Antarctica were also separate continents. Although there were glaciers in some montane regions, such as western North America, tropical and temperate conditions prevailed as in the Paleocene. Besides marsupials, almost all the principal orders of land-dwelling placental mammals had now made their appearance. A group known as the Creodonta flourished. They were rat-size to dog-size carnivorous creatures, somewhat squat, with heavy limbs, and gave rise to the vast array of today's carnivores. Whales also appeared in the Eocene, represented by *Zeuglodon*, 60 feet in length with a very long tail. Among the land-dwelling creatures was *Uintatherium*, so called because its fossil remains were first found in the Uinta mountains of Utah. This grotesque animal, as large as a rhinoceros, bore six horns on its elongated head, had two stout tusks, and was herbivorous. The forerunners of rhinos, tapirs, pigs, and cattle also arose in the Eocene, as did the ancestors of the elephants, then trunkless, which originated in Africa. This period likewise saw the arrival of the first precursor of the horse. This was *Hyracotherium*, or eohippus, the "dawn horse," which had four toes on its front feet and three on its hind feet, and was the size of a small dog. An Eocene skeleton of *Icaronycteris*, the oldest known bat, was found in Wyoming. Primitive primates——ancestors of the monkeys and apes yet to evolve——were widespread. These small, agile creatures gave rise to arboreal lemurs, lorises, and tarsiers. As we draw closer to present times and enter the Oligocene, 37 to 26 million years ago, we find many Eocene mammals being replaced by the ancestors of modern forms. Bats became diversified; elephants, still small, developed short trunks and bore four tusks. The little "dawn horse" was succeeded by its slightly larger descendant *Mesohippus*. The giant, hornless rhinoceros, *Baluchitherium*, lived in Asia during the Oligocene. It was the largest land mammal ever known, standing 16 to 18 feet high at the shoulders, and probably ate leaves. Even-toed ungulates, herbivorous animals having a pair of toes on each foot, became abundant. They included primitive camels in North America, ancestral deer, and many piglike and hippolike forms. Carnivores such as the forerunners of modern dogs, cats, bears, and the hyena preyed upon the Oligocene fauna; many of the prey doubtless were rodents and rabbits, similar to their present-day descendants.

The Age of Mammals reached its zenith in the Miocene epoch, 26 to 5 million years ago. It was a time of geologic and climatic upheaval, when the massive Himalayan and Alpine ranges were formed and the continents assumed dimensions similar to those of today. Tropical climates gave way to temperate, resulting in vast dry grasslands, or prairies, and even deserts. Great herds of herbivores spread through the woods and plains. There were now different sorts of horses, and there were rhinoceroses, giraffes, the first deer to wear antlers, giant pigs, cattle, camels, and antelopes displaying three or four horns, often in weird shapes. Elephants evolved into several types, had grown in size, and with many other species invaded new lands at a time when Europe was joined with Asia as well as with North Africa and North America, as a result of both land movements and changes in ocean depth. Just as the immense grasslands provided sustenance for the numerous species of grazing mammals, so too those creatures were themselves a food source for many carnivores——ancestral dogs, civet cats, bears and others. Foremost among them were small but effective sabertooth cats.

Diverse species of mammals declined during the subsequent Pliocene (5 to 1.8 million years ago) and Pleistocene (1.8 mil-

In the Cretaceous period, when mammals were beginning to develop, marsupials and placentals split into separate groups. The murine opossum (Marmosa) and the white-toothed shrew (Crocidura) are present-day examples of these groups.

lion to 10 thousand years ago) epochs. Primates, however, continued their adaptive radiation. It was in east Africa that the primates displayed those most interesting modifications that led to the first humans. Possibly the first creature leading directly to man was *Ramapithecus,* a Miocene ape that died out in Asia but survived in Africa. And it is the appearance of these primates that marked the beginning of the decline of mammals and ushered in the Pleistocene, in which we see the rise of man and the disappearance of many mammal species. These extinctions were caused mainly by the very harsh glacial conditions which four times prevailed over the northern third of the earth's surface. The last glaciation began to retreat northward about 10,000 years ago—at the close of the Pleistocene—and is still retreating. Only those species which could adapt to such a climate managed to survive—as did, for example, the woolly mammoth with its shaggy coat and heavy layer of fat. During the Pleistocene, however, mammalian evolution no longer continued in the direction of sophisticated specialization of different species, as had occurred in the Miocene, but rather pushed toward a smaller number of species that could adapt more satisfactorily to a changing environment—in other words, less specialized species. The birth and rise of man is the best example of this new strategy of adaptation. It was only in Africa that mammals continued to live as they had done for millions of years, and in fact the present-day African savanna is a typical Miocene setting. From ancient *Ramapithecus* and perhaps Pleistocene *Australopithecus,* via *Homo erectus*—who lived from 1.5 million to 300,000 years ago—we ultimately emerged as *Homo sapiens* some 100,000 years ago.

DISTRIBUTION

The mammals we see today, and *where* we find them, are results of a complicated process involving the formation and extinction of species, movements and migrations, and competition and balance between species. It is mandatory that a species disperse if it is to survive. Young animals move away from the home territory of their parents and establish their own home range in an area that may satisfy their needs. Such a move could be a few feet; it could be miles. The pressure of increasing populations forces a species to spread over ever-widening areas, so that in time it may occupy an entire region and have adapted to a variety of living conditions, or produced descendant species that have so adapted.

The capability for such dispersal depends upon a number of factors. Large, highly mobile mammals and those that fly can disperse over a greater distance than burrowers. The animals' tolerance for different environmental conditions is also important. If a prairie dweller, for example, can exist in wooded country, it may disperse farther from its origin than a species that cannot survive outside the grasslands. And finally, natural barriers impede dispersal. Such barriers may be rivers, lakes or seas, mountain ranges, different climates, or zones of different vegetation.

North America and Eurasia appear to be major centers where certain families of mammals originated; other families first appear in South America and Africa. Migrations of species must have occurred, and such movements could take place only when and where natural routes existed. A considerable exchange of fauna between Asia and Europe could be expected when the two continents were joined; a significant, though lesser, exchange would occur across land bridges only occasionally connecting continents, as between Siberia and Alaska; and very few land mammals would make it across an ocean to populate islands, perhaps by means of floating debris. For example, one species of bat was the only land mammal to reach Hawaii without the intervention of man.

Thus geologic changes and the dispersal process have contributed to the evolution of species and helped create today's picture of the earth's fauna. To put it simply, the fauna of each region in the world consists of descendant species whose ancestors came to the area in different periods, by different means, and from various regions.

The modern science concerned with the distribution of animal life is zoogeography. One of the cornerstones in this field was laid just over a century ago by the great English naturalist Alfred Russel Wallace, the codiscoverer, with Charles Darwin, of the principle of natural selection. In what Wallace himself considered his "most important scientific work," he delineated the six faunal realms into which the earth could be divided. Zoogeographers still use Wallace's divisions, which are:

Ethiopian Region. Embraces southern Arabia, Madagascar, and Africa north to the Atlas Mountains, but excluding the coastal strip north of the Sahara.

Oriental Region. Includes tropical Asia—that is, India, Indo-china and southern China, Malaya, the Philippines, and Indonesia east to an imaginary line approximately between Borneo and Celebes, and between Java and Lombok.

Palearctic Region. Made up of Africa north of the Sahara and the whole of Eurasia, except the Indian subcontinent and southeast Asia.

Nearctic Region. Constitutes the whole of North America north of the tropics in Mexico.

Neotropical Region. Embraces all the New World southward from tropical Mexico.

Australian Region. Includes Australia with Tasmania, New Guinea, Celebes, and the small islands of Indonesia east of Borneo.

When taken together, the Nearctic and Palearctic are termed the *Holarctic Region.* The world's oceans can be taken as an added *Oceanic Region.* There are no native land mammals inhabiting Antarctica.

The Ethiopian Region is joined to the Palearctic by Egypt and the Sinai Peninsula. It is composed of the most varied environments, from deserts to tropical forests, tundra to savanna. Because of this variety of habitats the fauna is also diversified. No fewer than 14 families of mammals are endemic to this region. Nearly all the genera of antelope are too. Two genera of great apes—the gorilla and the chimpanzee—are African, as is the

The zoogeographical regions

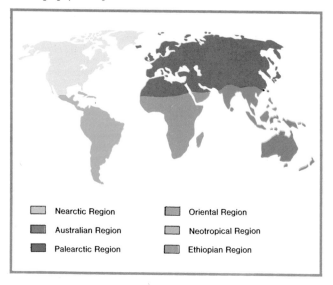

Nearctic Region

Australian Region

Palearctic Region

Oriental Region

Neotropical Region

Ethiopian Region

array of Old World monkeys. This region also includes the peculiar fauna of Madagascar, with lemurs being the most spectacular example of endemism, or the occurrence of an animal or plant in one area and nowhere else. The small viverrid carnivores (civets and mongooses) display their greatest variety of forms in the Ethiopian Region; 23 of the 25 genera are native.

The Oriental Region is characterized by tropical climates and forests. This region is separated from the Palearctic by deserts to the west and the Himalayan range to the north. The mammal fauna is similar to that of the Ethiopian Region, and in fact about 78% of the families are common to each. The presence in both these regions of rhinoceros, elephants, the great apes, and viverrid carnivores gives the impression of two very similar faunas, but there are also striking differences. The Oriental Region has no lemurs or their close kin, none of the numerous African antelope, or peculiarly African hystricomorph rodents such as cane rats, mole rats, and gundis. Four families—including tree shrews, "flying lemurs," tarsiers, and spiny dormice—are endemic.

The Palearctic Region is the largest in area. Its mostly temperate climate ranges from the hot deserts of North Africa and the Middle East to the severe cold of the Arctic tundra. The mammal fauna is diverse—40 families are represented—but only two families are endemic, the Spalacidae (mole rats) and the Seleviniidae (central Asian dormouse). About 78% of the families are shared with the Ethiopian Region and 70% with the

Oriental Region. Eurasia remained linked to North America by the Bering land bridge for part of the Tertiary, which facilitated migration of mammals in both directions. Today the two regions have many families, and even a few species, in common——Felidae (cats), Canidae (wolves and foxes), Soricidae (shrews), Muridae (voles), Ursidae (bears), Vespertilionidae (bats), Mustelidae (weasels), and Cervidae (deer).

The Nearctic Region is similar to the Palearctic. Here, too, glaciations in the Quaternary period had a decisive influence on the fauna, destroying much of what had existed before, and paving the way for a new fauna with a greater ability to adapt. Much of the mammal fauna is shared with the Neotropical Region (more than 75% of the families); only two families are endemic, the Aplodontidae (mountain beavers) and the Antilocapridae (pronghorn antelope).

The Neotropical Region consists largely of vast tropical rain forest in the lowlands, with highland cloud forests. Tropical savanna and grassland extend over southern South America and occur in patches in Central America. The extreme habitats of arid desert and high alpine tundra are found in both Central and South America. Although South America has been isolated through most of the geologic past since the Cretaceous, the Central American isthmus formed a land bridge late in the Pliocene, affording an interchange of fauna which persisted into modern times. The neotropics are rich in mammals, with 46 families represented. Twenty of these are endemic. Nonetheless, the Neotropical Region shares one-third of its families of mammals with the Palearctic, a sign of an ancient and active process of diffusion. Peculiar to the neotropics are cebid monkeys, all the edentates——anteaters, sloths, and armadillos——opossums, and certain hystricomorph rodents such as the capybara, cavy, chinchilla, and nutria or coypu. The Andean llama, alpaca, and vicuña are New World relatives of the camel. Tapirs are also found in both the Neotropical and Oriental Regions.

The Australian Region is unique. It has no land connection with any other faunal realm, and in fact is composed of an island continent——Australia proper——and several nearby, but isolated, islands. The northern part of the region, including extreme northern Australia, lies in the tropics and is covered by evergreen forest. The west and interior of Australia consist of vast arid land, much of it extreme desert, while the eastern and southeastern montane belt and Tasmania are temperate in climate, with eucalyptus forests and woodlands. The renowned Australian mammal fauna is likewise unique. It is the result of Australia's long isolation and the dramatic radiation of marsupials——the pouched mammals——during that time. Perhaps as far back as the Paleocene epoch marsupials first invaded Australia from their South American homeland via Antarctica, then a land bridge between the two regions. By the Eocene, Australia had broken away, become an island continent, and drifted northeast, carrying its marsupials with it. With no significant competition from placental mammals, the marsupials filled virtually all the ecological niches available, evolving into an array of forms unequaled in any other single order of mammals. Marsupials grew to superficially resemble their placental ecological counterparts of other regions. For example, the marsupial mole developed powerful and clawed front feet for burrowing; the predatory thylacine resembled the Holarctic wolf; gliders grew membranes between their limbs in imitation of ''flying'' squirrels; and so forth. The analogy, however, is not absolutely complete, for there are neither truly flying marsupials nor marine ones. Even in Australia these niches are occupied by true bats of many species, seals, whales, and dugongs. And these are not the only placental mammals inhabiting Australia. A number of rodents are also found there. Their ancestors probably arrived on floating debris from New Guinea. The dingo, a variety of domestic dog, was brought by man. The unique egg-laying mammals, the monotremes (the platypus and echidnas), are an order found only in the Australian Region.

CHARACTERISTICS OF MAMMALS

Mammals are complex organisms and share many features with other classes of animals with which they have a common origin. Two readily apparent features set mammals apart from any other living vertebrates: they nourish their young with milk secreted by special organs on the mother's body, known as mammary glands, and they have hair. Although it is the unique glands, or mammae, from which the name ''mammal'' is derived, the development of hair came first in the long evolutionary history of mammals.

Moving into unoccupied ecological niches was an advantage in the revolution of mammals. The development of hair in their reptilian ancestors made such adaptations possible, for hair and the unique sweat glands accompanying it allowed these small creatures to control their body temperature. They had become homeothermic, or warm-blooded. No longer dependent upon the warm daylight to rouse them from overnight torpor, these creatures with their newly acquired fur coats were now insulated against the cold and could maintain a more regular body temperature. This enabled them to feed at night and avoid reptilian predators, which were still active only by day. A muscular system developed that would allow mammals to raise or lower their body hairs, exposing the skin and thus regulating the insulatory effect of a fur coat. Seasonal changes—heavy coat for winter, light in summer—further enhanced the advantages of having hair.

The glands associated with hairs brought additional benefits. By secreting water from the bloodstream, sweat glands set up an evaporative cooling system. Sebaceous glands secrete oil to waterproof the hair. The modification of certain skin glands resulted in the mammary glands which allowed mammals to nourish their young directly. Such maternal care permits mammals to bear fewer offspring, yet enjoy a higher rate of survival. This efficient system was completed when mammals gave up laying eggs and were able to bear their young alive, nourished during fetal development. By maintaining a constant high temperature, mammals not only could become nocturnal in habit but could tolerate a variety of habitats. With these advances

Many large herbivores, such as these caribou, migrate seasonally to obtain food.

came more active, efficient, and alert mammals. Higher energy required greater efficiency in both the circulatory and respiratory systems, together with a larger and more complex brain. Structural improvements evolved in the heart and blood vessels, which in turn supplied well-oxygenated blood to the brain, while the volume of oxygen breathed was increased by the development of a muscular diaphragm separating the thorax and abdomen. Thus the agile mammal added intelligence to the many advances over its reptilian ancestors.

But such improvements demanded enhancement. Speed and agility depend upon limbs placed more effectively under the animal's body to support its weight and thrust it forward. As mammals began to radiate into a greater variety of habitats, their limbs continued to adapt to new ways of life. Long, narrow legs developed, giving browsing ungulates access to the tender leaves of trees, and multiplying their speed to escape carnivorous predators. Small arboreal mammals, as flying squirrels, evolved strong membranes between their limbs permitting them to glide from tree to tree. Burrowing mammals (moles) formed massive shoulders, heavy forearms, and sharp claws for digging. Perhaps the most extreme cases are the elongated fingers with sheer membranes that form the wings of bats and the limbs modified into flippers for marine species such as whales.

Competition among mammals themselves led to even further evolution. The senses became sharper. An array of special devices also evolved by which mammals could protect themselves from predators. Enormous girth and thick skin serve to protect elephants, rhinos, and hippos, while armadillos hid within a hard shell. If you have ever encountered a porcupine or handled a hedgehog, you are familiar with their protective device—sharp quills. And who has not experienced the ready defense of a skunk? Often, however, such animals do not have to resort to spraying potential enemies because their bright, contrasting coloration acts as a warning signal. Many mammals, particularly grazing or browsing forms, have evolved a striped coat color, or a spotted pattern as in cats and some other carnivores, to conceal themselves in grass or among shrubs. Protective coloration is widespread among virtually all orders of mammals.

In addition to protective needs and adaptation to new environments, the feeding habits of mammals also produced anatomical changes. Among them were improvements in the digestive system to make it more efficient and able to extract sufficient energy from the food consumed. Paramount among the adaptations to feeding habits are mammals' teeth. Instead of the simple spiked form that serves reptiles, mammalian teeth have differentiated into biting or gnawing incisors; sharp, flesh-stabbing canines; chewing or grinding premolars and molars. Indeed, the dentition, because of its many minute differences, is used by scientists to classify the thousands of species of mammals that once inhabited this earth or do so today.

Skin and hair

Skin consists of two layers, the outer protective layer being the epidermis, made up of dead cells, and the layer beneath, the dermis, which is attached to the muscles of the body. Where covered with hair the epidermis is usually soft; otherwise it is thick—as in elephants—or even cornified, as in the foot pads of dogs. Nails, claws, and hooves, and the horns of sheep, cattle, and antelope, are likewise cornified structures that grow continuously from the base. Horns have an inner core of bone for support. The antlers of deer and their relatives, however, are annual growths—shed each year—consisting of tissue that becomes calcified.

Hair is composed of dead epidermal cells and the protein keratin. The color of a hair is determined by the pigment it contains, and a single hair can be of one or several colors. Collectively, the hairs or fur of a mammal, or pelage, consists of a fine undercoat for insulation; scattered guard hairs—long, coarse hairs that help protect the pelage from wear; and special sensory hairs, or vibrissae, commonly called whiskers. These are extremely important to the rodents and carnivores whose faces they decorate, for at the base of each vibrissa are nerves that make the hair a delicate sensing device to help the animal feel his way about. The pelage is thickest on mammals that inhabit cold and temperate climates; sparse and short on tropical species. Elephants, rhinos, and hippos have few hairs. Whales and dolphins bear hairs around the mouth, but otherwise make up for the absence of hair with heavy layers of insulating fat, or blubber, beneath the skin. There is a naked, or practically so, mole rat—a burrowing rodent in east Africa—

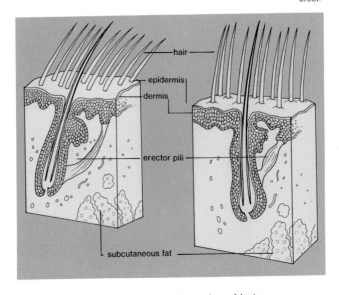

Hairs are typical of mammals, even though certain species have subsequently lost them as a result of adaptation to specific ways of life. Special muscles situated at the base of the hairs enable them to stand erect.

hair

epidermis

dermis

erector pili

subcutaneous fat

and there are two nearly unfurred species of bats.

Hair follicles are provided with sebaceous glands, which secrete an oily lubrication for the hairs and epidermis. Sweat glands in the skin help cool the body through evaporation and they eliminate wastes. The mammaries are modified sweat glands that secrete milk. In most mammals the mammary opens in a teat, or nipple, but the egg-laying monotremes have no such structure. Instead, the milk oozes from the glands and is sucked by the young from tufts of hair. The number of nipples on other mammals ranges from a single pair on the breast in bats and primates (including man), five or six pairs in some ungulates, to more in some rodents and marsupials, and a maximum of 11 pair in the tenrecs of Madagascar. They may extend from the breast to the abdomen or be concentrated in the female's abdominal area.

Bone structure

The hard parts of a mammal's body are the skeleton—a collection of some 200 bones—and it is the framework that supports the body. In the so-called lower animals, like lobsters or insects, an outer shell—the exoskeleton—holds the soft body together, but in mammals and all their cousins—fishes, amphibians, reptiles, and birds—the endoskeleton supports the body from within. Indeed, all such animals are known collectively as "vertebrates," or "backboned" animals, after part of this important feature. The skeleton is not simply a framework, however; it functions to protect the highly developed nervous

25

system and the digestive system from injury and to secure the muscles, which in turn move the bones that give the animal mobility and agility. In mammals the skeleton is simpler than that of reptiles through a greater fusion of bones. There is more actual strong, bony material than cartilage, permitting the more secure muscle attachment needed for the agility and greater speed of mammals. The skull together with the vertebral column and ribs form the axial skeleton; the limbs and the bones holding them are the appendicular skeleton.

The skull, or cranium, is made up of many bones fused together into a sort of box to house the brain. This braincase is large in mammals to accommodate the increased brain size over that of reptiles. The cranium provides a surface for attachment of the temporal muscles, which close the jaws. There is in many mammals, such as carnivores, a pronounced sagittal crest atop the cranium to permit firmer attachment of these strong muscles. The facial part of the skull forms the muzzle. It holds the upper teeth and protects the sense organs. The curved zygomatic arch, a bone structure dating back to the ancient mammal-like reptiles, forms the lower part of the eye socket and also articulates with the mandible, or lower jaw. On each side of the cranium are the tiny bones of the middle and inner ears; in many species the tympanic bone over the middle ear is enlarged and shaped like a round box, called the tympanic bulla. At the extreme rear of the cranium is a large opening, the foramen magnum, through which the spinal nerve cord is connected to the brain. On each side of this is the joint on

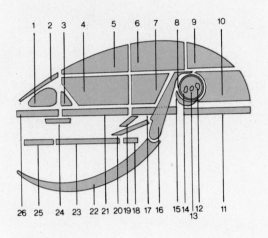

which the skull pivots on the first vertebra, or atlas. The fact that there are two such joints (one on either side of the skull) and the way the neck muscles are attached prevent the head from swiveling completely around.

The spinal column is composed of vertebrae which are jointed with each other by flexible discs, affording freedom of movement. The spinal cord passes through the center of the cylindrical vertebrae and is thus protected. Nearly all mammals have seven neck, or cervical, vertebrae, be they giraffes, mice, or men. The manatee and two-toed sloth have six, pangolins sometimes have eight, and the three-toed sloth has nine. The caudal vertebrae are tapered to form the tail, and in apes and man the four rudimentary bones are reduced to form the coccyx. The rib cage, attached to the thoracic portion of the spine and joined at the breastbone, protects the heart and lungs.

Except in highly modified marine forms—whales and sea cows—mammals have four limbs. The pectoral girdle—shoulder blade and collarbones—supports the forelimbs, and the pelvic girdle fixes the hind limbs to the axial skeleton. The upper-arm bone is the humerus; the corresponding upper-leg bone, the femur. These are followed by a pair of bones side by side—the radius in the forearm, the tibia and fibula in the shin, or lower leg. A variety of bones follow to form the carpals of the wrist and tarsals of the ankle, jointed with which, in turn, are metacarpals, or hand bones, and metatarsals, or foot bones. Fingers and toes are made up of phalanges. The length, shape, even number of these bones vary widely due to the re-

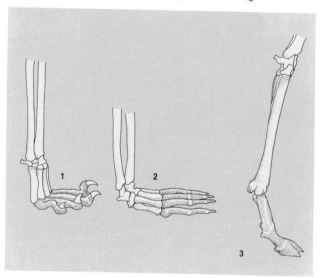

The bone structure of the foot has evolved into (1) the digitigrade mode of stealthy carnivores, (2) the plantigrade form, a basic posture for walking, and (3) the unguligrade, or hoofed type, for fast running.

markable adaptive radiation of mammals in all types of habitats, where their way of life demands quite specific types of limbs. Compare, for example, the lumbering rhinoceros, darting chipmunk, swinging gibbon, burrowing mole, flying bat, racing cheetah, and jumping kangaroo. Those mammals that walk by placing the entire sole and heel on the ground are called plantigrade, and include man and bears. We distinguish as digitigrade animals such as dogs and cats that walk on the undersurface of the digits, or toes. And horses, having evolved from five-toed through four- and three-toed ancestors, now walk on just a single toe or hoof on each foot; they are termed unguligrade.

Teeth

Nearly all mammals have teeth, although in the baleen whales they are absent or present only in the fetal stage and do not appear above the gums. An example of convergent evolution (that is, unrelated animals in the same ecological niche acquiring similar adaptive features) can be seen in African and Asian pangolins, true anteaters of the neotropics, and egg-laying echidnas of Australia and New Guinea. None of these unrelated creatures (aside from being mammals) has any teeth; they are all highly specialized ant or termite eaters.

Teeth vary according to their function and position. The usually small front teeth, incisors, bite or gnaw and are particularly prominent in rodents—beavers, especially—and in elephants the uppers are tusks. The eyeteeth, or canines, are the

Skulls and dentition of certain mammals: 1. aardvark (*Tubulidentata*); 2. bear (*Carnivora*); 3. bat (*Chiroptera*); 4. horse (*Perissodactyla*); 5. hare (*Lagomorpha*); 6. pocket gopher (*Rodentia*) (vertical section); 7. rat (*Rodentia*); 8. monkey (*Primates*).

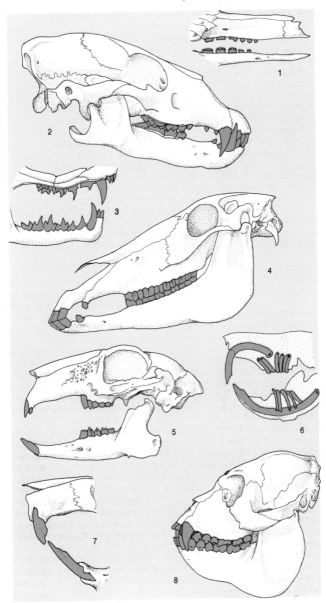

pointed, stabbing teeth adjacent to the incisors. They are most conspicuous in carnivores and in fact derive their name from dogs. They form the tusks of pigs. The canine teeth are used for tearing and for seizing prey. The cheek teeth, premolars and molars, are wider, with complex crowns, and are used for crushing and grinding.

During its lifetime a mammal will usually have two sets of teeth. The deciduous, or milk, teeth are shed as the animal grows, being replaced by the permanent set. Molars are not found among milk teeth. The incisors of rodents and molars of some herbivores are put to hard use and therefore continue to grow as the outer ends wear away.

While some marsupials have as many as 50 teeth and long-beaked dolphins may have up to 260 simplified teeth, as a rule the complete dentition in mammals does not exceed 44. The number and type of teeth, important diagnostic characters in classification, are expressed in a dental formula for each species. The number of each type of tooth in the upper jaw is written over the corresponding number for the lower jaw; for example, in the pig there are incisors 3/3, canines 1/1, premolars 4/4, molars 3/3. Since this applies only to one side of the jaw, the total is multiplied by 2 to arrive at the complete complement of teeth—in this case 22 × 2, or 44. The order is always the same and can be abbreviated, as in this dental formula for man: 2/2, 1/1, 3/3, 2/2 × 2 = 32.

Digestive system

Digestion of food begins in the mouth and is completed in the intestine. The premolars and molars break up the food in the mouth, where saliva begins to digest any starch and wets the fragmented food for easier swallowing. The food then passes through the gullet, in the chest cavity, and into the stomach, just beyond the diaphragm. Gastric juices in the stomach break the food down, but except for alcohol, it is not absorbed there. Some mammals have a compartmentalized stomach, especially well developed in ruminants as cattle, deer, and camels. In their case the huge bulk of herbage consumed is largely cellulose, which cannot be digested by any natural enzyme known in the animal's body. It therefore first passes into the rumen, where there are bacteria and protozoa that break down the cellulose. A soft, fermented cud then returns to the animal's mouth for continued chewing, or ruminating, then on to a second stomach compartment, the reticulum. The food passes in turn to two additional compartments, the omasum and abomasum, for further digestion. In all mammals the partly digested food leaves the stomach to enter the duodenum, where enzymes from the pancreas and bile from the liver via the gallbladder are added. Digestion and ultimate absorption of nutrients into the blood takes place in the long small intestine; the remaining matter passes into the relatively short colon, or large intestine, from which it is finally excreted. Many nonruminating herbivorous mammals, rodents in particular, have an appendage—the caecum—extending out from between the small and large intestines, in which bacteria break down the cellulose in their food.

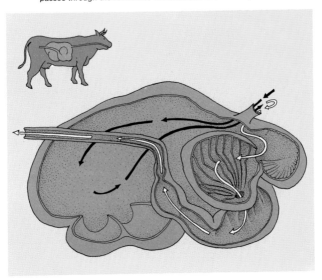

The large stomach of ruminants is divided into four connecting chambers. Ingested food first enters the rumen, or "paunch," (black arrows), from which it is regurgitated as a cud; after further chewing it passes through the reticulum, omasum and abomasum (white arrows).

Circulation and respiration

The nutrients absorbed into the bloodstream after digestion are circulated throughout the body via a highly efficient circulatory system. The heart in mammals, as in birds and some reptiles, is divided into four chambers—two auricles and two ventricles—whose muscular walls regularly contract to pump the blood. Refreshed blood is sent from the left ventricle through the aorta, the main artery, which branches into smaller arteries and finally tiny capillaries, thus circulating blood to all the cells of the body. Here the blood exchanges oxygen for waste gas—carbon dioxide; it then flows toward the heart through the veins and ultimately through the large vena cava, passing into the right auricle. The veins and heart are provided with valves to keep the blood flowing in the proper direction. The gas-laden blood journeys from the right auricle to the right ventricle, then goes directly to the spongelike lungs, where it now exchanges carbon dioxide for fresh oxygen. The newly oxygenated blood is then returned to the left auricle of the heart, flows into the left ventricle, and is once again pumped through the body. The rate at which the heart contracts, or beats, varies widely among diverse mammals; it can be as slow as 20 beats per minute in gigantic whales, or more than 1,300 beats per minute in a tiny shrew.

The heart and lungs together fill the chest cavity. When a breath is taken, the air passes down the trachea and into the paired bronchi, which branch into small passages, or bronchioles, that in turn spread into small alveolar ducts. The

31

The uterus, or womb, takes on various configurations in mammals: (1) double with an outlet shared with the intestine in monotremes; (2) double with two vaginas in marsupials; (3) bifid, or forked, in rodents; (4) two-pronged in carnivores and ungulates (5) single in the primates and bats.

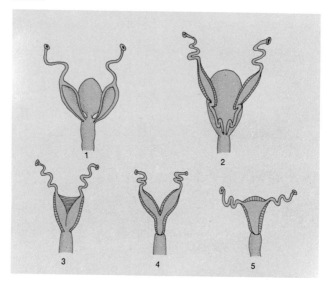

lungs, two porous masses side by side, consist of countless minute chambers, or alveoli, through whose membranes inhaled air is exchanged with the carbon dioxide waste in the blood. There are some 300 million alveoli in a human lung, collectively totaling more than 600 square feet of surface area for respiration. When you take a breath, it is the muscular expansion of the thorax which forces the lungs to inhale as the air pressure is reduced in an enlarged, sealed compartment, creating a partial vacuum. Although the muscles pulling the ribs outward help in each such expansion, it is the diaphragm which is really responsible for every breath taken. This muscle, a sophisticated development found only in mammals, seals off the thoracic cavity from the abdomen; when it contracts, it stretches backward (downward in man) into the abdomen, thereby expanding the chest for each new breath.

Reproduction

Animals must reproduce to ensure continuation of the species. In simple invertebrates this is merely a matter of the single-celled animal's dividing itself in two; in some others a new organism grows from the body of its parent and breaks off. By the time we reach mammals, however, the matter has become much more complex. Fundamentally, as in all other vertebrates, cells from two different individuals—an egg cell from the female and a sperm cell from a male—are united to grow and form a new individual. By reason of having two parents, the young is not an identical duplicate of another individual but

instead is a genetic combination of two, thus providing a greater potential for evolutionary advance. As in reptiles and birds, fertilization in mammals is internal.

Transfer of male sperm to the body of the female is made through the penis, the male copulatory organ. It is composed of erectile tissue and in many mammals, but not man, contains a bone known as the baculum. Sperm cells are produced in the paired testes which usually are situated together in the scrotum, a saclike appendage that serves to keep the testes at a cooler temperature than inside the body. The sperm pass during coitus through small tubes into the urethra, the connecting tube that runs through the penis and is also used for urination. In the female, the paired ovaries are situated in the pelvis and contain thousands of eggs, or ova. As each egg matures, it is released through the oviduct, or fallopian tube, through which it passes into the uterus for fertilization and subsequent development. The uterus opens into the vagina, the passage through which the male penis enters. There are two vaginas and two uteri in monotremes and marsupials. In placental mammals there is but one vagina; the uteri, however, are separate in rodents and incompletely fused in insectivores, carnivores, and ungulates. Primates have a single uterus.

Monotremes are oviparous, or egg-laying, mammals. Marsupials are ovoviviparous, which means the egg is large and has a yolk adequate to nourish the embryo during its early development, but it remains unattached to the wall of the uterus. Gestation in marsupials is necessarily short, therefore, and the

33

young are born in an immature, fetal stage. They make their way to the mother's pouch and continue to grow, nourished with milk. All other mammals, termed placental, are viviparous. Their small egg, lacking food substance, becomes attached to the uterine wall, and the developing embryo is nourished by the mother's blood passing through a placenta. This process allows longer gestation, and as a result the young are born in a more advanced state of development.

The reproductive cycles vary considerably among placental mammals, depending upon the length of gestation. In elephants the gestation period is as long as 22 months, although size alone is not the determining factor; the giant among all mammals, the blue whale, has a gestation period of only 11 months. Many bats and certain other mammals have a delayed implantation in which the fertilized ovum remains dormant or its development is retarded at first, thus considerably extending the gestation period and delaying birth until the optimal season of warm weather or abundant food. Thus the gestation period of the fisher, a small North American carnivore with delayed implantation, is 48 to 51 weeks, or about the same as that of the blue whale. The length of gestation varies from 22 to 45 days in squirrels, 2 to 7 months in New World porcupines, 6 months in bears, 14 to 15 months in giraffes.

Animals having long gestation periods or whose young mature slowly and are suckled for a long time do not breed as often as others. Some mice often breed throughout spring, summer, and autumn; have a gestation period of three weeks; and the females can breed at 21 days of age. Many mammals, as beavers, coyotes, and weasels, breed once a year. Many other species, however, are able to breed twice each year, and even three times in one year is not uncommon. Environmental conditions to which various species have adapted play a role in their breeding cycles. It is advantageous for the young to be born during the season of least severe weather and to be weaned when food is most abundant. Many tropical mammals breed throughout the year and young are born accordingly. In temperate and cold climates, the young are most often born in spring or summer.

Similar factors also influence the number of young born among different species. Their rate of growth until weaned, mortality rates, the adult activity cycles, and other factors no doubt help determine the litter size as well. Many rodents have three to six young per litter; a few species of mice can have as many as eighteen. Seals, whales, and most species of primates and bats bear only a single young at one time.

The senses

The sense of smell is not the same in all mammals. It is highly developed in some insectivores, whose olfactory lobes of the brain are proportionately large. They are also prominent in carnivores and rodents, but poorly developed in whales and higher primates. Our sense of smell as humans is obviously no match for that of our dogs. Porpoises and dolphins have no olfactory system. In other mammals, the olfactory nerves (which sense odors) are located on a moist mucous membrane over a

Among carnivores, such as bears, the young are first weaned onto food obtained by their mother, from whom they later learn how to catch their own prey.

complex set of folded bones, or turbinals, set far back in both nasal passages. As air is breathed in through the nose, some passes through the turbinal bones and contacts the olfactory nerves; thus odors are perceived. Many mammals smell odors that others cannot appreciate, and the sense of smell is important in identifying individuals, enemies, possible predators, and the state of sexual receptiveness as well as food sources. Taste is associated with the sense of smell; its receptors are the taste buds on the tongue. Humans distinguish only four distinct tastes—sweet, sour, bitter, and salt—and refinements come from our sense of smell.

The eyes are well developed in most mammals, except in some insectivores and dolphins and in burrowing rodents. Those of nocturnal mammals have a special reflective layer, the tapetum lucidum, which improves their vision in the dark by reflecting light back to the retina. It is this feature that makes their eyes shine when caught in a spotlight. Except for cetaceans and primates, almost all mammals have a nictitating membrane, or third eyelid, at the inner corner of the eyeball. It passes horizontally across the eyeball, inside the other two eyelids, to clean the cornea. Binocular vision affords perception of depth, an ability demanded by arboreal mammals such as gibbons that swing rapidly from branch to branch high in the treetops. Depth perception is most acute where the view overlaps between the two eyes, as in primates whose eyes look forward.

Hearing is more highly developed in mammals than among

other creatures whose lives may be less dependent upon this sense. Only mammals have external ears, or pinnae, to catch and direct sound waves. Although some insectivores and cetaceans, as well as certain seals, have lost their external ears through evolution, many mammals have large or extraordinarily shaped pinnae. Bats in particular have unique, sometimes bizarre, ears because they have developed the sense of hearing to the extreme. The tube leading from the pinna to the tympanic membrane, or eardrum, is very long in mammals, exceptionally so in whales and porpoises, and the middle ear has become highly specialized.

Nervous system and endocrine glands

The brain and spinal cord together constitute the central nervous system, which in mammals has reached its zenith in complexity. The human brain is a vast network of about 10 billion nerve cells, each of which is connected to an average of some 1,000 others. Although the mammalian brain is also larger, compared with body size, than that of any other animals, size alone does not determine intelligence. Nor does the amount of convolution. The brain of the sperm whale weighs nearly seven times as much as man's, and the porpoise's brain is more convoluted than man's. Although both factors contribute to the degree of intelligence reached, it is now thought that the ratio between the weight of the brain and that of the spinal cord more accurately indicates intelligence. In the "lowest" vertebrates, fish and amphibians, the ratio is about 1:1; in the "highest" mammal, man, it is 55:1. Gray matter, called the neopallium and found in the convoluted cortex, is a primary characteristic of the brain in mammals. It has grown into the control center and dominates the brain, receiving all conscious stimuli and originating actions. It is the memory bank and is the seat of the will and intellect.

While some nerves in the head pass through several small openings in the skull, the spinal cord is the connection between the brain and the nerves that extend throughout the body, transmitting stimuli to the brain and relaying messages from the brain. What are these messages? They are impulses and minute chemical changes from the sense organs—sight, scent, hearing, taste, touch, pain, and so on—for the brain to interpret and act upon.

But nerves are not the only way the body sends messages. Slower, long-lasting changes are wrought by chemical means—hormones—produced by endocrine glands and transmitted via the blood. This complicated and important biochemical system is largely controlled by the pituitary gland at the base of the brain. It produces five hormones to regulate other endocrine glands and one to govern growth of the body. The thyroid, found in the neck area, is the largest endocrine gland and secretes hormones to promote normal body growth and development of the nervous system. Located on the kidneys, the two adrenal glands produce adrenaline, a heart stimulant. Various other endocrine glands are distributed throughout the body, and their hormones play a wide range of roles to keep the entire organism functioning properly.

THE ORDERS OF MAMMALS

For convenience in discussing animal life biologists have given names to all the species known. Indeed, among invertebrates newly discovered species are still being named. Except, perhaps, for one or two new rodents or bats every year, virtually all mammals have been described and named. A species is defined as a natural population of individuals of common ancestry and close resemblance and which in nature interbreed and produce fertile offspring. Among mammals such a population—a species—may be confined to a single valley or mountain, or may range throughout a continent or even over most of the world. The name given a species is in Latin and remains unchanged no matter what language a biologist speaks. The name of a species consists of two words, almost like one's surname plus given name. The first word denotes the genus (the next higher rank of relationship) to which the animal belongs; the second denotes its species—as *Canis lupus*, the wolf.

The relationships of species are shown by grouping all like genera (the plural form of the word "genus") into a family, related families into an order, orders into a class. Subdivisions have been adopted to further indicate relationships of animals, and geographical variants are often named as subspecies, or varieties of a particular species. The wolf is classified as:

Class Mammalia
  Subclass Theria
    Infraclass Eutheria
      Order Carnivora
        Family Canidae
          Genus *Canis*
            Species *Canis lupus*

The mammals living today can be divided into 20 orders, which are briefly discussed in the following pages.

Monotremata

The most uncharacteristic of all mammals are the monotremes—the unique duck-billed platypus and two spiny anteaters, or echidnas, known only from the Australian Region. They are the most primitive of living mammals, retaining certain characteristics of their reptilian ancestors and displaying some features of birds as well. Although they have hair and suckle their young, monotremes lay eggs of a soft-shelled, reptilian sort and incubate them as do birds. They have no teeth, except in young platypuses, and the face terminates in a leathery bill or elongated beak. There are peculiarly reptilian features in the facial bones, skull, shoulder girdle, and ribs. And like birds and reptiles, monotremes have a cloaca, a single chamber serving both the excretory and reproductive systems. Their body temperature is also subject to considerable fluctuation. Little wonder that the first specimen of the platypus to reach the scientific world, late in the 18th century, was thought to be a hoax.

Thus the monotremes are living links between reptiles and mammals. They are not, however, the ancestors of more ad-

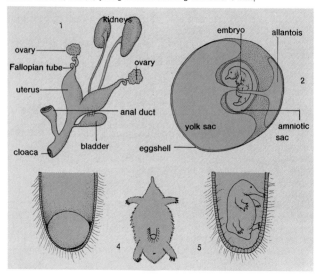

Reproduction in monotremes: (1) female urogenital system (2) embryonic development in the eggs (3,4) egg and temporary pouch of female echidna, and (5) young echidna suckling its mother's milk.

vanced mammals, but rather an early offshoot that developed along variant lines in long isolation. The fossil record is very scant. So distinctive are they from any other orders of mammals that the Monotremata form a separate subclass, Prototheria. The order is divided into two families: the Tachyglossidae, which has two members—the Australian spiny anteater and the giant echidna of New Guinea; and the Ornithorhynchidae, which has but one—the platypus.

Marsupialia

The second major division of mammals is the subclass Theria, which embraces the order of marsupials together with all the remaining mammals—the 18 orders of placentals. However, although marsupials join the ranks of other mammals as distinct from egg-layers, they are nevertheless a unique group deserving of recognition at a high level. The order Marsupialia, therefore, is set apart as an infraclass, Metatheria, while the orders of placental mammals collectively form the infraclass Eutheria. In a practical sense, such a classification emphasizes that marsupials are far more advanced than monotremes, yet differ considerably from placentals. The two infraclasses have evolved along different lines since their separation in the early Cretaceous or Jurassic.

The principal features distinguishing marsupials are, of course, the pouch, or marsupium, which gives the order its name, together with the entire reproductive system of which the pouch is only a part. The female reproductive tract is dou-

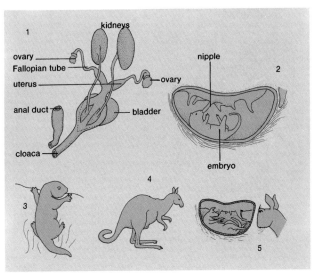

Reproduction in marsupials: (1) female urogenital system; (2) pouch-young attached to nipple; (3) young at birth, making its way to the pouch; (4) adult female kangaroo with abdominal pouch; (5) older offspring suckling.

ble, fusing at the time of birth into a single birth canal independent of the vagina. Embryonic marsupials have a yolk sac for nourishment, rather than the placenta of more advanced mammals, and are therefore born in an extremely immature state. They make their way unaided to the pouch, attach themselves to a nipple, and continue to develop. The number of nipples varies from 2 to 19 in different species, and the female pouch itself may be well developed or a mere fold in the abdominal skin. The pouch opens toward the front in some marsupials, toward the rear in others.

Marsupials have a small, relatively simple brain compared with that of placental mammals. The braincase is generally narrow. The broad radiation of marsupials into different ways of life is reflected especially in their limb structure. Long, powerful hind legs and specialized feet characterize the kangaroos, wallabies, and their kin, whose saltatorial, or hopping, habits are well known. The New World opossums have a clawless, opposable hallux (the big toe) on the hind foot which they use much like a thumb to gain a foothold. They are arboreal in habit. The Neotropical water opossum has webbed feet. The bandicoots of Australia are highly adapted to fast running; the digits of their hind feet are greatly reduced, except one enlarged toe which has somewhat the effect of a horse's hoof. Burrowing and gliding marsupials have likewise developed modified limbs.

We usually associate marsupials with Australia, where, indeed, the order displays its famous diversity of species. Of the

Sixteen orders of placental mammals with approximate number of living species in each.

Insectivora: 344 species

Chiroptera: 950 species

Cetacea: 76 species

Rodentia: 1,586 species

Carnivora: 273 species

Artiodactyla: 181 species

Proboscidea: 2 species

Hyracoidea: 5 species

Perissodactyla: 16 species

Sirenia: 4 species

Xenarthra: 29 species

Tubulidentata: 1 species

Lagomorpha: 54 species

Pholidota: 7 species

Dermoptera: 2 species

Primates: 179 species

approximately 251 living species, 170 are native to Australia and/or the adjacent islands. The remaining 81 species are the few living descendants of a once extensive marsupial fauna in the Americas. They are now relatively unobtrusive—the Virginia opossum and similar forms, and tiny mouse-opossums or rat-opossums—all greatly overshadowed by placental mammals. The array of marsupials in Australia is grouped in thirteen distinct families, from little honey possums, marsupial moles and bandicoots, through carnivorous "cats," gliders, and wombats, to the koala and the kangaroos.

Insectivora
Shrews, hedgehogs, moles, and a number of small animals native to Madagascar known as tenrecs, make up the Insectivora. These creatures have in common a diet of insects; actually, other small invertebrates such as worms and crustaceans are eaten too. And aquatic species may add small fish and even amphibians to their meals. Seven families of Insectivora are recognized—some 359 species. They are widely distributed, found throughout most of the world except in the polar and Australian regions. Only five species of shrew (*Cryptotis*) inhabit the South American continent, and there they are limited to the northwestern corner. One entire family, consisting of only two species, is confined to the Caribbean islands of Cuba and Hispaniola (Santo Domingo). These rare, endangered species are the solenodons, relict forms that are apparently unable to survive agriculture and the introduction of

dogs, cats, house rats, and the mongoose. Together with the European water shrew (*Neomys fodiens*) and North American short-tailed shrew (*Blarina brevicauda*), solenodons are among the only venomous mammals known (the male platypus has a poisonous spur on its hind feet).

Insectivores are the most primitive of the Eutherian, or placental, mammals living today, and many, in fact, are probably fairly close facsimiles of early ancestral forms. They have a small brain and unspecialized teeth. Most insectivores have poorly developed eyes, small ears, and a long, pointed snout. They are small plantigrade animals, from among the very smallest of living mammals to about the size of a house cat. A certain degree of specialization does exist among this rather generalized order. Hedgehogs and some tenrecs have developed a spiny coat, underlying which is a set of special muscles to control erection of the spines. They may further protect themselves by then rolling into a tight, sharp spiny ball. Some species of hedgehogs hibernate in winter, and desert-dwelling species may estivate——that is, reduce their body temperature and metabolic rate, thereby entering a state of torpor——during extremely hot weather. The pectoral girdle and front limbs of moles are modified for burrowing, and they have developed large, spadelike front feet with broad, heavy claws enabling them to nearly "swim" through moist topsoil. The European desman, an aquatic mole, has webbed feet and laterally flattened tail—aids to actual swimming.

Macroscelidia

The elephant shrews are the only members of this order. In many ways similar to the insectivores (in fact, formerly classified as a family of that order), these peculiar African animals are highly specialized for running. Their legs are long and slender; the back legs are somewhat longer than the front ones, giving them an almost kangaroolike appearance as they make their speedy bounds.

Dermoptera

Only two living species, in a single genus, compose the entire order of flying lemurs. Their scientific name, Dermoptera, means "skin-winged." They do not have true wings, but have the most complete gliding membrane: a furred skin extending from behind the ears outward to the digits, embracing the tail, stretching along the sides and base of the body. One species, *Cynocephalus volans*, is found in the Philippines; the other, *C. variegatus*, from southeast Asia to Java and Borneo.

Flying lemurs, or colugos, most probably evolved from ancient insectivores. Indeed, because of their apparent close relationship colugos were once placed in the order Insectivora; they have also been classified as bats. They do not fly and are not lemurs. They are about the size of a domestic cat, and their large eyes and pointed face lend them a certain resemblance to lemurs. So highly specialized are colugos to their life in the treetops——they have long, curved, sharp claws on hands and feet——that they are clumsy crawlers on the ground. At dusk

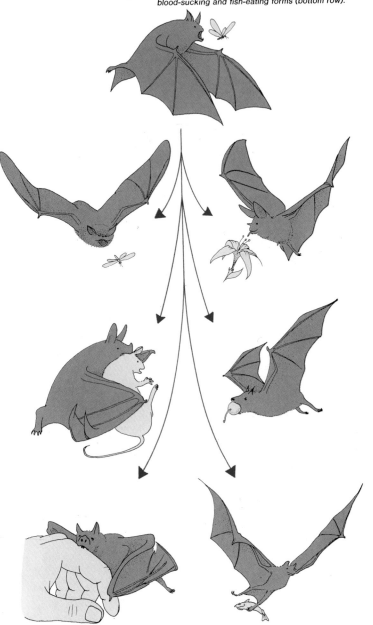

The Chiroptera (bats) have evolved forms adapted to the most varied of ecological niches, and consequently, to different types of diets: from primitive insectivore (top), to insectivore and feeder on pollen and nectar (second row), to carnivore and frugivore (third row), to the blood-sucking and fish-eating forms (bottom row).

they emerge from their daytime retreat in a tree hollow to glide from tree to tree until they reach favored foraging areas, where they feed upon leaves, flowers, and fruit.

Chiroptera

The world's only true flying mammals, bats, are all gathered in the order Chiroptera. Probably derived from arboreal insectivores, bats are known from rare fossil remains dating back to the early Eocene; they probably originated at least as long ago as the Paleocene. Second only to rodents, they are the largest order of mammals, numbering about 950 species. Bats are found in every part of the world except the polar regions. The order is clearly divisible into two very distinct suborders: the Megachiroptera, consisting of 173 species of flying foxes and other fruit bats; and the Microchiroptera, which embraces all the other, generally insectivorous, bats. So diverse are the latter that they are classified into 16 different families, while the fruit bats are all contained in a single family. The Megachiroptera inhabit the tropics and subtropics of the Old World—Africa and Australasia; the Microchiroptera are worldwide.

Flight clearly distinguishes bats from other mammals. Their entire bone structure is modified for flight, and as we should expect, this is most noticeable in the limbs. The wings are formed by elongated finger bones, over which is stretched an extremely thin skin membrane arising from the sides of the body and enclosing the legs and tail. In the Megachiroptera, the membrane does not extend across the legs down to the feet, as it does in the Microchiroptera. The wing membrane is naked, although in some species the body fur may grow barely onto the wing, and when the wing is not extended the membrane folds up along countless creases more efficiently than an umbrella.

Rather than displaying quick maneuvers, flying foxes have a powerful and steady type of flight. They use their acute vision, even when flying at night. All other bats—that is, the Microchiroptera—have reasonably good eyesight but do not depend upon it in flight. Instead they have developed a remarkable sense of hearing and guide themselves by echolocation, or sonar. The bat constantly emits high-frequency clicking sounds, up to 200 per second and beyond the human range of hearing. As such sound waves strike objects in their path, the echo is returned to the bat, which literally hears its way about. Bats in flight also perceive insects in this manner, which accounts for their sudden darting twists, turns, and dives while pursuing dinner. As bats are believed to have evolved from insectivores, echolocation as a means of finding flying insects in the dark probably developed early. Bats eat all sorts of nocturnal insects; beetles and moths probably top the list. Some species have cultivated other tastes. Like their distant relatives the flying foxes, a few species of Microchiroptera feed on ripe fruit, and others, on nectar and pollen. These diets are common to leaf-nosed bats, Phyllostomidae, of the New World tropics. In the same region, two species, *Noctilio leporinus* and *Pizonyx vivesi*, catch and eat fish from the water's surface. There are carnivorous—indeed, cannibal—bats: two species in tropical America, *Phyllostomus hastatus* and *Vampyrum spectrum* (not a vampire bat), prey upon birds, rodents, and

The pangolin covered with sharp-edged scales, protects itself by curling into a tight coil.

other bats. African and Asian false vampires (*Megaderma*) and Australian ghost bats (*Macroderma gigas*), the largest of the Microchiroptera, likewise devour frogs, birds, and small mammals, including other species of bats. But perhaps the most bizarre feeding habits belong to the true vampire bats. They are three species, constituting the subfamily Desmodontinae. Vampires feed exclusively on the blood of large mammals and even birds, and are the only vertebrates with such a diet. They do not suck blood, as is commonly believed, but bite a neat wound through the skin from which they lap the blood. The vampire's saliva contains an anticoagulant to keep the blood flowing.

Pholidota

In the tropical and subtropical regions of southern Asia and Africa are found seven species, all of the genus *Manis,* that constitute the entire order Pholidota. These are pangolins, or scaly anteaters, strange arboreal or terrestrial creatures that look like walking pinecones. They are of medium size, weighing about 10 to 50 pounds; with a long, narrow nose, long body, long tail; covered with large, flat, overlapping, brown scales. The scales are modified hair and shield the animal from enemies, especially when it curls itself into a tight coil or ball. The pangolin can erect its razor-edged scales, and inflict nasty wounds by lashing with its tail. Some species spray a foul-smelling liquid produced by glands near the anus.

Its limbs are strong, and the heavy tail acts as further support when the pangolin rears up on its hind legs while tearing at

45

The platyrrhine monkeys of the New World have widely separated flattened nostrils; whereas the catarrhine monkeys of the Old World have nostrils set close together and turned downward.

termite mounds or fallen logs with its sicklelike claws to literally scratch up a meal during its nocturnal forays. Ants and termites are its principal diet, although other insects are eaten as well. Since the pangolin has no teeth, its stomach is provided with thick, muscular walls and contains small pebbles used to grind its food, much like a bird's gizzard. The exceptionally long, whiplike tongue is anchored to the pelvis.

Many of the peculiar adaptations to its specialized diet of ants, such as long snout and tongue, sharp digging claws, absence of teeth, and even its protective shell of scales and ability to roll up into a ball are very suggestive of xenarthrans. It is interesting to note, however, that the two orders are not closely related. They are prime examples of convergent evolution.

Scandentia

The tree shrews, all in one family (Tupaiidae) are placed in an order of their own, Scandentia. They were formerly classed as Insectivora, and some today consider them primates of the suborder Prosimii because of certain internal similarities to the latter. All zoologists are agreed, however, that they are intermediate between the insectivores and the lower primates, and that they form a link between the two orders—although in appearance they look like pointed-nosed squirrels. They live in deciduous forests in the Oriental Region, are arboreal and terrestrial. and consume both plant and animal matter.

Primates

Some195 species of lemurs and their kin, monkeys, apes, and man, together constitute the primates. They are essentially

Complex social structures are very common in primates. Baboons maintain a heirarchic order by continual play and comparison of strength.

tropical in distribution, found in the Americas, Africa, and southern Asia. Primates evolved from ancient insectivores and for the most part retained their arboreal habits. There has been considerable development of the brain, and a rounded braincase to go with it. The sense of sight is acute, the eyes being large and facing forward to provide depth of vision, while the senses of hearing and smell are reduced. A relatively flattened face has resulted. Grasping hands and feet with flat nails rather than claws occur in most primates, as do diurnal activity and an omnivorous diet. Many primates are capable of breeding the year around and usually bear only one young per year. They have evolved a comparatively complex social organization to provide for breeding and particularly for the raising of young, which are born in a quite helpless state and develop very slowly.

The more advanced monkeys and apes form the suborder Anthropoidea, and all other primates—those less advanced—are given their own suborder, Prosimii. A wide variety of small and intermediate-sized primates constitute the six families of prosimians. They are the mouse lemurs, true lemurs, indris, the aye-aye, lorises and bushbabies, and tarsiers. The first four are found only on the island of Madagascar, the loris family inhabits southern and southeastern Asia and Africa, and the three species of tarsiers are native to Sumatra and Borneo, Celebes, and the Philippine island of Mindanao. Second to the tiny tree shrew, the smallest of the prosimians is the mouse lemur (*Microcebus murinus*). As its name implies, it is the size

47

of a mouse. Some species of lemurs and indris are diurnal in habit and active on the ground, but most prosimians are nocturnal and at home in the trees. Their diets are varied. The indris eat leaves, as do the mouse lemurs, who add fruit and insects to their meals. All other prosimians are insectivorous; lorises prey upon small birds and lizards as well. The aye-aye has specially adapted fingers for extracting insect larvae from crevices, and several other prosimians have remarkably specialized hands and feet or hind limbs. Owing to the clearing of their forest habitat for agriculture, the unique prosimians of Madagascar may not survive much longer in the wild state.

The more advanced primates, or anthropoids, are conveniently classified in five families. Almost all species are diurnal in habit, in contrast to the prosimians, and are among the more familiar primates. The New World primates are classed in the family Cebidae. The most common in the tropical forests of South America belong to the subfamily Callitrichinae, comprising marmosets and tamarins. The tiny marmosets range from mouse- to squirrel-size, and scamper, twittering, through the trees in small family groups searching for fruit, insects, lizards, small birds, and eggs. Also in the family Cebidae are the New World monkeys: the small squirrel monkey, the larger nocturnal owl monkey and sakis, spider monkeys, and the 20-pound howler monkey. All have long, well-haired tails except the rare uakaris. Cebids have long, narrow limbs; some lack an opposable thumb; but all have a strongly opposable big toe. Their eyes face forward, but the nostrils are usually widely separated and face to the side—the so-called platyrrhine characteristic sometimes cited as a distinction between New World and Old World monkeys. Another difference is the lack of colorful calluses on the rump seen in some Old World species. Cebids, particularly male howler monkeys, are often heard rather than seen as they call in resounding voice while roaming in large troops through the forest. Primarily fruit-eaters, although cebids enjoy other plant matter too, and some eat insects, lizards, small mammals, and birds' eggs as well.

All Old World monkeys, but not apes and man, are grouped in a second family—and the largest: the Cercopithecidae. All together some 76 species, the family ranges from northwest Africa through Africa south of the Sahara, southern Arabia, and southern and southeastern Asia to Timor, the Philippines, and Japan. Old World monkeys obviously tolerate greater cold than do their New World cousins, as is demonstrated by the Japanese macaque (*Macaca fuscata*) which lives in the snow of northern Honshu. Cercopithecids are fairly large, weighing from about 3 pounds to a record 119-pound male mandrill, and are distinguished by a catarrhine feature—that is, having the nostrils close together and opening downward. They also have large, sometimes exceptionally long, upper canines; opposable thumb and big toe, except in colobus monkeys, whose thumb is vestigial or lacking; and in many species, large, bare, red calluses on the rump. They eat a variety of foods, depending upon the species. Although most are arboreal in habit, baboons are terrestrial, and macaques are equally capable in trees or on the ground. Cercopithecids are mainly diurnal and

often live in large social troops. Besides baboons, mandrills, macaques, and colobus monkeys, this family includes mangabeys, the gelada, guinons, patas monkeys, and langurs. The colobus and langurs are leaf-eaters and have more elaborate digestive systems than other cercopithecids, so they are placed in a distinct subfamily, the Colobinae. (The others are placed in the subfamily Cercopithecinae.)

Six species of gibbons make up a separate family, Hylobatidae, distinguished from the great apes in particular by their highly developed brachiating ability—that is, the ability to travel rapidly through the trees swinging by their arms from branch to branch. They range throughout southeast Asia to Sumatra and Borneo.

The most highly advanced primates next to man are in the family Pongidae: the orangutan, two species of chimpanzees, and the gorilla. The orangutan, rapidly disappearing, is native to Sumatra and Borneo. The chimpanzees and gorilla inhabit west and central equatorial Africa. Pongids have a fairly rounded skull, large braincase, and the same dental formula as man. The great apes are mostly vegetarian in diet, and known to be carnivorous on occasion. Unlike the gibbons, these apes are terrestrial, and although able to walk bipedally are usually quadrupedal.

Human beings are the only living species of the family Hominidae—truly bipedal primates with opposable thumps, large braincase and enlarged cerebrum, and with the skull opening downward as a result of standing upright.

Sievelike plates of baleen strain out the plankton on which toothless whales live.

Rodentia

Almost anywhere you look, except in the polar ice, you can find a rodent. The Rodentia are the most abundant land mammals, climbing or gliding among trees, darting across the landscape, burrowing beneath the soil, or even swimming in lakes or streams. They consume all sorts of plant material, primarily seeds, but also stems, leaves, flowers, and roots, and insects and other invertebrates. Some are partially carnivorous. Rodents number about 1,600 species in 30 separate families. They are, in short, a very successful order of mammals. Besides certain internal features, they have in common one conspicuous characteristic: a pair of long and prominent incisors, upper and lower. The chisel-like incisors, kept sharp through wear, since there is hard enamel only on their front surface, are ever-growing and extremely effective for gnawing. The beaver's commendable industry in felling trees is a classic example. All rodents have a large empty space in place of canine teeth to allow maneuverability with their incisors. Some species are provided with pouches or pockets, opening either inside or outside their mouths, for carrying seeds or other food as gathered. And it is habitual with many rodents to store food for future use.

Rodents range in size from that of mice and rats, the smallest being the Eurasian harvest mouse (*Micromys minutus*) which weighs as little as 0.14 ounce; the largest, the South American capybara (*Hydrochaeris hydrochaeris*), weighing over 100 pounds. Their success as a group is no doubt due, at least in part, to their generally small size and high rate of reproduction. The survival of some species is further aided by the ability to hibernate in extreme cold or estivate in hot climates.

Perhaps because the order is so vast, rodents have developed certain specialized traits repeatedly in unrelated species. For example, North American kangaroo rats (*Dipodomys*), Australian hopping mice (*Notomys*), and north African jerboas (*Jaculus*)—all in different families—dwell in sandy desert regions and have evolved exceedingly long, narrow hind legs and feet with a correspondingly long tail used for hopping over the sandy expanses like miniature kangaroos. They all have keen hearing, small front limbs, similar pale coloration, and even the same hair tuft at the tip of the tail.

Cetacea

In every ocean of the world, and in a few rivers, are found whales, dolphins, and porpoises—the cetaceans. There are 76 species, some exceedingly rare. The largest living animal and probably biggest ever to live is the blue whale (*Balaenoptera musculus*), averaging some 80 to 100 feet in length and 90 to 130 tons in weight. The smallest cetaceans are a number of dolphins and porpoises about 4.5 to 6 feet long when adult and weighing only 80 to 100 pounds.

Cetaceans are, of course, highly modified for life at sea. Hind limbs are absent, forelimbs are flippers, and the tail is flattened; most have a dorsal fin. The nasal openings, or blowholes, are at the top of the head (there is one opening in toothed whales and two in baleen whales). There are no external ears. Hair is virtually lacking and the skin is slick. It is fatal for cetaceans to become stranded on land—even the young are born at sea.

Dolphins, porpoises, and other toothed whales, the most abundant of the Cetacea, have from one pair to 260 simple teeth. In the male narwhal, the upper left canine is a spiraled tusk that projects straight forward eight or nine feet. Most eat fish and invertebrates; the killer whale hunts in packs of up to fifty individuals and preys upon birds, seals, smaller cetaceans, and other marine animals. The toothless baleen whales have long plates of stiff hairlike material—whalebone, or baleen—hanging from each side of the palate that act as sieves to strain out the plankton on which they subsist.

Cetaceans are intelligent, social animals. They utter a vast repertoire of sounds by which they communicate with one another, and they navigate in the water by sonar, or echolocation, much as bats do in flight.

Carnivora

Just as rodents identify themselves by their long incisors, members of the order Carnivora are distinguished by their prominent canine teeth. These are long, curved, pointed, very strong, and particularly effective for stabbing. Most carnivores are predatory meat-eaters with small but sharp incisors, good for nipping. A special adaptive feature lies in the fourth upper premolar and the first lower molar, specialized teeth that form

Dentition of some carnivores: 1. upper half-jaw of a dog, showing three incisors, one canine, four premolars, and two molars; 2, 3. incisor of a dog (2. front surface; 3. lateral surface); 4. upper half-jaw of a dog; 5. of a bear; 6. of a marten; 7. of a Eurasian badger; 8. of a mongoose; 9 of a hyena; 10. of a lion. In the half-jaws on the right there are no incisors shown: the vertical line indicates the fourth premolar.

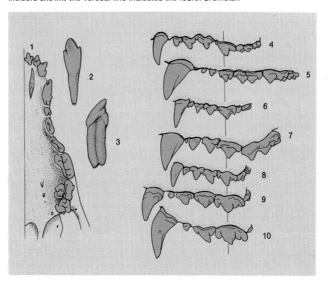

shearing blades to cut up meat guillotine fashion. Called carnassials, they are common to meat-eating Carnivora, but least developed in those species whose diets have become less carnivorous. Aquatic members of the order lack carnassials. The Carnivora have strong jaws, powerful muscles, and heavy skulls to put their teeth into action.

They are an ancient order, having evolved from early Paleocene creodonts, and have spread successfully to all parts of the world, including the Arctic and Antarctic, but are not native as land dwellers to Australia, New Zealand, or many oceanic islands. (The dingo is a domestic dog introduced into Australia by aboriginal man.) The Carnivora have become widely diversified; some species are nocturnal in habit, while others are diurnal, and many are active both day and night. There are 239 terrestrial and semiaquatic species of so-called fissiped carnivores, whereas the truly aquatic forms (34 species) make up three families of pinniped carnivores.

The most familiar family of fissipeds is the Canidae—dogs, jackals, wolves, and foxes—found in a variety of habitats from the Arctic to the tropics. They are highly predatory and often hunt over great distances, being endowed with either great speed, as in the coyote, or endurance, as in wolves. Some canids hunt in packs; many eat carrion, fruit and other plant material, or almost any edible matter available. Closely related to the dog family are bears, the Ursidae, which are the largest

The leopard often drags its prey up into a tree to be eaten at leisure.

living terrestrial carnivores. Although there are tropical species, for the most part bears inhabit cold northern regions. In temperate climates they may take refuge in caves but do not actually hibernate. Bears have become omnivorous and lost the shearing capacity of their carnassials, but the polar bear is still a meat-eater. The giant panda, often classified in the bear family, has a unique diet of bamboo. Raccoons and their kin are medium-sized carnivores, also related to canids, and are New World species except for the lesser panda of China, Burma, and Nepal. The procyonids, as they are called, are omnivorous and arboreal. Their carnassials are modified for crushing. Mustelids are small animals with short legs and long bodies, and have well-developed scent glands. This family includes weasels, badgers, skunks, and otters and has a wide distribution in all climates, in both the Old and New Worlds. They seek out and prey upon various vertebrate animals smaller than themselves, such as rodents, and are known to eat insects as well. Similar to the mustelids in general appearance is a family of carnivores found in Africa and southern Eurasia, the Viverridae. They are the civets and genets. Like mustelids, viverrids have strong scent glands and feed upon smaller animals. They do not tolerate cold climates, however. Again unlike mustelids, they have retractile or semiretractile claws. Mongooses, the Herpestidae, were until recently placed in the Viverridae, but their distinctness has recently become

Walruses are highly gregarious, aquatic carnivore, which prefer shallow coastal waters. Their herds can number up to 2,000.

more convincing. The hyenas of Africa and southern Asia constitute a separate family. These strong, heavy animals are dog-sized; they have longer forelegs than hind, nonretractile claws, and well-developed carnassials. They are predatory and also feed on carrion. The aardwolf, in a family by itself, prefers a diet of ants, termites, and insect larvae. The well-known felids, or cat family, range worldwide except in Australia, Antarctica, and certain islands. They are the acme of predators, with strong limbs and sharp, curved, retractile claws, able to stalk, run down, and kill prey of their own size or very much larger. The cheetah's claws are only semiretractile.

The seals, sea lions, and walrus—the pinnipeds—are highly aquatic carnivores, found along nearly all coastal regions of the world, including the Arctic and Antarctic. Their bodies are streamlined and their limbs are modified for swimming, but unlike cetaceans, they have kept their hind limbs. They breed and give birth on land; in fact, some species spend considerable time ashore. All are carnivorous, the diets varying from fish to marine invertebrates, birds, or even other seals. Most pinnipeds are diurnal, and some are highly gregarious.

Proboscidea

The sole present-day survivors of a once prevalent order are just two species of elephant—those colossal pachyderms which inhabit Africa south of the Sahara and India, Sri Lanka,

The smaller Indian elephant is the species commonly domesticated, although large African elephants were also used for transport in ancient Roman times.

and southeast Asia. They are the largest living land mammals and can exceed six tons in weight. Their now extinct relatives were dozens of species of remarkable animals known from fossils and included the mammoths hunted by ancient man.

Elephants are easily recognized by their immense size and long trunk—really an extraordinary modification of the nose. The trunk is strong and sensitive; the tip is used to pick up small objects with great facility. The tusks are elongated upper incisors. Elephants have no canines or premolars, and the molars used to grind their herbaceous food are replaced successively from behind as they wear down. Their large external ears act as coolers in hot weather; heat is dissipated from the extensive surface area by fanning. Their legs are like pillars supporting great weight and bulk. When elephants walk, at either a slow or a fast rate, they must keep two legs on the ground at all times; they cannot jump.

Elephants travel in herds and forage on trees, shrubs, and grasses. An adult male elephant consumes 300 to 400 pounds of herbage per day, for which he must forage widely—covering up to 20 miles a day.

Hyracoidea

The hyrax, or dassie, is an odd mammal that superficially resembles a rodent and is about the size of a rabbit. It is neither, however, but is more closely related to elephants and manatees. Hyraxes are found in Africa and in the Arabian peninsula, living in diverse habitats. There are five species which together make up the order Hyracoidea.

Hyraxes have a short, rather blunt head; small ears; and a pair of widely separated, protruding, and pointed upper incisors which grow continuously from the base. In place of canines there is a wide gap, similar to that in rodents and lagomorphs. Their plantigrade feet are peculiar, with peglike toes that are united to the last joint, and soles with moistened pads that can be drawn in like suction cups to provide traction. This is an especially useful adaptation, as hyraxes scurry among the rocks or over upright tree trunks with ease. They live in colonies of five to fifty individuals, and are herbivorous in diet.

Sirenia

The sirenians are just four living species——one dugong and three manatees. The last of the sea cows, formerly seen in the north Pacific, was slaughtered by man and has been extinct for two centuries. Manatees and the dugong are completely aquatic, inhabiting the tropical coastal waters and certain adjacent rivers of the Caribbean Sea and Atlantic South America, as well as Africa and southern Asia to northern Australia.

They are large mammals, up to 10 feet long and 450 to 500 pounds in weight, somewhat resembling cetaceans in shape and modifications for marine life. The forelimbs are paddles, hind limbs are absent, the tail is wide and flat; there are no fins. The skin is thick, wrinkled, and practically hairless except for strong vibrissae around the mouth; the nose is blunt. Sirenians have no external ears. Only the cheek teeth are functional; manatees have a single upper incisor on each side, dugongs have none, and neither has canines. The molars are replaced from behind in the manatees, somewhat as in elephants. The stomach is complex, with three chambers.

Dugongs and manatees are slow, placid, quite defenseless creatures who spend their time browsing on marine plant life. Despite their external appearance and aquatic habit, like hyraxes they are most closely akin to elephants, with which they have a common ancestry.

Perissodactyla

All the hoofed mammals, thought to be closely related, were once placed together in a vast order labeled Ungulata. We now know that there are two quite distinct groups, taxonomically separated on the basis of their toes, though we often still speak of "ungulates" for the sake of convenience. First of the two orders is the Perissodactyla, or odd-toed ungulates, which refers to the fact that their weight is borne by the longer middle, or third, digit on each foot. Horses and their kin, tapirs, and rhinoceros make up this order of some 16 living species. These are only the few survivors of a once vast assemblage of mammals, today distributed in tropical America, eastern and southern Africa, and southern Asia to Borneo. Members of the horse family——asses and zebras——and rhinos live in open scrub or savanna, whereas tapirs are usually found in tropical forests. All perissodactyls are large animals and herbivorous in diet. Their cheek teeth are massive, strong, and modified for

Today, the horse is a thoroughly domestic animal, even though some breeds, like these from the Camargue in France, have regained their liberty. Its wild ancestor now numbers very few specimens in the mountains of southwestern Mongolia.

grinding. They do not have tusks or true horns; those of rhinos are cornified skin without a bony core.

Tapirs are the most primitive of the order and in many ways probably resemble the early ancestors of the Perissodactyla back in Eocene times. Tapirs and rhinos both are heavy-bodied with short legs.

Of the entire order it is the horse family——the equids——that are truly modified for fast running. Their limbs are long and slender for striding and their toes have evolved into a single digit——a hoof——on each foot. And their musculature has developed to make the best use of these features. They are thus able to avoid predators on the open grasslands, where shelter is scarce or nonexistent, and they can seek food and water over great distances. We have a very complete fossil record of the horse's evolution in North America, where this animal apparently originated but disappeared long before the advent of man. Wild horses roamed Eurasia within historic times.

Artiodactyla

All the remaining ungulates belong to the order Artiodactyla. These are even-toed, which means the axis of the foot lies between the ''third'' and ''fourth'' digits, or their weight is borne equally by the middle toes. The first digit has been lost in evolution and can be seen only in fossil forms. The second and fifth toes, those on the sides, are also lacking in certain living species——''beasts of cloven hoof''——or are vestigial in others, thereby leaving two prominent, functioning toes on each foot.

A duel between two ibex. In order to impose their superiority within the group, or to lay claim to a particular female, or to defend a harem, males often engage one another in fierce duels, particularly during the mating season.

This is the important diagnostic feature of artiodactyls. A further distinction setting the two apart is the development of true horns or antlers among the even-toed ungulates.

These are the more successful ungulates, too, as the order embraces some 181 living species and is found on all continents except Australia and Antarctica, and on some islands. A vast array of mammals are the artiodactyls—pigs and peccaries, hippos, camels and llamas, chevrotains and deer, giraffes, pronghorns, and antelope of every description, together with cattle, sheep, and goats. They can be as small as a five- or six-pound mouse deer (*Tragulus javanicus*) or dik-dik (*Madoqua*), as tall as a giraffe, or as heavy as a nearly one-ton giant eland (*Tragelaphus derbianus*) or Indian gaur (*Bos gaurus*). Overall, however, there is considerable uniformity in their anatomy. The cheek teeth are large, often complex, and effective for grinding since artiodactyls are herbivores. The upper incisors and canines are reduced or absent, although in a few species they are elongated like tusks. Pigs, peccaries, and hippos have a two- or three-chambered stomach and are not ruminating animals; camels and their South American cousins the llamas, as well as chevrotains, are cud-chewers but have a three-chambered stomach; all other even-toed ungulates are ruminants and have a four-chambered stomach. Many artiodactyls, such as antelope of various kinds, are highly cursorial—that is, fast-running—animals. Like horses among the Perissodactyla, these are often grazing species found in enormous herds on open grasslands. They too have long, slender limbs and are built for speed.

It is from among the artiodactyls—animals which primitive man doubtless hunted—that man selected his domestic livestock several millenia ago.

Xenarthra

New World in their distribution, the xenarthrans consist of 29 species in four distinct families—anteaters, sloths (two families), and armadillos. Anteaters are toothless; sloths and armadillos lack incisors and canines, but do have simple cheek teeth that lack enamel and grow continuously from the roots as the tops wear down. Armadillos have up to 100 such teeth.

The skull is elongated and the brain small and narrow. The vertebrae of the lumbar region have an extra articulation, a skeletal feature peculiar to this order. Their specially strengthened backbone may have evolved from the defense posture that anteaters assume. If threatened, the animal stands erect on its hind legs and braces itself with its strong, heavy tail, forming a tripod. It then proceeds to lash out with its powerful arms, slashing with its formidable claws. Giant ancestors of today's anteaters may have defended themselves in this manner against such attackers as sabertooth cats.

The xenarthrans that we know in present times are but a remnant of their Cenozoic past. While in Argentina, in 1833, on the famous voyage of the *Beagle,* Darwin collected fossils of one of the most fantastic mammals ever to live—a glyptodont. Glyptodonts were ancient armadillos, but of giant proportions; some were about 12 feet long. They were completely armored, having a bony helmet on the head, a great bony mosaic covering the back and sides of the body, and jointed armor plate over the tail, terminating in a defensive, multispiked club. They once roamed the region from Arizona to Florida, as well as Central and South America. The giant ground sloth, as big as a rhinoceros, lived throughout the New World and was another of the fossil xenarthrans Darwin picked up in South America. Ground sloths became extinct near the end of the Pleistocene, only about 10,000 years ago, and were known to early man in the Americas.

Today, except for the armadillos, xenarthrans are tropical dwellers—found in Central and South America. The nine-banded armadillo (*Dasypus novemcinctus*) ranges into the southwestern United States, and other armadillo species live in temperate, even near-desert, regions in South America. Like their ancestors, though perhaps less extreme, armadillos are armored with jointed, bony plates covered with cornified epidermis. Sparse hair grows between the plates and on unarmored parts of the body and limbs. Anteaters and sloths are well furred, without armor.

Lagomorpha

Who is not familiar with rabbits and hares? They have been among the first mammals we learn about in childhood since the time of Aesop. Together with the pikas, they form a small but distinct order known as Lagomorpha. The lagomorphs are strictly ground-dwelling and inhabit all continents, except Antarctica; they were introduced by man, with dire consequences, into Australia and New Zealand. There is no extreme variation among lagomorph species; all are about the size of domestic cats, give or take a few pounds. All have short tails. Pikas have short, round ears; hares and rabbits, long, narrow ears. Similar to rodents, to which lagomorphs are *not* closely related, they have ever-growing incisors, but the uppers total four, two of which are small and located behind the two larger ones. They also have a large gap behind the incisors. All are herbivorous. Pikas, fourteen species in all, live in colonies among rocks, often in cold, montane regions. They are diurnal. The forty species of hares and rabbits inhabit grassy areas, where they generally forage at dawn and dusk, that is, they are crepuscular. They live in burrows.

Tubulidentata

Perhaps we think of the aardvark only as being the first word in the dictionary, but it is so extraordinary among mammals that it is placed in an order all by itself. The aardvark is a beautiless beast that looks something like a long-nosed, rabbit-eared pig Its name means "earth-pig" in Afrikaans. It is found in Africa in areas where its only foods——ants and termites——are in good supply. Well adapted to such a specialized diet, its strong limbs and heavy claws easily dig into termite mounds. It has a long, sticky tongue, thick skin, and an acute sense of smell. Incisors and canines are absent, but the aardvark has on each side five upper and four lower cheek teeth which are peculiarly tubular in structure. It is from this feature that the name of the order is derived. Skeletal evidence suggests that the aardvark descended from primitive ungulates.

OF MAMMALS AND MEN

From the very beginning, man's relationship with other mammals can be put in one word: predatory. For like his ancestors before him, Paleolithic, or Old Stone Age, man was a hunter. He was carnivorous in diet——or more precisely, omnivorous, since his feeding habits were really opportunistic. Primitive man ate whatever came to hand: fruit and other herbaceous matter along with insect grubs, shellfish if available, small vertebrates, and certainly mammal meat. *Homo sapiens* used his superior intelligence to fashion weapons and his communicative ability to hunt together in groups. He killed not only small mammals, but the very largest. He ate their meat, used their bones for tools and weapons, clad and sheltered himself with their skins. Primitive man depended upon wild mammals for his very survival. His efficiency——making better weapons, setting traps, and lighting fires——had devastating effects. It now appears that ancient man learned to drive large game animals to the slaughter by deliberately burning grasslands and scrub, destroying hordes of wildlife and their habitat in the process. There is a growing body of evidence indicating that between 30,000 and 10,000 years ago, at the very time and place predatory human populations increased, a vast fauna of large mammals coincidentally became extinct. Great mammoths, the woolly rhinoceros, the Irish elk, the cave hyena, the cave lion,

the cave bear, and others disappeared from Europe; antelope of several kinds, a giant deer and giant baboons, several species of boar, and the scimitar-toothed cats became extinct in Africa; and ground sloths, the giant beaver, an antelope and other species died out in the New World. Climatic changes may have had a part in the passing of so many great mammals in so short a time, but most probably man played the leading role as exterminator.

By the end of the Ice Age man had grown more sophisticated, his wants and needs more varied. It was probably some 12,000 years ago, if not before, that two predators—man and dog—became allies: the wolf was domesticated. By about 9,000 years ago, in western Asia man had begun to plant crops and raise his own livestock. He domesticated, from wild species, sheep, goats, cattle, and pigs, possibly in that order. These species, together with the Asian horse—which was not tamed until the third millennium B.C.—are today still the principal species around which man has built his life. So thorough was the taming of the wild beast, in fact, that certain species no longer exist in the wild state and can be found only in manmade varieties. The great ox, or aurochs (*Bos primigenius*), ancestor of domestic cattle, and the unknown progenitor of the dromedary, or Arabian camel, are two examples.

Thus man came to exploit other mammals not just for their meat and leather, but as beasts of burden as well. They supplied his transportation, plowed his fields, cleared timber. Some even provided milk for his children. Modern man, following in the footsteps of his forebears, domesticated additional species to meet his modern needs. Mice, rats, guinea pigs, rabbits, and monkeys became experimental animals in medical research. Foxes, minks, chinchillas, nutrias, and others are bred in captivity to produce pelts for the fur trade.

It was not by breeding captives, however, that man decimated so many species of mammals. He accomplished this by treating wild populations as ever-growing, unending stores that would always supply his wants, be they hides, glandular secretions for perfume manufacture, ivory for carving, or merely sport—killing for the joy of killing. Considerably more fur-bearers are taken in the wild than are ever raised in captivity. Seals, leopards and ocelots, sables, martens, ermines, beavers and muskrats, even moles, monkeys, and opossums have supplied literally millions of pelts to the fur market. And they are but a few of several hundred such species. In the north Pacific, 18th-century fur hunters in quest of seals and sea otters completely obliterated Steller's sea cow (*Hydrodamalis gigas*) in just 27 years after its discovery. This animal was the giant among sirenians, up to 30 feet in length, and was slaughtered for both its meat and its hide. Today about 1,000 of its near relatives—dugongs—are killed annually in Indonesia; their teeth are fashioned into cigarette holders for the export trade. In the past 400 years no fewer than forty full species of mammals have become extinct at the hands of man. Several hundred others now face the same end.

Above all else, the native habitats upon which all wild creatures depend are being forever destroyed at an alarming rate, faster today than ever before. Tropical and temperate forest lands alike, even sandy deserts, are cleared for their timber or to plant crops, build cities, or lay out golf courses.

Men of foresight have tried to preserve wildlife for posterity by controlling the quantities of game animals that may be hunted each season or marine species that may be harvested; by regulating the poisoning of species harmful to cultivated crops; and by breeding rare animals in zoos. By far the greatest hope lies in setting aside vast natural areas where all plant and animal life is protected. Such an idea was first implemented just over a century ago, in 1872, when Yellowstone National Park was created. It was too late to save species already annihilated, but offered the chance to forestall further extinctions. The Canadians followed immediately with Glacier and Banff National Parks in 1886 and 1887, respectively. By the turn of the century the nucleus of South Africa's Kruger National Park had been set aside. Today, countries on all continents maintain some sort of wildlife preserves, though far too inadequate to prevent the death of more species. Poachers still take their toll: elephants are still slain for their ivory, South American monkeys are still captured for pet dealers, kangaroos are still shot as "pests," American bighorn sheep are still killed for trophy heads, whales are still harpooned for dog food . . . .

Perhaps man has found it easier to destroy than to nurture his fellow mammals.

A CLASSIFICATION OF LIVING MAMMALS

Order	Family	Common names	Entry numbers
SUBCLASS PROTOTHERIA			
Monotremata	Tachyglossidae	Echidnas	1
	Ornithorhynchidae	Platypus	2
SUBCLASS THERIA			
Infraclass Metatheria			
Marsupialia	Didelphidae	Opossums	3–5
	Microbiotheriidae	Monito del monte	
	Caenolestidae	Rat opposums	
	Dasyuridae	Marsupial mice, quoll	6–10
	Myrmecobiidae	Numbat	11
	Thylacinidae	Thylacine	
	Peramelidae	Bandicoots	12
	Thylacomyidae	Rabbit bandicoots	
	Notoryctidae	Marsupial moles	
	Phalangeridae	Possums, cuscuses	13–14
	Petauridae	Gliders, ringtails	17–19, 22–23
	Burramyidae	Pygmy possums	15–16
	Macropodidae	Kangaroos, wallabies	25–32
	Tarsipedidae	Honey possum	20
	Vombatidae	Wombats	24
	Phascolarctidae	Koala	21
Infraclass Eutheria			
Insectivora	Solenodontidae	Solenodons	33
	Tenrecidae	Tenrecs, otter shrews	34–37
	Chrysochloridae	Golden moles	38
	Erinaceidae	Hedgehogs, moonrats	39–40
	Soricidae	Shrews	43–48
	Talpidae	Moles, desmans	49–51
Macroscelidia	Macroscelididae	Elephant shrews	41–42
Dermoptera	Cynocephalidae	Flying lemurs	52
Chiroptera	Pteropodidae	Fruit bats, flying foxes	53–59
	Rhinopomatidae	Mouse-tailed bats	
	Craseonycteridae	Hog-nosed, or bumblebee, bat	
	Emballonuridae	Sheath-tailed bats	60
	Nycteridae	Slit-faced bats	
	Megadermatidae	False vampire bats	62–63
	Rhinolophidae	Horseshoe bats	64–65
	Noctilionidae	Bulldog bats, fisherman bats	61
	Mormoopidae		
	Phyllostomidae	New World leaf-nosed bats	66–70
	Natalidae		
	Furipteridae		
	Thyropteridae		
	Myzapodidae		
	Vespertilionidae	Common bats	71–80
	Mystacinidae	Short-tailed bat	
	Molossidae	Free-tailed bats	81–82

1 TACHYGLOSSUS ACULEATUS
Echidna, spiny anteater

Classification   Order Monotremata, Family Tachyglossidae.

Description   A heavy, round-bodied animal; covered with short, pointed spines mixed with coarse hairs except on underparts; small tail; long, narrow beak with tiny, toothless mouth; 5 toes on each foot with strong, broad claws and long, curved claw on second toe of hind feet. Males about 35–45 cm (13.5–17.5 in) in length, weight 3–6 kg (6.5–14.5 lb); females somewhat smaller.

Distribution   Throughout Australia including Tasmania, and in southern New Guinea.

Habitat   Virtually all terrestrial situations.

Behavior   The crepuscular and nocturnal echidna digs out ants and termites which adhere to its long sticky tongue. It has a keen sense of smell and good hearing, but weak vision. Its long hind claw is used to clean between its spines. The echidna shelters among rocks or in hollow logs rather than digging tunnels, but quickly burrows straight down into the soil to escape enemies or rolls into a prickly ball for protection. It can fast for long periods. Usually 1 (rarely 2 or 3) egg is laid and incubated for 10 days in a temporary pouch on the female's abdomen, where the naked young remains until its spines begin to appear. The mother then deposits it in a sheltered place, returning daily for about 3 months to suckle it until it is weaned.

2 ORNITHORHYNCHUS ANATINUS
Platypus, duckbill

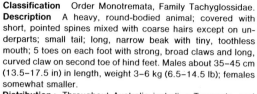

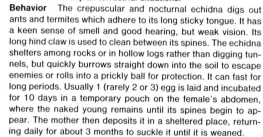

Classification   Order Monotremata, Family Ornithorhynchidae.

Description   Long, flat-bodied animal covered with short, velvety brown fur; muzzle is a flexible, leathery, ducklike bill; short, wide tail; webbed feet, male with poisonous spur on hind feet. Males about 61 cm (24 in) total length, weight 2 kg (4.4 lb); females about 46 cm (18 in).

Distribution   Eastern Australia including Tasmania.

Habitat   Freshwater streams, rivers, and lakes.

Behavior   The crepuscular platypus is aquatic and burrows extensively into riverbanks, usually leaving an entrance below water and another above. It subsists on small aquatic animals, vertebrate and invertebrate, taken from the muddy stream bottom. The food is located by touch with the sensitive bill and collected in cheek pouches, wherein sand and grit probably help mastication as the adult platypus has no teeth; food is also crushed between horny plates inside the bill. A platypus stays submerged for about 1 minute with eyes and ears closed. From 1–3, usually 2, small eggs are laid from annual breeding, August–October, and incubated by the mother in a grass-and-leaf nest in the burrow for 12–14 days. Young platypuses leave the burrow and swim at 17 weeks of age. The venomous spur on the male's hind feet may be used for defense and helps in the capture of prey such as frogs.

3 MARMOSA MURINA
Mouse opossum, murine opossum

Classification   Order Marsupialia, Family Didelphidae.
Description   Mouselike creature with rather pointed muzzle; long, hairless, prehensile tail; thin, moderate-sized, naked ears. Dense, lax fur of brown to cinnamon color dorsally, buff on underparts, and pronounced black patch surrounding the large eyes. Head and body length 10–22 cm (about 4–8 in); weight about 250 g (0.6 lb).
Distribution   Amazon and Orinoco River basins and adjacent lower parts of the Andes.
Habitat   Principally tropical rain forest.
Behavior   The murine opossum is one of 41 recognized species of mouse opossums widespread from southern Mexico to Patagonia. This species is solitary, nocturnal, and arboreal in habit. Its opposable hallux and prehensile tail help it to grasp small twigs and vines while climbing. Daytime hours are spent sleeping in an abandoned bird's nest or a tree hollow. Murine opossums eat fruit and insects. Although a true marsupial, the female has no pouch. The offspring, 5 or more in a litter, each cling to a teat or, when older, hold fast to the fur of their mother's back. Murine opossums breed throughout the year and have a gestation period of about 14 days.

4 DIDELPHIS VIRGINIANA
Virginia opossum

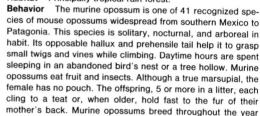

Classification   Order Marsupialia, Family Didelphidae.
Description   About house-cat size with short legs; opposable, clawless hallux; long, flattened, pointed muzzle; small, thin, hairless ears; long, nearly naked, scaly, prehensile tail. Pelage is long, gray or brown, with numerous white guard hairs throughout. Head and body length 38–51 cm (15–20 in), weight 4–6 kg (9–13 lb); females smaller than males.
Distribution   United States east of the Rocky Mountains, through Mexico and Central America to Costa Rica; introduced and well established in Pacific coastal North America from San Diego, California, to Crescent Beach, British Columbia.
Habitat   Virtually all situations; prefers wooded areas.
Behavior   The only marsupial species found in the United States, and still hunted for its meat and fur, the Virginia opossum is solitary and nocturnal in habit. It is both arboreal and terrestrial, and builds its nest of leaves in tree hollows. Its omnivorous diet includes fruit, insects, eggs, small vertebrates. Individuals in the northern reaches of its range often lose portions of tail and ears to frostbite. When pursued, the opossum can feign death; that is, "play 'possum." Females have a well-developed pouch and produce an average of 7 young per litter, once or twice a year. Gestation is 12–13 days; young are weaned at 100–101 days of age and carried on their mother's back.

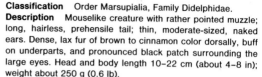

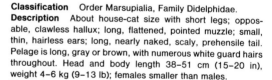

5 CHIRONECTES MINIMUS
Yapok, water opossum

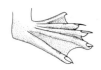

Classification　Order Marsupialia, Family Didelphidae.

Description　A long-legged opossum with relatively broad muzzle; long, almost hairless, scaly tail except at its base; a modified wrist bone simulating a sixth digit on the forefeet, webbed hind feet. Short, dense fur with round black patches on back and head, contrasting with gray; white beneath. Head and body about 28 cm (11 in) long; weight 610–790 g (1.3–1.7 lb).

Distribution　Southern Mexico to northern Argentina.

Habitat　Freshwater rivers and lakes.

Behavior　Known from lowland rivers to mountain streams of at least 6000 feet elevation in the eastern Andes, the yapok is the only truly aquatic marsupial. It burrows into stream banks, leaving an entrance just above water level, and with a nesting chamber dug at the end of a descending tunnel. It may also have a nest of leaves or grass on the ground surface for an occasional daytime retreat. An expert swimmer and diver, it eats crustaceans, fish, and other small aquatic animals, and is nocturnal in habit. The female's pouch can be closed by a sphincter muscle surrounding its edge, rendering it waterproof for the young carried inside while the mother swims. The male yapok has a ventral pouch protecting the scrotum. An average of 2 or 3 young are born in December–January.

6 ANTECHINUS FLAVIPES
Yellow-footed antechinus, mardo

Classification　Order Marsupialia, Family Dasyuridae.

Description　A marsupial the size of a large mouse with pointed muzzle; short-haired, moderately long tail; short, broad feet of buff to yellow-brown color. Fur on back and sides red-brown, with gray hairs on head. Head and body length about 10–13 cm (4–5.2 in); weight about 30 g (1 oz).

Distribution　Eastern, southeastern, and southwestern Australia.

Habitat　Rain forest, eucalypt forests, and woodlands.

Behavior　These semi-arboreal, primitive little marsupials live in hollow trees, fallen logs, and rock crevices, and particularly favor sandstone caves. Active at night, the antechinus feeds upon insects and small vertebrates. It is a common form throughout most of its range, though rarely seen, and is preyed upon by owls, snakes, and the larger carnivorous members of its own family. During the breeding season the antechinus builds an intricately woven nest of eucalypt leaves. Annual mating occurs in the winter, July–September, with a gestation period of 23–27 days, after which 10–12 minute young are born and attach themselves to the mother's teats. There is no pouch in this species, but the area around the teats is surrounded by a slightly raised edge. Among the 12 species of *Antechinus* related to *A. flavipes,* the pouch may be completely absent, partially or well developed.

7 DASYUROIDES BYRNEI
Crested-tailed marsupial rat, kowari

Classification Order Marsupialia, Family Dasyuridae.
Description A ratlike marsupial with a distinctive black brush on distal half of its long tail; body covered in dense, soft, grayish hair, tinged yellow-brown with creamy white underparts; feet white and without hallux on hind feet; the ears are long and hairless. Head and body 16.5–18.4 cm (6.5–7.3 in) long; weight around 75 g (2.6 oz).
Distribution Central Australia—junction of Northern Territory, Queensland, and South Australia.
Habitat Sandy and rocky desert; arid grassland.
Behavior The desert-dwelling kowari burrows in the ground wherein it constructs a nest of dry grass. It is most active at night, though also about by day. It is predatory, feeding upon small vertebrates such as rodents, as well as on insects. Although terrestrial, the kowari can climb with agility and can leap at least 18 inches vertically. The animals are known to bask in the sun and clean their fur by sand bathing. The female pouch is poorly developed, being simply 2 low, lateral folds between which are 6 or 7 teats to accommodate the same number of young per litter. Young are born from May to October after a gestation period of 30–35 days. Maturity is reached by 12 months of age. Females can bear 2 litters in succession per year.

---

8 SMINTHOPSIS CRASSICAUDATA
Fat-tailed dunnart, narrow-footed marsupial mouse

Classification Order Marsupialia, Family Dasyuridae.
Description A delicate mouselike marsupial with wide face, yet sharply pointed muzzle; small, slender limbs and feet; large ears; tail of moderate length. Pelage soft and fine, ashy gray in color dorsally, lighter beneath. Head and body length 7.5–8.5 cm (3–3.5 in); weight 15–25 g (0.5–0.9 oz).
Distribution Australia: southern and interior southeastern regions; southwest.
Habitat Dry scrub, woodland, and grasslands; sandy and rocky areas.
Behavior This active, common little animal is nocturnal and terrestrial. Consuming as much as its own weight daily, it lives entirely upon small insects and other arthropods but, unlike some of its close relatives, will not catch vertebrates. Under stress of starvation it may become torpid; however, it can draw upon fat stored in its tail to see it through times of food scarcity. The dunnart burrows in the ground, lives under rocks, or builds nests of leaves and grass in sheltered places such as hollow logs. It breeds year round. A female may produce successive litters, of up to 10 young each, constantly for a 6-month period. Gestation is 13–16 days. The female pouch is well developed. The young leave the pouch at 40–43 days, are placed in the nest, and become entirely independent when 61–69 days old.

9 DASYURUS MACULATUS
Tiger cat

Classification   Order Marsupialia, Family Dasyuridae.
Description   A muscular, red-brown, white-spotted marsupial the size of a large house cat; with long tail, also spotted; short, thick fur; comparatively blunt muzzle; short, rounded ears; 5 toes on hind feet. Head and body 40–77 cm (16–31 in) long; weight about 1.1 kg (2.4 lb).
Distribution   Eastern and southeastern mainland Australia; common in Tasmania.
Habitat   Rain forest and eucalypt forests.

Behavior   Largest of the 5 ''native cats'' of the Australian Region and closely related to the Tasmanian devil, the tiger cat is sometimes placed in a separate genus *Dasyurops*. It is a highly carnivorous marsupial, not a placental cat. A forest inhabitant, it is arboreal and has serrated foot pads and long, sharp claws to aid in climbing. The tiger cat is nocturnal and preys mostly upon smaller mammals and birds but is able to kill small wallabies. It is extremely agile, leaping from limb to limb or to the ground to pounce upon its prey. The female's pouch is a flap of skin covering the front and sides of the mammary area, forming a pocket. The breeding season is in winter; gestation approximately 21 days. Litters are of 4–6 young who become independent when about one-third adult size, at about 18 weeks of age.

10 SARCOPHILUS HARRISI
Tasmanian devil

Classification   Order Marsupialia, Family Dasyuridae.
Description   Stocky animal about the size of a small dog, with large head and wide neck; short muzzle; heavy limbs; rounded ears; tail of medium length. Pelage short, dense, soft; uniformly black, sometimes with white crescent on chest and white patches on shoulders or rump. Head and body length, 53–76 cm (21–30 in); weight up to 11.8 kg (26 lb).
Distribution   Tasmania.
Habitat   Eucalypt forest.

Behavior   Largest of the dasyurids—family of carnivorous marsupials—the Tasmanian devil has powerful jaws to devour its prey, including the bones. It feeds on small mammals, reptiles, fish, and invertebrates, and often eats carrion. It is crepuscular and nocturnal in habit, primarily terrestrial though able to climb. The animal is slow but cunning and strong, smells out its prey, and takes it by surprise. Daytime shelter is in a hollow log or rock crevice where a nest is built of bark or grass. The breeding season is during March–May, and 1–4 young are born after a gestation of some 31 days. There are 4 teats in the pouch. When 15 weeks old the young are left in the nest or are carried on their mother's back. They are weaned at 20 weeks of age.

11 MYRMECOBIUS FASCIATUS
Numbat, banded anteater

Classification Order Marsupialia, Family Myrmecobiidae.
Description A squirrel-sized, delicately formed animal with long, pointed snout and long, well-haired tail. Colorfully marked, grizzled red-brown dorsal pelage bears transverse white stripes; a dark band, with parallel white stripes above and below, runs from the ear through the eye to the nose; white beneath. Head and body length about 25.5 cm (10 in); weight 280–450 g (9.8–15.8 oz).
Distribution Southwestern Australia, northwestern South Australia.
Habitat Eucalypt forest and desert.
Behavior The solitary, terrestrial, and diurnally active numbat inhabits a woodland of scattered wandoo trees—an open forest with much litter of fallen logs and limbs, riddled with termites. The numbat lives on the termites, which it collects with its long, narrow, darting tongue; and takes shelter in the hollow logs where it nests. The animal is deliberate in its search for termites which, once located, it digs out quickly. It frequently sunbathes during winter. When it suspects a predatory eagle overhead, the numbat runs for shelter, first stopping to stand on its haunches and survey the situation. Breeding is from December–April; the 2–4 young per litter are born between January and May. The female is pouchless but her offspring cling to the 4 teats available. Young are weaned in about 6 months.

12 PERAMELES NASUTA
Common long-nosed bandicoot

Classification Order Marsupialia, Family Peramelidae.
Description A small, slender marsupial with long, tapered muzzle; long, narrow, pointed ears; short tail; hind legs with second and third toes united. The dorsal fur is coarse, thin, gray-brown in color; lighter beneath. Head and body 31–42.5 cm (12.3–16.5 in) long; weight about 500 g (1.1 lb).
Distribution Eastern coastal Australia.
Habitat Rain forest, eucalypt forest, and woodland.
Behavior The nocturnal and strictly terrestrial common bandicoot, one of 15 species in the Australian Region, eats insects, grubs, and earthworms, which it finds by scratching through ground litter and digging shallow holes in the soil. It is solitary and builds a nest by piling up humus, twigs, and leaves under shelter of thick brush. Though not a burrowing animal the bandicoot will nest in abandoned rabbit tunnels, as well as in hollow logs or among rocks. It breeds throughout the year. Gestation is about 12 days. As a rule there are no more than 4 young per litter; that is, half the number of the mother's teats. A second litter is often born before the first litter is weaned at approximately 60 days of age, the newcomers attaching themselves to the vacant teats. The well-developed pouch opens backward in all species of bandicoots.

13 PHALANGER MACULATUS
Spotted phalanger, spotted cuscus

Classification   Order Marsupialia, Family Phalangeridae.
Description   A monkeylike possum with strong, prehensile tail which is naked over the terminal half; small ears. Fur thick and woolly; gray to rust color, often with cream or white blotches, or entire animal sometimes nearly white. Head and body length about 65 cm (25.5 in); weight about 6 kg (13 lb).
Distribution   Cape York peninsula of Australia; New Guinea, New Britain, and Admiralty Islands.
Habitat   Tropical rain forest.
Behavior   Largest of the possums, the cuscus is a slow-moving, sluggish animal, a bit larger than a house cat, strictly arboreal in habit. By day it rests in a tree, curled up among dense foliage or in a hollow. At night the cuscus climbs through the trees, feeding upon leaves and fruit; it will also attack and devour birds or small reptiles. Man is its principal enemy; the natives of New Guinea catch cuscuses to eat. Breeding is believed to be throughout the year rather than seasonal. Gestation is reported to be about 13 days and 2–4 offspring may be born, with only 1 surviving a short time later in the pouch. The spotted cuscus is one of several species occurring in the Celebes and eastward to the Solomon Islands.

---

14 TRICHOSURUS VULPECULA
Brushtail possum

Classification   Order Marsupialia, Family Phalangeridae.
Description   A large, stout possum with long, bushy, prehensile tail that lacks fur on the terminal half of the underside; large, erect ears; face foxlike. The dense, woolly fur is silvery gray, often nearly black, dorsally; yellow or buff beneath; tail tipped black or white; completely white or cream individuals are not uncommon. Head and body length 32–58 cm (12.2–23 in), weight up to 5 kg (11 lb).
Distribution   Throughout most of Australia (except parts of the interior), including Tasmania; introduced in New Zealand.
Habitat   All wooded and forested areas.
Behavior   Despite being hunted for its fur, the brushtail is one of Australia's most common marsupials. It is found virtually everywhere eucalypts grow, even in the arid interior where scattered trees hug the riverbanks. Primarily arboreal, the brushtail spends the day sleeping inside a tree hollow, venturing short distances at night to feed upon leaves and buds. Insects and small animals are also eaten. In the absence of trees it will seek shelter in shrubs or abandoned rabbit burrows. Usually a single young is born after a gestation period of 17 days. Breeding is once or twice per year. Offspring leave the pouch at about 5 months of age.

15 ACROBATES PYGMAEUS
Feathertail glider, pygmy glider

Classification Order Marsupialia, Family Burramyidae.
Description A tiny, mouse-sized possum with a fold of skin from wrist to ankle that forms a gliding membrane; long, prehensile, evenly fringed, featherlike tail. The silky pelage is chocolate or grayish brown on the upper parts and white beneath. Length of head and body about 6–7 cm (2.4–2.8 in); weight 12–16 g (0.4–0.6 oz).
Distribution Eastern and southeastern Australia.
Habitat Forests and woodlands.
Behavior Smallest of the marsupial gliders, the tiny and delicate feathertail is a strictly arboreal inhabitant of eucalypt forests. By day it sleeps curled up in a small, spherical nest—about 3½ inches diameter—ingeniously woven of leaves transported under its curled tail, and built inside a tree hollow or knothole. Solitary or sometimes found in small groups, the nocturnal feathertail eats insects, nectar, and blossoms. It crawls along narrow branches and twigs, and when it reaches the outside edge of a branch, the tiny creature suddenly leaps out and slightly downward, spreading its gliding membranes, and, with tail outstretched as a rudder, it speeds through the air like a projectile, landing on a neighboring tree. The young number from 1 to a maximum of 4 per litter. The reproductive habits of this species are little known.

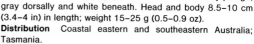

16 CERCARTETUS NANUS
Eastern pygmy possum

Classification Order Marsupialia, Family Burramyidae.
Description A small, mouselike possum with large, thin, sparsely haired ears; long, prehensile tail. Soft woolly pelage, gray dorsally and white beneath. Head and body 8.5–10 cm (3.4–4 in) in length; weight 15–25 g (0.5–0.9 oz).
Distribution Coastal eastern and southeastern Australia; Tasmania.
Habitat Eucalypt forests.
Behavior Solitary, arboreal, and nocturnal in habit, the pygmy possum nests in small hollows or knotholes, using a soft bark, which it will collect up to a quarter mile away if necessary, for nesting material. It consumes nectar and insect larvae, as well as beetles and moths which it catches in flight. Activity is regulated by outside temperature; thus the pygmy possum eats less in winter and grows thin but consumes more in summer months when its body and tail become swollen with fat. Curled into a tight ball, it hibernates during cold weather but for only a few days at a time. When active it often winds its tail around the branch, climbing in the manner of a European dormouse. When not in use, the tail may be carried tightly coiled. Pygmy possums breed in the spring and have a maximum of 4 young per litter. Six species are known, 2 of which inhabit New Guinea.

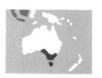

17 GYMNOBELIDEUS LEADBEATERI
Leadbeater's possum

Classification   Order Marsupialia, Family Petauridae.
Description   A squirrel-like possum with long, furred tail, bushy near tip; spatulate digits with short claws. Thick, soft pelage gray-brown dorsally, white or buff beneath; dark band from forehead to rump, dark patches at base of ears and above and below eyes. Head and body length 15–17 cm (6–6.8 in), weight 150–250 g (5.3–8.8 oz).
Distribution   Southeastern Victoria, Australia.
Habitat   Dense wet eucalypt forest.
Behavior   Known from only 5 specimens collected before 1910, Leadbeater's possum was thought to be extinct until 1961, when several were seen alive and 2 specimens subsequently collected by Australian scientists. The species resembles the closely related sugar glider (*Petaurus breviceps*, **18**) but lacks the gliding membrane. Leadbeater's possum is highly arboreal and lives in heavily wooded forests, where it nimbly scrambles from branch to branch during the night. It makes a nest of loose bark in a tree hollow, and is known to eat beetles and a species of nocturnal flightless cave cricket that lives under bark, and it probably consumes other insects as well. Reproductive habits of the species are not yet known, though young have been found in the pouch in October–November, suggesting a breeding season in September. There are 4 teats and 2 young are believed average per litter.

---

18 PETAURUS BREVICEPS
Sugar glider

Classification   Order Marsupialia, Family Petauridae.
Description   A squirrel-sized possum with lateral gliding membrane from wrists to ankles; long, fluffy tail; slender, long-clawed digits. Fine, short, dense fur, ash gray dorsally, paler beneath; dark stripe from nose to rump. Head and body about 17 cm (6.8 in) long, weight 70–100 (2.5–3.5 oz).
Distribution   Coastal northern, eastern, and southeastern Australia; New Guinea and adjacent islands; introduced in Tasmania.
Habitat   Eucalypt forests and woodlands.
Behavior   Called sugar glider because of its fondness for the sweet sap exuded from the bark of certain eucalypt trees, this common arboreal marsupial uses its strong incisors to strip bark in search of its food. It also eats blossoms and insects. Nocturnal in habit, and with limbs and membranes outstretched, it glides as far as 150 feet between trees. The sugar glider carries leaves under its curled tail to the nesting site—a hollow trunk or limb. Sugar gliders are social, living in small family groups, and communicate by marking each other and their territory with glandular-secreted scent; they also mark their nests with urine. In addition, they use a variety of vocal sounds. Breeding year round, the sugar glider bears 1–3 offspring after a gestation of about 16 days. The young become independent at 4 months of age.

19 DACTYLOPSILA TRIVIRGATA
Striped possum

Classification   Order Marsupialia, Family Petauridae.
Description   A conspicuously marked, squirrel-like marsupial with dense, coarse fur and a long, bushy tail. General color white with black longitudinal stripes around eyes, down back and sides to the rump; tail often tipped white. Hands with fourth digit elongated, as are fourth and fifth toes. Head and body length 23.5–30 cm (about 9–12 in); weight about 170 g (6 oz).
Distribution   New Guinea; Cape York peninsula of Queensland, Australia.
Habitat   Tropical rain forest and gallery forest.
Behavior   This strikingly colored, strictly arboreal species spends the day asleep in a tree hollow, emerging at night to search for food. In contrast to the slow pace of other possums, its actions are quick and darting. Although it eats fruit and leaves, the striped possum feeds principally on insects and their larvae found inside dry, dead branches, which the possum easily rips open with its chiseled incisors. Detecting a grub or other morsel in a crevice, it probes with its extra-long, specialized fourth finger and extracts its prey much in the manner of the Madagascan aye-aye (**88**). The striped possum does not use its tail when climbing, but holds it upright. It often feeds while hanging upside down by its hind feet. Its breeding habits are unknown.

20 TARSIPES SPENCERAE
Honey possum, noolbenger

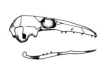

Classification   Order Marsupialia, Family Tarsipedidae.
Description   A mouse-sized, delicate possum with very long, whiplike prehensile tail and elongated, narrow, pointed muzzle. Short, coarse, gray-brown fur with 3 dark longitudinal stripes on back, light beneath; tail sparsely haired with naked tip. Head and body about 7.5 cm (3 in) long; weight 12–25 g (0.4–0.9 oz).
Distribution   Southwestern corner of Australia.
Habitat   Sandy plains, tree and shrub heathlands.
Behavior   With no known close relations, the unique, nimble honey possum is highly modified to feed on the nectar of flowers such as bottlebrush, banksia, and grivillea. Its skull is elongated and narrow, its teeth degenerated, the snout greatly lengthened, and its lips have overlapping flanges that form a strawlike tube through which it sucks nectar, pollen, and minute insects. The tongue, specially adapted to reach inside flowers, bears bristles and a tuft at the tip, is very thin, and can extend an inch beyond the tiny animal's nose. The nocturnal honey possum may move seasonally in colonies to favored plant species when in flower. By day it sleeps in a grass nest in thick shrubbery or in an abandoned bird's nest. The breeding season is probably June–August; litters contain 1–4 young, usually 2. At 4 months the young leave the pouch, nursing for 2 more weeks.

21 PHASCOLARCTOS CINEREUS
Koala

Classification   Order Marsupialia, Family Phascolarctidae.

Description   A heavy-bodied, tail-less animal with large tufted ears; bulbous, naked nose; thumb and forefinger opposable to other 3 digits. Pelage is thick and woolly, generally gray, whitish ventrally. Head and body about 80 cm (31.5 in) in length; average weight of males 10.5 kg (23 lb), females 8 kg (18 lb).

Distribution   Eastern and southwestern coastal Australia.

Habitat   Eucalypt forest and woodlands.

Behavior   Though heavy and clumsy, the arboreal koala is otherwise well adapted with strong limbs, sharp claws, and 2 opposable digits on its hands. Living alone or in small groups, it sleeps in the fork of low branches, without a nest, ascending at night to eat. Its diet is highly specialized—some 2.5 pounds daily of about 12 particular species of eucalypt leaves, some of which are avoided at certain seasons when they contain fatally poisonous prussic acid. The koala has a caecum 6–8 feet long, to aid digestion of bulky fiber. It also eats earth to obtain calcium and other minerals. Breeding is in September–January; gestation is about 35 days. The single young per year leaves the pouch after 8 months and clings to its mother's back, being weaned when 1 year old. Koalas are sexually mature at 3–4 years.

22 PSEUDOCHEIRUS PEREGRINUS
Common ringtail

Classification   Order Marsupialia, Family Petauridae.

Description   A relatively slender possum of house-cat size with long, tapering, prehensile tail; thumb and adjacent forefinger opposable to the other 3 digits. Coloration variable, generally gray-brown above, light beneath, with white patch behind the ears; tail tipped white. Head and body length, 29–36 cm (11.5–14.3 in); weight up to 1.3 kg (2.9 lb).

Distribution   Eastern and southeastern coastal Australia, through Great Dividing Range; Tasmania.

Habitat   Rain forests, eucalypt forests, and woodlands.

Behavior   Most common of 13 species found in New Guinea and Australia, the arboreal ringtail is active mostly between dusk and midnight. Its name is derived from its habit of holding its tail curled when not in use for climbing. It builds a large spherical nest—a foot in diameter—of leaves, grass, and twigs placed among branches or forks of heavy shrubs or trees, often within clumps of mistletoe. Both males and females work on the nest, built at any time of the year. The ringtail is strictly herbivorous, feeding on leaves and buds of trees, primarily eucalypt and acacia. There is usually 1 litter per year, born May–August; there may be 1–3 young in a litter, but most commonly 2, which permanently leave the pouch at about 120 days of age.

23 SCHOINOBATES VOLANS
Greater glider

Classification Order Marsupialia, Family Petauridae.
Description Large glider with prominent ears; tail longer than head and body; lateral gliding membrane from wrist to ankle but narrow along forearm and lower leg. Long, silky hair usually black, gray, or white dorsally, white or cream beneath; tail well haired, underpart naked at tip. Head and body 30–48 cm (nearly 12–16 in) in length; weight about 1.2 kg (2.6 lb).
Distribution Eastern coastal Australia, from Cairns, Queensland, to Dandenong Range, Victoria.
Habitat Eucalypt forests.
Behavior Largest of all 5 species of marsupial gliders, this species is solitary and lives high in the forest trees, where at night, unlike other gliders, it feeds exclusively on the tender leaves, shoots, and blossoms of certain eucalypts. It is most closely related to the ringtail, *Pseudocheirus,* of similar feeding habits. The greater glider can travel long distances. One was observed to cover 590 yards in 6 successive glides among trees spaced 70 to 120 feet apart. By day the animal shelters in a hollow trunk or branch, sometimes adding a nest of bark or leaves. Greater gliders are believed to live up to 15 years in the wild. A single young is born in April–August, leaves the pouch in 15½ weeks, and is independent at 31 weeks of age.

24 LASIORHINUS LATIFRONS
Southern hairy-nosed wombat

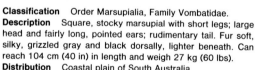

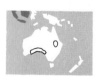

Classification Order Marsupialia, Family Vombatidae.
Description Square, stocky marsupial with short legs; large head and fairly long, pointed ears; rudimentary tail. Fur soft, silky, grizzled gray and black dorsally, lighter beneath. Can reach 104 cm (40 in) in length and weigh 27 kg (60 lbs).
Distribution Coastal plain of South Australia.
Habitat Arid scrub, grassland, open woodland.
Behavior Strong, stout limbs and digging claws make the wombat an efficient burrower. Its long, complex tunnels provide shelter from daytime heat, though in cool weather the wombat sunbathes. Mostly crepuscular and nocturnal, it eats only a few selected species of plants. Unlike any other marsupials, wombats have a single pair of ever-growing upper and lower incisors. Adapted to a desert climate, the hairy-nosed species does not sweat or drink water, and it concentrates the feces to conserve moisture. It may also recycle urea. This species is usually solitary, except during the breeding season, apparently summer. A single young occupies the pouch, which opens toward the rear. The future of this species is in doubt. Further human encroachment upon its already restricted native habitat may diminish its population beyond recovery. Two related species have been reduced to very small numbers, isolated in Queensland. The common forest wombat, *Vombatus ursinus,* is comparatively abundant.

25 PETROGALE PENICILLATA
Brush-tailed rock wallaby

Classification   Order Marsupialia, Family Macropodidae.
Description   A small, kangaroolike, gray-brown marsupial with long, dark-colored tail of even thickness; relatively short ears with yellow edges; dark eye band with light cheek stripe; large, well-padded hind feet with granular pads. Average head and body length 76 cm (30 in), weight about 7 kg (15 lbs).
Distribution   Australia except Tasmania; introduced in New Zealand and Oahu Island, Hawaii.

Habitat   Rocky outcrops, boulders, caves.
Behavior   Of the 7 species of rock wallaby, this is the most widespread. Confined strictly to rocky areas, it shelters in caves or large crevices that offer relief from the heat. Its agility is astounding, particularly for an animal that uses only its hind feet (and tail as a rudder), bounding rapidly among boulders, up cliffs, and off slightly leaning tree trunks. The rock surface of its trails and cave floors are often highly polished from its rough foot pads. Living in colonies of up to 50 or more, rock wallabies graze on grass and are most active at night, early morning, and late afternoon. They survive periods of drought by eating bark or roots as a grass substitute and to obtain moisture. Little is known about its breeding habits, but a single young has been recorded in the pouch in February and August.

---

26 THYLOGALE BILLARDIERI
Red-bellied wallaby, Tasmanian pademelon

Classification   Order Marsupialia, Family Macropodidae.
Description   Comparatively short-tailed, small, kangaroolike marsupial with relatively small, rounded ears, and hind foot only about 13–13.7 cm (5.2–5.4 in) long. Pelage long, thick, and soft, grizzled gray-brown on upper parts, yellow-orange underparts. Average length of head and body 60–65 cm (23.5–25.5 in); weight about 6 kg (13 lb).
Distribution   Tasmania; formerly in southeastern Australia.
Habitat   Dense, low scrub and tall grass.

Behavior   Closely related to rock wallabies, the small pademelons number 4 species ranging from New Guinea through eastern Australia into Tasmania. The gregarious red-bellied form, now extinct on the mainland, lives in large colonies throughout much of Tasmania, where it has long been hunted for its fur. In damp areas it inhabits thick underbrush through which it makes extensive tunnel-like runways. The pademelon is crepuscular, foraging at dawn and dusk on grass—its principal diet—though leaves and shoots are also eaten. It seems to depend on sound rather than sight for protection: it thumps the ground with its foot, probably as an alarm signal, when it hears someone approach. The Tasmanian pademelon usually has one young; births have been recorded in January, February, and July. Delayed implantation is known in this species.

27 MACROPUS RUFUS
Red kangaroo

Classification   Order Marsupialia, Family Macropodidae.
Description   Large kangaroo with long hind legs and feet; long, thick, tapering tail; heavy frame. Short, thick pelage of red, gray, or both colors combined; black mark on side of muzzle; sexes are often of opposite colors in any locality. In males, head and body length about 165 cm (65 in), maximum weight 82 kg (180 lb); females much smaller.
Distribution   Throughout inland continental Australia.
Habitat   Arid grassland, shrub steppe, and salt pans.
Behavior   Largest living marsupial, the red kangaroo lives in groups, called ''mobs,'' and is mainly nocturnal, especially in hot weather. Although it grazes on grass and selected short green plants, it is not in direct competition with sheep or cattle, as often assumed (this misinformation is cited as the rationale for mass slaughter by graziers). Red kangaroos will remain active throughout the day in cool weather. The animal can jump 6–8 feet high, though 4–5 feet is usual. It covers a 12–14-foot distance per leap. In short bursts of speed it can attain 35–40 mph, but normally 8 mph is its fast pace. The red kangaroo breeds year round and has delayed implantation. Normal gestation is 33 days; the single young leaves the pouch permanently at about 235 days of age but continues to suckle until 12 months old.

28 MACROPUS GIGANTEUS
Eastern grey kangaroo, forester, great grey kangaroo

Classification   Order Marsupialia, Family Macropodidae.
Description   Large kangaroo with hind limbs and feet of intermediate length; heavy, long, tapering tail. Fur short, fine, silver-gray in color in both sexes, frequently darker on hands, toes, and tip of tail. In males, head and body length about 150 cm (59 in), maximum recorded weight 91 kg (200 lb); females much smaller.
Distribution   Eastern Australia, Tasmania.
Habitat   Forests and woodlands.
Behavior   Slightly smaller than the red kangaroo, but perhaps heavier, the great grey occupies a different habitat even where the 2 species overlap in range, preferring heavy scrub and forest of the damp coast and mountains. By day, groups or mobs of grey kangaroos rest under the trees, foraging from evening until early morning. This species eats grass and a few small plants. Like all large terrestrial kangaroos, it crawls slowly with its 4 feet flat on the ground when grazing; the paired limbs are moved forward in unison. The tail is used as a prop and becomes a balance when the animal hops. Grey kangaroos breed throughout the year; gestation is 29–38 days, varying regionally. Delayed implantation occurs infrequently. The single annual young has the longest pouch life known in marsupials, 300 days or more, and it suckles until 18 months old.

29 MACROPUS ROBUSTUS
Wallaroo, euro, hill kangaroo

Classification   Order Marsupialia, Family Macropodidae.
Description   A stocky kangaroo with relatively short hind legs and long, tapering tail. Long, coarse fur of dark gray to red-brown; may be lighter in females; coloration varies among subspecies. In males head and body length 100–125 cm (39.5–49.3 in), average weight 40 kg (88 lb); females much smaller.
Distribution   Most of continental Australia.
Habitat   Stony ground, rock outcrops, eroded scrubland.
Behavior   Discontinuous in range across Australia, the several subspecies of euro all have a predilection for rocky areas affording daytime shelter in caves or crevices. In their absence, a euro may dig under mulga bushes to escape daytime heat. With adequate shelter it is known to survive for long periods without water, deriving moisture from its diet of grass. Its urine is concentrated to conserve body water. The euro is nocturnal in hot weather, active diurnally as well in cool seasons. It is sedentary and the most solitary of kangaroo species, sometimes seen in pairs or a mother with young. The euro has delayed implantation, postponing birth until after a drought has passed. Normal gestation is 31–33 days; breeding and births are throughout the year. The single young leaves the pouch permanently when 240–254 days old.

30 DENDROLAGUS LUMHOLTZI
Lumholtz's tree kangaroo

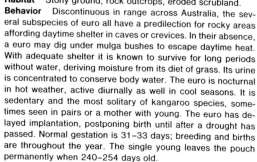

Classification   Order Marsupialia, Family Macropodidae.
Description   A large, heavy-bodied marsupial with powerful limbs; long, cylindrical tail equal to length of head and body; short, rounded ears. Short, soft fur grizzled gray dorsally, lighter ventrally, with black muzzle, toes, and tail tip. Average head and body length 66 cm (26 in), maximum weight about 10.5 kg (23 lb).
Distribution   Atherton Tableland, northern Queensland, Australia.
Habitat   Rain forest.
Behavior   With front limbs enlarged, hind limbs reduced, rough foot pads and long sharp claws, the tree kangaroo is specially adapted to arboreal life. It climbs tree trunks, leaps 10–20 feet from branch to branch using its nonprehensile tail as a rudder, and normally descends slowly by shinning tail first down the trunk. If alarmed, however, it will quickly leap down from a 50–60-foot height, landing unharmed, rather than attempt escape through the treetops, as it is equally at home on the ground. Crepuscular and nocturnal, it eats leaves and bark high in the trees and browses on seedling trees and shrubs. By day it sleeps curled up unprotected on a branch, even during rain. Lumholtz's tree kangaroo is one of 2 species confined to diminishing ranges in northeastern Queensland; 5 species inhabit New Guinea. Its breeding habits are unknown.

31 AEPYPRYMNUS RUFESCENS
Rufous rat kangaroo

Classification Order Marsupialia, Family Macropodidae.

Description A small kangaroolike marsupial with long hind legs, hind feet lacking first toe; well-haired, nonprehensile tail long and tapering; ears fairly long. Pelage long, coarse, grizzled red-gray, lighter below, with white hip stripe. Head and body length 48–53 cm (19–21 in), average weight 3 kg (6.5 lb).

Distribution Eastern coastal Australia from northern Queensland to mid New South Wales; formerly in Victoria.

Habitat Eucalypt forests and woodlands.

Behavior Largest of about 6 living species of Australian rat kangaroos, the rufous form inhabits open forests and woodlands. Strictly terrestrial, it prefers dense underbrush, tussock grass, and bracken through which it forages in the evening and at night. It eats grass, roots, and possibly fungi, which it is well able to scratch from the soil with its large, curved claws. During the day the rufous rat kangaroo sleeps curled up in a large nest of grass built against a fallen log, grass tussock, or similar shelter. Little is known of reproduction in this species. Females with young in pouch have been captured in January–March; the usual litter is a single young although 2 occasionally occur. The species is apparently extinct in Victoria, victim of the introduced fox.

32 POTOROUS TRIDACTYLUS
Southern potoroo, long-nosed rat kangaroo

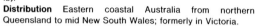

Classification Order Marsupialia, Family Macropodidae.

Description Small, rabbit-sized marsupial with relatively long hind legs, pointed muzzle, short round ears, and short, tapering, prehensile tail. Fur long, soft, and straight, grizzled redgray or near black, underparts whitish; tail often has white tip. Average head and body length 40.5 cm (16 in), weight 1–1.75 kg (about 2–4 lb).

Distribution Eastern and southeastern coastal Australia; Tasmania.

Habitat Wet eucalypt forests.

Behavior Smallest of the macropods, the southern potoroo inhabits dense undergrowth and tall grass in well-forested areas. Its nest is of dry grass. In motion it is a diminutive kangaroo, moving slowly on its hind legs only, covering about 12–18 inches with each bound. Strictly nocturnal, the southern potoroo eats mostly grass and fungi, together with other plant material, and consumes insects when abundant during spring and summer. It scratches shallow holes in the ground to obtain food, which it then eats squirrel fashion, using its hands. Breeding is throughout the year but most young are born in September–October or January–February. Gestation is 38 days, and this species has delayed implantation. The single offspring is weaned when 115–120 days old.

33 SOLENODON PARADOXUS
Hispaniolan, or Haitian, solenodon

Classification   Order Insectivora, Family Solenodontidae.
Description   The size of a large rat, this animal has a distinctive long, tubular snout with nostrils on the sides; small eyes and ears; long, nearly naked tail, and hairless 5-toed feet bearing sharp, slightly curved claws. Pelage is long, coarse, buff to yellow, often mixed with black. Total length about 30–31 cm (12 in); weight about 600 g (1.3 lb).
Distribution   Island of Hispaniola (Santo Domingo).
Habitat   Wooded and rocky areas.
Behavior   The rare terrestrial solenodon is a slow-moving, nocturnal animal that feeds on ants, other insects, grubs, small reptiles, fruit and other plant matter, for which it roots about on the ground, through forest litter, and finds by ripping open rotten logs. By day, in family groups of up to 8 individuals, it shelters in caves, rock crevices, or hollow logs. Its elongated cartilaginous snout and scent glands in the armpits and groin suggest that smell is the solenodon's predominant sense. The female's 2 teats are placed on the edge of the buttocks near the tail. The solenodon has poisonous salivary glands with ducts opening at the base of its large second lower incisors, which are deeply grooved on the inner sides to inject venom when biting. There may be 2 litters of 2 young each per year.

34 TENREC ECAUDATUS
Tail-less tenrec

Classification   Order Insectivora, Family Tenrecidae.
Description   A large, shrewlike creature with elongated snout, vestigial tail, short limbs. Pelage thin and coarse, almost spiny; red-brown with scattered long, black hairs on back, lighter beneath. Head and body length 26.5–39 cm (about 10.5–15 in), weight 1.5–2 kg (about 3–4.5 lbs); females much smaller.
Distribution   Throughout Madagascar, Comoro Islands; introduced on nearby islands.
Habitat   Undergrowth in rain forests and gallery forests.
Behavior   The tenrec is terrestrial and fossorial. In winter it hibernates deep in its burrow with the entrance plugged. Active mostly at night, usually alone or in family groups, it eats earthworms, grubs, grasshoppers, and possibly small vertebrates. The tenrec forages with its nose to the ground, probing the forest litter and soil, digging out prey once located. When faced with an enemy, it responds by raising the stiff hairs at the crest of its head and along the middle of its back, stamping its forefeet, hissing, and it may open its mouth very wide as a threatening gesture. The tenrec defends itself with quick, slashing bites. Breeding is in spring, October–November; gestation is 58–64 days. There is usually only 1 litter per year of 16–32 offspring (21 on average), which are weaned at 25–30 days of age. The tail-less tenrec was formerly the genus *Centetes*.

35 HEMICENTETES SEMISPINOSUS
Streaked tenrec

Classification   Order Insectivora, Family Tenrecidae.
Description   A small insectivore with long snout and limbs, vestigial tail. Pelage black with yellow longitudinal stripes dorsally, light beneath; scattered quills, some barbed and detachable. Head and body 12–16.5 cm (4.8–6.5 in) in length, weight about 200 g (7 oz).
Distribution   Northern and eastern Madagascar.
Habitat   Tropical lowland rain forest.

Behavior   This small, terrestrial creature lives in long, shallow burrows dug in the damp humus and usually occupied by family groups. The streaked tenrec is active during the day and night, feeding primarily upon earthworms. It has warning coloration and effective defense. If threatened by a predator, such as a mongoose or fossa, the tenrec erects the barbed quills on its back and on the crest around its head, pointing them completely forward, and drives them into the attacker's nose or paws with body and head movements. Its nonbarbed quills, clustered in the middle of the back, produce a faint chattering sound when vibrated, and are used to communicate within family groups. Breeding is in October–December and possibly other times, depending upon local food supply and temperature. Gestation is 58 days and litters usually vary between 5–8 young which are weaned at 18–25 days. A related, less spiny species, *H. nigriceps,* inhabits the Madagascan plateau.

36 ECHINOPS TELFAIRI
Lesser hedgehog tenrec

Classification   Order Insectivora, Family Tenrecidae.
Description   A small, stout-bodied animal similar to the hedgehog, with short tail; limbs and muzzle of moderate length; prominent ears; entire dorsum covered with sharp spines. Color usually yellow buff; individuals range from near white to almost black. Head and body length 13–17 cm (5–6.8 in), weight about 200 g (7 oz).
Distribution   Southwestern Madagascar.
Habitat   Arid savanna, baobab, and brush.

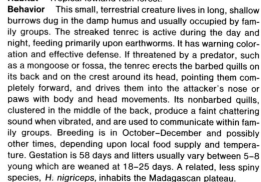

Behavior   The lesser hedgehog tenrec is both terrestrial and arboreal, spending daytime hours resting under a log or in a hollow tree, although trees are widely scattered in its native habitat. In hot weather it sleeps with its body extended but otherwise lies in a curled position. It hibernates in winter. *Echinops* and the greater hedgehog tenrec, *Setifer setosus,* are the only tenrec species completely covered with spines dorsally, including the head, and able to roll into a tight ball for defense. Hedgehog tenrecs feed upon insects and other invertebrates as well as on small vertebrates, and usually forage alone except for a mother with young. Breeding is known to occur in October but may depend on warm weather first arousing the animals from winter torpor and on an available food supply. Gestation is 62–65 days; litters average 7 offspring (1–10), which are weaned at 18–22 days of age.

37 POTAMOGALE VELOX
Giant otter shrew

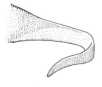

Classification Order Insectivora, Family Tenrecidae.
Description A long-bodied squirrel-sized animal with long, thick, tapered and laterally compressed, rudderlike tail; broad, flattened muzzle bearing numerous long, stiff whiskers; nostrils concealed by a flap of skin on the nose. Fur dense and soft; glossy chocolate brown dorsally, white beneath. Head and body length 29–35 cm (11.5–13.8 in), weight about 1 kg (2.2 lb).
Distribution Congo basin and western Uganda.
Habitat Mountain streams, coastal rivers, and swamps.
Behavior Adapted strictly for aquatic life, the giant otter shrew is equally at home in fast-flowing streams or sluggish swamps. Its rapidly undulating tail propels the animal through the water while it holds its feet close to the body. Though primarily sensory in function, the abundant whiskers also act as a hydrofoil to stabilize the head and streamlined body in motion. The whiskers are also used to locate food in the water, which is then eaten on land. The giant otter shrew's favorite food is freshwater crabs; 20–25 can be eaten in one night. Fish are also commonly consumed, as are frogs and mollusks. This nocturnal animal, found solitary or in pairs, burrows in the riverbank, often leaving the entrance below water level. Its breeding habits are not known; apparently a litter is 2 young.

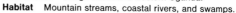

38 CHRYSOCHLORIS ASIATICA
Cape golden mole

Classification Order Insectivora, Family Chrysochloridae.
Description A small, round-bodied animal lacking external tail; rudimentary eyes covered with skin; ears are simple openings; nose flat and fleshy; hands bear 4 digits, outer 2 small and middle 2 large with strong, pointed claws; hind feet small with 5 toes. The pelage is thick, has heavy underfur, and is brown to gray in color with a strong yellow or green iridescent sheen. Total length about 11.5–12.5 cm (4.5–5 in), weight about 30 g (1 oz).
Distribution Western Cape Province, South Africa.
Habitat Soft or sandy soil in grassy or scrub areas.
Behavior Although its habits are similar to those of true moles, the 6 genera and numerous species of golden moles are not closely related to them. This fossorial animal is blind. It burrows extensively, making both deep and shallow tunnels. Those cut through the humus or topsoil raise a visible ridge along the ground. Digging is done by butting with the nose while pushing soil away with the foreclaws, an activity for which the wedge-shaped skull and short, muscular neck are especially adapted. The golden mole eats earthworms and other small invertebrates. Its breeding habits are little known. The young are born in a grassy nest and suckled for 2–3 months until almost fully grown.

39 ECHINOSOREX GYMNURUS
Moonrat, Raffle's gymnure

Classification   Order Insectivora, Family Erinaceidae.
Description   A narrow animal the size of a house cat, with a long, pointed muzzle; long, tapering, sparsely haired, scaly tail; short limbs. Pelage short and soft with long, coarse guard hairs throughout; usually black with white head and neck, occasionally almost entirely white coat. Head and body length 25.5–44.5 cm (10–17.5 in), weight 0.5–1.4 kg (about 1–3 lb).
Distribution   Peninsular Burma and Thailand, Malaya to Sumatra and Borneo.
Habitat   Tropical lowland and foothill forests.

Behavior   The largest living insectivore, Raffle's moonrat was previously the genus *Gymnurus;* white specimens from Borneo were thought to be a separate species, *G. alba.* This strictly terrestrial animal shelters among tree roots, in hollow logs, or under rocks, and frequents moist areas such as stream edges. It is solitary and active both day and night, foraging for earthworms, beetles, roaches, termites, insect larvae, millipedes and centipedes, spiders, scorpions, and various aquatic invertebrates and larval amphibians. The moonrat is notorious for its characteristic onion or rotten-garlic odor, produced by an anal glandular secretion. Little is known of its reproductive habits. Pregnant females have been recorded in May, June, September, and November, suggesting either year-round or twice-yearly breeding. There are usually 2 young per litter.

40 ERINACEUS EUROPAEUS
Western European hedgehog, common hedgehog

Classification   Order Insectivora, Family Erinaceidae.
Description   A large, stout insectivore with short tail and short ears; head, back, and sides evenly covered with dense, sharp spines. Color brown with yellow spine tips, paler on face and underparts. Head and body 21–30 cm (8.3–11.8 in), weight about 0.8–1 kg (2 lb).
Distribution   British Isles, western Europe, Mediterranean islands; introduced in New Zealand.
Habitat   Deciduous forest, open woodlands, grassy heath, scrub, and sand dunes.

Behavior   This common terrestrial animal builds a nest of grass and leaves among tree roots or under a bush. It forages from dusk to dawn, noisily sniffing out worms, insects, snails, and small vertebrates, including snakes. Its eyesight is poor, but hearing and smell are acute. When alarmed it rolls into a tight, spiny ball for protection. A hedgehog will sometimes lick a strange object of pungent odor until its saliva becomes frothy, then with its tongue anoint its spines with the froth. The purpose of this behavior is unknown. Hedgehogs hibernate in cold climates. Litters of 1–7 young, usually 4 or 5, are produced twice a year, May–June and August–September. Gestation is 34–49 days. The offspring are weaned at 4 weeks. Similar, related species range throughout Africa and Eurasia.

41 ELEPHANTULUS ROZETI
North African elephant shrew

Classification   Order Macroscelidia, Family Macroscelididae.
Description   A small, ratlike insectivore with long, sparsely haired tail; very long hind limbs; long, sharply pointed snout; prominent ears. Pelage dense, soft, buff to light brown on back, white beneath. Head and body length 9–13 cm (3.5–5.2 in); weight 25–50 g (0.9–1.8 oz).
Distribution   Northwestern Africa: Morocco to Tripolitania.
Habitat   Semidesert.

Behavior   About 15 species of elephant shrews are found throughout much of Africa, where they occupy a variety of habitats. The family is ranked by some authorities as a separate order because it is such a distinctive group. Though the terrestrial elephant shrews resemble miniature kangaroos with long, hopping hind limbs, they use all 4 legs for walking and hop only when running. The isolated North African species, *E. rozeti*, lives in dry open country where it burrows, often under rocks, for shelter. It is diurnal in habit but spends the midday hours in its burrow. It is primarily insectivorous in diet. The reproductive habits of this species are unknown. The related East African spectacled elephant shrew, *E. rufescens*, bears 1 or 2 young per litter, following a gestation of 50 days. Pregnant females have been found in April and May. The young are weaned when 1 month old and attain adult size at 2 months.

42 RHYNCHOCYON CIRNEI
Giant elephant shrew

Classification   Order Macroscelidia, Family Macroscelididae.
Description   Long-legged and hunch-backed, this animal is about the size of a large rat; with long, thin, tapering tail; long, pointed proboscis; 4 toes on hind feet. Pelage buff, orange, or nearly black, usually with longitudinal stripes or rows of light-colored splotches. Length of head and body 24–31 cm (9.6–12.4 in), weight 80–120 g (2.8–4.2 oz).
Distribution   Central and eastern Africa, including Zanzibar.
Habitat   Tropical and subtropical forests and woodlands.

Behavior   This, the largest elephant shrew, lives where there is shaded leaf litter, in which it feeds by sniffing and probing with its proboscis and scratching with its feet to locate ants, termites, and other small creatures. Often in pairs or small groups, giant elephant shrews are active mostly during the day and occasionally at night, uttering constant squeaks to keep in touch and rapping their tails when alarmed. Both sexes mark stones and twigs with scent from a gland at the base of the tail. The nest is a discreet mound of leaves piled in a shallow depression in the ground. The giant elephant shrew bears 1 fully haired young at a time, giving birth 4 or 5 times a year. The offspring stays in the nest for about 3 weeks, then follows its mother for another week.

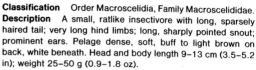

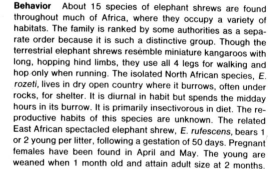

43 SOREX CINEREUS
Masked shrew

Classification   Order Insectivora, Family Soricidae.
Description   A very small, mouselike insectivore with sharply pointed muzzle; minute eyes; long tail. Velvety fur of gray-brown color, pale gray beneath. Length of head and body 4.5–6 cm (1.8–2.5 in), weight 2.4–7.8 g (0.08–0.25 oz).
Distribution   Throughout most of North America, north of central Rocky Mountains and southern Appalachians; northeastern Siberia; introduced in Newfoundland Island.
Habitat   Virtually all moist areas and dry forest floors.

Behavior   This long-tailed form is the most widespread of 30 species of shrews in North America. Active both day and night, mostly after dusk and at dawn, the masked shrew forages in the forest litter and even under winter snow since it does not hibernate. Its diet consists of insects and other small invertebrates such as worms, sowbugs, and snails, and it will also eat salamanders, young mice, nestling birds, and some vegetable matter. This particularly voracious shrew consumes its own body weight or more daily and has a fast metabolism——800 heartbeats per minute. Generally solitary, it will fight viciously and often kill another of its own species. Breeding is April–October. After gestation of about 18 days, 1 or 2 litters of 2–10 young, usually 4 or 5, are born during the season. The young are weaned at about 20 days. Total life span is 14–23 months.

---

44 SOREX ARANEUS
Eurasian common shrew

Classification   Order Insectivora, Family Soricidae.
Description   A mouse-sized creature with tail of moderate length; pointed muzzle; small eyes; ears nearly concealed by fur. Pelage dense and brown or blackish dorsally, gray beneath, and intermediate on sides. Head and body length 6.5–8 cm (2.5–3.2 in); weight 5–16 g (0.2–0.6 oz).
Distribution   Britain, Europe from Arctic to Mediterranean, east to Lake Baikal in central Asia.
Habitat   Forest and woodland, scrub, grassland, and tundra.

Behavior   This tiny, quick animal lives in the leaf litter where it has extensive runways. It also digs tunnels and uses those of other species. Its roughly spherical nest of woven grass is placed underground or under natural shelter on the surface. Solitary and pugnacious, the common shrew is active day and night, mostly at night, feeding on invertebrates such as worms and beetles, located by touch with its sensitive whiskers. Common shrews have poor eyesight. After first biting and disabling its prey, the shrew stores morsels not immediately consumed. Breeding season is May–October, a female often becoming pregnant again upon the birth of a litter, thereby producing 2, and possibly more, litters per season. Average litter size is 6. Gestation is 13–19 days and young are weaned at 19 days. Complete life span is 14–16 months.

45 NEOMYS FODIENS
Eurasian water shrew

Classification Order Insectivora, Family Soricidae.
Description Mouse-sized insectivore with moderately long, pointed snout; a long tail with distinct keel formed of stiff hairs; large feet with hairy fringe; small eyes and ears. Fur dense, velvety, gray dorsally and whitish beneath. Length of head and body, 7–9.5 cm (2.8–3.8 in), weight 12–18 g (0.4–0.6 oz).
Distribution Britain, Europe from Arctic to montane south, central Asia to Lake Baikal, eastern Siberia.
Habitat Wet forest, streams, marshes.

Behavior The water shrew is particularly adapted to aquatic habits. It can live at least 2 miles away from water but usually inhabits stream banks in which it burrows extensively. Entrances are above or below water and tunnels are made narrow to squeeze water from the animal's fur. The shrew is solitary and active day and night throughout the year. It swims fast, remaining submerged up to 20 seconds, hunting frogs, fish, snails, mollusks, and insects, which it immobilizes with its venomous saliva. The shrew propels itself in the water with its fringed hind feet, using its keeled tail as a rudder. Its ear passage is closed by 2 valves. Breeding is in April–September, with 2 or more litters of 3–8 young per season. Gestation is about 24 days, longer in nursing females. Offspring are weaned in about 37 days.

---

46 BLARINA BREVICAUDA
Northern short-tailed shrew

Classification Order Insectivora, Family Soricidae.
Description A small, mouse-sized insectivore with very short tail; short limbs; muzzle somewhat pointed; tiny eyes; ears concealed by fur. Pelage dense, slate gray with slightly lighter underparts. Head and body length 7.5–10.5 cm (3–4 in), weight 15–30 g (0.5–1 oz).
Distribution Southeastern Canada and eastern United States from Nebraska to the Atlantic, south to Kentucky and Alabama; also in central Gulf-coast Florida.
Habitat Deciduous or coniferous forests, fields, grassy areas near water, salt marshes.

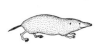

Behavior The abundant short-tailed shrew digs through the forest litter or tunnels in moist soil, and is active mostly during early morning and late afternoon. Its diet is principally earthworms, snails, and insects; fungus, various invertebrates, and occasionally small vertebrate animals are also eaten. This species paralyzes its victims with its poisonous saliva, and is known to store surplus food. Males are territorial and mark their burrows with glandular secretions, the odor of which keeps other males out. During the breeding season, March–September, the short-tailed shrew builds a nest of dry leaves and grass under a log or other shelter. Gestation is 21 days or more, and 2 to possibly 4 litters, each of 5–7 young, are born per year.

47 CROCIDURA LEUCODON
Bicolored white-toothed shrew

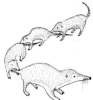

Classification Order Insectivora, Family Soricidae.

Description A medium-sized shrew with short tail; moderately pointed muzzle; small eyes; small but clearly visible ears. Short, dense fur of gray or reddish brown color with silvery reflections above, whitish beneath; tail dark dorsally, light beneath. Length of head and body 7–9 cm (2.8–3.5 in); weight 10–28 g (0.4–1 oz).

Distribution Central and southern Europe, from France to southern Russia.

Habitat Open fields, forest edge, brushland.

Behavior One of the common European representatives of a widespread genus of shrews—containing about 120 species ranging across the Palearctic, Ethiopian, and Oriental Regions—the bicolored form is terrestrial and prefers dry situations. Its grass nest is built at the base of bushes or under similar shelter. Like many other shrews, it alternates short periods of rest and activity, each of about 2–3 hours, throughout the day and night. It forages in leaf litter for earthworms, insects, and other invertebrates. Breeding from spring through autumn, 2 or more litters are born each year. Gestation is about 28 days. The young number 3–7 per litter and mature in 2–3 months. The mother leads her growing offspring to safety by "caravanning." In line behind the mother, each shrew grips the one ahead with its teeth holding the fur just above the tail, the young one in front gripping its mother's fur.

48 SUNCUS ETRUSCUS
Savi's pygmy shrew, Etruscan shrew

Classification Order Insectivora, Family Soricidae.

Description A minute, pointed-nosed insectivore with moderately long tail, thick at its base; prominent ears; small eyes. Pelage soft, short, drab brownish gray in color, very slightly lighter beneath. Head and body length 3.6–5.2 cm (1.4–2 in), tail length 2.4–2.9 cm (about 1 in), weight 1.5–2.5 g (0.05–0.09 oz).

Distribution Southern Europe and southern Asia to Burma; Sri Lanka; North Africa, Nigeria, Ethiopia.

Habitat Deciduous, coniferous, and riverine forests, and dense brush.

Behavior The Etruscan shrew is one of the smallest living mammals; only a minute bat from Thailand is smaller (see Introduction). Some adult specimens of Hoy's pygmy shrew, *Microsorex hoyi*, of Canada and the northern United States, are almost as tiny as *S. etruscus*. Shrews of the genus *Suncus* are sometimes called "musk shrews" because of their strong, unpleasant odor, derived from a gland on the skin of the flanks. Savi's pygmy shrew nests in rock crevices and under tree roots. Foraging at night and probably during the day as well, its diet consists of insects, spiders, and other invertebrates of which it daily consumes 2–4 times its own body weight. Its breeding habits are unknown.

49 DESMANA MOSCHATA
Russian desman

Classification   Order Insectivora, Family Talpidae.

Description   A rat-sized insectivore with short limbs, webbed hind feet; long, laterally flattened, scaly tail; long, proboscislike snout. Pelage soft and dense, chestnut brown dorsally, lighter beneath. Head and body about 20 cm (8 in) in length, tail about the same; weight 100–200 g (3.5–7.7 oz).

Distribution   Volga, Don, and Ural river basins, Russia.

Habitat   Slow-moving rivers and streams.

Behavior   Well equipped for its aquatic life, the Russian desman burrows extensively into riverbanks, leaving entrances well below water level for access under winter ice. Grass nests are placed in chambers above water level. This nocturnal and crepuscular animal swims efficiently, often using its proboscis as a snorkel or as an underwater sensor to search out food such as mollusks, worms, water insects, fish, and frogs. Water plants are also eaten. The species was hunted almost to extinction but is now strictly protected. Its fur was used for trimmings, and the strong musk from glands at the base of the tail was used in perfume manufacture. After a gestation of 40–50 days, a litter of 3–5 young is born in early summer or autumn. The offspring are weaned when about 1 month old and become fully grown in a year. A smaller species, the Spanish, or Pyrenean, desman, *Galemys pyrenaicus*, lives in the Pyrenees.

50 TALPA EUROPAEA
European mole

Classification   Order Insectivora, Family Talpidae.

Description   Tubular-shaped and rat-sized, this creature has a conical muzzle; minute eyes; no external ears; short, thick, sparsely haired tail; short limbs with broad, spatulate hands having wide claws and a sesamoid bone forming a sixth "finger." Fur short, dense, and velvety, dark gray with metallic iridescence. Head and body length of male about 14 cm (5.5 in); weight about 125 g (4.4 oz); females slightly smaller.

Distribution   Britain, Europe except some Mediterranean areas, east through Russia.

Habitat   Meadows, grassland, forests.

Behavior   With powerful shoulders and forefeet specially adapted for digging, the mole virtually "swims" through the soil as it makes long tunnels just beneath the surface. Deep, complicated burrows are also dug. The mole is active day and night. It sometimes forages aboveground in leaf litter, though most of its food consists of the worms and other subterranean invertebrates that drop into its tunnels. The European mole has extremely poor vision and sense of smell. Apparently it hears reasonably well, but relies more on tactile senses. The breeding season is February–May and gestation is 28 days. An average of 4 young are born in a nest of dry grass or leaves in an underground chamber. There is usually only 1 litter per year, and young are weaned after 1 month.

51 CONDYLURA CRISTATA
Star-nosed mole

Classification   Order Insectivora, Family Talpidae.
Description   A round-bodied insectivore of rat size, with long muzzle and nostrils surrounded by a naked, fleshy disc bearing 22 tapering tentacles; small, concealed eyes; no external ears; long, scaly tail; fairly long limbs; large hands surrounded by a row of bristles. Pelage fine, short, black or near-black. Head and body length 12–13 cm (4.8–5.2 in); weight 70–120 g (2.5–4.2 oz).

Distribution   Southeastern Canada; eastern United States from North Dakota to Indiana, east to Atlantic, south through Appalachians to southeastern Georgia.
Habitat   Marshes, stream banks, lake shores, wet meadows.
Behavior   The startling nose appendages immediately set this mole apart from the 5 other North American species, which more closely resemble the European mole. Less fossorial and more aquatic than other species, the star-nosed mole forages on the surface, mostly at night, and excavates shallow tunnels through wet soil. An able swimmer, it uses its tentacles to cover the nostrils in water, as well as to keep dirt out when digging. The nasal tentacles also serve as sensitive feelers. This colonial species eats aquatic insects, worms, crustaceans, and mollusks. Breeding begins in February; gestation is about 45 days. The single annual litter of 2–7 young are born in late March–June, and leave the nest when 3 weeks old.

52 CYNOCEPHALUS VARIEGATUS
Malayan flying lemur, colugo

Classification   Order Dermoptera, Family Cynocephalidae.
Description   Nearly house-cat size, a flat-bodied animal with ample gliding membrane from the neck, along sides of body to the fingers, toes, and tail tip; large eyes; long limbs; feet with sharp, curved claws; lower incisor teeth comblike. Fur mottled gray or brown with white spots dorsally. Head and body length 33–38 cm (13–15 in); weight 1–1.5 kg (over 2–3 lb).
Distribution   Southern Burma, Cambodia, Vietnam to Sumatra, Java, and Borneo.
Habitat   Tropical forests and woodlands.

Behavior   Strictly arboreal, the well-camouflaged colugo roosts in hollow trees or among palm fronds, emerging to spend its active hours—usually nocturnal but sometimes diurnal—in the trees as well. Its flight from tree to tree, often about 200 feet or more, is actually a glide with membranes outstretched. It climbs awkwardly up vertical trunks, pulling itself up with both arms at once, followed by both legs. Colugos eat leaves, shoots, and fruit. A single offspring is born after a 60-day gestation period. Females have been found pregnant while still nursing young. The offspring is carried on the mother's abdomen, protected by her gliding membrane.
Note   The only other member of this tiny order is a species of the same genus, the very similar C volans, which inhabits the Philippines.

53 ROUSETTUS AEGYPTIACUS
Egyptian rousette

Classification   Order Chiroptera, Family Pteropodidae.
Description   A medium-sized fruit bat with simple, doglike face and ears; large eyes; very short tail projecting beyond an incomplete tail membrane. Brown pelage is often tinged with gray. Length of head and body 13–15.5 cm (5.2–6 in), forearm about 9.5 cm (3.8 in); weight 100–140 g (3.5–4.9 oz).
Distribution   Throughout sub-Saharan Africa, the Nile Valley, Arabia, and the Near East.
Habitat   Prefers wooded areas; common in all habitats in its range.

Behavior   Originally found in the Great Pyramid at Gizeh, this bat was also depicted on the walls of ancient Egyptian tombs. Unlike most fruit bats, the rousette roosts in caves, tombs, and similar dark daytime shelters, often in colonies of up to several thousand individuals. The genus *Rousettus* is also an exception among the suborder Megachiroptera in its ability to guide its agile flight by echolocation, or sonar, in the dark, although it also has keen vision. Nocturnally active, rousettes feed on soft fruits of many kinds and ingest the juice of hard fruits and certain leaves. Figs and dates form its diet in arid regions. The bat finds its food by smell. Breeding is year round in Egypt, twice yearly in East Africa, and once annually in southern regions. Gestation is 105–107 days. A single young is usual, but twins are not rare.
Note   All members of the suborder Megachiroptera (**53–59**) belong to the single family Pteropodidae.

54 PTEROPUS GIGANTEUS
Indian flying fox

Classification   Order Chiroptera, Family Pteropodidae.
Description   Very large bat with foxlike head and ears, large eyes, 2 claws on wings, no tail. Coarse pelage; head reddish brown with dark muzzle, neck and shoulders yellow, back brown, yellowish brown beneath. Length of head and body about 23 cm (9 in), forearm about 17 cm (6.8 in); weight 568–625 g (20–22 oz).
Distribution   India to Burma, west China, Sri Lanka, Maldive Islands.
Habitat   Tropical and subtropical forests.

Behavior   With a wingspan of about 4 feet, this is one of the largest of the 67 species of flying foxes, but is exceeded by *P. vampyrus* of Burma to Java and the Philippines, which has 5-foot wingspan. The Indian species is commonly seen by day roosting in large colonies, or ''camps,'' high in the trees. They spend the morning bickering vociferously for preferred roosting sites, branches where they hang by their feet head-downward; they pass most of the day asleep with their wings wrapped around themselves. At night they fly to favored foraging areas, where they feed in the trees on ripe fruit of all sorts (except citrus). The flying fox ingests only the juice, chewing and spitting out the pulp. The single young is born in February, after a gestation of 140–150 days, and clings to its mother for some 2 months until nearly adult size.

55 DOBSONIA MOLUCCENSIS
Greater naked-backed bat

Classification Order Chiroptera, Family Pteropodidae.
Description A large fruit bat with doglike face and ears; wings continuous across the back, attached along the spinal line; short tail; no claw on first finger. Fur is brownish with black shading on head. Length of head and body 19–20 cm (7.5–8 in), forearm 13–15 cm (5–6 in); weight up to 450 g (15.8 oz).
Distribution Moluccas, New Guinea, northern Queensland, Australia.

Habitat Tropical forests and woodlands.
Behavior This highly specialized fruit bat, the largest of 12 species of *Dobsonia* inhabiting the island region from the Philippines to the Solomons, usually roosts in caves or mine tunnels. It has also been seen hanging by day in mango trees. It is unique among flying foxes and their kin by having its wing membranes attached along the mid-back, thus appearing to be dorsally naked; there is fur under the wings, however, covering the bat's back. Such extended wing mass—about 3.5 feet—apparently increases the bat's agility in flight, as it is able to maneuver through thick rain forest which other bats of equal size cannot manage. This species also hovers, flapping its gigantic wings while foraging among forest trees at night. It eats fruit, including native figs, and in open mixed woodlands in Australia feeds on nectar of gum-tree blossoms. Its breeding habits are unknown.

---

56 EPOMOPHORUS GAMBIANUS
Gambian epaulet bat

Classification Order Chiroptera, Family Pteropodidae.
Description Of medium size, with long, pointed muzzle and small, rounded ears. Fur is long and soft, light or reddish brown with large white tufts ("epaulets") on the shoulders of males; white patches at base of ears. Length of head and body about 16 cm (6.3 in), forearm 8.5 cm (3.3 in); weight 100–150 g (3.5–5.3 oz).
Distribution Across Africa from Senegal to southern Ethiopia on the north, and southern Zaire, Zambia, and Zimbabwe on the south.

Habitat Open woodland and savanna; occasionally rain forest.
Behavior This species derives its common name from the showy white shoulder patches of the males which can be exposed or inverted into large pockets. Its function is unknown but believed to be for sexual signaling. Gambian epaulet bats roost during the day in mango or other trees, or in bamboo. They hang singly and in small groups of up to 20. This species feeds on fruit, such as mangos and wild figs, but more important, eats the nectar of baobab, sausage tree, and locust-bean trees. Evidence indicates that certain flowering trees may depend upon this bat for pollination, and in turn, the bat's distribution may be linked to the occurrence of such flowering, nectar-producing trees.

57 HYPSIGNATHUS MONSTROSUS
Hammer-headed bat

Classification   Order Chiroptera, Family Pteropodidae.
Description   This large fruit bat has short brown fur over its body and head, with little on its wing membrane. The head is large and rectangular, with pointed ears, an inflated nose, and thick, folded lips. It has no tail. Length of head and body 22–28.5 cm (about 8.5–11.3 in), forearm 12–14 cm (4.8–5.5 in), weight 228–450 g (8–16 oz); females smaller.
Distribution   Senegal, through Congo basin, to southwest Sudan.
Habitat   Wet, tropical, lowland forest; riverine woods; mangrove swamps.
Behavior   This species, in a genus by itself, is the largest bat in Africa and is immediately recognized by its peculiarly raised muzzle. More pronounced in males, this feature, in combination with its huge larynx, thick vocal chords, and special air chambers in the throat and head all serve to resonate the voice. At different seasons in various parts of its range, male hammer-headed bats spend the night calling incessantly, about every second uttering a loud, monotonous, and disturbing croak or clanging sound, something like *kwok,* that can be heard over a great distance. Several males may call in chorus; the purpose is thought to be to attract females. By day the hammer-headed bat, singly or in small groups, roosts in shady trees. It feeds at night, sucking the juice of tropical fruits. Breeding may be year round, though births peak in February and July. One young is usual.

58 SYCONYCTERIS AUSTRALIS
Southern blossom bat

Classification   Order Chiroptera, Family Pteropodidae.
Description   Tiny, delicate fruit bat resembling a miniature flying fox, with long, tapering snout; large eyes; tail absent. Long, reddish brown fur. Length of head and body about 5 cm (2 in), forearm 4 cm (1.6 in); weight 15–20 g (0.4–0.7 oz).
Distribution   Eastern New Guinea; coastal Queensland and extreme northeastern New South Wales, Australia.
Habitat   Tropical forests and woodlands.
Behavior   Together with the closely related genus *Macroglossus,* these are the smallest creatures among the Megachiroptera suborder of fruit bats. Their wing span is under 10 inches. Queensland blossom bats rest in trees by day, hanging upside down with feet clinging to a tiny branch. They often roost singly; sometimes several are found in one tree. This species may also form sizable camps, like flying foxes, for short periods in the spring. At night as many as a dozen fly about flowering trees, including bloodwood and paperbark, feeding on nectar and pollen. Their tongues are long and narrow, with hairlike papillae forming a brush near the tip. Southern blossom bats may help pollinate trees as their relatives in Indonesia are known to do. The southern species is not exclusively a nectar feeder; it also eats fruit such as wild figs. Its breeding habits are unknown.

59 NYCTIMENE ALBIVENTER
Common tube-nosed bat

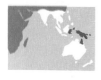

Classification   Order Chiroptera, Family Pteropodidae.
Description   Of medium size, a robust fruit bat with large, rounded head; large eyes; prominent, long, tubular nostrils extending sideways; short tail. Fur soft and long, gray-brown above, darker along mid-back and on spinal stripe; underparts yellowish white; neck and sides tinged with yellow-orange; wings and ears speckled with irregular yellow spots. Length of head and body about 8–9 cm (3.2–3.5 in), forearm 5.5–6 cm (2.2–2.4 in); weight up to 45 g (1.6 oz).
Distribution   Moluccas, New Guinea, Admiralty and Solomon Islands; Cape York peninsula, Australia.
Habitat   Tropical forests.
Behavior   Ten species of tube-nosed bats are recognized, of which 2 inhabit the rain forests of northeastern Australia. By day these bats roost singly on tree trunks or hanging from branches, well concealed by their protective coloration. The spots on the wings and ears look like splattered enamel paint and are sometimes chartreuse, a color common to tropical vegetation. At night tube-nosed bats feed on soft fruits and nectar, while either hovering in front of the blossoms or climbing among flower clusters. Their peculiar nostrils may be an adaptation to their feeding habits or may function in sound production. The nasal tubes stretch and vibrate when the bat utters its high whistling call in flight.

---

60 TAPHOZOUS MAURITIANUS
Mauritian tomb bat

Classification   Order Chiroptera, Family Emballonuridae.
Description   The back is grayish brown with white speckling, but the underside of the body is almost completely white. The male has a large sac on the throat. There is also a sac or pouch at the base of the wings. The wing membranes are unusually tough. Length of head and body 9 cm (3.6 in), forearm 6.1–6.5 cm (2.4–2.6 in); weight 25 g (0.9 oz).
Distribution   Sub-Saharan Africa, including Madagascar, and the islands of Mauritius, Reunion, and Assumption.
Habitat   Forests and woodland.
Behavior   This tomb bat lives in small groups in places not necessarily shielded from the light, such as among rocks, or hanging in trees or from walls or eaves. It emerges before nightfall to hunt, rising into the air to a height of 200–300 feet, and then slowly making its way downwards as darkness descends. It feeds on flying insects. Reproduction may be confined to a single season where alternations in the climate are more accentuated. It hibernates only in colder regions. In these parts it accumulates a large amount of fat beneath its skin as an energy reserve.

61 NOCTILIO LEPORINUS
Fisherman bat, bulldog bat

Classification   Order Chiroptera, Family Noctilionidae.
Description   A large, robust bat with wedge-shaped head and pointed muzzle; large, pointed ears; wrinkled upper lip; tail about half as long as the tail membrane. Fur short; dorsally bright reddish yellow in males, gray or brown in females; lighter beneath. Length of head and body about 10 cm (4 in), forearm 8 cm (3.2 in); weight 40–70 g (1.4–2.5 oz).
Distribution   Lowland western and southern Mexico from Sinaloa; Central and South America to northern Argentina; West Indies.
Habitat   Tropical and subtropical forests; woodlands and rocky cliffs near inland waters or the sea.
Behavior   Fisherman bats are gregarious; several dozen often roost together by day in caves, rock crevices, or hollow trees, frequently shared with other species of bats. In late afternoon and at night, they feed upon small fish caught by gaffing with the bats' large, sharp, curved claws. By echolocation, or sonar, the bats detect the ripples caused by fish swimming near the water's surface. The strong hind legs and large feet of fisherman bats are modifications to their feeding habits. They can swim well, using their wings as oars. These bats also eat insects and aquatic crustaceans. The single young may be born during the period December–March and possibly later.

---

62 MEGADERMA COR
African false vampire, heart-nosed bat

Classification   Order Chiroptera, Family Megadermatidae.
Description   A bat of medium size, with very large ears joined across the top of the head; relatively large eyes; heart-shaped noseleaf; no external tail. Pelage long, fine, blue-gray. Length of head and body about 7.5 cm (3 in), forearm 5.5–6 cm (2.2–2.4 in); weight 30–50 g (1–1.8 oz).
Distribution   Throughout east Africa from Eritrea to northern Zambia; Zanzibar.
Habitat   Dry acacia bushland.
Behavior   Sometimes placed in a genus of its own, *Cardioderma*, and closely related to the 2 species of bat-eating bats of India (also *Megaderma*) and Australia (*Macroderma gigas*), the African false vampire is primarily an insect-eater. Much of its diet consists of flightless insects, which the bat sees from its hunting roosts on low branches of bushes, flies to the ground to capture, and returns to its perch to devour. The bats begin hunting at dusk and are low fliers. They rest during the day, remaining alert, hanging in caves. Widely spaced individuals roost in small colonies and rarely share their quarters with bats of other species, whose dead remains have been found under their roosts (suggesting that the false vampires killed and ate them). A protracted breeding season apparently peaks in August; gestation is about 3 months. The single young clings to its mother for some 2 months.

63 LAVIA FRONS
Yellow-winged bat

Classification   Order Chiroptera, Family Megadermatidae.
Description   Similar to *Megaderma cor* but with bright yellow or orange wings and ears; bluish fur. Enormous ears with long, forked tragus; tall, pointed noseleaf. Length of head and body 6–8 cm (2.4–3.2 in), forearm 5.5–6.5 cm (2.2–2.5 in), weight 35–40 g (1.2–1.4 oz).
Distribution   From Senegal to Somalia, south to Zambia.
Habitat   Lowland savanna and open woodlands near water; occasionally riverine gallery forests.

Behavior   This strikingly colored bat is most abundant in open country around lakes, marshes, rivers, or the sea, below 6700 feet elevation. In pairs or groups of 4 or 5, yellow-winged bats roost by day in bushes and trees, sometimes in direct sunlight; with their faces covered with their wings, they look like dry leaves. They are restless and will change roosting sites during broad daylight. They feed at dusk and during the night. The bat hangs on a low branch in the open. Very alert, it sees or hears an insect on the ground or flying, swoops down and captures it, and returns to the roost to eat its catch leisurely. Large and small insects, including moths and butterflies, beetles, grasshoppers, flies and mosquitoes, are its prey. Following a gestation of about 3 months, most births of the single offspring occur in April.

---

64 RHINOLOPHUS FERRUMEQUINUM
Greater horseshoe bat

Classification   Order Chiroptera, Family Rhinolophidae.
Description   A bat of medium size, distinguished by its large, pointed ears and flattened face; a horseshoe-shaped fleshy disc surrounds the nostrils, forming the base of a pointed noseleaf. Pelage fine, silky, tawny brown in color, sometimes grayish. Length of head and body about 6.3 cm (2.5 in), forearm 5.5 cm (2.2 in); weight 16–28 g (0.5–1 oz).
Distribution   Entire southern Palearctic Region.
Habitat   Caves and woodlands; montane areas in warm regions.

Behavior   The peculiar horseshoe noseleaf acts as a megaphone for the ultrasonic echolocating cries of this species, which, unlike many other bats, emits such sounds through the nostrils rather than the mouth. Its larynx extends into the back of the nasal passages. It forages at night, often taking large beetles and other insects from the ground. Daytime retreats are usually caves, mines, hollow trees, or buildings; during the winter this species hibernates in caverns where it is found hanging in small clusters. Although breeding occurs in the autumn, fertilization is delayed until spring; actual gestation is about 6 weeks. The single offspring is born in June–July and by autumn attains adult size and can fly. While little, it clings to its mother's fur and to her false teats—2 abdominal fleshy protuberances.

65 HIPPOSIDEROS COMMERSONI
Commerson's leaf-nosed bat

Classification   Order Chiroptera, Family Rhinolophidae.
Description   A large, robust bat with short tail enclosed in the tail membrane; leaf-shaped ears and broad, rounded noseleaf on base of 3 or 4 fleshy leaflets. Pelage may be either of 2 color phases: red-orange or sepia-brown above, gray or white beneath. Length of head and body about 11 cm (4.3 in); forearm 10 cm (4 in); weight 130 g (4.6 oz).
Distribution   Throughout Africa south of the Sahara; Zanzibar and Madagascar.
Habitat   Savanna and woodlands; occasionally forests.
Behavior   With a wingspan of nearly 2 feet, the giant leaf-nosed bat is one of the largest insectivorous species in Africa. It is eaten in Tanzania. Large colonies, sometimes hundreds of individuals, roost by day in caves, though hollow trees and even shrubs sometimes provide shelter. At night, Commerson's bat flies at low levels foraging for the variety of insects upon which it feeds. It spits out the hard parts of insects, consuming only the soft portions. This bat is known to gorge on flying termites. Gestation is thought to be 5 months; the single offspring is usually born in October, at the beginning of the rainy season. Although the young bat grows rapidly, it is not weaned until over 5 months of age, and only reaches sexual maturity when 2 years old.

66 PHYLLOSTOMUS HASTATUS
Spear-nosed bat

Classification   Order Chiroptera, Family Phyllostomatidae.
Description   Of fairly large size, a heavy-bodied bat with short tail; short muzzle; pointed ears widely separated; large, broad, tapering noseleaf; and V-shaped groove in lower lip. Thick fur, dark gray- or red-brown above; paler beneath. Length of head and body 10–13 cm (4–5.2 in), forearm about 9 cm (3.6 in); weight up to 100 g (3.5 oz).
Distribution   Honduras to southeastern Brazil; east of the Andes.
Habitat   Tropical forests and woodlands.
Behavior   Spear-nosed bats are highly gregarious, usually roosting together in clusters in caves or tree hollows, sometimes forming colonies of several thousand individuals sharing one cave. Groups often fly together from their diurnal retreat to their evening foraging areas. This species is quite omnivorous in diet, eating fruit, possibly nectar and flowers, insects, birds, and small rodents. A large bat with a 2-foot wingspan, it will also attack, kill, and devour other bats. It is itself prey to an even larger cannibal bat, the false vampire (*Vampyrum spectrum*), which is the largest bat in the Americas. The spear-nosed bat gives birth to a single offspring, apparently seasonally, either once or twice per year. Pregnant females have been captured in March and April; nursing mothers have been recorded in each month from April through August.

67 GLOSSOPHAGA SORICINA
Pallas' long-tongued bat

Classification Order Chiroptera, Family Phyllostomatidae.
Description A small, brown bat with long, narrow snout; small eyes; short, rounded ears; simple, erect, pointed noseleaf; very short tail with its extreme tip free on the upper surface of the tail membrane. Length of head and body 4.8–6.4 cm (1.9–2.5 in), forearm 3–4 cm (1.2–1.6 in); weight about 9 g (0.3 oz).

Distribution Southern Sonora and Tamaulipas, Mexico, south to northern Argentina; Bahamas, Trinidad, Jamaica.
Habitat Tropical and subtropical forests; woodlands.
Behavior One of the most common Neotropical bats in warm regions, this species roosts by day in caves, mine tunnels, and buildings, often sharing its quarters with other species. It is gregarious, forming colonies of several hundred, but is also found in only small clusters; individuals roost separated from one another. A noisy, fast-flying bat, Pallas' long-tongued bat feeds at night on nectar, fruit, and insects. Similar to Australasian blossom bat (of an entirely distinct suborder), this species is endowed with a particularly long, narrow, extensible tongue with a brush of hairlike papillae arising from the sides at the tip. This helps in lapping nectar from flowers of plants, including calabash tree and night-blooming cacti. This species may give birth to its single offspring twice each year, the seasons of birth varying geographically.

---

68 URODERMA BILOBATUM
Yellow-eared bat

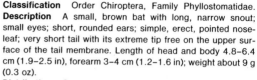

Classification Order Chiroptera, Family Phyllostomatidae.
Description A small bat with erect, pointed noseleaf with rounded sides on a fleshy, horseshoe-shaped base; no visible tail. Pelage gray-brown with 4 white facial stripes, a median stripe down the lower back, and yellow ear margins. Length of head and body about 6 cm (2.4 in), forearm 4.2 cm (1.6 in); weight up to 22 g (0.8 oz).
Distribution Lowland southern Mexico, Central America, northern South America to São Paulo, Brazil; Trinidad.
Habitat Tropical forests.

Behavior The yellow-eared bat subsists on a wide variety of tropical fruits and consumes insects as well. Solitary individuals, or small clusters of 10 or more, roost by day in tree hollows or more often under the broad leaves of banana plants or palm trees. Like many tropical bats, they remain alert while resting. Unlike most bats, which make no nest or shelter of any sort, the tent-making bat is known to cut a row of small holes in a palm frond so the edges droop, forming a sort of tent under which the bat hangs. Bats of a closely related Neotropical genus *Artibeus*, and a distantly related genus of fruit bats (*Cynopterus*) in Sri Lanka, have similar roost-making habits. A single young is usual; peak periods of birth are March–April and July–August.

69 CENTURIO SENEX
Wrinkle-faced, or lattice-winged, bat

Classification Order Chiroptera, Family Phyllostomatidae.
Description A small, brownish bat with a white spot on each shoulder. Short muzzle; crown of the head raised; naked face covered with wrinkled skin; wing membranes marked with numerous transverse parallel dark bands. Length of head and body 5.5–7 cm (2.2–2.8 in), forearm about 4.5 cm (1.8 in); weight up to 28 g (1 oz).

Distribution Sinaloa and Tamaulipas, Mexico, through Central America to Panama; Venezuela; Trinidad.
Habitat Tropical and subtropical forests and woodlands.

Behavior The grotesque facial appearance immediately sets this species apart from all other bats. Most of its close relatives have a noseleaf, but instead, the wrinkle-faced bat has a mass of fleshy growths covering its face. When roosting during the day, the bat covers its face with a mask of skin by drawing it upward from its attachment at the chin and hooking it on a protrusion at the top of its head. Even the ears are thus covered. In some individuals there are 2 translucent patches in the mask, allowing the bat to perceive light or moving forms. Wrinkle-faced bats roost among the leaves of trees, usually singly or in small groups of fewer than a dozen. They are fruit-eaters. One offspring is usual and females breed more than once each year; the gestation period is unknown.

---

70 DESMODUS ROTUNDUS
Common vampire bat

Classification Order Chiroptera, Family Phyllostomatidae.
Description A medium-sized, dark gray-brown bat with short, blunt muzzle; small, rounded protuberance in place of a noseleaf; deep groove in lower lip; short ears with pointed tragus; long, strong thumb with short, curved claw; no tail. Length of head and body about 8 cm (3.2 in), forearm 6 cm (2.4 in); weight 18–42 g (0.6–1.5 oz).

Distribution Sonora and Tamaulipas, Mexico, to central Chile, northern Argentina, and Uruguay; Trinidad.
Habitat Tropical and subtropical forests; temperate scrub and woodlands; cactus deserts.

Behavior Cave-dwelling common vampires roost in colonies of up to 1000, but usually about 100. They feed on blood, mainly on cattle and other livestock, often attacking the same animal night after night. Humans are seldom bitten. The bats' large, razor-sharp upper incisors cut a small wound from which the blood is lapped through a "drinking straw" formed by grooves under the bats' tongues and in their lower lips. Vampires transmit paralytic rabies and other livestock infections. Common vampire bats breed throughout the year, bearing a single young after an 8-month pregnancy. The 2 other species of vampire bats are *Diaemus youngi* in eastern Mexico to Brazil, and the hairy-legged vampire (*Diphylla ecaudata*), known from Val Verde County, Texas, to southern Brazil.

71 MYOTIS LUCIFUGUS
Little brown bat, little brown myotis

Classification Order Chiroptera, Family Vespertilionidae.
Description A small bat with simple nose; moderately long ears with long, pointed tragus; tail extending to edge of tail membrane; long hairs on toes. Fur long, silky, glossy; tan, reddish, or dark brown; paler beneath. Length of head and body 4–5.4 cm (1.6–2.2 in), forearm 3.3–4.1 cm (1.3–1.6 in); weight about 8 g (0.3 oz).

Distribution Most of Canada and continental U.S.A. (except coastal southern California, central Nebraska through Texas, and Gulf Coast region), and Sierra Madre Occidental to near Mexico City.
Habitat Temperate forests and woodlands near fresh water.

Behavior This very common nocturnal species eats flying insects caught on the wing. Seasonal in habit, little brown bats roost in colonies of up to several thousand, choosing warm sites such as attics or caves in summer. They breed in late summer and autumn, though fertilization is delayed until spring, and migrate up to 290 miles to form winter colonies in caves where temperatures remain just above freezing. There they hibernate, rousing themselves about every 2 weeks to move to more favorable positions. Again migrating in spring, the females form large maternity colonies, males usually roosting alone. After gestation of 50–60 days, the single offspring is born May–July. It flies and forages as an adult when 1 month old.

---

72 MYOTIS MYOTIS
Large mouse-eared bat

Classification Order Chiroptera, Family Vespertilionidae.
Description A heavily built, small bat with simple nose; moderately long, leathery ears and long, round-tipped, simple tragus; fairly long tail with only extreme cartilaginous tip free of tail membrane. Fur short, brown dorsally, grayish white beneath. Length of head and body up to 8 cm (3.2 in), forearm about 6 cm (2.4 in); weight up to 45 g (1.4 oz).

Distribution Central and southern Europe; Lebanon and Israel.
Habitat Nearly all situations.

Behavior Abundant on the Continent but seldom found in England, this bat is the largest of the 11 *Myotis* species in Europe. The genus is the most widespread in the world, with nearly 100 species recognized (over 20 of them in North America). The large mouse-eared bat eats insects caught in flight as well as beetles taken on the ground. The species is migratory, traveling up to 160 miles between its summer and winter roosts. In summer, nursery colonies of several hundred inhabit buildings, tunnels, or caves; smaller winter colonies hibernate in caves. Most single offspring, rarely twins, are born in June following a gestation of 50–70 days, reaching maturity and migrating with their parents by August.

73 PIPISTRELLUS PIPISTRELLUS
Common pipistrelle

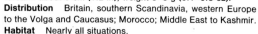

Classification Order Chiroptera, Family Vespertilionidae.

Description Small and robust, this bat has a short, dark muzzle; small ears, tragus straight with broadly rounded tip; glandular swelling on each side of face; tip of long tail free from tail membrane. Fur long, uniformly brown, may be slightly lighter beneath. Length of head and body about 4 cm (1.6 in), forearm about 3 cm (1.2 in); weight 3–8 g (0.1–0.3 oz).

Distribution Britain, southern Scandinavia, western Europe to the Volga and Caucasus; Morocco; Middle East to Kashmir.

Habitat Nearly all situations.

Behavior The most abundant bat in the British Isles and one of the most common in Europe, the tiny pipistrelle roosts singly or in small colonies up to several hundred in number, often with other species. It favors hollow trees or under loose bark, buildings, under roofs, but is rarely found in caves. It forages throughout the night, and in spring and autumn may be seen flying about in midday as well, seeking small insects such as gnats and crane flies. Common pipistrelles hibernate in winter and sometimes migrate more than 1000 miles between seasonal roosting sites. Most young are born in July after a gestation period of about 6 weeks, and reach sexual maturity in 2 years. A single offspring is usual in Britain; twins are common in northern and central Europe.

---

74 EPTESICUS FUSCUS
Big brown bat

Classification Order Chiroptera, Family Vespertilionidae.

Description A bat of medium size with dark, broad muzzle; simple nose; ears of moderate length, with rounded tips and blunt tragus. Fur long, pale to dark brown, may be lighter on underparts. Length of head and body about 7 cm (2.8 in), forearm 4–5 cm (1.6–2 in), weight 15–24 g (0.5–0.8 oz); females larger than males.

Distribution Southern Canada to Colombia and Venezuela; West Indies.

Habitat Nearly all situations.

Behavior Originally a forest dweller, the big brown bat has adapted to urban life and is frequently found in buildings, under bridges, and in other artificial structures, as well as in tree hollows and sometimes caves. It may roost singly or in small colonies; it rarely migrates, and then only short distances. The big brown bat forages at night, following a habitual course of flight. It eats mostly beetles, and although many other flying insects are also taken, moths are not among them. This species hibernates in winter in the coldest parts of its range. Breeding begins in autumn with fertilization delayed in hibernating females; gestation is about 2 months. The young are born during mid-May to June, usually a single offspring in western North America and twins in the East. The young are weaned and can fly when 1 month old.

75 VESPERTILIO MURINUS
Particolored bat

Classification   Order Chiroptera, Family Vespertilionidae.
Description   Small and robust, a bat with short, broad, rounded ears; simple but prominent nose; long tail with tip extending beyond tail membrane. Fur short, dense; dark brown with whitish tips, giving a frosted appearance. Length of head and body about 5 cm (2 in), forearm up to 4.5 cm (1.8 in); weight about 15 g (0.5 oz).
Distribution   Central Europe to Siberia; Scandinavia to Iran and Afghanistan.
Habitat   Forests, woodlands, and steppes.
Behavior   This hardy bat favors cold climates. Abundant in southern Sweden and central Russia, it is also common in the Alps and lives in the Himalayas to at least 10,000 feet elevation. Two vagrants, probably brought by boat, have been found in England within the past 100 years. Particolored bats roost in rock crevices and hollow trees and are often found in the walls and attics of buildings, both large summer colonies of up to several thousand bats or when hibernating in winter. They forage for insects late at night, flying back and forth or in circles 60 feet or more above the ground through their habitual hunting areas, which are open places 300–1000 feet across. Their migrations are usually only short distances between seasonal roosting sites. Gestation is 40–50 days; the young, frequently twins, are born May–June.

76 LASIURUS CINEREUS
Hoary bat

Classification   Order Chiroptera, Family Vespertilionidae.
Description   A heavy-bodied bat of medium size with short, rounded ears edged with black; simple nose; tail membrane dorsally furred. Pelage thick, face and throat buff to yellow, body brown with hairs tipped white, giving a frosted appearance. Length of head and body about 8.5 cm (3.4 in), forearm about 5 cm (2 in); weight 20–35 g (0.7–1.2 oz).
Distribution   Throughout the Americas from southern Canada to central Chile and Argentina; Hawaii; Hispaniola.
Habitat   Forests and woodlands.
Behavior   Largest bat in eastern North America (and the only bat native to Hawaii), this species breeds in its northern summer range and winters in the southern U.S. and possibly in Mexico. Some South American populations may also migrate. Its complex migratory habits are incompletely known. Vagrants, probably blown off course, have been found in Iceland, Orkney, and Bermuda. Individuals remaining far north in winter may hibernate during the coldest weather. The hoary bat, usually solitary, roosts in leaf clusters in trees, at 10–15 feet above the ground, and emerges in late evening to forage. Fast-flying, these bats catch and eat insects (mainly moths) on the wing. In North America the young are born in May–June, after what is probably an 8-month gestation period; there are usually 2 per litter (occasionally 1).

77 BARBASTELLA BARBASTELLUS
Western barbastelle

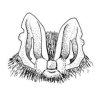

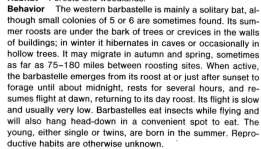

Classification   Order Chiroptera, Family Vespertilionidae.
Description   A small bat with flat face; ears long and broad with notched outer edge and inner margins joined at their base, pointed tragus half height of ear. Long, blackish fur with light tips giving a grizzled appearance. Length of head and body about 4.7 cm (1.8 in), forearm 4 cm (1.6 in); weight 6–8 g (0.2–0.3 oz).
Distribution   England; throughout Europe from Norway south to Spain, east to the Volga and Caucasus; Morocco.
Habitat   Forests and woodlands.
Behavior   The western barbastelle is mainly a solitary bat, although small colonies of 5 or 6 are sometimes found. Its summer roosts are under the bark of trees or crevices in the walls of buildings; in winter it hibernates in caves or occasionally in hollow trees. It may migrate in autumn and spring, sometimes as far as 75–180 miles between roosting sites. When active, the barbastelle emerges from its roost at or just after sunset to forage until about midnight, rests for several hours, and resumes flight at dawn, returning to its day roost. Its flight is slow and usually very low. Barbastelles eat insects while flying and will also hang head-down in a convenient spot to eat. The young, either single or twins, are born in the summer. Reproductive habits are otherwise unknown.

78 PLECOTUS AURITUS
Common long-eared bat

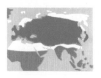

Classification   Order Chiroptera, Family Vespertilionidae.
Description   Of small size, this delicate bat has a moderately long muzzle bearing a pair of protuberances above the nose; extremely long ears joined across the forehead with a long, simple, narrowly rounded tragus; tail tip free beyond tail membrane. Pelage long, grizzled; brownish in color except gray-white beneath. Average head and body length 4.7 cm (1.8 in), forearm 4 cm (1.6 in); weight 5–15 g (0.2–0.5 oz).
Distribution   British Isles; Scandinavia south to the Pyrenees, east as far as Japan.
Habitat   Forests and woodlands.
Behavior   This possibly migratory species is very common in the temperate parts of the Palearctic Region, and often roosts in colonies of 50–100 in its summer daytime retreats, such as under roofs or in hollow trees. It is generally more solitary in winter while hibernating in caves. Foraging at dusk and through the night, the long-eared bat eats moths and beetles caught in flight, and captures other insects, spiders, and wood lice by hovering in trees and climbing on branches or walls. Long-eared bats breed in autumn and spring. Pregnant females form nursery colonies of 100 or more in early summer, and the single young or twins are born in June–July. Four similar species of *Plecotus* inhabit North America.

79 EUDERMA MACULATUM
Spotted or pinto bat

Classification   Order Chiroptera, Family Vespertilionidae.

Description   Immediately recognized by its striking coloration, this small, delicate bat is black with a contrasting white patch on each shoulder and the rump; white at base of ears; underparts with black hair tipped white. Ears are enormous, rounded at tip; tragus simple. Length of head and body 6–6.5 cm (2.4–2.6 in), forearm 5 cm (2 in); weight 10–20 g (0.4–0.7 oz).

Distribution   Western North America from interior southern California east to New Mexico, from Montana south to Querétaro, Mexico.

Habitat   Rocky cliffs and canyons; coniferous forest and woodland; scrub and desert.

Behavior   The spotted bat is rare, perhaps a relict species, and is known from only a few dozen specimens collected since its discovery in 1890. It has been found in mixed coniferous forest at 6000–8000 feet, as well as in arid desert below sea level. It is probably solitary and roosts in crevices high up in rocky cliffs and canyons. It may hibernate in caves during winter in northern latitudes and otherwise migrate, perhaps vertically. Foraging late at night, it eats mostly moths, discarding the wings and hard parts, and occasionally consumes other insects. Little is known of its reproductive cycle, but it apparently bears a single young in June (possibly in July–August in the northern parts of its range).

---

80 MINIOPTERUS SCHREIBERSI
Bent-wing, or Schreiber's long-fingered, bat

Classification   Order Chiroptera, Family Vespertilionidae.

Description   A small bat with short, broad muzzle; ears low, wide, rounded; long second joint of third finger. Pelage short and dense; color ranges from reddish to grayish, but is generally brown. Length of head and body about 5–6 cm (2–2.4 in), forearm 4.5 cm (1.8 in); weight up to 20 g (0.7 oz).

Distribution   Southwestern Europe to Japan; throughout Africa including Madagascar; southern Asia, through the islands to Australia.

Habitat   All situations except desert.

Behavior   The cave-dwelling bent-wing bat roosts in small clusters or large colonies up to 50,000, often sharing its quarters with bats of other species. Migrations can cover about 100–200 miles between summer and winter retreats. This bat hibernates in cold climates or otherwise curtails activity during cold weather. Foraging flights begin soon after sunset, the insect-eating bats flying high and fast. Bent-wings mate in the autumn; fertilization is immediate, but growth of embryo varies according to climate. In Europe, births are in April. In eastern Australia, young are born in December–January. In the tropics, gestation is rapid with births following in late November–December. The single offspring can fly when 7 weeks old.

81 CHEIROMELES TORQUATUS
Hairless, or naked, bulldog bat

Classification   Order Chiroptera, Family Molossidae.
Description   A medium-sized bat with small ears, long muzzle and simple nose; tail long, thick, and extending well beyond tail membrane. Loose, heavy, dark gray or brown skin is nearly naked, with only sparse hairs around scent gland on throat, and bristles on first toe. Length of head and body 13–14.5 cm (5.2–5.8 in), forearm 8–8.6 cm (3.2–3.4 in); weight about 180 g (6.3 oz).
Distribution   Southern Thailand to Sumatra; Java, Borneo.
Habitat   Tropical forests.
Behavior   In addition to its hairless condition, the naked bulldog bat is peculiar in having a pocket of skin along its sides, into which its wings are folded when the bat rests. The haired gland on its throat produces a strong, foul odor. The bat cleans its skin with the brushlike bristles on its big toes, which are opposable to the others, and have a flat nail instead of a claw. These bats are gregarious, having been found in colonies of nearly 1000 roosting in hollow trees or sometimes caves, often with other free-tailed bats. Emerging at dusk, they fly fast and purposefully, foraging for flying termites above the forest treetops or in clearings. The breeding habits of this species are not known.

82 TADARIDA BRASILIENSIS
Brazilian free-tailed bat

Classification   Order Chiroptera, Family Molossidae.
Description   A small, robust, gray-brown bat with long tail, half of its length free beyond the tail membrane; long, stiff hairs on the toes; short, broad muzzle with wrinkled lips; ears bonnet-shaped. Length of head and body 4.7–6.5 cm (1.9–2.6 in), forearm 3.7–4.6 cm (1.5–1.8 in); weight 10–15 g (0.4–0.7 oz).
Distribution   Southern half of U.S. to mid Chile and Argentina; West Indies and Bahamas.
Habitat   Scrub and woodlands.
Behavior   Summer nursery colonies of this highly gregarious bat number up to 10 or 20 million per cave in Texas, Oklahoma, New Mexico, and Arizona. At one time, nearly 9 million inhabited the Carlsbad Caverns; now only some 250,000 bats summer there. These vast populations migrate as far as 800–1000 miles into Mexico for the winter, whereas in southeastern and western North America, the free-tails remain throughout the year, roosting in buildings and possibly hibernating in cold weather. Flying 35 to 50 mph, free-tails emerge at dusk to feed on small moths. Gestation is 77–84 days in Florida, about 100 days in California (unknown for other parts of the range). The single offspring is born in June–July and is able to fly in about 5 weeks.

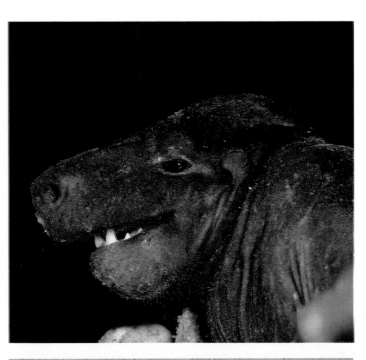

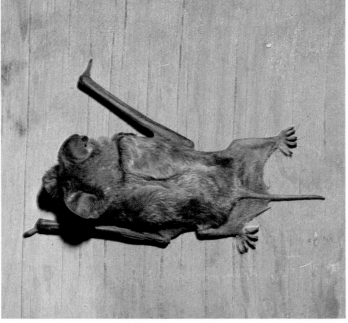

83 TUPAIA GLIS
Common tree shrew

Classification   Order Scandentia, Family Tupaiidae.
Description   In both appearance and size it closely resembles the squirrels. Pelage is soft and dense, ranging in color from gray to green with dark coloring uppermost, and whitish or dark chestnut-brown on the underside. The snout is pointed; the ears are small and bare and set close to head. The toes are clawed, and the "thumb" is not opposable. The tail is covered with long hairs. Length of head and body 14–23 cm (5.5–9 in), tail about the same; weight 100–200 g (3.5–7 oz).
Distribution   Southern China, the Indochinese Peninsula, India between Ganges River and the Himalayas, and offshore islands.

Habitat   Secondary forest, shrubby areas, and montane forest.
Behavior   The common tree shrew feeds on insects, fruit, seeds, and leaves. When eating it sits on its hind legs and holds its food with its front feet. It is active by day, and appears to be constantly on the move and searching for food. It lives mainly on the ground, building its nest among tree roots or in fallen trunks. Tree shrews live in pairs, and the male delimits his territory with a strong-smelling substance secreted from glands situated in the throat. Gestation requires 46–50 days; the litter usually consists of 2 young, which become sexually mature at 4 months.

84 LEMUR MACACO
Black lemur

Classification   Order Primates, Family Lemuridae.
Description   The snout is pointed and foxlike. The hind legs are considerably longer than the front legs and the toes all have claws. The coat is long and soft, black in males, reddish in females. There is a dense collar of long hairs around the neck and close to the ears. Length of head and body 30–45 cm (12–18 in), tail 40–50 cm (16–20 in); weight 2–2.8 kg (4.4–6.2 lb).
Distribution   Northern Madagascar.
Habitat   Tropical forests.

Behavior   The black lemur feeds on fruit and insects; it is essentially arboreal and can leap as far as 26 feet. It is most active in the morning and toward nightfall. It gathers in groups of about 10 (4–15) individuals and is territorial. In order to delimit its territory it rubs its front legs against things, thus leaving its scent on them, or it may use vocal signals. Its shrieks are quite terrifying when the whole group cries in unison. It takes great care of its own coat, and spends many hours a day cleaning it, using its claws and its lower incisor dental comb to do so. The female usually gives birth to just a single offspring, after a gestation period of about 128 days, in March–June. The young are suckled for about 6 months and remain with their mother at all times, clinging tightly to the coat of her back.

85 LEMUR CATTA
Ring-tailed lemur

Classification   Order Primates, Family Lemuridae.
Description   A cat-sized animal with a fairly agile, sleek body and pointed snout. The soft, relatively long coat is gray with reddish coloring uppermost; very pale on the underside; clearly marked black and white rings on its long tail. On the forearms there are glands which secrete a strong-smelling substance. Length of head and body about 42.5 cm (16.6 in), tail about 50 cm (20 in); weight 2.3–3.5 kg (5–7.7 lb).
Distribution   Southern and southwestern Madagascar.
Habitat   Rocky mountains with sparse vegetation.
Behavior   Mainly active by day, this lemur lives principally on the ground. It feeds on wild fruit, leaves, and flowers. It holds fruit with its front feet and bites into it with its molars, holding its head in such a way that the juice falls directly into its mouth. The ring-tailed lemur lives in large groups, with approximately equal numbers of each sex. When the weather is cold these animals draw close to each other to generate warmth; they also "sun" themselves in the treetops. The territory is delimited by using the secretion of the glands on the forearm and in the anal region. It spends a great deal of time preening and cleaning its coat, combing it with its lower incisors and its claws. During the mating season, aggression increases in the otherwise social males, involving "spat call" vocalizations and "stink fights" involving their tail and forearm glands. The female usually gives birth to a single young, in March–April, after a gestation period of 120–136 days. The young are suckled for about 6 months.

86 MICROCEBUS MURINUS
Gray mouse lemur

Classification   Order Primates, Family Cheirogaleidae.
Description   This and *Cebuella pygmea* (**104**) are the smallest of all the primates. The legs are very sturdy; the tail is not prehensile, but is used to maintain balance. Eyes and ears are large. Coat dense and woolly; gray or sometimes reddish gray uppermost, paler on the underside. Length of head and body 11–13 cm (4.4–5.2 in), tail 12 cm (4.8 in); weight 50–80 g (1.8–2.8 oz) varying with the season.
Distribution   The west, south, and southwest coasts of Madagascar.
Habitat   Damp woodland and grassy, lightly wooded areas.
Behavior   This is a nocturnal animal which sleeps in groups low in the trees, in a nest made of leaves and twigs and lined with fur, or in tree hollows. It forages singly, feeding on fruit, flowers, insects, and small animals, which it holds tightly with its front feet. Before the dry season (July–September), it accumulates fat at the base of the tail and in the front legs, which it metabolizes during the 3 dry months when food is scarce. (The capacity to accumulate fat appears unlimited: captive animals have weighed up to 6 ounces. Gestation lasts 54–68 days; litters consist of 2 or 3 young, most born after the dry season, in September–March. The mother "sticks" them to the sides of her body with her mouth, and carries them about. By the time they are 3 weeks old, they are completely independent.

87 INDRI INDRI
Indri

Classification   Order Primates, Family Indriidae.

Description   The coat of this primate, the largest of the prosimians, is long and rather bristly; dark brown-gray or black, with distinctive white areas around the ears, the shoulders, the arms, and the hindquarters. The snout is pointed and completely hairless; the eyes are large. The feet and hands have very strong big toes and thumbs, respectively. Length of head and body 60–90 cm (24–36 in), tail only 5–6 cm (2–2.4 in), weight 5–7 kg (11–15.4 lb); female somewhat smaller.

Distribution   Northeastern Madagascar.

Habitat   Forest, from sea level to 6000 feet.

Behavior   This may be the only Malagasy primate that is exclusively diurnal. Its diet is entirely vegetarian, made up of leaves, fruit, and flowers. During certain times of year, especially when other foods are scarce, the indri uses its tooth comb to obtain bark and dead wood, to add nutrition and roughage to its diet. It lives in trees in small groups, alone, or in pairs. It is territorial and in order to delimit its territory it makes shrill cries. It rarely descends to the ground and when it does so it walks in an upright position, making its way forward by hopping. Little is known about its reproductive habits, but the female generally gives birth to a single offspring after a gestation period of about 60 days.

Note   This species is threatened with extinction because of the changes to which its natural environment has been subjected.

88 DAUBENTONIA MADAGASCARIENSIS
Aye-aye

Classification   Order Primates, Family Daubentoniidae.

Description   The pelage consists of a short, soft, white layer overlaid by a layer of extremely long, coarse blackish brown hairs, resulting in paler areas here and there, especially on the snout and the underside of the body. Both hands and feet have long, tapering fingers and toes; the third finger on the hand is particularly long and slender, and almost skeletal. All the digits have pointed, curved clawlike nails except the first, which has a flat nail. The dentition is like that of the rodents, with incisors which grow as they are worn down and a broad diastema (space), which separates the incisors from the premolars, in place of the missing canines. Length of head and body about 45 cm (18 in), tail 55 cm (22 in); weight about 2 kg (4.5 lb).

Distribution   Eastern Madagascar.

Habitat   Forest, bamboo forests, mangrove swamp, dry scrub forest, and cultivated areas (especially coconut groves).

Behavior   This nocturnal animal sleeps hidden among vegetation or in tree hollows. In late afternoon, hopping from branch to branch, it hunts for larvae, beetles, and certain other insects. The conspicuously long and slender third finger is used to extract larvae from beneath the bark of trees and, together with its specialized incisors, enables the aye-aye to get at coconut meat. It lives alone or as a pair. In February–March the female gives birth to a single young.

89 PERODICTICUS POTTO
Potto

Classification　Order Primates, Family Lorisidae.

Description　Its color varies, depending on the age, sex, and type, ranging from reddish brown to black. The fur is very thick and woolly. The very short tail is barely visible beneath the coat. The round head has a short, wide face. The cervical vertebrae are protruding and form a series of spiny processes beneath the bare skin. Length of head and body 30–45 cm (12–18 in), tail 6 cm (2.4 in); weight 1–1.5 kg (2.2–3.3 lb).

Distribution　West Africa (coastal zones) and central Africa as far east as the Rift Valley.

Habitat　This species is restricted to equatorial forests, including rain forest and montane forest.

Behavior　The rarely sighted potto is nocturnal; it spends the daylight hours dozing in the branches of trees, curled up with its head between its legs. It clings tightly to its branch and is not easily removed. It can defend itself most effectively with powerful bites. It never descends to the ground, and feeds mainly on fruit and plant matter, but also on insects and slugs. It lives a solitary existence, and even its courtship and mating period is a brief one. Its main enemy is the palm owl. When it moves from one branch to the next, or one tree to the next, it places one foot after the other, alternately, as if on a tightrope, but always with great caution. Little is known about the potto's breeding habits, but there is usually only a single young.

90 LORIS TARDIGRADUS
Slender loris

Classification　Order Primates, Family Lorisidae.

Description　The slender loris is tail-less, with soft, dense fur that is brown in color, with the underside silver-gray. The nose is pointed and the eyes are very large. The ears are round and prominent, and hairless at the edge. The hands and feet are prehensile; the thumbs and big toes opposable; and there are small flat nails on all digits except the second toe, which is reduced and has a specialized grooming claw. Length of head and body about 25 cm (10 in); weight up to 350 g (12.3 oz).

Distribution　Southern India and Sri Lanka.

Habitat　Tropical forests, swampy forests, and woodlands.

Behavior　This is a nocturnal creature which spends the hours of daylight in tree hollows or among the branches of trees, curled up tightly with its head tucked between its hind legs, and its feet clinging to a branch. Its movements are very slow indeed; it spends the hours of darkness moving among the branches of trees hunting insects, geckoes, and lizards. It lives a solitary life and is territorial; it soaks its hands and feet in its own urine (this activity is called "urine-washing") so that it leaves a scent wherever it goes, which helps it to find its way as well as to mark its territory. A single offspring is born after a gestation period of (apparently) about 6 months. At birth the young loris is covered with hair, and achieves independence from its mother after about a year.

91 NYCTICEBUS COUCANG
Slow loris

Classification Order Primates, Family Lorisidae.

Description The coat is dense, woolly and soft, tawny in color with a black stripe along the back; its short tail is entirely concealed by the fur. The face is rounded, the eyes large, and the ears small. The fingers and toes are short and thick, equipped with nails, and the second toe on each hind foot has a long grooming claw. Length of head and body 23–37 cm (9–14.5 in); weight 0.5–1.5 kg (1.1–3.3 lb).

Distribution Southeast Asia.

Habitat Tropical forests.

Behavior This is a nocturnal, tree-dwelling creature, feeding on fruit and insects. Its movements are even slower than those of *Loris tardigradus* **(90);** but like that species, the slow loris lays an ambush for its prey and then, at the opportune moment, seizes it with a swift movement. The powerful musculature of the hands and feet enables it to keep a tight grip on the branches of trees, on which it hangs, asleep, throughout the daylight hours. It is a territorial animal and uses urine to mark its territory. It uses its tongue, grooming claw, and dental comb to clean its fur. Gestation lasts between 90 and 180 days, at the end of which the female, which has 4 nipples, gives birth to a single young.

92 GALAGO SENEGALENSIS
Senegalese bushbaby

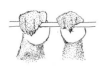

Classification Order Primates, Family Lorisidae

Description This bushbaby is generally gray with yellowish highlights and with a light-colored stripe between the eyes. Some are various shades of brown. The fur is short and very soft. The very long tail has a darker tip. The back feet are elongated, with short toes. The ears are very large, naked, and mobile, and the face is flattened. Length of head and body 20 cm (8 in), tail 25 cm (10 in); weight 500 g (1.1 lb).

Distribution Various parts of Africa south of the Sahara.

Habitat Scrub-strewn savanna and dry forests.

Behavior The Senegalese bushbaby is nocturnal and lives in groups, sometimes in large numbers, especially when sleeping *en masse* during the hours of daylight. By night, when it is active, it moves about either alone or in pairs, creeping nimbly among the branches of trees. It is essentially tree-dwelling, but can also move about on the ground without any difficulty, sometimes jumping as far as 10–13 feet. Its specially adapted hands enable it to cling firmly to branches. It also uses its hands to seek out and catch insects on the wing, to defend itself, and to build its nest. Its favorite foods are grasshoppers and other insects, but it also eats fruit, small birds, tree sap, and eggs. After a gestation period of about 110 days a single young (occasionally twins) is born. For 2 weeks the young are carried about clinging to the back of their mother.

93 TARSUS SYRICHTA
Philippine tarsier

Classification Order Primates, Family Tarsiidae.
Description The head is very rounded, with large, slender, almost entirely hairless ears, and very large eyes. The front legs are short, the hind legs very long. The toes and fingers are enlarged to form flat, soft discs with flattened nails except for the second and third toes, which bear grooming claws. The thumbs and big toes are opposable. Length of head and body 15–18 cm (6–7.5 in), tail 22–25 cm (8.7–10 in); weight 80–140 g (2.8–4.9 oz).
Distribution The Philippines.
Habitat Forested areas, but also found in agricultural areas, as fields and plantation.

Behavior This tarsier's diet consists mainly of insects, but it also hunts small fishes and crabs in fresh waters. It lives in trees, and spends the daylight hours clinging to the vertical branches of trees with its pupils contracted; if disturbed it moves its ears in the direction of the noise, and then slowly turns its head. At night its eyes dilate and it descends to the ground to hunt for prey. On the ground, it hops about like a frog, thrusting off from the ground with its long hind legs and then clinging to branches with the help of the suckerlike discs of its toes. It seizes its prey with both hands after making a lightning jump. Mating is preceded by mutual grooming; 1 well-developed infant is born, weighing slightly less than 1 ounce.

94 AOTUS TRIVIRGATUS
Night monkey, owl monkey

Classification Order Primates, Family Cebidae.
Description This is the only nocturnal monkey in the New World. The coat is dense and woolly, varying in color, but usually tending to gray, with three stripes on the head. The face looks like that of an owl, with large, round eyes. Length of head and body 24–47 cm (9.5–18.5 in), tail 40 cm (16 in); weight 0.5–1 kg (2.2–4.5 lb).
Distribution From Panama to northeastern Argentina, and from Guyana and Brazil to Ecuador and Peru.
Habitat Forests, from sea level to an altitude of 7000 feet.

Behavior This nocturnal animal lives in family groups of 2–5, and spends the hours of daylight hidden in hollows in trees or in vine tangles. At sundown the night monkey starts moving about with great ease in search of food. It eats fruit, leaves, insects, small birds, and even small mammals. As the following day starts to dawn, it returns to one of its few established hideouts. When in danger it emits a high-pitched shriek as an alarm signal. It can make a large variety of sounds, depending on the situation in which it finds itself, ranging from shrill cries to small squeaks, and from loud hoots to sharp clicks. Owl monkeys do not groom each other except immediately preceding copulation. The single offspring (occasionally twins) is a family affair—the father, or sometimes an older sibling, will carry the infant on his back, except during nursing.

95 ALOUATTA PIGRA
Guatemalan howler monkey

Classification   Order Primates, Family Cebidae.

Description   The howler monkeys are the largest of the group of platyrrhine monkeys (named after their widely separated nostrils). It is covered with a long, silky coat of black fur, which is longest on its throat, hiding the monkey's prominent vocal organ. Its legs and arms are long but stout, and its tail is prehensile. The thumbs and big toes are opposable to the other fingers and toes. Length of head and body 55–91 cm (22–36.4 in), tail 58–91 cm (23–36 in); weight 7–9 kg (15.4–20 lb).

Distribution   Southern Central America.

Habitat   Tropical forests.

Behavior   This howler monkey usually lives in groups ranging in number from 4–30 individuals of both sexes and all ages. Although group territories overlap, the strongest male, and sometimes all the males together demarcate the space around the group with their "howls." This monkey is mainly active in the morning and the evening, but can also remain busy throughout the day; at night it emits its distinctive howl which can be heard up to 2 miles away. It feeds on fruit (especially figs) and leaves. Gestation lasts about 140 days, after which the female gives birth to a single young, which she carries about clinging to the fur on her back for almost a whole year.

---

96 CEBUS CAPUCINUS
White-throated capuchin

Classification   Order Primates, Family Cebidae.

Description   The capuchin's body is nimble and slender, the limbs thin. The thumbs and big toes are opposable to the other fingers and toes. The head is round with short hairs at the back which are darker than the rest of the coat; the long tail is covered with hair and is partly prehensile. Length of head and body 32–56 cm (12.8–22.4 in), tail about the same; weight 1.5–4 kg (3.3–8.8 lb).

Distribution   Southern Central America.

Habitat   Forests, but these species have also adapted to places colonized by man.

Behavior   It lives in quite large groups, hidden among the dense arboreal vegetation of the forest; it descends to the ground only to drink. Each group has its own home range—often quite extensive—in which the members move about in search of the most abundant feeding grounds. The various members of the group remain in contact with one another by calling. In order to keep their sense of direction and mark territory they leave a scent among the foliage of the trees by soaking their feet and hands in their urine (urine-washing). They feed on fruit, insects, leaves, small birds, and possibly also on small mammals. After a gestation period of about 6 months, the female gives birth to a single young, which she weans after a few months.

97 SAIMIRI SCIUREUS
Common squirrel monkey

Classification   Order Primates, Family Cebidae.
Description   This species is known as the squirrel monkey because of its small size. The eyes are large, and the tail very long, though not prehensile in adults. Its fine coat is varied in color, often gray with yellowish or orange hue, sometimes marked with black on the legs. Length of head and body 30 cm (12 in), tail 40 cm (16 in); weight 750–1100 g (1.6–2.4 lb).
Distribution   Northern South America.
Habitat   Tropical forest, gallery forest, and forest edge.
Behavior   It lives in the treetops in the forest, in quite large groups of up to 100 in some areas. It rarely descends to the ground in search of food. It feeds on berries and fruit, insects, frogs, and other small animals. When demarcating its own territory it leaves a scent by soaking its body, especially its tail, in its urine. When assuming a commanding attitude toward the members of the group it stands up and displays its genitalia. During the mating season, the males achieve the "fatted male condition," almost doubling their body weight. Only 1 young is born in each litter.

---

98 ATELES GEOFFROYI
Black-handed spider monkey

Classification   Order Primates, Family Cebidae.
Description   This monkey has a prominent face, which is hairless with white rings around the eyes. The body is covered with pale-colored, bristly fur. The legs are long; the hands have virtually no thumb. The clitoris in the female is very protuberant, and can be mistaken for the male penis. Length of head and body 38–63 cm (15–25 in), tail 50–89 cm (20–35.5 in); weight about 6 kg (13 lb).
Distribution   Southern Central America.
Habitat   Tropical forests.
Behavior   It lives in groups of 2–8 individuals with the group splitting up during feeding. The group roams around its own territorial area following fixed routes, in search of fruit and nuts. If an alien monkey or other animal enters the territory, the members of the group approach it emitting shrill cries to scare it away. But the aggressivity of these monkeys is something of a façade, because if the intruder holds his ground, the spider monkeys simply move off in the opposite direction. The gestation period lasts for about 140 days, and the female gives birth to a single young, which remains dependent on its mother for about 10 months.

99 LAGOTHRIX LAGOTHRICHA
Woolly monkey

Classification Order Primates, Family Cebidae.
Description The most distinctive feature of this animal is its extremely prehensile, very flexible tail, which acts like a fifth hand (it can actually grasp objects). The body is covered with a dense, woolly, pale gray-brown coat. The legs and arms are quite long. The head is round and large, and the face is hairless. Length of head and body 50–60 cm (20–24 in), tail 60–70 cm (24–28 in); weight about 6 kg (13 lb).
Distribution Amazon Basin, Orinoco River, upper reaches of the Amazon, eastern slopes of the Andes.
Habitat Equatorial forests.

Behavior This monkey feeds mainly on fruit and leaves. It lives in large groups which split up while feeding. During the day it methodically makes its way from one tree to the next, making frequent use of its prehensile tail, in search of trees with a more plentiful supply of food. When eating it sits, or hangs by its tail to reach food out of reach of its hands. It rarely descends to the ground, and when it walks it assumes an upright position. The gestation period lasts for about 5 months, after which a single offspring is born.

---

100 CACAJAO CALVUS
Red uakari

Classification Order Primates, Family Cebidae.
Description Of all the New World monkeys, the uakaris have the shortest tails. They have a distinctive vermilion face, with the forehead and upper part of the cranium hairless. The rest of the coat is reddish-brown, and the hands, feet, and ears are brown. Length of head and body 57 cm (22.5 in), tail 16 cm (6.2 in); weight about 5 kg (11 lb).
Distribution In the upper reaches of the Amazon.
Habitat Dense, flooded forests.

Behavior The red uakari lives in large groups of 15–30, with reports of 100. It is mainly active during the daylight hours, when it moves among the branches of trees in search of fruit, leaves, insects, and other small creatures. It moves nimbly, but does not make spectacular leaps; it does not emit many sounds, and is otherwise rather quiet. In fact, these monkeys can easily go unnoticed in the forest, and it is only their bright red face which draws attention to them. They spend almost all their lives in the treetops, and almost never descend to the ground, which is flooded for most of the year in their preferred habitat.
Note This monkey has become very rare, because of overhunting. They usually survive for very short periods in captivity.

101 CHIROPOTES SATANAS
Black-bearded saki

Classification   Order Primates, Family Cebidae.
Description   This species is unmistakable because of the long, very thick beard on its chin, temporal swellings on the skull, and for its long and very densely coated tail. Its head, beard, and tail are all black; the shoulders and back vary from reddish brown to blackish; the hands and feet are black or reddish. Length of head and body up to 50 cm (20 in), tail slightly less; weight about 4 kg (8.8 lb).
Distribution   Guyana, Venezuela (southern part), and Brazil, north of the Amazon.
Habitat   Dense forests.
Behavior   It lives in groups of 8–30 or more, but the group splits up to search for food. We have very little information about its biology. It feeds on fruit, and on the seeds of unripe fruit. It emits a whistlelike sound which is differently modulated depending on the various situations in which the monkey happens to find itself.
Note   The saki has a limited geographic range. It was recently reported as having been observed in Peru, but this has as yet to be confirmed. It is a very rare species, and is actively hunted by the local Indians for the fur and hair on its tail and beard, which are used for ornamental purposes.

102 SAGUINUS IMPERATOR
Emperor tamarin

Classification   Order Primates, Family Cebidae, Subfamily Callitrichinae.
Description   The emperor tamarin has a distinctive long, white, drooping mustache. The dense coat is blackish (but reddish on the chest), there are tufts of hair on the ears. The very long tail is not prehensile, but it does help keep the monkey balanced while moving around in trees. Length of head and body up to 30 cm (12 in), tail to 35 cm (14 in); weight 250–500 g (8.75–17.5 oz).
Distribution   In the Amazon.
Habitat   Dense forests.
Behavior   This animal belongs to the subfamily Callitrichinae (102–105) which consists of 21 species of small primates distributed throughout South America. The emperor tamarin lives in small groups, sometimes in association with different species of monkey as well. It is diurnal and keeps constantly on the move with swift, nervous movements. It is very agile and can move from branch to branch with great ease; it can also make impressive leaps, and will sometimes make drops from a considerable height. It feeds mainly on fruit and plant matter, but also eats sap from wounds in trees, catches insects and small vertebrates, and robs birds' nests of their eggs. Gestation lasts about 5 months; the female delivers 1 (but sometimes 2) young.

103 CALLITHRIX JACCHUS
Common marmoset

Classification   Order Primates, Family Cebidae.
Description   Another member of the Callitrichinae, this species is easily identified by the two white tufts of hair at the sides of the head and a white blaze on the forehead. Its body is covered with soft, thin hair, grayish in color, with darker stripes. The tail has lighter- and darker-colored rings. Length of head and body 20–25 cm (8–10 in), tail 29–35 cm (12–14 in); weight about 400 g (14 oz).
Distribution   Eastern Brazil.

Habitat   Tropical forests.
Behavior   It lives in family groups of 3–8, but may be seen in groups of considerable size. It feeds on fruit, insects, small birds, and birds' eggs, and also feeds on tree gums and saps by gouging holes in the bark with its specialized incisors. It devotes much time to mutual grooming. By night it sleeps in hollows in trees or hidden among vegetation. The female delivers 1–3 young (usually twins) after a gestation period of 142–150 days. Only one female per group reproduces. The others are somehow inhibited from reproduction. The father is very involved in parental care, carrying the young twins on his back except during nursing.

---

104 CEBUELLA PYGMAEA
Pygmy marmoset

Classification   Order Primates, Family Cebidae.
Description   This callitrichine and *Microcebus murinus* **(86)** are the smallest of all the primates. The coat on the head and neck is dark brown and gray, the body is gray and black with a yellowish hue, the legs yellowish, and the tail has delicately shaded black and gray rings. The most distinctive feature is the almond shape of its eyes. The ears are completely hidden by the mane. Length of head and body 14–16 cm (5.5–6.5 in), tail 15–20 cm (6–8 in); weight 50–80 g (1.8–2.8 oz).
Distribution   The upper reaches of the Amazon River (Ecuador, Colombia, northern Peru, and western Brazil).

Habitat   Tropical forests.
Behavior   It feeds on fruit and insects, but most of its time is spent clinging vertically to trees while feeding on saps and gums, gouging holes in the bark with its specialized incisors. It lives among the branches of trees and is very agile and active. Unfortunately, because of its small size and its swift movements, it is very hard to observe in the wild. When frightened, it clambers up a tree trunk, following a rapid, spiral-like route. Its cry is like that of a songbird. Little is known of its reproductive biology, but the usual number of offspring appears to be 1 or 2.

105 LEONTOPITHECUS ROSALIA
Golden lion marmoset, golden lion tamarin

Classification   Order Primates, Family Cebidae.

Description   The distinctive feature of this species of callitrichine is the thick lionlike mane which conceals the ears. The dense, bristly coat is of an almost uniformly golden color. The hands and feet are very long, and the second, third, and fourth digits are joined together by skin which extends to the middle joint. The face is hairless. All digits bear clawlike nails except the big toe, which has a flat nail. Length of head and body up to 50 cm (20 in), tail 22–38 cm (8.5–14.8 in); weight (in captivity) 600–800 g (1.3–1.8 lb).

Distribution   Coastal mountains southwest of Rio de Janeiro.

Habitat   Lowland tropical forests.

Behavior   This marmoset is virtually omnivorous; it eats fruit, insects, lizards, and even small birds. It lives in small groups in the tops of trees, moving nimbly through the branches in search of food. It rests in tree hollows. Gestation lasts 132–134 days; the female bears 1–2 young (usually twins), which are then looked after by the father, except when the mother suckles them. They start to be self-sufficient at about 3 months of age.

Note   The three distinct subspecies of this species are all threatened with extinction because of changes wrought by human encroachment and colonization.

106 MACACA MULATTA
Rhesus macaque

Classification   Order Primates, Family Cercopithecidae.

Description   This macaque has a long, light brown coat, which is paler on the underside. The head is round, the eyes oval, and the ears small. The front legs are longer than the hind legs. It has red ischial callosities (horny areas). Length of head and body about 50 cm (20 in), tail about 25 cm (10 in), weight 6–10 kg (13–22 lb); females smaller than males.

Distribution   Northern India, Afghanistan, Assam, Burma, China.

Habitat   Forests, woodlands, rocky terrain. It has also adapted to the human environment, and is often found living near dwellings.

Behavior   The macaques belong to a large subfamily of Old World monkeys, Cercopithecinae (**106–114**), which are not primarily leaf eaters. The rhesus macaque feeds on fruit, seeds, and berries, and also on insects and other small creatures. It moves about during the day alone or in groups of up to 35 individuals, composed of several geneological units, each headed by a founding female. It is territorial and will defend its own territory but subordinate groups usually avoid dominant groups, so physical battle is rare. It is equally at ease on the ground and in trees (where it sleeps). After the gestation period of 130–180 days, the female delivers a single young, which she nurses for several months.

107 MACACA SILENUS
Lion-tailed macaque

Classification Order Primates, Family Cercopithecidae.
Description Of the 16 species of macaques, this one is the most striking, because of the 2 large, dense tufts of pale gray hair that contrast so vividly with the rest of its coat, which is a shiny brown-black color. The tail is covered with shorter hairs. The face, which looks quite large because of the tufts, is somewhat elongated as well; the body structures and musculature are quite powerful. Length of head and body up to 65 cm (26 in), tail up to 45 cm (18 in), weight 6–9 kg (13–20 lb); females about one third smaller.

Distribution Southwestern India.
Habitat Forests.

Behavior The lion-tailed macaque lives in quite large groups of 20–30 individuals, made up of both sexes and members of all ages. It moves nimbly among the branches of trees as well as on the ground, and is also an able swimmer. It is active mainly during the daylight hours, which is when its cry is most frequently heard. It feeds on a large variety of plants and plant matter, including fruits, but will often pursue insects and small vertebrates as well. Gestation lasts for about 6 months, then the female delivers a single young, or in rare cases twins. The young are looked after and suckled by their mother for more than a year, and take at least 4 years to reach maturity.

---

108 CERCOCEBUS TORQUATUS
Sooty, or white-collared, mangabey

Classification Order Primates, Family Cercopithecidae.
Description The body is powerful although its form is slender, with very long legs; the relatively short tail is stiff and held raised at an acute angle with the back. The coat on the back is gray, the underside is white, and on the head there is a reddish brown cap. Length of head and body up to 65 cm (26 in), tail 70 cm (27 in); weight up to 12 kg (26.5 lb).

Distribution Coastal zone of Guinea Bissau and the forests of the Cameroons and Gabon.
Habitat Tropical forests.

Behavior The sooty mangabey, another cercopithecinid, lives in small groups of 4–12 individuals, preferably on the ground and among the lower layers of the forest. It moves nimbly among the branches of trees, but its movements are always unhurried and sure-footed. The tail is partly prehensile and helps it to keep hold of branches. It feeds on plant matter, but also eats insects and birds' eggs. It is a very social animal and the group has a highly developed ''domestic'' communications system, which functions by means of shrieks and other sounds as well as by means of expressive facial gestures. Nothing is known about its reproductive biology or behavior. Its main enemy is the leopard.

109 THEROPITHECUS GELADA
Gelada baboon

Classification   Order Primates, Family Cercopithecidae.
Description   The deeply grooved face is dark brown and the nostrils, which are set well back in the nose, are turned upward. The body has 3 hairless areas: a central area beneath the throat, and 2 symmetrical red areas on the chest (hourglass-shaped in females). There are 4 round, gray calluses at the rear. The short tail has a dark brown tuft of longer hairs at the tip. The male has a thick mane that hangs halfway down his back. Length of head and body up to 75 cm (30 in), tail to 50 cm (20 in), weight to 25 kg (51 lb); females about half the size of males.

Distribution   Mountainous regions in northern Ethiopia.
Habitat   Rocky upland areas.
Behavior   The gelada baboon forms groups numbering up to 400 individuals, but the basic social unit is a family, consisting of a large adult male, his female entourage (up to a dozen or more "wives"), and their young. The group does not have a clearly defined territory, and will move as much as half a mile a day, in a line parallel to a cliff. By day the gelada baboon descends to grasslands or pastures foraging for roots, bulbs, grass, other green plants, and small animals; it only rarely eats insects. It remains closely associated with the rocky terrain. At night the groups split up to sleep on small ledges on vertical cliffs.

Note   This species is threatened with extinction.

---

110 PAPIO HAMADRYAS
Baboon

Classification   Order Primates, Family Cercopithecidae.
Description   The baboon, although a large monkey, is quite slender. Its coarse coat is dark olive-green, with the underside slightly paler and often bare. The calluses at the base of the tail are small and gray. The face has an elongated muzzle with a very marked angle where the nose meets the forehead. Length of head and body up to 100 cm (40 in), tail 70 cm (27 in), weight up to 45 kg (100 lb); females somewhat smaller.

Distribution   From Senegal to Somalia and southward in Africa, and in southern Arabia.
Habitat   Rocky terrain in savannas, and cliffs at the seashore.
Behavior   These cercopithecinids live in large groups, numbering up to 150–200 individuals, in which there is a strict hierarchical order. The size of the group depends on the availability of food and varies from habitat to habitat. When the group is on the move it can travel up to 6 miles a day. The young males take up positions to the front and rear of the group, with the adult males remaining in the middle with the females and young. If attacked, all the males will engage in fierce combat. Their last form of defense is to flee into trees. Each group occupies a different territory, in which it moves about in search of food. Baboons eat early in the day and at dusk, feeding mainly on plant matter, but also eating small mammals and birds.

111 MANDRILLUS SPHINX
Mandrill

Classification   Order Primates, Family Cercopithecidae.
Description   In the adult male the face, which is deeply grooved, is scarlet in the central area and blue at the sides. His hindquarters are hairless and vividly colored: the area around the anus is scarlet, and the calluses are pink and violet; the genitals themselves are pink and red. The pelage in both sexes is grayish brown. The female is less colorful, lacking the red on the nose and having smaller bluish areas on the sides of face. In both, the tail is short, and the neck and shoulders are covered by a thick mane (thicker in the male). Length of head and body up to 95 cm (38 in), tail 75 cm (29 in), weight about 45 kg (100 lb); females much smaller.

Distribution   Tropical forests in the Cameroons and Gabon.
Habitat   Primary tropical forests.

Behavior   The mandrill lives in primary forest, which has frequent clearings and allows this species to roam freely on the ground. It is in fact a ground-based monkey, feeding on the ground and only retreating into the trees to defend itself or to sleep at night. It lives in large groups, numbering up to 50 individuals, and it occupies fairly small areas as a group. It is omnivorous, although plant matter forms the bulk of its diet. Its principal enemy is the leopard, but it is also actively hunted by humans because it often causes considerable damage to crops. Gestation lasts about 250 days and the usually single offspring is carried about by its mother, clinging to her back or belly.

112 CERCOPITHECUS AETHIOPS
Savannah, or vervet monkey

Classification   Order Primates, Family Cercopithecidae.
Description   This single species consists of various geographic subspecies, or races, more or less well defined. The face is usually black and the coat surrounding it, which is usually white, takes on a variety of patterns in the different subspecies. The body coat is pale olive-green, sometimes with rust-colored shading. Its long tail is carried at an angle to the back. Length of head and body 40–60 cm (16–24 in), tail 50–87 cm (20–35 in); weight about 7 kg (15 lb).

Distribution   Most of Africa south of the Sahara, with the exception of the central areas in southern Africa. This monkey has been introduced to some Caribbean islands.
Habitat   Savanna and scrubland, right up to the edge of forests.

Behavior   Among the various cercopithecinids, the vervet monkey is one of the most adaptable, and often occupies environments frequented by man. It usually lives in open areas where it can move about easily. It lives in small groups of up to 2 dozen individuals, but groups numbering more than 100 members have also been observed. It is a quiet animal, and will only send out an alarm call when in danger. It has separate alarm calls for bird predators, snakes, and leopards. It feeds on soft fruits, seeds, and flowers, and often raids cultivated land and gardens. It almost never drinks any liquid.

113 CERCOPITHECUS HAMLYNI
Owl-faced monkey

Classification   Order Primates, Family Cercopithecidae.

Description   This average-sized monkey has a relatively short tail which is gray with a black tuft at the tip. The face resembles that of an owl, the two large eyes encircled by long lashes. Its face is black with reddish highlights, and there is a conspicuous white strip running from the forehead to the upper lip. The whole head is surrounded by a thick mass of dark green fur which completely covers the ears. The bare horny areas on the rear end are light blue in color. Length of head and body about 55 cm (22 in), tail 58 cm (23.2 in); weight about 7.5 kg (17 lb).

Distribution   Eastern Zaire and neighboring forests.

Habitat   Dense forest up to an altitude of more than 15,000 feet.

Behavior   Observations of this monkey in the wild are few. It stays permanently among the topmost branches of trees and feeds on a wide variety of plant matter. It lives in small groups and does not appear to make any sounds or noises to indicate its presence. Nothing is known about its reproductive biology.

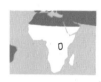

114 ERYTHROCEBUS PATAS
Patas monkey

Classification   Order Primates, Family Cercopithecidae.

Description   This is one of the most elongated monkeys, with long, slender legs and a slight body. The short, coarse coat is brick-red in color, and more vividly colored on the head. The long tail is carried arched over the back. The face is pink in the western part of the species range, and gray with a white marking in the eastern parts. Length of head and body about 55 cm (22 in), tail 50–70 cm (20–28 in), weight up to 10 kg (22 lb); female about half the size of the male.

Distribution   The Sahel, from Senegal to the Sudan and Tanzania.

Habitat   Very dry savanna to the edge of true desert.

Behavior   The patas monkey lives in groups, usually consisting of a male and his harem, plus the newborn and young, but in some cases these groupings can number up to 100 individuals. It is essentially terrestrial but can climb trees with no difficulty. If attacked it runs away at great speed. It is very social, but quite taciturn; communication consists principally of gestures and facial expressions. By day it goes in search of food—almost entirely plant matter—and by night the group splits up and sleeps in various trees. The gestation period lasts for 160 days, after which a single young is born. The mating season and the period when the young are born are closely synchronized in any one group.

115 PRESBYTIS ENTELLUS
Entellus, or Hanuman, langur

Classification   Order Primates, Family Cercopithecidae.
Description   Slender body and arms, long fingers and toes, except for the small but opposable thumbs. Consists of various subspecies, which differ in coat color, usually gray or brown, and in the varying position of the tufts of hair around the face. The face and hands are black. Length of head and body 43–79 cm (17–31.5 in), tail 54–107 cm (21.5–42.5 in), weight 9–20 kg (20–44 lb); female about 70% of male weight.

Distribution   Southern Asia (from Sri Lanka to southern Tibet and Sikkim).
Habitat   Forests, but also in open terrain.
Behavior   The subfamily Colobinae (**115–117**) is distinguished from the other subfamily of Old World monkeys, Cercopithecinae, by their leaf-eating specializations, such as complex stomachs and better developed cross ridges on the teeth. Feeds on young leaves, fruit, and flowers, and is the most terrestrial colobine, descending to the ground to drink, gather food, or move from one area to another. It lives in socially organized groups, each with its own territory, headed by one or more males. In one-male groups, takeovers by a new male occur every few years, sometimes resulting in the death of infants. Gestation lasts 196 days. All the females in the group take part in the care of the single newborn young.

Note   This is the Indian sacred monkey. Because it does not feel threatened by human beings, the langur plunders trees in gardens and steals people's food.

116 NASALIS LARVATUS
Proboscis monkey

Classification   Order Primates, Family Cercopithecidae.
Description   The strangest feature of this monkey is its nose, which in the male adult is much enlarged and may hang down over the mouth. The female has a much smaller and upturned nose, although it is still longer than that of other species. The color of the coat varies from brown to pale reddish; the lower parts of the body are gray-cream-colored. The limbs, as is generally true of colobines, are relatively long. The feet are well furred and have dark soles; the second and third hind toes are connected by a web of skin. Length of head and body 66–76 cm (26–30 in), tail 55–76 cm (22–30 in), weight 12–24 kg (26–53 lb); females about half this weight.

Distribution   Borneo.
Habitat   Near waterways and in mangrove forests.
Behavior   The proboscis monkey eats leaves and the shoots of aquatic plants. It lives in loosely cohesive groups of 12–24 and moves with great agility among the branches of trees. Most activity is early in the morning. It is a good swimmer. Loud nasal "honks" are emitted by the males and are given particular resonance by the long proboscis which straightens out during each honk. The flesh of the proboscis monkey is regarded as something of a delicacy and it is actively hunted by the natives of Borneo with little success because these monkeys are wary and flee at the slightest sign of danger.

117 COLOBUS GUEREZA
Black-and-white colobus monkey

Classification   Order Primates, Family Cercopithecidae.
Description   This colobus is a large creature; its coat is basically black, with white running from its shoulders down the sides of its back to its tail. The callused areas on its hindquarters are surrounded by a broad white ring. The tail, which varies in shape from subspecies to subspecies, is black at the base, becoming fairly consistently white. The many subspecies of this colobus are determined on the basis of the tail and color of the coat. Length of head and body up to 75 cm (30 in), tail about 80 cm (32 in); weight up to 11 kg (24 lb).
Distribution   Central Africa from the Cameroons to Ethiopia and Tanzania.
Habitat   Forests, especially riverine and secondary.

Behavior   This arboreal monkey rarely descends to the ground except to obtain salts and water plants from swamps. It moves with great ease among the highest treetops in the forest, making spectacular leaps between branches. The color of the coat camouflages this monkey effectively in the foliage, and it can stay silent for hours if need be in the event of danger. It lives in territorial groups of about 7 individuals, with 1 adult male. It is exclusively vegetarian and feeds on leaves and fruit.
Note   Populations of this species were much reduced in the 19th century by relentless hunting for its highly prized fur.

---

118 HYLOBATES SYNDACTYLUS
Siamang

Classification   Order Primates, Family Hylobatidae.
Description   Like the other gibbons of the genus *Hylobates,* the coat is very dense and long. The pelage of the siamang is black and has dark red on the eyebrows. Its arms are very long (150 cm/4 ft); its head is small; and it has no tail. The second and third toes of the hind feet are joined together by a fold of skin; they also have a laryngeal sac which is hairless and puffs up when sounds are emitted. Length of head and body about 90 cm (36 in); weight 8–13 kg (17.5–28.5 lb).
Distribution   Sumatra and Malaysia.
Habitat   Tropical forest at an altitude of 2000–7000 feet.

Behavior   The siamang feeds on leaves, fruit, and other plant matter, often hanging by one long arm while reaching with the other. Like other gibbons it is a nimble brachiator. In spite of their great locomotor skill, the rapidity and energy of their movements is such that broken bones do occur from time to time. When it descends to the ground, which is an extremely rare occurrence, it walks in an upright position. It lives in a family group, which has its specific territory. This is demarcated with shrill cries that resemble barking. The female initiates the cries and the male then joins in. Gestation lasts for about 7 months and the female usually delivers a single offspring, which she nurses for several months.

119 HYLOBATES LAR
Common, lar, or white-handed, gibbon

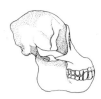

Classification   Order Primates, Family Hylobatidae.
Description   Tail-less and long-limbed like all other gibbons, this small ape has long and tapered hands. The coat is long and dense, varying in color from black to pale brown and yellowish. The face is black, surrounded by white hair. The tops of the hands and feet are white. Length of head and body 45–63 cm (18–25 in); weight 5–8 kg (11–17.5 lb).
Distribution   Sumatra, Malaysia, southwestern Thailand, and Cambodia.
Habitat   Equatorial forest, from sea level up to an altitude of 8000 feet.
Behavior   This gibbon lives in family groups, consisting of a male, one female, and several young. The group has its own territory, varying in area from 30–100 acres. The members of the genus *Hylobates* are the most agile and fastest-moving of all the primates. They are greatly helped by their long, strong arms, and virtually "fly" from branch to branch among the tallest treetops in the forest in a type of locomotion termed brachiation. Early in the morning they begin loud vocal battles and chases at territorial boundaries, they take a break during the hottest hours of the day, and wind up the day in the evening among the branches of their favorite tree, where they spend the night. They are solely vegetarian, often hanging by one long arm while reaching with the other for food. Gestation lasts 200–212 days, and the female usually delivers a single young, which she nurses for several months.

120 PONGO PYGMAEUS
Orangutan

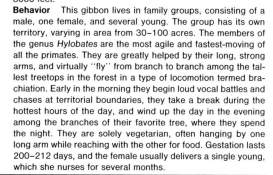

Classification   Order Primates, Family Pongidae.
Description   The orangutan is tail-less, with small ears and a small nose. The coat is long and soft, and reddish brown in color. The arched eyebrows are not very conspicuous, and the jaws are prominent. The head is pear-shaped, the eyes small, and the lips mobile. The arms are very long and strong, and its prehensile feet give it a 4-handed appearance. On the head of the adult male there is a "crest" to which the powerful temporal muscles are attached. Length of head and body averages 96 cm (38.4 in), standing height 137 cm (54.8 in), weight 75 kg (165 lb); females about 80–85% of height and 50% of weight of males.
Distribution   Borneo and Sumatra.
Habitat   Tropical forests.
Behavior   The orangutan feeds mainly on fruit, especially on figs, but it also eats leaves, bark, shoots, and flowers. It is arboreal, rarely descending to the ground. It usually lives a solitary life, with mothers and offspring forming the only long-term bond. The adult males live on their own, and only join a female and her young on a temporary basis for mating. There is no evidence of fighting between adult males, and they do not appear to display any territorial behavior. The gestation period lasts between 233–263 days, and the single infant is nursed for many months.

121 PAN TROGLODYTES
Chimpanzee

Classification   Order Primates, Family Pongidae.

Description   The color of the coat and face varies somewhat depending on age, sex, and environment of the individual. Some old males are silver-gray with an almost totally black face, but members of this species are typically blackish brown. The ears are large and, as in all apes, bare. Length of head and body 77–92 cm (30–36 in), standing height up to 115 cm (46 in), weight about 50 kg (112 lb); females slightly smaller.

Distribution   Senegal and Guinea, and in Central Africa from the Cameroons as far east as Tanzania.

Habitat   Varied: from the edge of the savanna to the forest; also in secondary and semideciduous forests.

Behavior   This is both a tree-dwelling and terrestrial animal, and it moves with equal ease in both environments—brachiating in the trees and "knuckle-walking" on the ground. At night it sleeps in large nests built in trees. It lives in groups that are not strictly organized, and can number up to 40 individuals; but the basic relationship is between the mother and her offspring, which remain with her for many years. The chimpanzee is one of the most communicative animals and has a complex repertoire of gestures and vocal sounds. It is a fruit-eater, but has been observed, in Tanzania, to prey on colobus monkeys and antelopes, and to shape and use twig tools to obtain termites from termite mounds. The gestation period lasts about 236 days. A closely related species, the bonobo (*P. paniscus*) of the Congo Basin, is smaller, much darker, and mostly arboreal.

122 GORILLA GORILLA
Gorilla

Classification   Order Primates, Family Pongidae.

Description   The gorilla is the largest and heaviest of the primates; the head is especially large, and it has highly developed chest muscles. The shape of its face varies somewhat, as do its facial expressions. Its ears are relatively small; the nostrils are always flared. The coat is black, but has silver and gray highlights in adult males. When a gorilla is older than 10 years the whole coat tends to turn gray. In colder parts of the gorilla's range, the coat tends to be shaggier, and longer. Length of head and body 140–185 cm (4.62–6.10 ft), standing height up to 2 m (6.7 ft), weight to 220 kg (500 lb); female smaller.

Distribution   Lowland gorilla in Cameroons, Gabon, Zaire; mountain gorilla in Uganda, Rwanda, Tanzania.

Habitat   Lowland and montane tropical forest.

Behavior   The gorilla lives mainly on the ground, and adults only venture into trees to build nests, though young gorillas often play in trees. On the ground it is quadrupedal and the weight of the body rests at the front on the central phalanges of the fingers in a kind of locomotion called knuckle-walking. The gorilla is a peaceful creature, and will only attack if attacked. A diurnal vegetarian, it lives in groups of 2–30 individuals, always dominated by a large male. The gorilla has a rich vocal repertory and a wide range of gestures. After a 251–289-day gestation, a single offspring (rarely twins) is born.

123 MYRMECOPHAGA TRIDACTYLA
Giant anteater

Classification Order Xenarthra, Family Myrmecophagidae.
Description The giant anteater's nose is elongated and cylindrical in shape; its ears, eyes, and mouth are all small; both neck and head are tapered. The coat is hispid (bristly and shaggy), quite short on the head, and very long on the back where there are silver-white stripes. The distinctive front feet are very strong and have 5 specially adapted toes: the fifth toe is not visible; the second and third toes are strong, set well apart, and have long claws; and the fourth toe is much smaller. This animal has a very long tongue (60 cm/24 in) covered with a sticky coating. Length of head and body 100–130 cm (40–52 in), tail 65–90 cm (26–36 in); weight 8–23 kg (17.5–50.5 lb).
Distribution Guatemala to northern Argentina.
Habitat Open forest and savanna.
Behavior The diet consists of ants and termites (preferably those species without pincers or stings). The anteater's body is well adapted to this diet: the strong front limbs are able to destroy the solid hills built by termites, and the long, thin, sticky tongue can easily find its way into many of the inner recesses of an ant nest. Its strong front legs are also used to defend itself from predators such as pumas and jaguars, the anteater's natural enemies. After a gestation period of about 190 days, a single young is born; it is carried about on its mother's back for a long period.

---

124 TAMANDUA TETRADACTYLA
Tamandua, collared anteater

Classification Order Xenarthra, Family Myrmecophagidae.
Description The tamandua's nose is elongated, but much less so than the giant anteater's; its eyes and mouth are small. The coat is bristly and brown-yellow in color, with black, red, and brown markings. The tail is partly prehensile and covered with hair for a third of its length; the end of the tail is completely hairless and covered with scales. The legs are strongly built: the front feet have 4 toes (hence its name, *tetradactyla*), the third being the largest and strongest, with a very long claw. The hind feet have 5 toes. Length of head and body about 55 cm (22 in), tail about the same; weight 4–7 kg (9–15.5 lb).
Distribution South America.
Habitat Savanna and on the edge of woodlands; also found on cultivated land.
Behavior Like *Myrmecophaga tridactyla* **(123)**, the tamandua feeds on ants and termites which it catches with its long, sticky tongue. Unlike the giant anteater, however, it can climb nimbly up trees in search of its prey. A distinctive feature is the unpleasant smell it emits when in danger, and the posture it assumes to scare away its enemies; it stands upright on its hind legs with its front legs spread wide in front of it. In spring the female gives birth to a single offspring, and for a long period carries it clinging to her back or flanks.

125 BRADYPUS TRIDACTYLUS
Three-toed sloth

Classification   Order Xenarthra, Family Bradypodidae.
Description   The head is round, the neck quite long and flexible, the eyes and ears small. The coat is hispid, or bristly and dense, gray-brown in color with white and orange markings on the back. The legs are long, particularly the front legs, and the feet have long, curved claws (three on the front foot, and four on the hind foot); the underside of each foot is covered with hair. Length of head and body 50–60 cm (20–24 in), tail 6–7 cm (2.4–2.8 in); weight 4–4.5 kg (8.8–10 lb).

Distribution   Central and South America (from Honduras to northern Argentina).
Habitat   Woodland and along riverbanks, in areas where the plant *Cecropia lyratiloba* (a species of trumpetwood) grows.
Behavior   This sloth feeds only on trumpetwood leaves and fruit, which it finds by using its sense of smell. It lives in trees, moving very slowly among the branches in search of food; it will often spend many hours hanging from a horizontal branch, using the curved claws on all four feet as hooks. Sloths often look greenish because of algae growing on their long thick hair. The sloth rarely descends to the ground. It makes an unmistakable "ay-ay" cry, which increases in frequency during the mating season (March–April). After a gestation period of 120–180 days, the female delivers a single young.

126 CHOLOEPUS DIDACTYLUS
Two-toed sloth

Classification   Order Xenarthra, Family Megalonychidae.
Description   The face is quite flattened and hairless; the eyes are small, set within black rings; the ears are also small and almost completely hidden beneath the long, bristly, gray-brown coat. The tail is little more than a stump. The front legs are slightly longer than the hind legs, and have feet with long curved claws (on the second and third toes of the front feet, and on the second, third, and fourth toes of the back feet). Unlike the three-toed sloth, the underside of the foot is hairless. Length of head and body 60–64 cm (24–25.5 in); weight about 9 kg (20 lb).

Distribution   Northern South America.
Habitat   Tropical forests.
Behavior   This species has a vegetarian diet that is less specialized than that of *Bradypus tridactylus* **(125).** It moves about more swiftly than the three-toed sloths. It lives in trees, rarely descending to the ground, and spends much of its time hanging from branches, or resting in the fork between branches. A single offspring is born after a 5–6-month gestation period. In the first 4 weeks of its life the young sloth remains firmly attached to its mother, hidden in her coat. At 9 months it is almost completely independent, but does not reach full maturity until 2.5 years of age.

127 DASYPUS NOVEMCINCTUS
Common long-nosed armadillo

Classification   Order Xenarthra, Family Dasypodidae.
Description   The body is covered with armor consisting of bony plates in the form of shields, except for the belly, which is hairy. The body is rounded and the legs are short. The feet have strong claws. The eyes are small and the ears pointed. Length of head and body 40–50 cm (16–20 in), tail 25–40 cm (10–16 in); weight 4–8 kg (8.8–17.6 lb).
Distribution   Southern United States south to Argentina.

Habitat   Semidesert areas and arid grasslands.
Behavior   This armadillo (1 of 6 species in the genus Dasypus) feeds mainly on insects, especially the larvae, but also eats worms, millipedes, and berries. In the hot summer months, it is active only in the evening and at night; in the colder months, it is usually active only during the warmest part of the day. It relies on its keen sense of smell to find food, and is able to detect prey hidden deep in the ground. It lives in burrows in the ground, which are lined with leaves. Mating usually takes place in July but implantation is delayed until November. These animals are polyembryonic; 120 days after implantation, the female gives birth to 4 identical young which all originate from the division of a single egg.

128 CHAETOPHRACTUS VILLOSUS
Hairy armadillo

Classification   Order Xenarthra, Family Dasypodidae.
Description   The armor on this small armadillo consists of a first section on the head, a narrow strip on the neck between the ears, and a large carapace which covers and protects the entire body. This carapace consists of 18 strips, of which only 8 are mobile and articulated with each other. The lower parts of the body are covered with long, bristly hairs. Length of head and body 28 cm (11 in), tail less than 10 cm (4 in); weight 1.5–3 kg (3.3–6.6 lb).
Distribution   Bolivia, Chile, Argentina, and Uruguay.

Habitat   Grasslands and steppelike regions.
Behavior   With the powerful claws on its feet, the hairy armadillo can dig swiftly into the ground, making deep holes. When one attempts to pull it out, the armadillo anchors itself inside the hole by pressing its legs against the walls, or bracing its carapace against the side of the hole. If it is pursued on open ground and is unable to take refuge in a hole, it draws in its legs and lets the edge of its carapace rest on the ground; in this way it offers little access to its foe. It lives a solitary life. It is active at night when it feeds on insects, snakes, and some plants. Two young are born after a gestation period of 2 months.

129 MANIS TEMMINCKII
Cape pangolin

Classification   Order Pholidota, Family Manidae.
Description   This animal has a cone-shaped head with tiny ears; its body is squat, with a tail which is enlarged at the base, and completely covered with scales. Three of the 5 toes on the forefeet are well developed and have long, strong, large claws; the claws on the 5-toed hind feet are shorter. Length of head and body 50 cm (20 in), tail 35 cm (14 in); weight about 9 kg (20 lb).
Distribution   East Africa, Sudan, Central African Republic, and the southern region of Africa with the exception of the coastal Cape region.
Habitat   Arid zones with little vegetation and preferably with sandy ground.
Behavior   The cape pangolin lives on the ground. It moves slowly, often on just the hind legs, balancing itself with its tail. It generally leads a solitary existence, and forms pairs for only a brief time during the mating season. It has a highly developed sense of smell which it uses to find the ant and termite colonies which provide its diet. It is toothless but has a long, sticky tongue with which it captures these insects. It is a nocturnal creature, only rarely seen in daylight. The female delivers a single young after a 140-day gestation period, and carries it on the base of her tail. She protects it by wrapping herself around it. If attacked, the pangolin curls into a ball; its very sharp scales can inflict serious injury on its foes.

---

130 ORYCTEROPUS AFER
Aardvark

Classification   Order Tubulidentata, Family Orycteropidae.
Description   This fairly large creature has a distinctive shape, with a curved back and a cylindrical, rather piglike snout. Its ears are long and tough; it has strong feet with four toes on the front foot and five on the back. All toes have large claws. The grayish skin is thick and bare except for a few scattered hairs. Length of head and body 100–150 cm (40–60 in), tail 45–61 cm (18–24 in); weight 80–100 kg (175–220 lb).
Distribution   Africa south of the Sahara.
Habitat   Savanna, grasslands, and open forests where the ground is soft.
Behavior   The only living representative of the Tubulidentata, the aardvark is a completely nocturnal creature and very difficult to observe. It spends the day in its burrow. It is a very efficient digger, and can disappear underground rapidly. The tunnels are sometimes very long and complex, with numerous openings, but they invariably end in a large chamber. These tunnel systems are also used by other denizens of the savanna. It feeds on termites, which it sucks into the mouth with its sticky tongue. It is a solitary animal, except when the female is accompanied for a while by 1 or more young. Gestation lasts 7 months, after which a single offspring is born. Although the young is nursed for only a few months, it will often remain with its mother for many more months.

RODENTS

131 OCHOTONA PRINCEPS
Pika

Classification   Order Lagomorpha, Family Ochotonidae.
Description   This rat-sized animal is grayish or brown, with short, wide, rounded ears. The short tail is not visible. There are 26 teeth and the female has 4 or 6 nipples. Length of head and body up to 21 cm (8.3 in); weight up to 180 g (6.3 oz).
Distribution   Northwestern United States and western Canada.
Habitat   Rocky terrain and moraines in mountainous regions on the edge of woodland, but also down to sea level in the most northerly areas.

Behavior   The northern pika lives in large colonies, within which each individual seems to maintain its own territory, at least in the autumn months and possibly throughout the year. It is active by day and spends much time gathering its food in small piles of ''hay.'' It feeds on grass. It does not hibernate, and reproduces in spring and possibly in summer as well. Gestation lasts about 30 days and the female gives birth to 2–5 young at each delivery, in May–June and July–August. The northern pika makes a short squeak which is very distinctive and unmistakable. It lives in areas where man's presence is very limited.

132 ROMEROLAGUS DIAZI
Volcano rabbit

Classification   Order Lagomorpha, Family Leporidae.
Description   This is one of the smallest of the Leporidae in the Americas. The color of the coat is uniformly dark brown mixed with scattered yellowish parts of hairs on the back and dark brownish gray below. The rounded ears are 4–4.4 cm (1.6–1.8 in) long; the tail is virtually nonexistent. In appearance the volcano rabbit looks more like a large vole or pika than a hare or rabbit. The coat is shed once a year. Length of head and body about 30 cm (12 in); weight about 1 kg (2.2 lb).
Distribution   Mexico (limited in distribution to the slopes of certain volcanoes to the southeast of Mexico City).
Habitat   On the slopes of volcanoes, probably in close association with 2 species of tall grasses, usually at an altitude of 9000–10,500 feet.

Behavior   It lives in the densest grass available, where it maintains paths along which it moves. It is mainly nocturnal, but also is active in daylight on cloudy or overcast days. It feeds on shoots and the tenderest blades of grass. It has a high-pitched voice. It digs burrows in which to take refuge but as soon as a ray of sunlight appears it is quite common to see this rabbit lying on the ground to warm itself. Nothing is known about its reproductive biology and behavior.
Note   This species is strictly protected, but it is nevertheless hunted by local people for its flesh or simply for sport.

133　SYLVILAGUS AUDUBONII
Desert cottontail

Classification　Order Lagomorpha, Family Leporidae.
Description　The hind legs of this rabbit are quite long, with slender feet. The pointed ears are about 7 cm (2.8 in) long, and sparsely furred in the inner part. The vibrissae, or whiskers, are usually black. The tail is broad, black above and white beneath. The female has 4 pairs of nipples: 1 pair in the pectoral region, 2 pairs in the abdominal region and 1 inguinal pair. Length of head and body 32–39 cm (12.6–15.4 in), tail 4.5–6 cm (1.8–2.4 in); weight 0.7–1.2 kg (1.5–2.6 lb).
Distribution　Western North America, from the Canadian border to Central Mexico.
Habitat　Arid woodlands, prairies, and deserts.
Behavior　This rabbit feeds on grass and roots. It is most active early in the morning and at dusk, but its activities become limited if it is raining or windy. It swims well if necessary, paddling with its legs like a dog. It can also climb trees. If danger threatens, it can hold itself motionless; but if truly alarmed, it scampers off into the nearest bush. The position in which the tail is held can serve as a warning signal for fellow cottontails. If the tail is raised showing the white underside, danger is indicated. Gestation lasts for 28 days, after which the female delivers 4–7 young in a burrow dug in the ground and lined with grass and fur.

134　LEPUS AMERICANUS
Snowshoe hare

Classification　Order Lagomorpha, Family Leporidae.
Description　One distinctive feature of the snowshoe hare is the seasonal change in coat color. In summer it is reddish brown above and white underneath; but in winter, it becomes white, with only the tips of its ears (up to 7.5 cm/3 in long) remaining black. Another unmistakable feature is its hind feet, which are quite broad and, in winter, they are covered with a dense coat, which makes them even larger and facilitates movement on the snow-covered ground. Length of head and body 37.5–55 cm (15–22 in), tail 3–5 cm, (1.2–2 in), weight 1.4–1.8 kg (3–4 lb).
Distribution　Northern United States and Canada.
Habitat　Evergreen woodlands with plenty of vegetation.
Behavior　It is completely vegetarian, feeding on many plant species in summer, and bark and shoots in winter. Like the other species of *Lepus*, the snowshoe hare is essentially a solitary animal. Its home range includes various burrows and tracks which are regularly used. The reproductive period occurs between March and August. Gestation lasts 30–38 days, at the end of which the female delivers a litter of 2–6 young, 2 or 3 times a year. The young are very precocial: they crawl at 1 day, nibble grass at 10 days, and are weaned after 1 month. The main predators of the snowshoe hare are coyotes, bobcats, Canada lynxes, red foxes, and weasels—and man.

135   LEPUS TIMIDUS
Arctic hare

Classification   Order Lagomorpha, Family Leporidae.
Description   Its general appearance is like the hare familiar in Europe, *L. capensis* **(137)**, but stockier; its fur is less dense and its ears are shorter, measuring 6–8 cm (2.4–3.1 in). Like the snowshoe hare **(134)**, it has a coat that varies with the season: brown with gray and sometimes reddish shades dorsally in the summer, white in the winter (although in the most northerly regions its coat remains white year round. Its small round tail is permanently whitish. Length of head and body up to 60 cm (24 in), tail up to 8 cm (3.1 in); average weight 3.5 kg (7.7 lb) but up to 5.5 kg (12.1 lb).

Distribution   Northernmost Europe, Asia, and North America.
Habitat   Arctic tundra and mountainous environments, up to timber line.
Behavior   It sometimes lives in small groups but is more commonly found alone. It feeds on the sparse vegetation of the tundra, and on aromatic herbs. In winter, it nibbles the bark of young trees. The female gives birth 2 or 3 times a year to 2–5 leverets. The young do not reach sexual maturity until they are a year old. The population numbers of this hare fluctuate widely, but the species is nevertheless becoming increasingly rare. The main predator is the arctic fox.

136   LEPUS CALIFORNICUS
Black-tailed jackrabbit

Classification   Order Lagomorpha, Family Leporidae.
Description   The coat is gray-brown, with white markings on the forehead, around the eyes, and on the backs of the ears, which are 10–13 cm (3.9–5.1 in) long. The tip of the stumpy tail and the tips of the large ears are black. Length of head and body 40–50 cm (15.7–19.7 in), tail 5–10 cm (2–4 in); weight 1.5–3 kg (3.3–6.6 lb).
Distribution   Western United States and northern Mexico.
Habitat   Desert plateaus, grasslands.
Behavior   In winter the diet is based chiefly on bark and buds of bushes, and in summer it tends to eat tender grasses. In very dry periods of the year it will eat cacti, which are quite plentiful in some parts of its range. It is a solitary animal, and its behavior is much like that of the other members of the genus *Lepus*. Gestation lasts 41–47 days, and the female gives birth to a litter of 1–6 young. These are born covered with fur and with their eyes already open. The female does not make a nest or burrow, and mating occurs throughout the year, except possibly in the months September–December in the southernmost parts of its range.

137 LEPUS CAPENSIS
Brown hare

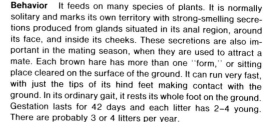

Classification Order Lagomorpha, Family Leporidae.
Description The body is covered with cinnamon-brown fur, which is more reddish on the back, neck, and sides. The long (10 cm/4 in) ears are black-tipped, and the upper part of the tail is also black; on the lower part and on the sides, the tail is white. The hind legs are longer than the front legs. Length of head and body 49–67 cm (19.3–26.4 in), tail 7–12 cm (3–4.7 in); weight 1.5–6.5 kg (3.3–14.3 lbs), varying with locale.
Distribution Europe (except Ireland), across central Asia, and south through most of Africa. It has been introduced to Australia, New Zealand, Chile, and parts of North America.
Habitat Varied, but has a preference for flat areas and terrain near cultivated land; rarely in coniferous woodland.
Behavior It feeds on many species of plants. It is normally solitary and marks its own territory with strong-smelling secretions produced from glands situated in its anal region, around its face, and inside its cheeks. These secretions are also important in the mating season, when they are used to attract a mate. Each brown hare has more than one "form," or sitting place cleared on the surface of the ground. It can run very fast, with just the tips of its hind feet making contact with the ground. In its ordinary gait, it rests its whole foot on the ground. Gestation lasts for 42 days and each litter has 2–4 young. There are probably 3 or 4 litters per year.

138 ORYCTOLAGUS CUNICULUS
Old World rabbit

Classification Order Lagomorpha, Family Leporidae.
Description This is the ancestral species of all domestic rabbits. The coat varies considerably in color; it is usually gray with reddish highlights on the back and almost white underneath. The lower part of the tail is white. The ears are 7 cm (2.8 in) long, shorter than those of hares, and have a rather indistinct black edge at the tips. Length of head and body up to 40 cm (18 in), tail 6 cm (2.5 in); weight 1.3–2.25 kg (2.9–5 lb).
Distribution Europe; introduced into Australia, Chile, and elsewhere.
Habitat Sandy terrain, with scrub and bushes; coniferous woodland.
Behavior This species is most active at night. It lives in large colonies, and has shared burrows with various entrances and numerous chambers. It rarely strays more than 60 feet from its burrow. It feeds on tender plants, and in winter, will eat the bark of trees. It is very prolific: it can produce 3–4 litters a year, each one with 6–8 young (sometimes as many as 12). Gestation lasts about 30 days. Most litters are delivered January–June. The young are born in a burrow at a distance from the main colony, in nests which consist of a single chamber lined with fur. In areas of high density, this species is an agricultural pest.

139 APLODONTIA RUFA
Mountain beaver

Classification Order Rodentia, Family Aplodontidae.
Description *Aplodontia rufa* is a chunky rodent with short neck, nose, ears, tail, and legs. The coat is dense and woolly, and has bristles; it is brown, speckled with black. The sewellel (another name) has small eyes and ears, and the tail is but a small tuft of hairs. The molar teeth are rootless. It has prehensile hands and feet, and the 5 toes on each foot are clawed. Length of head and body 33–47 cm (13–18.5 in), tail 2–3 cm (1 in); weight 900–1800g (2–4 lb).
Distribution Western North America.
Habitat Near waterways, and in woodlands.

Behavior This nocturnal rodent feeds on the leaves and branches of broadleaf trees, conifers, and aquatic plants. It eats holding its food in its front feet. It is very fond of washing itself, and when so occupied sits by the bank of a stream or river, dips its front feet into the water, and then washes its body thoroughly all over. It lives alone or in loose colonies and digs its own den near running water. The gestation period lasts for 42–48 days and the single yearly litter has 2–6 young in it.

---

140 SCIURUS CAROLINENSIS
Eastern gray squirrel

Classification Order Rodentia, Family Sciuridae.
Description The ears are not especially large and do not have the distinctive tufts of hair of the common European squirrel, *Sciurus vulgaris* **(142)**. The hind legs are longer than the front legs and the hind feet have 5 toes (the front feet have only 4 functional toes), all with long claws. The coat is gray on the back, and white underneath. In summer, the long, dense tail is edged with white hairs. Length of head and body 20–30 cm (8–12 in), tail 16–30 cm (6.3–11.8 in); weight up to 700 g (1.5 lb).
Distribution Eastern United States, from Maine south to Florida and west to Texas; introduced into England.
Habitat Woodlands, but also farmlands and parks.

Behavior This species of squirrel is strictly diurnal. At night, it retreats into hollows in trees or into its nest, made of branches and leaves, in a fork in a tree. It feeds on pine cones, nuts, berries, and also on insects, birds' eggs, and young birds. The mating season is December–August; after a gestation period of about 40 days the female gives birth to 2–5 young which are blind and furless. They leave the nest after 6 weeks. There are usually 2 litters per year.
Note This species was introduced into Britain and spread so rapidly that it is now considered as a dangerous pest in some agricultural areas.

141   SCIURUS NIGER
Eastern fox squirrel

Classification   Order Rodentia, Family Sciuridae.

Description   The coat is orange-brown in color, with the underside paler and orange-yellow. The tail is bushy and edged with reddish-tipped hairs. Like the other members of the genus *Sciurus*, the eastern fox squirrel has a short, pointed nose, long vibrissae, and long ears. Length of head and body 25–38 cm (10–15 in), tail 25–35 cm (10–14 in); weight 750–1000 g (1.5–2 lb).

Distribution   Southeastern United States.

Habitat   Oak, beech, pine, and cypress forests with clearings.

Behavior   This squirrel feeds on nuts, seeds, berries, birds' eggs, and bark. It is active during the day and, although mainly arboreal, spends much time feeding on the ground. It builds its nest in trees, in hollows in the trunk or in forks in the branches; in the latter case the nest is round and made of leaves and twigs. It is an adept, nimble climber. It does not go into hibernation but becomes less active in the winter months. The young are born February–April. The female usually gives birth to 1–6 (usually 4) young after 44 days of gestation, and rears them for 2–3 months.

---

142   SCIURUS VULGARIS
Eurasian red squirrel

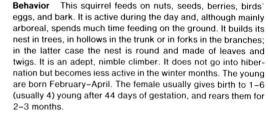

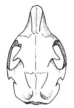

Classification   Order Rodentia, Family Sciuridae.

Description   The coat is reddish brown, and sometimes black. The tail is long and plume-shaped. In winter there is a tuft of hairs on the ears. The front foot has 4 large toes; the hind foot has 5. Length of head and body 19–28 cm (7.6–11 in), tail 14–24 cm (5.6–9.6 in); weight 250–500 g (8.8–17.5 oz).

Distribution   Europe and Asia.

Habitat   Coniferous and deciduous woodlands.

Behavior   It feeds on seeds, fruit, bark, insects and will sometimes eat eggs and small birds. When plenty of food is available, it stores food for times of scarcity. It does not hibernate. It builds numerous, round nests which are made of twigs stripped of leaves and covered with grass, leaves, and moss. The nest is built at the top of a tall tree. This diurnal is extremely agile and climbs around trees with ease; it is just as quick to dart back down to the ground again headfirst. It can swim. When it walks on the ground the tail is held upright; when it jumps the tail billows out behind it to maintain balance. The tail is also used as a means of communication with other squirrels, and expresses its state of mind. It emits a distinctive squeak, and chatters. It mates in April and after 28–42 days of gestation the female delivers 3 or 4 young which are hairless and have their eyes closed. They are weaned at 2–3 months.

143 SCIURUS ABERTI
Tassel-eared squirrel

Classification   Order Rodentia, Family Sciuridae.

Description   The back of this squirrel is reddish; the sides of the body, gray; the belly, black or white; and the tail varies from dark to completely white (in the distinctive population on the Kaibab Plateau of Arizona). The tufts on the ears are black and very conspicuous. In some populations completely black individuals occur, as is the case in a number of species of tree squirrels. Length of head and body up to 30 cm (12 in), tail to 23 cm (9 in); weight about 900 g (2 lb).

Distribution   Southwestern United States and Mexico.

Habitat   Coniferous forests between 6500–8300 feet.

Behavior   This solitary and diurnal creature emits a shrill bark when it is excited. It builds large nests in pine trees and feeds on pine cones and the new wood of tender young pines. It also eats mushrooms and fungi. Mating takes place in March and April, and the young are born a month later, usually 3 or 4 per litter.

Note   This species is a special tourist attraction wherever it lives. As a result it is also one of the best known of the squirrel family.

144 TAMIASCIURUS HUDSONICUS
American red squirrel

Classification   Order Rodentia, Family Sciuridae.

Description   The coat usually has a reddish hue on the back; the underside of the body is whitish. Black stripes are usually evident on each side where darker dorsal color meets paler ventral color. The ears, which are relatively larger than in most tree squirrels, have a tuft of hair in winter. Length of head and body 18–20 cm (7.2–8 in), tail 10–15 cm (4–6 in); weight 200–250 g (7–8.8 oz).

Distribution   Northern United States and Canada.

Habitat   Coniferous woodlands.

Behavior   The diet of this species is based mainly on pine seeds, but also includes apples, nuts, and grain. It is an arboreal creature and is active by day. Its scolding chatter is a common sound in northern woods. It mates in March and April and gestation lasts about 38 days. A secondary mating period may occur in August and September. The female then gives birth to 2–6 (usually 4 or 5) young in a nest made in the hollow of a tree trunk or in a fork in the branches. The young are born blind and hairless and open their eyes when they are 2–3 weeks old.

145 RATUFA BICOLOR
Black giant squirrel

Classification   Order Rodentia, Family Sciuridae.
Description   It has distinctive coloring; the coat on the underside is pale yellow, and the back is black. The ears are short and round; the front feet and the hind feet are quite broad and have strong claws. Length of head and body 25.5–45.5 cm (10–18 in), tail about the same; weight up to about 2 kg (4.4 lb).
Distribution   From Nepal, Burma, to Malaysia and the East Indies as far east as Java and Bali.

Habitat   Tropical and temperate forests.
Behavior   This animal lives alone or occasionally in a pair. It is arboreal and feeds on fruit, nuts, bark, insects, and birds' eggs. It frequently makes forays into coffee, banana, and fig plantations. It rarely descends to the ground; when it does, it is only to chase away another member of its species or to pursue a female in heat. When at rest it hides in tree hollows. When the mating season comes, it builds a large nest the size of an eagle's nest, in which it rears its young. Gestation lasts about 28 days, and the female gives birth to 1 or 2 young.

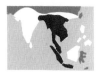

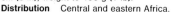

146 FUNISCIURUS PYRRHOPUS
Cuvier's tree squirrel

Classification   Order Rodentia, Family Sciuridae.
Description   The overall body color varies from dark brown to olive yellow-green, but the underside of the body is always paler; the brightness of the white stripes on the back varies according to the subspecies and the distribution area. The tail is long, the ears small and round, and the female has only 4 nipples. Length of head and body up to 19 cm (7.6 in), tail to 20 cm (8 in); weight to 450 g (1 lb).
Distribution   Central and eastern Africa.

Habitat   Woodlands and stands of palms.
Behavior   This animal is solitary or else lives in pairs; it lives mainly in trees, but descends to the ground from time to time to gather food. It eats fruit, seeds, and various plants, and also likes insects, eggs, and small vertebrates. It makes its nest in palm trees, usually where the leaf joins the trunk, about 6–7 feet above the ground. It is active at dawn and dusk and rests during the hottest part of the day. The female gives birth to 2 or 3 young. The time of year when the young are born is variable.

147 CALLOSCIURUS PREVOSTI
Prevost's squirrel

Classification   Order Rodentia, Family Sciuridae.
Description   The coat of this squirrel has 3 different colors; the top of the head, the back, the sides, and the tail are black; the underside of the body is red-brown; and the strip where the 2 colors meet is white. Length of head and body 20–27 cm (7.9–10.6 in), tail slightly shorter; weight up to about 500 g (1.1 lb).
Distribution   Malay Peninsula, Sumatra, Borneo, Sulawesi, and smaller islands nearby.
Habitat   Forests.
Behavior   Prevost's squirrel is solitary, lives in trees, and is active during the hours of daylight. Its diet consists of seeds, nuts, fruit, flowers, birds' eggs, and insects. At night it rests in hollows in trees or in nests built of leaves and twigs. The gestation period is unknown, but we do know that the female gives birth to 3 or 4 young per litter.
Note   The genus *Callosciurus* (Oriental tree squirrels) comprises about 20 species. They are the most brightly colored of all the squirrels. The coat ranges from white to gray tinted with brown: the lower parts of the body are red-brown, and in some species the legs are brown.

148 ATLANTOXERUS GETULUS
Barbary ground squirrel

Classification   Order Rodentia, Family Sciuridae.
Description   The coat is short and hard and there is a conspicuous white stripe along each side of the body; sometimes there is also a white stripe down the back. The coat is often reddish brown but is quite variable in color. The whitish stripes may be separated by blackish stripes. Length of head and body 30 cm (12 in), tail about the same; weight about 800 g (1.8 lb).
Distribution   Algeria and Morocco.
Habitat   Arid and rocky environments; scrub.
Behavior   This is the only species of squirrel that is found in Africa north of the Sahara, and it is not well known. Believed to be solitary, it is active in the early morning and toward dusk, and spends the rest of the day in its burrow or den. It feeds on seeds and fruit, especially those of a species of tree with which it is often associated—*Argania sideroxylon*. It is thought that it undertakes migratory journeys whenever the population has become too large for the foodstock available in a given environment.

149 XERUS ERYTHROPUS
Geoffrey's ground squirrel

Classification   Order Rodentia, Family Sciuridae.
Description   The overall color of this species is reddish brown, but there is a conspicuous pale stripe along each side of the body. The tail is dark brown and bushy except near the base. Young individuals have a patch of white at the tip of the tail. The general color of this ground squirrel often echoes that of the terrain in which it lives because particles of earth cling to the short, bristly coat. It has no undercoat. Length of head and body up to 31 cm (12.4 in), tail 28 cm (11.2 in); weight 350–650 g (.8–1.4 lb).
Distribution   Africa south of the Sahara, in a broad band eastward to Kenya.
Habitat   Forest and scrub.
Behavior   This species has adapted well to the life of a terrestrial—as opposed to arboreal—animal both in the form of its body and in certain specific features like its small ears. It is active during daylight. It seems to be quite unafraid of people, since one may easily get close to its lair without the animal fleeing. Nevertheless it is constantly on the alert for possible enemies and is quick to take refuge in the burrow it digs in the driest available soft ground. The number of young per litter probably does not exceed 2 since the female has only 2 nipples.

---

150 MARMOTA MONAX
Woodchuck

Classification   Order Rodentia, Family Sciuridae.
Description   The body of this animal is quite stocky and the legs are short. The coat is shiny and yellowish brown, and paler on the underside of the body. The legs are covered with a darker, almost black fur. The thumb has been reduced to a short stump which has a blunt claw. The female has 8 nipples. Length of head and body 40–51 cm (16–20.4 in), tail 10–18 cm (4–7.2 in); weight 2.2–4.5 kg (4.8–10 lb).
Distribution   Eastern United States and Canada.
Habitat   Woodland.
Behavior   The woodchuck feeds on grass, berries, fruit, vegetables, and cereal crops. It is mainly active by day, but in the spring, it may also be active at night. It lives alone and in winter falls into a deep hibernation, which lasts from October to February. Its burrow is dug among the roots of trees or rocks, and usually has 2 or more entrances. The mating season occurs in March–April and after a gestation period of about 30 days the female delivers 2–9 young (usually 4–6) which are blind and hairless. The young nurse for about 6 weeks. The fox is one natural enemy of this animal.

151 MARMOTA MARMOTA
Alpine marmot

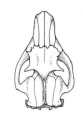

Classification   Order Rodentia, Family Sciuridae.
Description   The coat is short and smooth; it is yellowish brown on the body, gray on the head and nape, and the nose is white. The head is large and round, the ears small, and the legs rather short. The tail is short and hairy, ending in a black tuft. There are thick whiskers on the upper lip. Length of head and body 50–60 cm (20–24 in), tail 13–16 cm (5.2–6.4 in); weight 4–8 kg (8.8–17.6 lb).
Distribution   The Alps and Carpathians. Introduced to the Tatra mountains, the Black Forest, and the Pyrenees.
Habitat   Open spots in mountainous country at an altitude of 4700–9000 feet, with a preference for fairly flat terrain.
Behavior   It feeds on plants, which it nibbles at like a rabbit. It lives in groups of 10–15 individuals and is easy to spot in the early morning near the permanent snow line searching for food. At the slightest hint of danger a "sentry" emits a distinctive whistle to alert the group members. In winter it hibernates, taking up its position with the whole group in a deep, large burrow (which consists of a long tunnel and a chamber). When it re-emerges from its dormant state the mating season begins. Gestation lasts 35–42 days and the litter contains 2–6 young. They nurse for about 5–6 weeks and reach sexual maturity only in the second year of their life.

152 CYNOMYS GUNNISONI
Gunnison's prairie dog

Classification   Order Rodentia, Family Sciuridae.
Description   The coat is yellowish buff intermixed with blackish hairs. There are darker areas on the head, and the belly is paler. The distal half of the tail has a grayish color and its hairs are tipped with grayish white. The body is stout, the legs short, and the toes clawed. The female has 5 pair of nipples. Length of head and body 30–38 cm (12–15 in), tail 3–8 cm (1.5–3.5 in) weight 700–1100 g (1.5–2.4 lb).
Distribution   Western United States.
Habitat   Prairie in mountainous regions at an altitude of 5000–11,500 feet.
Behavior   This creature is active by day and lives in colonies. The name "prairie dog" comes from its distinctive call, which is like the yapping of a dog, and is emitted when the animal is alarmed. It feeds mainly on grasses but will eat grasshoppers and other insects. Its burrow is deep in the ground and has many chambers which are connected by long passages. The whole colony lives in one large burrow system. In winter it hibernates, from October–November to late March. The mating season begins in late March and continues throughout April. After a gestation period of 28–32 days, 3 or 4 young are born. They remain within the burrow for about 1 month.

153   AMMOSPERMOPHILUS LEUCURUS
White-tailed antelope squirrel

Classification   Order Rodentia, Family Sciuridae.
Description   The coat is pinkish gray with a white stripe on each side of the body. There are 2 molts each year: the winter coat has more fine underfur; the summer coat has a harsher feel. The underside of the tail is white. The female has 10 nipples. Length of head and body 14–16 cm (5.6–6.4 in), tail 5–7.6 cm (2–3 in); weight 90–150 g (3.2–5.3 oz).
Distribution   Southwestern United States, and northwestern Mexico.
Habitat   Desert terrain with sparse vegetation.
Behavior   This squirrel feeds on seeds, insects, and flesh, and leads a mainly solitary existence. It does not hibernate, and is active even when the ground is covered with snow. It is diurnal and remains active even when temperatures are high. The white part of the tail is exposed when the antelope squirrel runs and is often used as a visual signal to communicate with other individuals of the same species that danger is imminent. Like the other ground squirrels, this species stores food in its underground burrow. As a rule the female gives birth twice a year and has a litter of 6–10 young.

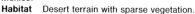

154   SPERMOPHILUS TRIDECEMLINEATUS
Thirteen-lined ground squirrel

Classification   Order Rodentia, Family Sciuridae.
Description   The back is covered with brown fur which has a series of continuous, alternating with broken, white stripes running longitudinally. The underside of its body is whitish. The female has 10 nipples. Length of head and body 11.4–16.5 cm (4.5–6.5 in), tail 6–13 cm (2.4–5.2 in); weight 140–250 g (4.9–5.8 oz).
Distribution   Canada to the southern United States.
Habitat   Prairies, golf courses, cemeteries, and other open areas.
Behavior   It eats many insects, especially grasshoppers, plant matter, and sometimes the meat of vertebrates. (It will even eat other ground squirrels that have been killed by automobiles.) It is active during the day and is generally solitary. It stores food in the burrow and builds round nests of vegetation. It digs a relatively simple burrow in the ground, with a well-hidden entrance. Mating takes place in April, after emerging from hibernation. The gestation period lasts about 28 days and each litter has 5–13 young, which are born blind, hairless, and toothless. Weaning occurs in about 4–6 weeks, then the young fend for themselves. Among its many predators are foxes, weasels, cats, dogs, badgers, hawks, and snakes.

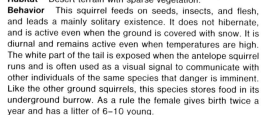

155 SPERMOPHILUS PARRYII
Arctic ground squirrel

Classification Order Rodentia, Family Sciuridae.
Description The coat is brown-yellow or reddish brown with white speckling, and the legs are tawny. There is some black coloring on the tail. Length of head and body 21.5–35 cm (8.6–14 in), tail 7.6–15 cm (3–6 in); weight 450–1150 g (1–2.5 lb).
Distribution From Alaska to Hudson Bay in North America, and in eastern Siberia.
Habitat Arctic tundra.
Behavior This diurnal squirrel is mainly vegetarian but will eat insects, eggs, mice, and other small rodents. It digs a burrow deep in the ground with several different chambers and "larders." There is usually just one entrance, and before the period of winter hibernation, which lasts from October to May, this is blocked off with a "plug" made of damp earth. When this species enters hibernation it is quite awkward because of all the subcutaneous fat it has accumulated. In the event of danger, or when frightened, it lets out a strident call, which also acts as a warning signal to other members of the same species. The gestation period lasts for about 25 days and the 4–8 young are born in June–July.

---

156 SPERMOPHILUS BEECHEYI
California ground squirrel

Classification Order Rodentia, Family Sciuridae.
Description The dense coat is brown with small white spots on the back. The head is brown and the sides of the body whitish. The tail is thick and bushy with a tuft at the end. The female usually has 12 nipples. Length of head and body 23–28 cm (9–11 in), tail 13–23 cm (5–9 in); weight 450–1000 g (1–2.2 lb).
Distribution California and Oregon.
Habitat Pastureland with short-stemmed vegetation; slopes of mountains with scattered trees.
Behavior This squirrel lives in colonies. It is active during the day and feeds on seeds, fruit, berries, insects, and birds' eggs. It stores food in its underground burrow, which has several entrances. Between these entrances on the surface of the ground there is a network of connecting tracks and paths. The chambers built to contain the nest itself are lined with dry vegetation. This is where this species hibernates from October–November to January. The young are born in spring, summer, and autumn. The gestation period lasts for 25–30 days and there are on average 7 young per litter. More than 1 litter may be born in a year.

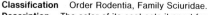

157 SPERMOPHILUS LATERALIS
Golden-mantled ground squirrel

Classification   Order Rodentia, Family Sciuridae.

Description   The color of its coat sets it apart from the other ground squirrels. It has a copper-colored head, the back is gray-brown, the belly yellow-brown and on the sides of the body there is a white stripe edged with black as is seen in chipmunks. It lacks the distinct black and white stripes seen on chipmunk faces, however. The female has 8–10 nipples. Length of head and body 15–20 cm (6–8 in), tail 6–12 cm (2.4–4.8 in); weight 170–270 g (6–9.5 oz).

Distribution   From southwestern Canada to the southern slopes of the Rocky Mountains.

Habitat   Mountainous areas with woodlands of fir, Norway spruce, and pine.

Behavior   Like other ground squirrels, this species feeds on seeds, fruit, insects, and eggs, and has the same habit of storing food in its nest. It is colonial in favorable habitats, but occasionally solitary. Its nest is in a burrow dug in the ground near a fallen tree trunk, bush, or rock. It hibernates from October–November to March–April. Breeding takes place after emerging from hibernation; gestation lasts about a month, and 2–8 young are born in late spring. This squirrel is a frequent visitor in campsites and shows little fear of people where it is not disturbed, such as in the national parks in its range.

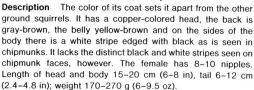

158 TAMIAS STRIATUS
Eastern chipmunk

Classification   Order Rodentia, Family Sciuridae.

Description   The coat is grayish, and the back has black longitudinal stripes on either side of a pale stripe on each side. There is a white stripe above and below each eye. It has internal sacs, or pouches, in its cheeks. The female has 8 nipples. Length of head and body 12–15 cm (4.8–6 in), tail 9–11 cm (3.6–4.5 in); weight 60–120 g (2–4 oz).

Distribution   Eastern United States.

Habitat   Deciduous forests.

Behavior   The eastern chipmunk leads a more or less solitary existence and is active during the hours of daylight. It seems alert and shows the typical squirrel behavior pattern of quick movements and sudden pauses to look about. It feeds on seeds, fruit, nuts, and insects, and carries food in the pouches in its cheeks, then hoards it back at its burrow, which is dug in the ground. It hibernates in the winter months, but sometimes emerges from its burrows in this period. Mating takes place in March–April and sometimes again in July–August. Gestation lasts 31 days and each litter has 2–8 (usually 4 or 5) young in it; these are born blind and hairless. When they reach about 8 weeks of age they are two thirds grown and fend for themselves.

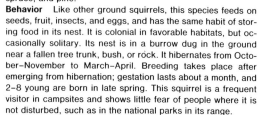

159 TAMIAS MINIMUS
Least chipmunk

Classification   Order Rodentia, Family Sciuridae.
Description   The color of the fur varies depending on the geographical location: from gray-yellow to pale yellow with black and pale stripes, which extend to the base of the tail. When it runs, the tail is held upright. It has large pouches in its cheeks. The female has 8 nipples. Length of head and body 9–11 cm (3.6–4.4 in), tail 7.5–11 cm (3–4.4 in); weight 30–60 g (1–2 oz).
Distribution   North America from Alaska to Mexico.
Habitat   Varied: from desert terrain to coniferous forests at high altitude, but mainly in areas with bushes.
Behavior   It feeds on seeds, fruit, insects, and reptiles. It uses its large cheek pouches to carry food back to its nest, which it builds among rocks, behind fallen tree trunks, or in burrows dug in the ground. Summer nests may be different from and less well sheltered than winter nests in deeper burrows. The latter nests are carefully constructed of grass and other fibrous or downy material. It can climb nimbly and swiftly in trees and is a very busy creature in spring, summer, and autumn. In winter it hibernates. It may have 2 litters a year, with 2–7 (usually 5 or 6) young in each one. Gestation lasts about 30 days.

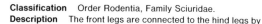

160 GLAUCOMYS VOLANS
Southern flying squirrel

Classification   Order Rodentia, Family Sciuridae.
Description   The front legs are connected to the hind legs by a hairy patagium, or fold of skin, which enables this animal to glide skillfully through the air. The pelage is a dense, thin, silky coat which varies somewhat in color: on the back it ranges from pinkish cinnamon to brown; the underside from white to creamy. The tail is flat and plume-shaped. The eyes are large. Length of head and body 20–25 cm (8–10 in), tail 8–12 cm (3.2–4.8 in); weight 50–80 g (1.8–2.8 oz).
Distribution   Central and eastern United States and parts of Mexico and Central America.
Habitat   Temperate and subtemperate forests.
Behavior   This mammal is nocturnal, remaining hidden all day in hollows or nests in trees (which may have been taken over from tree squirrels, woodpeckers, or other birds). The inside of the nest is lined with soft bark, moss, lichens, and feathers. Flying squirrels feed on fruit, leaves, insects, birds' eggs, and other small animals. It moves from tree to tree by gliding, and can cover up to 30 feet in a single flight. It is solitary (except for mother-offspring groups), but there may be a fairly dense population in suitable areas. It is less active in the winter months, but does not hibernate. Mating occurs in February–March, and after a gestation period of about 40 days the female delivers 2–6 young.

161 THOMOMYS BOTTAE
Botta's pocket gopher

Classification Order Rodentia, Family Geomyidae.

Description The color of the coat varies depending on the habitat: from almost white in the desert to almost black in coastal areas. In most areas the coloring is some shade of dull brown. The eyes and ears are small. At each side of the mouth is a large fur-lined cheek pouch, as in all geomyids and heteromyids. The large, powerful, yellowish incisor teeth are visible even when the mouth is closed. The feet have long, strong claws, particularly the front feet. Length of head and body 12–18 cm (4.8–7.2 in), tail 5–9 cm (2–3.6 in); weight 70–250 g (2.5–8.8 oz). Males are larger than females.

Distribution Southwestern United States and northern Mexico.

Habitat Varied: large valleys, mountains, and coastal regions.

Behavior The western pocket gopher spends almost all of its life underground. It digs out long tunnels with its strong claws. When it digs it also uses its incisors for shifting earth. Its large burrow, which is usually lived in by a single gopher or a female and her young, consists of various chambers and larders, and tunnels leading to these. It feeds on roots, beets, seeds, and various cereal crops, sometimes causing considerable damage; but at the same time it aerates and mixes the soil, thus making it more fertile. The 2–6 young are born in October–June, after a gestation period of about 19 days. There is usually 1 litter, but occasionally 2.

162 PEROGNATHUS SPINATUS
Spiny pocket mouse

Classification Order Rodentia, Family Heteromyidae.

Description The coat, which has many spiny hairs on the back, is pale yellow mixed with brown. The tail has longer hair on top. The head is pointed and the ears are small. At the sides of the mouth there are cheek pouches. This species has 20 teeth and the toes are all clawed. Length of head and body 7.5–9 cm (3–3.6 in), tail 8–12 cm (3.2–4.8 in); weight about 20 g (0.7 oz).

Distribution California and Baja California in Mexico.

Habitat Desert; rocky slopes.

Behavior Like the other members of the genus *Perognathus* (pocket mice), this species is typically nocturnal. During the day it remains inside a burrow it has dug in the ground; by night it emerges to feed on seeds. The cheek pouches are used for carrying food into special larders dug below ground. After a probable 3–4-week gestation, 2–6 young are born; they nurse for a few weeks. There is usually only 1 litter per year, but occasionally 2.

Note This genus has 25 species and numerous subspecies distributed from British Columbia to Mexico.

163 DIPODOMYS DESERTI
Desert kangaroo rat

Classification   Order Rodentia, Family Heteromyidae.
Description   The coat is pale yellow and differs from most other members of this genus in having a white-tipped tail. The hind legs are much longer than the front limbs, thus enabling it to make impressive bounds. The hind feet have 4 toes. There are cheek pouches at the sides of the mouth. Length of head and body 12–16 cm (5–6.5 in), tail 17–21 cm (7–8.5 in); weight 95–135 g (3.3–4.7 oz).
Distribution   Southwestern United States and extreme northwestern Mexico.
Habitat   Desert.
Behavior   Kangaroo rats are typically nocturnal, lead a solitary existence, dig burrows and storage chambers in the ground. It feeds primarily on the small seeds of many desert plants. Its water requirements are met chiefly by eating plants that contain water and by conserving metabolic water produced by oxidation of carbohydrates. Mating takes place in February–June and after a gestation period of about 30 days the female gives birth to 2–5 young which nurse for a few weeks. There are 2 or more litters each year.

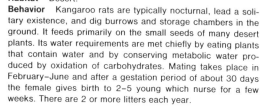

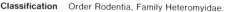

164 CASTOR CANADENSIS
American beaver

Classification   Order Rodentia, Family Castoridae.
Description   The coat ranges from yellowish brown to black. The tail is wide (9–20 cm/3.6–8 in), flattened, covered with scales, and almost completely hairless. The feet are all 5-toed, and the hind feet are webbed. The front feet are relatively small and all the front toes are clawed. The beaver closes its ears and nose when it dives. The female has 4 nipples in her pectoral region. Length of head and body up to 1.2 m (48 in), tail 25–32 cm (10–12.8 in); weight 14–25 kg (31–55 lb).
Distribution   North America, with the exception of the Arctic tundra, Florida, and the deserts in the southwest.
Habitat   Streams and at the edges of lakes.
Behavior   The beaver is colonial, usually with 4–8 individuals in each colony. It feeds on bark and leaves of trees growing beside lakes or streams, or on aquatic plants. It builds elaborate dams and "houses" out of mud, branches, and tree trunks, which it gnaws through with its powerful incisors. The house has 2 or more entrances below the water level and an internal chamber slightly above the water level. Along larger streams it digs dens in the banks. The beaver reproduces once a year; mating occurs in January–February. After a gestation period of about 107 days the female gives birth to 3 or 4 young which remain with their parents for at least a year.

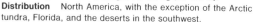

165 ANOMALURUS PELI
Pel's flying squirrel

Classification Order Rodentia, Family Anomaluridae.
Description The body is covered with a dense and bristly coat which is black on the back and almost white on the underside. A fold of skin forms a broad membrane and enables this rodent to glide through the air. The membrane joins a cartilaginous protuberance on the front limbs to the hind legs and the base of the tail. All four feet have long, sharp claws. On the bottom of the tail, near where it joins the body, there are sharp-edged scales which probably serve to brace the tail against bark. Length of head and body 45 cm (18 in), tail 35 cm (14 in); weight up to 750 g (1.7 lb).
Distribution Guinea, Liberia, and the Ivory Coast.
Habitat Tropical forests.
Behavior This arboreal rodent moves around trees with surprising agility, clinging with its long claws and gliding from tree to tree, covering distances of up to 165 feet. It takes refuge in trees, and uses hollows for its lair. It eats berries, seeds, and fruit which are found in trees. It is mainly active at night. There is little information about its reproductive behavior, but the female probably gives birth to 2 or 3 young per litter.

---

166 PEDETES CAPENSIS
Cape springhare

Classification Order Rodentia, Family Pedetidae.
Description The springhare resembles a small kangaroo, with its small front legs and very powerful hind limbs. It has large eyes and long ears. The coat is long and soft and yellow-brown in color with blackish highlights on the head and back. The terminal half of the tail is black. Length of head and body up to 42 cm (16.2 in), tail 40–50 cm (16–20 in); weight to 4 kg (9 lb).
Distribution Specific areas from Tanzania through the tip of South Africa.
Habitat Arid, open terrain, preferably where the soil is sandy.
Behavior The nocturnal springhare lives in complex burrow systems with a great many different openings to the surface which may be blocked off from the inside in some cases. When it emerges from its burrow it appears to leap into the air, possibly to avoid any enemy lurking near the exit. It is completely vegetarian and feeds on bulbs, tubers, and roots. It can cause great damage to crops. It covers several miles a night, especially when there is little water about and food is scarce. The 2–4 young are born in the burrow. The female has 2 pair of nipples.

167 ORYZOMYS PALUSTRIS
Marsh rice rat

Classification   Order Rodentia, Family Muridae.
Description   The color of the upper body is grayish brown, but the lower parts are usually gray. The tail is long and has conspicuous scales; it is gray on top, and paler on the underside. The coat is soft and the fur short. The female has 8 nipples. There are 16 teeth. Length of head and body up to 15 cm (6 in), tail 11–16 cm (4.3–6.3 in); weight to 80 g (2.8 oz).
Distribution   Southeastern United States as far west as Texas.
Habitat   Marshlands and wetlands.

Behavior   This is a gregarious species which is primarily nocturnal but can be seen frequently during the day. Its presence is closely associated with water, and it is a skillful swimmer and diver. It builds a nest of grasses and sedges which is located in vegetation above the highest water level. It occasionally digs a burrow in the ground. It feeds on seeds, grass, fruit, and possibly insects. It reproduces several times throughout the year. Gestation lasts 25 days. Three or four blind and hairless young are born in each litter. The populations of this species are subject to dramatic numerical fluctuations. This rat can cause considerable damage in southern rice paddies.

168 REITHRODONTOMYS MEGALOTIS
Western harvest mouse

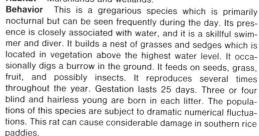

Classification   Order Rodentia, Family Muridae.
Description   The color of the coat varies somewhat, ranging from pale gray to brown. In appearance, the harvest mouse somewhat resembles the house mouse (*Mus musculus*, **194**). It has 16 teeth and the female has 6 nipples. Length of head and body about 7 cm (2.8 in), tail 5–8 cm (2–3.2 in); weight 9–18 g (0.3–0.6 oz).
Distribution   Western United States and Mexico.
Habitat   Prairies and deserts.

Behavior   It feeds on seeds, grass, and occasionally insects, and is most active at night. It does not hibernate. It builds distinctive spherical nests of grass, on the ground in thickets of tall vegetation, in fallen logs, and in abandoned woodpeckers' nests. There is no specific period when mating occurs. Gestation lasts for about 24 days, then the female gives birth to 2–4 young which are blind and hairless. At 5 weeks the young are fully developed, and the young females are capable of reproducing at 3–4 months of age.
Note   The native New World rats and mice of the subfamily Sigmodontinae are represented by **167–172**.

169 PEROMYSCUS MANICULATUS
Deer mouse

Classification Order Rodentia, Family Muridae.

Description The coat is variable in color due to different conditions in different parts of the large geographic area occupied by this species. The color ranges from pale gray to dark reddish brown. The tail is white underneath and dark on top. The feet are white; the eyes and ears are relatively large. Its general appearance is similar to the species of the widespread European genus *Apodemus*; *A. sylvaticus* (**188**) is shown in this book. Length of head and body 7–10 cm (2.8–4 in), tail 5–12 cm (2–5 in); weight 25–30 g (0.9–1 oz).

Distribution North America from Alaska to Mexico.

Habitat Varied: forest, prairie, rocky terrain, and even near buildings in suburban areas.

Behavior This mouse feeds on seeds, nuts, and insects. The nest is dug in the ground or built in the hollow of a tree, in rocks, or in buildings. Food is stored in "larders" in the nest complex. Mating usually takes place February–November and varies with the latitude; gestation lasts 25–27 days. There can be up to 4 litters a year, each with 3 to 5 young. (The female has 6 nipples; 1 pair is pectoral, 2 pair are inguinal.)

Note The genus *Peromyscus* (deer mice) is quite large and highly speciated, having 49 distinct species occurring in various parts of North America. The species *P. maniculatus* is the most widespread and variable of the species.

---

170 ONYCHOMYS LEUCOGASTER
Northern grasshopper mouse

Classification Order Rodentia, Family Muridae.

Description The fur on the back is pinkish pale cinnamon and on the underside completely white. The soles of the feet except for tubercles are covered with hair; the front feet have four conspicuous toes, the hind feet five. The ears and eyes are of average size. The female has 6 nipples, 2 in the pectoral region and 4 in the inguinal region. Length of head and body 11–19 cm (4.4–7.6 in), tail 3–6 cm (1.2–2.4 in); weight 30–40 g (1–1.4 oz).

Distribution Central and southwestern United States to northern Mexico.

Habitat Prairie with low grass, desert, and pastureland.

Behavior It feeds on grasshoppers (whence its common name), other insects, lizards, mice, and also on seeds and grass. It is solitary and nocturnal. After a gestation period of 29–38 days the female gives birth to 2–6 young in March–August; these are born hairless and with their eyes closed. After about 4 days they start to move about outside the nest, and after 9 days their eyes are open. They are weaned in 3–4 weeks, and reach sexual maturity when they are about 90 days old. A female may produce 3–6 litters in a year. Under controlled conditions in the laboratory individuals have lived as long as 4 years, but the average life expectancy of one born in the wild is a few weeks or months.

171 SIGMODON HISPIDUS
Hispid cotton rat

Classification   Order Rodentia, Family Muridae.

Description   The dorsal pelage ranges from gray-brown to black-brown and has a distinctive grizzled appearance because of a mixture of hairs of different colors. The underside is paler and more uniform in color. The ears are almost completely hidden by long hairs. The female has 8–10 nipples. Length of head and body 12–20 cm (3.2–6.4 in); weight 120–200 g (4.2–7 oz).

Distribution   Southern United States, Mexico, and Central America.

Habitat   Areas with tall grass.

Behavior   This diurnal rodent feeds on green plants and eggs of ground-nesting birds. Its nest is either under or on the surface of the ground. When it moves about it uses cleared paths which are easily recognizable. It can reproduce all year round; the gestation period lasts for 27 days and each litter has 1–15 young. (In northern populations litters average about 7; in southern populations, 3 or 4.) Young grow rapidly and may be weaned 10–15 days after birth. Up to 9 litters can be born in a single year. As a result, in years when climatic conditions are good, there is a marked increase in the population and these rats can cause severe damage to sugarcane, corn, and other crops.

172 NEOTOMA LEPIDA
Desert wood rat

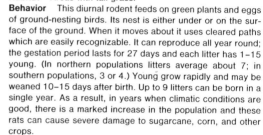

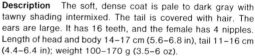

Classification   Order Rodentia, Family Muridae.

Description   The soft, dense coat is pale to dark gray with tawny shading intermixed. The tail is covered with hair. The ears are large. It has 16 teeth, and the female has 4 nipples. Length of head and body 14–17 cm (5.6–6.8 in); tail 11–16 cm (4.4–6.4 in); weight 100–170 g (3.5–6 oz).

Distribution   Southwestern United States.

Habitat   Desert plains or rocky slopes with cactus and scrub.

Behavior   These wood rats are nocturnal and rarely seen in daylight. They feed on seeds, acorns, and cactus. The nest, which is made with a wide variety of materials, may be built on open ground or in crevices among rocks. Wood rats are not colonial, but where the habitat is favorable they may be common and live fairly close together. They are not highly territorial. Habitats that are favorable may occur only at widely scattered local areas. The desert wood rat gathers all sorts of things in its nest. This and other wood rats are sometimes called pack rats on account of this collecting habit. It can have up to 4 litters a year, each consisting of 1–5 young, after 30 days of gestation. The young reach sexual maturity at the age of 2 months.

173 MESOCRICETUS AURATUS
Golden hamster

Classification Order Rodentia, Family Muridae.

Description The back is a deep golden or reddish brown, and the underside is paler. The cheek pouches can extend as far as the shoulders and when they are full they seem to double the size of the hamster's head. The female has 14–16 nipples and is slightly larger than the male. Length of head and body up to 18 cm (7.2 in), tail only to 12 mm (0.5 in); weight to 130 g (4.6 oz).

Distribution From Rumania and Bulgaria throughout the Middle East, the Caucasus, and the northwest corner of Iran.

Habitat Steppe and grassland.

Behavior This animal is mainly nocturnal and lives in burrows dug in the ground, usually alone or in small family groups. It feeds on a large variety of foods and can reproduce during any month in the year, at least when it is in captivity. Gestation lasts only 16 days. The number of young averages 6 or 7, although litters of 15 young have been recorded.

Note The 25 species of Old World hamsters make up the subfamily Cricetinae, 2 species of which **(173–174)** are treated here. This species is well known throughout the world as a household pet and is widely studied in scientific laboratories. All the golden hamsters presently living in captivity originate from a single female with 12 young which were dug from one burrow in Syria in 1930.

---

174 CRICETUS CRICETUS
Common hamster

Classification Order Rodentia, Family Muridae.

Description The coat on the back is reddish brown, and black on the underside of the body. This is quite unusual for most mammals are paler beneath. Over the cheek pouches, which open within the month, there are white markings. The snout is somewhat pointed as in rodents generally, the eyes are of average size, the ears are rounded and membranous. Length of head and body 24–34 cm (9.6–13.6 in), tail 3–6 cm (1.2–2.4 in); weight 150–380 g (5.3–13.3 oz).

Distribution Central eastern Europe, to the north as far as Siberia and to the south as far as Iraq.

Habitat Steppe and cultivated land.

Behavior The stocky common hamster feeds on cereal crops, potatoes, and beets, and also on small birds and rodents. It makes large stockpiles of food within its burrow system, which is dug in the ground and has an intricate network of tunnels. The food for storage is carried in the cheek pouches, which can hold remarkable amounts of food. This solitary animal is most active in the morning and evening, and hibernates through the winter in all parts of the range. There may be 2 or more litters a year, with 5–12 young which nurse for about 3 weeks. Gestation lasts 18–20 days.

175 LOPHIOMYS IMHAUSI
Crested rat

Classification   Order Rodentia, Family Muridae.
Description   This is a brightly colored rat with long, soft fur. There is an erectile strip of fur that runs from the head to the tail along the central part of the back. The head has a broad white band across it and the long, bushy tail is blackish with a white tip. On each side of the body, along a line of lateral skin glands, there is a thin stripe of whitish fur. The head and ears are small, as are all the limbs. Length of head and body up to 35 cm (14 in), tail 14–17 cm (5.6–6.8 in); weight 2–3 kg (4.4–6.6 lb).
Distribution   Sudan, Ethiopia, Somalia, and Kenya.
Habitat   Thick forest, and also on the edge of scrub-covered terrain.
Behavior   With its partly opposable thumb this solitary, slow-moving rat has adapted well to tree-climbing, and it can descend head first. Although it spends a great deal of its time in trees, it makes its nest among rocks or in holes dug in the ground. It is vegetarian, with a preference for shoots and tender young leaves. It is completely nocturnal. It has a specific cry, 1 or 2 hisses followed by a short snarl. Nothing is known about its reproductive biology or behavior.
Note   This unusually distinctive rodent is the only species in its own subfamily, the Lophiomycinae.

176 DICROSTONYX GROENLANDICUS
Greenland collared lemming

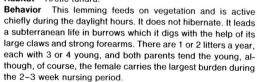

Classification   Order Rodentia, Family Muridae.
Description   The coat is long and soft, gray-brown with a dark dorsal stripe in summer, and completely white in winter. The ears are small and almost completely hidden in the fur. The third and fourth toes of the front feet have large claws which grow in the spring and drop off in the autumn. Length of head and body 10–14 cm (4–5.6 in), tail only 1–2 cm (0.4–0.8 in); weight 45–70 g (1.4–2.5 oz).
Distribution   The Arctic regions of North America, as far east as Greenland.
Habitat   Arctic tundra.
Behavior   This lemming feeds on vegetation and is active chiefly during the daylight hours. It does not hibernate. It leads a subterranean life in burrows which it digs with the help of its large claws and strong forearms. There are 1 or 2 litters a year, each with 3 or 4 young, and both parents tend the young, although, of course, the female carries the largest burden during the 2–3 week nursing period.
Note   The subfamily Arvicolinae (**176–182**) includes about 100 species of voles and lemmings and is widely distributed in northern parts of both the Old and New World.

177 LEMMUS LEMMUS
Norway lemming

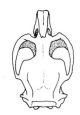

Classification Order Rodentia, Family Muridae.

Description The body is quite rotund, with short legs. The ears are almost completely covered by the coat, and the eyes are small. The coat varies somewhat in color, but is generally yellowish brown with darker markings. Length of head and body 13–15 cm (5.2–6 in), tail 1–2 cm (0.4–0.8 in); weight 50–90 g (1.8–3 oz).

Distribution Scandinavia.

Habitat Tundra and mountains, especially areas with birch and conifers.

Behavior This vegetarian rodent feeds on grass, lichens, and roots. It lives hidden beneath boulders and tree stumps, digging out a complicated system of tunnels quite near the surface. About every 2 or 3 years the numbers of this communal species increase considerably, which forces it to migrate *en masse* in search of food. On these migratory journeys few obstacles will stop them. They cross streams and even throw themselves into the sea, where they drown (whence the common misconception that lemmings "commit suicide"). They are active by day and by night, and do not hibernate. Gestation is about 23 days, and they probably have more than one litter a year, with 5 or 6 young in each. The young are born in the spring, nurse for 2–3 weeks, and are capable of reproduction by the end of the summer.

178 CLETHRIONOMYS GLAREOLUS
Bank vole

Classification Order Rodentia, Family Muridae.

Description The coat is reddish chestnut on the back, and yellowish white on the underside; the legs are gray. The ears and eyes are small. The molar teeth tend to wear down with use, but grow continuously. Length of head and body 8–12 cm (3.2–5 in), tail 4–5.5 cm (1.6–2.2); weight 15–35 g (0.5–1.2 oz).

Distribution Europe (except for Spain, the Balkans, Ireland and the Hebrides) and east to central Asia.

Habitat Broadleaf woodlands; hedgerows; terrain with bushes.

Behavior This solitary vole is diurnal but is sometimes active at nightfall and just before dawn. It feeds on grass, roots, fruit, and seeds, and also on insects, earthworms, and other animal matter. When food is scarce it climbs into trees to nibble the bark. It is a nimble climber and can run fast. It usually builds a nest in the ground, quite near the surface, with tunnel systems, but it will occasionally build a nest on top of the ground; these nests are spherical in shape, and made with soft materials such as grass, moss, leaves, and feathers. After about 18 days of gestation, the female gives birth to 3–5 young which are blind and hairless; these reach full maturity after about 9 weeks. The breeding season is in the warmer months of the year, and several litters are possible.

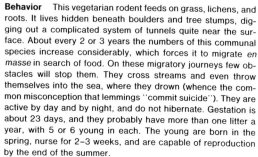

179 ARVICOLA TERRESTRIS
European water vole

Classification   Order Rodentia, Family Muridae.

Description   The coat is dense and dark brown, but some individuals are light gray or black. The head is quite thickset, the snout relatively short and rounded as in other voles, the eyes small, and the ears short. Length of head and body 12–19 cm (4.8–7.6 in), tail 7.5–12.5 cm (3–5 in); weight 80–170 g (2.8–6 oz).

Distribution   Europe, central northern Asia.

Habitat   Cultivated land, orchards; also by the shores of lakes and along riverbanks.

Behavior   This vole feeds on roots, which it finds by digging tunnels which are similar to those dug by moles. It also eats fruit, vegetables, and bulbs. When it finds its way into an orchard it can severely damage fruit trees, by gnawing through the roots. The tunnel system also includes a burrow with a nest chamber and in most cases a storage chamber. It is a solitary animal, but the population may be dense at times in favorable habitats. Reproduction occurs in summer; in this period the males mark out their territory with a substance secreted by glands located on the sides of the body. After a gestation period of 21 days the female delivers 2–8 young, which nurse for about 4 weeks. There may be as many as 4 litters in the course of a single summer.

180 ONDATRA ZIBETHICUS
Muskrat

Classification   Order Rodentia, Family Muridae.

Description   Its appearance is that of a large rat with a scaly tail that is flattened at the sides and acts as a rudder when it swims. The coat is dark brown and waterproof. Near the genitals there is a gland which produces a strong-smelling musky secretion. The female has 3 pair of nipples. Length of head and body about 26–40 cm (10.4–16 in), tail 20–26 cm (8–10.2 in); weight 600–1600 g (1.3–3.5 lb).

Distribution   North America; introduced to Europe and now found in Germany, Austria, Poland, Switzerland, Yugoslavia, Rumania, Bulgaria, and parts of the U.S.S.R.

Habitat   Marshland and swamps with fresh and salt water; streams and rivers.

Behavior   The solitary muskrat is active at all hours. It feeds mainly on aquatic plants, but will also eat frogs and fish. It swims by using its hind legs and tail. It builds "houses" of vegetation in shallow ponds; alternatively it digs underground burrows in the banks of waterways (these burrows have an entrance under the water and sometimes another one on the water level). Mating usually occurs in the water. The female may produce several litters each year—gestation lasts 25–30 days—each of 6–8 young. The offspring are weaned by about 4 weeks and reach sexual maturity the spring following their birth.

181 PITYMYS SAVII
Savi's woodland vole

Classification Order Rodentia, Family Muridae.
Description The body is reddish brown, sometimes tending to yellowish. The eyes are very small; the ears are almost completely hidden beneath the fur; tail very short. These features occur in many fossorial species. Length of head and body up to 10 cm (4 in), tail only to 3.5 cm (1.4 in); weight 12–20 g (0.4–0.7 oz).
Distribution Northern Spain, southern France, Italy, and a small area in the Balkans.
Habitat Pastureland and moist fields.

Behavior This vole lives in small colonies. It spends much time building tunnels and nests. It is a fast runner, but rarely climbs or jumps. It is mainly nocturnal, but in some cases it is active by day as well. Its tunnels may be dug near the surface or as much as, but never below, 12 inches deep. The storerooms it builds are filled with food, and the nesting rooms are lined with dry leaves and grass. The entrances to the burrow are closed off when it snows or rains, and any wet earth is quickly removed. When alarmed it emits a whistle. Gestation lasts about 20 days, after which usually 4–6 young are born. Litter follows litter year round, except during the winter months, at roughly 21-day intervals. Female offspring reach sexual maturity at 5 weeks, while still occasionally nursing.

182 MICROTUS NIVALIS
Snow vole

Classification Order Rodentia, Family Muridae.
Description The coat is dense, soft, and pale gray; the tail is white. There are long vibrissae on the snout. Length of head and body 9–13 cm. (3.6–5.2 in), tail 2–4 cm (0.8–1.6 in); weight up to 45 g (1.6 oz).
Distribution Europe, in the Pyrenees, Alps, Carpathians, the Balkans, Asia Minor, and the Caucasus.
Habitat Above the timberline on rocky mountainsides in sunny places.

Behavior This vole is active both by day and by night. By day it is easy to spot, especially on fine sunny days. It feeds on alpine plants (the roots of various roses, primroses, carnations, etc.). It digs a system of tunnels with numerous exits, plus a nest chamber and a storeroom. It does not hibernate in winter and often takes shelter in cellars or barns or haylofts to protect itself from the cold. When it runs it is easily identifiable by the fact that it holds its tail in an upright position. During the short mountain summer after a gestation period of 21 days the female gives birth to 2–7 young which she suckles for 3 weeks. She may bear 2 litters per season.

183 GERBILLUS CAMPESTRIS
Large North African gerbil

Classification   Order Rodentia, Family Muridae.
Description   The body is long and light, and the soles of the hind feet are covered with fur. The entire body is light or dark brown, depending on the environment, but the tip of the tail is often darker. The eyes and ears are large in proportion to the body. Length of head and body up to 13 cm (5.2 in), tail slightly shorter; weight 20–30 g (0.7–1 oz).
Distribution   Northern Africa, from Morocco east to Libya and Somalia.
Habitat   Grasslands and semidesert areas.
Behavior   This gerbil lives in a simple burrow which it digs itself and which has a single entrance. Several individuals may build their nests so close to one another that a colony is formed. It is active at night but when the weather becomes too harsh it prefers to stay in its burrow. It feeds on seeds, roots, and grass. Gestation lasts 20 days and the female usually gives birth to 4 young. Its main enemies are snakes, which find the gerbil easy prey when attacked inside the burrow.
Note   The subfamily Gerbillinae comprises 15 genera. *Gerbillus* has 34 species; *Meriones* (of which *M. libycus*, **184**, is an example) has 14. All 82 different species of gerbillines dwell in dry regions.

184 MERIONES LIBYCUS
North African jird

Classification   Order Rodentia, Family Muridae.
Description   The back is pale in color but tends to have a brown marking running along the middle. The sides of the body and the underside are paler, and the tail is darker. The coat on the upper part is longer than on the rest of its body. Length of head and body up to 13 cm (5.2 in), tail to 10 cm (4 in); weight to about 60 g (2.1 oz).
Distribution   Libya and other parts of North Africa and eastward in Asia to Sinkiang, China.
Habitat   Desert and arid environments in general.
Behavior   This jird may live in large colonies which dig and share burrows in sand and soft soil, with many entrances and passages. It may also be solitary. It moves about by day and by night in search of seeds, roots, bulbs, and leaves. Gestation lasts 28 days and reproduction occurs several times a year, but mainly in the summer months. There are 3–7 young per litter. This species may hibernate in the coldest months of the year; this is certainly the case with other species in the same genus which live in the upland plateaus of Asia.

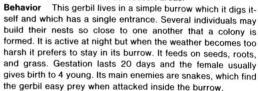

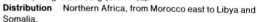

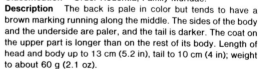

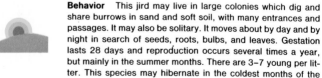

185 TACHYORYCTES SPLENDENS
East African mole rat

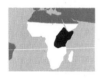

Classification   Order Rodentia, Family Muridae.

Description   The head resembles that of a pocket gopher and the strength of the legs and feet also indicates a creature which burrows. The upper incisors are broad and are used in digging as well as in cutting roots and other food items. The coat is thick, short, and soft, and varies from black to various shades of brown; some individuals have white splotches. On the snout there are a few long whiskers, the function of which is undoubtedly tactile. Length of head and body up to 25 cm (10 in), tail 7 cm (2.8 in); weight to 300 g (10.5 oz).

Distribution   East Africa, in scattered local areas.

Habitat   Plains and forests up to an altitude of 12,500 feet.

Behavior   This animal lives permanently underground, digging a burrow and a network of passages and tunnels through which it hurries incessantly; in one tunnel it builds a sort of nest lined with dry leaves. It digs with its front feet and then gets rid of the earth with its hind feet. When the amount of earth to be pushed to the surface is excessive it also uses its chest to push it. Its diet chiefly consists of the underground parts of plants—roots, tubers, bulbs, rhyzomes—and shoots. It can cause considerable damage to crops and is hunted by the rural inhabitants where it occurs. Nothing is known about its reproductive habits except litter size: 1–4 offspring (but usually only 1).

Note   The mole rats belong to the subfamily Rhizomyinae, which comprises 6 species.

186 SPALAX LEUCODON
Lesser mole rat

Classification   Order Rodentia, Family Muridae.

Description   The coat is dark gray or yellowish gray. The body is stocky and cylindrical in shape; the legs are short; and the tail virtually nonexistent. The toes of the feet do not have especially strong claws, which is not what one might expect in a fossorial animal. The incisors, on the other hand, are powerful and stick out conspicuously. There is no pinna (external parts) of the ear and the eyes are atrophied and covered with fur. Length of head and body 15–30 cm (6–12 in); weight 150–300 g (5.3–10.1 oz).

Distribution   Northern Africa, Middle East north to the Caucasus, Europe to the Danube basin.

Habitat   Varied, from sea level to 8500 feet.

Behavior   This member of the subfamily Spalacinae is solitary. Active both day and night, it spends its life building tunnels and underground burrows, almost never going into the open. Its head, which is thickset and strong, and the powerful incisors are excellent tools for digging. Its feet are used for removing the earth. The tunnels, which are not very deep, run among the roots, tubers, and bulbs of the plants on which it feeds. In autumn, in the mating period, the female builds mounds of earth, about 16 inches high, in the middle of which there is a chamber, where she delivers and rears 2–4 young, born in January–March after a 1-month gestation.

187 MICROMYS MINUTUS
Harvest mouse

Classification   Order Rodentia, Family Muridae.
Description   The coat is reddish yellow dorsally, and white on the underside. The eyes are of average size. The ears are round. The hind feet have 5 toes, the front feet only 4. Length of head and body 58–76 cm (2.3–3 in), tail 51–72 mm (2–2.9 in); weight 5–9 g (0.2–0.3 oz).
Distribution   Europe (except Ireland, Spain and Scandinavia), Siberia, China, and Taiwan.
Habitat   Fields of grain (temporarily), terrain with tall grass.
Behavior   The harvest mouse feeds on seeds, grain, and sometimes insects. It is active by day and by night. It climbs nimbly up and down the stalks of tall grass, where it builds its round, birdlike nest. It uses its tail, which is partly prehensile, to help it climb. When building its nest it uses leaves and stalks, which it tears off with its teeth. For the winter it builds either a larger nest situated higher up the stalk or a nest under the ground. It does not hibernate, but survives the winter on food it has stored. Gestation lasts about 21 days and there can be several litters a year, each with 3–7 young, which nurse for about 18 days. The sound it emits is shrill, almost like a shriek.
Note   The most common and generalized rats and mice of the Old World (and introduced elsewhere) belong to the subfamily Murinae (**187–196**, and **199**).

---

188 APODEMUS SYLVATICUS
Wood mouse

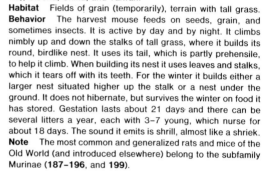

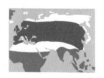

Classification   Order Rodentia, Family Muridae.
Description   The coat on the back is shiny and tawny, on the underside dirty white. On the throat there is often a small white marking. The eyes are large and the ears conspicuous. The hind legs are longer than the front legs. Length of head and body 9–10 cm (3.6–4 in), tail 7–11 cm (2.8–4.4 in); weight 15–25 g (0.5–0.9 oz).
Distribution   Europe east to central Asia; North Africa.
Habitat   Woods, cultivated land, and orchards.
Behavior   This somewhat gregarious mouse feeds on seeds, berries, fruit, and roots. It stores large quantities of food in storerooms in its burrow. In winter it often takes up residence in people's homes, on the lower floors, and is fond of flour and grain. It does not enter hibernation, but when a winter is particularly severe it falls into a sort of torpor. It is mainly active during darkness. It walks in small hops and is a good climber. It reproduces 4 times between March and September. After a gestation period of 23–26 days the female gives birth to 5–9 young in a spherical nest made with dry grass. The offspring are independent at about 3 weeks, and reach sexual maturity at about 2 months.

189 LEMNISCOMYS STRIATUS
Striped grass rat

Classification Order Rodentia, Family Muridae.

Description The bristly coat is tawny olive, with paler stripes on the back. In this species some stripes are broken into spots. The ears are of average size, round, and reddish in color. The feet are 5-toed, with the first and fifth smaller in size. Length of head and body 9–14 cm (3.6–5.6 in), tail up to 15 cm (6 in); weight 30–70 g (1–2.5 oz).

Distribution Africa, south of the Sahara.

Habitat Savanna and forest.

Behavior This gregarious rodent often forms large colonies. It is mainly diurnal and feeds on seeds, sweet potatoes, leaves, and other plant matter. The nest is made of grass and is built in a hole dug in the ground, in an abandoned termite nest, or on the surface of the ground (concealed among vegetation). Various ''paths'' lead from the nest to places where food is available. The female gives birth to 4 or 5 young, after about 28 days of gestation. The female offspring are sexually mature at 2 months.

190 OENOMYS HYPOXANTHUS
Rufous-nosed rat

Classification Order Rodentia, Family Muridae.

Description The body is gray-brown with reddish and blackish areas above and white below. There are two noticeable areas of reddish fur on the sides of the snout. The coat is quite long, especially on the hind half of the animal. The legs may be white, reddish, or brown. Length of head and body up to 18 cm (7.2 in), tail to 20 cm (8 in); weight 70–120 g (2.5–4.2 oz).

Distribution Central Africa, and eastern and southern Africa as far south as Angola.

Habitat Virgin forest, dense vegetation, and cultivated fields.

Behavior This solitary rat is active both day and night. It can cause damage in paddy fields and to cereal crops. It climbs around in vegetation above the ground as well as foraging on the ground. It builds a rounded nest between branches or in clumps of grass, usually with only one entrance. The average litter has 2 or 3 young, rarely 4, and several litters may be produced by a female in the humid parts of one year. Sexual maturity is not reached until 4 months of age.

191 RATTUS RATTUS
Black, or roof, rat

Classification   Order Rodentia, Family Muridae.
Description   The tail is hairless and covered with rings of scales. The snout is pointed, and the eyes and ears are large. The coat is black or gray-brown. The feet are 5-toed; however, the first toe of the front foot is very small. The female has 10 or 12 nipples. Length of head and body 16–22 cm (6.3–8.7 in), tail 17–25 cm (6.7–9.8 in); weight 150–230 g (5.3–8 oz).
Distribution   Worldwide in suitable habitat, not in colder regions.

Habitat   The black rat has adapted to almost every conceivable habitat apart from colder regions and deserts. It is usually found in places where human beings are present.
Behavior   This is a gregarious, mainly nocturnal rat. It usually feeds on fruit and grain, but in general it is omnivorous. It prefers warm places; beneath roofs and in barns and granaries. It is very agile, and a skillful climber, but it dislikes swimming. It is less prolific than *Rattus norvegicus* (**192**); however it does breed several times a year. Gestation lasts 21–30 days. Each litter has 5–8 young which are born blind and hairless. This rat creates major economic and health problems because it destroys foodstuffs and transmits infectious diseases, as plague and typhus, to humans.

---

192 RATTUS NORVEGICUS
Brown rat, Norway rat

Classification   Order Rodentia, Family Muridae.
Description   Not quite so slender as *Rattus rattus* (**191**), its tail is relatively shorter, the snout is less pointed, and the ears are shorter. The coat is dark gray on the back and off-white underneath. The tail is covered with rings of scales. The female has 10 or 12 nipples. Length of head and body 21–27 cm (8.3–10.6 in), tail 16–22 cm (6.3–8.6 in); weight 280–520 g (10–18.2 oz).
Distribution   Worldwide.
Habitat   Like the black rat, this species has adapted to more or less every habitat except the desert.
Behavior   This species lives communally, and preferably close to or in contact with man, although it can still be found in natural environments. Its favorite haunts are sewers, stables, cowsheds, and cellars. It is mainly active at night. This rat is not as good a climber as the black rat, but is an excellent swimmer. It prefers food of animal origin, such as fish, mice, and chickens, but it is highly omnivorous. The female bears 2 or 3 litters a year, each with 6–12 young, after a gestation period of 21–26 days.
Note   This rat is a serious pest because of the health hazards caused by its presence, including the transmittal of such diseases as bubonic plague and murine typhus. This species includes the familiar white laboratory rats.

193 UROMYS CAUDIMACULATUS
Giant naked-tailed rat

Classification   Order Rodentia, Family Muridae.
Description   The not very dense coat is gray-brown on the back and gray-white on the underside. The tail has flattened, non-overlapping scales and the distal half is white. The incisor teeth are strong and large. The ears are of average size; the feet are large and have powerful claws. The female has 4 nipples. Length of head and body 30–35 cm (12–14 in), tail 25–35 cm (10–14 in); weight 430–850 g (0.9–1.9 lb).
Distribution   New Guinea and northern Australia in Queensland.
Habitat   Forests, clearings, coconut plantations, and even rocky areas.
Behavior   It is arboreal and builds its nest in hollows in trees. It is a nimble and excellent climber, and is helped in this activity by its long scaly tail which can be wrapped around branches to provide a firm hold. It feeds mainly on coconuts which have fallen from palms. It is familiar as a camp robber and is omnivorous. It eats eggs and some insects but is mainly vegetarian. Litter size is 1–3 and the offspring weigh about 20 g at birth. They begin to eat solid foods at about 30 days of age but are not of adult size until about 8 months. Gestation lasts 41 days.

194 MUS MUSCULUS
House mouse

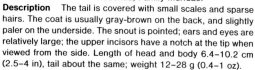

Classification   Order Rodentia, Family Muridae.
Description   The tail is covered with small scales and sparse hairs. The coat is usually gray-brown on the back, and slightly paler on the underside. The snout is pointed; ears and eyes are relatively large; the upper incisors have a notch at the tip when viewed from the side. Length of head and body 6.4–10.2 cm (2.5–4 in), tail about the same; weight 12–28 g (0.4–1 oz).
Distribution   Worldwide.
Habitat   This mouse lives in fields, among bushes, and in woodland, but it is also commensal with man, and is thus found in homes and buildings.
Behavior   The house mouse eats anything and everything, but prefers grain and other vegetable matter. It is usually active at night, but will also venture forth during the day. It is an agile little animal; it climbs well and swims fairly well. It lives alone, in large family groups, or in definite colonies. In nature it builds nests of relatively fine fibers from plants and other sources; in buildings it lives in the space between the walls. It reproduces virtually all year round. After about 13–21 days of gestation, the female gives birth to 6 or 7 young which are blind and hairless; they are weaned at 3–4 weeks.

195 NOTOMYS MITCHELLII
Mitchell's hopping mouse

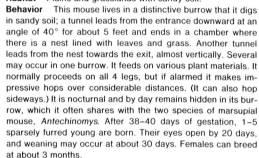

Classification   Order Rodentia, Family Muridae.

Description   The short, soft pelage is invariably pale in color, either sand-colored or pale brown, with the underside of the body grayish; the tail has a dark tuft of hair at the tip. The large ears are a distinctive feature. The hind legs are slender and long. Length of head and body up to 12.5 cm (4.9 in), tail to 15.5 cm (6.1 in); weight 40–60 g (1.2–1.7 oz).

Distribution   Southern Australia.

Habitat   Plains and grasslands with sandy soil.

Behavior   This mouse lives in a distinctive burrow that it digs in sandy soil; a tunnel leads from the entrance downward at an angle of 40° for about 5 feet and ends in a chamber where there is a nest lined with leaves and grass. Another tunnel leads from the nest towards the exit, almost vertically. Several may occur in one burrow. It feeds on various plant materials. It normally proceeds on all 4 legs, but if alarmed it makes impressive hops over considerable distances. (It can also hop sideways.) It is nocturnal and by day remains hidden in its burrow, which it often shares with the two species of marsupial mouse, *Antechinomys*. After 38–40 days of gestation, 1–5 sparsely furred young are born. Their eyes open by 20 days, and weaning may occur at about 30 days. Females can breed at about 3 months.

196 ACOMYS CAHIRINUS
Egyptian spiny mouse

Classification   Order Rodentia, Family Muridae.

Description   The upper parts of the body are brown, gray, or beige; the lower parts and underside are always white. The ears are large; the tail is hairless with large, conspicuous scales which are often split or broken. The coat has a hispid, or bristly appearance because of the presence of a great many hard and spiny outer hairs. Length of head and body 12 cm (5 in), tail the same; weight 60–90 g (2.1–3.2 oz).

Distribution   North Africa and the Middle East.

Habitat   Rocky areas, sometimes with dense vegetation.

Behavior   The ecology of this gregarious mouse is similar to that of the house mouse (*Mus musculus*, **194**), with which it competes for territory and sources of food. It prefers to eat plant matter, but adapts to anything edible. In desert and sandy areas it also competes with gerbils, and often uses their burrows. It is active early in the day and late in the afternoon and evening. Gestation lasts 36–40 days, and the young (2 or 3, at most 5) are born mainly in the spring and summer months; there are several litters each breeding season. The female has 6 nipples and the male is sexually mature at the age of 7 weeks.

197 CRICETOMYS GAMBIANUS
Giant Gambian pouched rat

Classification   Order Rodentia, Family Muridae.

Description   This is one of the largest of all the rats, with large ears and a long, hairless tail. The coat is long and hispid. It is gray above and white beneath and has a sharp separation of the color zones. The cheek pouches can be inflated to a considerable size. Length of head and body 30–42 cm (12–16.8 in), tail 30–48 cm (12–19.2 in); weight about 1.5 kg (3.3 lb).

Distribution   Together with the other species of giant rat (*Cricetomys emini*), from the Gambia to the Sudan and south as far as northern Transvaal.

Habitat   Wooded plains.

Behavior   This nocturnal rat often lives in close association with man, even though it is rarely found in houses. It digs long tunnels with various entrances and several different chambers; the most remote of these is used for nesting and is lined with plant matter of various sorts; the others are used as storerooms for food reserves—seeds and other plant matter. The females live in a group with their newborn young and older young (up to 30 individuals per group), but the males are more solitary. Gestation lasts 42 days, and 2–4 young are born at each delivery. The female probably bears more than one litter a year.

Note   This animal is considered to be a delicacy by many Africans and is hunted a great deal. This is one of 6 species of the subfamily Cricetomyinae.

---

198 DENDROMUS MESOMELAS
African climbing mouse

Classification   Order Rodentia, Family Muridae.

Description   The color of the upper parts of the body is gray-brown with a distinct black line running lengthwise down the body. The underside is white. The coat is soft and woolly. The tail has very small scales and a few scattered hairs and is extremely mobile and somewhat prehensile. The front feet have just 3 toes which are large and well developed, the other 2 toes are much reduced in size; the hind feet have the normal number, 5. The female has 8 nipples. Length of head and body up to 10 cm (4 in), tail about the same; weight 11–17 g (0.4–0.6 oz).

Distribution   Africa south of the Sahara.

Habitat   Grassland and scrub, but must be near water.

Behavior   This solitary mouse is mainly nocturnal and arboreal; it can move with great agility through the branches of trees and bushes, and also through the tallest types of grasses. But if threatened it returns quickly to the ground. It builds its nest with plant matter, sometimes hanging it from branches but it can also dig burrows and tunnels in the ground. It feeds on fruit, seeds, insects, and birds' eggs. It can easily be caught in the hands because it does not bite. Details about its reproduction are unknown.

Note   This is one of the 20 species of the subfamily Dendromurinae.

199 HYDROMYS CHRYSOGASTER
Golden-bellied water rat

Classification   Order Rodentia, Family Muridae.
Description   The coat is dense and very soft, and often varies in color between males and females; the male has a golden yellow ventral area. In both sexes the back is a fairly dark brown, tending to black or yellowish; the tip of the tail is white. The eyes and ears are small; the nostrils can be partly closed, and the hind feet are broad with the toes partly joined together by a web for swimming. Length of head and body up to 39 cm (15.4 in), tail 32 cm (12.6 in); weight to 1.3 kg (2.9 lb).
Distribution   Australia and New Guinea.
Habitat   Freshwater streams and lakes.

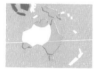

Behavior   This nocturnal and somewhat diurnal rat lives in family groups sharing a burrow system, which is a complex network of tunnels. These may be longer than 6.5 feet. There may be two main chambers, one used as a storeroom, the other as a residence. Food includes molluscs, crabs, frogs, fishes, and birds. The mating season occurs in the (southern) spring and, after a 35-day gestation period, the female gives birth to 4 or 5 young, which she nurses for about 34 days.
Note   The fur of this animal is highly prized and as a result the species has been almost wiped out in many parts of its range.

---

200 MYOXUS GLIS
Fat, or edible, dormouse

Classification   Order Rodentia, Family Gliridae.
Description   The body is covered with a gray coat on the back and is white on the underside; around the eyes there are two darker-colored markings. The tail is unusually bushy for a rodent. Length of head and body 13–19 cm (5.2–7.6 in), tail 11–15 cm (4.4–6 in); weight 70–180 g (2.5–6.3 oz).
Distribution   Northern Spain, southern central Europe, and eastern Europe as far as Asia Minor.
Habitat   Broadleaf woodland, gardens, orchards; rarely found at an altitude of more than 3300 feet.

Behavior   This dormouse feeds on berries, fruit, and insects, which it eats while holding them between its front feet. It is nocturnal but can sometimes be seen moving about in the daytime as well. It is very agile, and can even climb up and down relatively smooth surfaces with ease. In the autumn, before entering hibernation, and when food is plentiful, it accumulates a reserve of fat. Hibernation starts in September–October and is spent curled up (usually alone) in a tight ball in a tree hollow or in a burrow in the ground. As soon as it rouses itself from its lethargy, around April, the mating season starts. In a nest lined with moss and other plant material, the female gives birth to 2–7 young which reach their adult size within 3 months. In some instances several families unite to form a colony.

201 MUSCARDINUS AVELLANARIUS
Hazel, or common, dormouse

Classification Order Rodentia, Family Gliridae.
Description The coat is tawny on the back, yellowish under-neath, and the throat is white. The tail is covered with short, dense, tawny fur. The eyes are black; the ears small. The front legs are shorter than the hind legs. There are 4 toes on the front foot and 4 on the hind foot, all having short claws. Length of head and body 6–9 cm (2.4–3.6 in), tail 7–7.5 cm (2.8–3 in); weight 15–40 g (0.5–1.4 oz).
Distribution Europe, from the Pyrenees to the Volga.

Habitat Mountains and hilly regions; in woodlands, conifer-ous forests, and among mountain pine.
Behavior This tiny dormouse feeds mainly on hazelnuts, and occasionally on insects, birds' eggs, and nestlings. It is mainly nocturnal and sleeps through the day. It is solitary, or found in family groups of female and young. It hibernates from October or November until the latter half of April. It lives in a spherical nest made of grasses, moss, feathers, and hair, located on the ground hidden in undergrowth or in bushes at a height of up to 6.5 feet. The female delivers 1 litter a year after a 4-week ges-tation. The 3–7 young become independent when they are about 35 days old.

202 GRAPHIURUS MURINUS
Common African dormouse

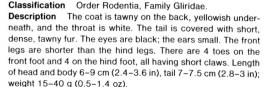

Classification Order Rodentia, Family Gliridae.
Description The general color of the body is some shade of gray and there are various black and white markings on the face. The hairs on the tail are quite long, and are dark on the top and paler beneath. There is much variation in color from place to place. The cranium has a flattened shape, and the ears are large and rounded. Length of head and body up to 10 cm (4 in), tail slightly shorter; weight about 160 g (5.3 oz).
Distribution Africa south of the Sahara.

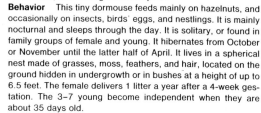

Habitat Forests or open savannas; ranges from river valleys to arid rocky highlands.
Behavior This solitary dormouse is mainly nocturnal but in areas of dense vegetation it may also be active during the day. It builds its nest in vegetation, on branches, in hollows of trees, in the thick of a bush, or in some cases among rocks. It often comes into houses and dwells in ceilings or under the roof. It feeds on fruit and seeds, as well as on eggs, lizards, and in-sects. Its vocalizations may be loud and shrill. Litters of 2–5 may be born several times a year after a gestation period of about 4 weeks. The offspring are independent by about 5 weeks of age.

203 ELIOMYS QUERCINUS
Garden dormouse

Classification   Order Rodentia, family Gliridae.

Description   Reddish brown in color on the back and off-white on the belly. The tail is black at its base and white towards the much thicker tip. A black stripe runs from the side of the snout, around the eye and behind the ear. The ears are large. Length of head and body 10–17 cm (4–6.7 in), tail 9–12 cm (3.5–4.7 in); weight 50–120 g (1.8–4.2 oz).

Distribution   Europe except for Scandinavia, Ireland, England, and the coastal regions of the north, extending eastward past the Ural mountains; North Africa.

Habitat   Broadleaf woodlands, sometimes also coniferous woods; parks and orchards.

Behavior   It lives at low altitudes, preferably in sunny areas. Although the dormouse is a good climber it more often moves about on the ground—normally only during the night. Generally solitary, it may be found in small, very noisy groups. Its nest may be among stones on the ground or in natural hollows in trees. Dormice hibernate throughout the winter and mate on waking. The female gives birth to 2–7 young between the end of May and June, after a gestation period of about 20 days. It feeds on fruit and small animals and often enters houses in search of food.

204 JACULUS JACULUS
Desert jerboa

Classification   Order Rodentia, Family Dipodidae.

Description   Like the other members of this family, Dipodidae, the overall appearance of the desert jerboa is like that of a kangaroo, mainly because of the very long hind legs. Its coat is cream or beige dorsally, white below. The tail is long and has a tuft of white hairs at the tip; it is used rather like a tiller or rudder when the jerboa jumps. Length of head and body 10–15 cm (4–6 in), tail 15–25 cm (6–10 in); weight 50–70 g (1.8–2.5 oz).

Distribution   North Africa, Arabia, central Asia.

Habitat   Desert and steppe.

Behavior   This solitary nocturnal rodent starts moving about in search of food after sundown. It eats seeds, roots, and insects, from which it extracts the water required for its survival. It is agile and has highly developed senses of smell, sight, and hearing. Gestation lasts about 30 days, and the female usually gives birth to 3 young. There may be more than 1 litter a year; the young are independent after a few weeks. The courting behavior of the male is interesting. He puts himself in an upright position in front of the prospective mate, then lowers his face to the height of the mate, and finally, slaps her rhythmically with his front legs.

205 HYSTRIX CRISTATA
Crested porcupine

Classification   Order Rodentia, Family Hystricidae.
Description   On the back and the tail it has distinctive spines which are elastic and erectile and can reach a length of 30–40 cm (12–16 in). The snout is short and flattened and covered with soft hair; the eyes are small and the ears short. The soles of the feet are hairless and the big toe is very small. Length of head and body 57–68 cm (22.8–27.2 in), tail 5–12 cm (2–5 in); weight 18–26 kg (39.6–57.2 lb).
Distribution   Central southern Italy, North Africa, and central western Africa.
Habitat   Dry, rocky hill country, with vegetation.
Behavior   This porcupine is mainly nocturnal; by day it rests among rocks or in holes in the ground. It feeds on fruit, roots, and bulbs—it nibbles while holding the food between its front feet. When in danger the porcupine erects the spines on its back and tail and makes them vibrate with a distinctive, rattling sound. It is a solitary animal. Gestation lasts for about 8 weeks and the litter has 2–4 young in it. At birth the young have soft spines but by the time they are 10 days old the spines have hardened and taken on the texture of those of an adult individual. The young nurse for about 3 months. There may be 2 litters in a year.

---

206 ERETHIZON DORSATUM
American porcupine

Classification   Order Rodentia, Family Erethizontidae.
Description   The body is stout and the legs and tail are short. The body and tail are covered with yellowish white spines with brown-black tips. The spines are longest on the lower part of the back and the hindquarters, and shortest on the cheeks. The pelage is quite variable in color, ranging from yellow to nearly black. The soles of the feet are hairless; the front foot has 4 clawed toes and the hind foot has 5 clawed toes. Length of head and body 64–103 cm (25.2–40.5 in), tail 14–30 cm (5.5–12 in); weight 9–18 kg (20–40 lb).
Distribution Canada, the United States, and northern Mexico.
Habitat   Varied: northern forests to tundra and desert regions.
Behavior   In the winter months this porcupine's diet consists mainly of the inner bark of trees, but in summer the diet includes roots, leaves, berries, flowers, and seeds. It nests in trees and climbs well. For much of the year it is solitary but in winter, several individuals may share a nest, which is generally made in a hollow tree, a cave, or a log. It is active during the day and at night. Mating occurs in autumn; after a gestation period of 205–217 days the female, which has four nipples, gives birth to a single young (2 on rare occasions). The offspring is well developed at birth: it is born with its eyes open and can climb almost immediately. One hour after birth the quills have hardened. It is completely independent after a few weeks.

207 COENDOU PREHENSILIS
Prehensile-tailed porcupine

Classification   Order Rodentia, Family Erethizontidae.
Description   The body is covered with short, thick spines which are whitish or yellowish in color, mixed with darker hair, while the underside is grayish. The tail is less spiny and is prehensile, with the tip curling upward so as to get a better grip on the branches of trees. All four feet are also able to hold on to branches firmly; all are 4-toed and have claws. Length of head and body up to 55 cm (22 in), tail to 45 cm (18 in); weight to 4 kg (9 lb).
Distribution   From Mexico throughout much of South America.
Habitat   Tropical forests.
Behavior   This shy, nocturnal porcupine is solitary or else lives in a pair in the branches of trees, from which it rarely descends to the ground. It shows little fear if it happens to be caught. It is not aggressive but will defend itself ferociously if attacked. Its diet consists of leaves, fruit, and small fresh twigs and shoots. As a rule the female gives birth to a single young in the spring. The newborn porcupine is covered with red hairs and small spines which harden shortly after birth. This creature can easily be tamed enough to keep in captivity.

---

208 CAVIA PORCELLUS
Domestic guinea pig

Classification   Order Rodentia, Family Caviidae.
Description   The coat varies a great deal in color: white, black, gray, and also spotted or dappled with white, yellow, and black. Like the wild guinea pig, from which the domestic form derives, it has a large head, large eyes, and round ears; and like the other species belonging to the family Caviidae, its molar teeth are rootless and permanently growing. The front feet have 4 toes and the hind 5. The female has 2 nipples. Length of head and body 22–34 cm (8.8–13.6 in), tail very short; weight 450–700 g (1–1.5 lb).
Distribution   In labs and as pets around the world; as farm animals in Latin America. The map represents what is believed to have been its original distribution before domestication—in Brazil and Paraguay.
Habitat   In areas with dense vegetation.
Behavior   The domestic guinea pig is widely used as a laboratory animal for various types of research, especially in the fields of medicine and pharmacology. In the natural state, a closely related wild guinea pig, *Cavia aperez*, is a nocturnal creature which feeds on all types of plants. It lives in groups of 5–10 individuals, and uses well-established paths in its search of food. In the domestic state it is extremely adaptable. Gestation lasts for 68 days and each litter has 2–4 young which reach sexual maturity when they are 55–70 days old.

209 DOLICHOTIS PATAGONUM
Patagonian cavy

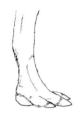

Classification Order Rodentia, Family Caviidae.
Description Its appearance reminds one of a hare because of its long ears and its long, slender legs. The shape of the claws also resembles that of a hoof. The coat is gray-brown, but white on the inside of the tail, which serves as an alarm signal when the members of the group are threatened. Length of head and body 69–75 cm (27.6–30 in), tail about 4 cm (1.6 in); weight 9–15 kg (20–33 lb).
Distribution Patagonia.
Habitat Pampas.
Behavior This diurnal creature feeds on grasses and other plants and lives in small groups of 10–15 individuals. It is a swift runner and makes leaps of up to 6.5 feet. It digs its den in the ground, or else uses burrows of other animals, such as armadillos. Inside the den the female prepares a nest in which she gives birth to 2 or 3 young after a gestation of 80–90 days. Her 4 nipples are situated on the sides of her body (2 axillary, and 2 inguinal) and this enables her to suckle her young sitting on the hind legs with the front legs extended forward. The offspring are independent after a few weeks, and reach sexual maturity at about 2 months.

210 HYDROCHAERIS HYDROCHAERIS
Capybara, carpincho

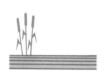

Classification Order Rodentia, Family Hydrochaeridae.
Description The head is large with a rounded snout; the eyes are conspicuous and the ears are small and round, it is almost completely tailless. Its overall appearance is one of bulkiness. The front feet are 4-toed, the hind 3-toed, and the toes on the hind feet are joined together by a membrane. The molars are extremely complex, rootless, and in a state of constant growth. The female has 10 nipples. Length of head and body, 100–130 cm (40–52 in); height up to 50 cm (20 in); weight to 50 kg (110 lb).
Distribution Panama south to northern Argentina and Uruguay.
Habitat Forests and pampas near water.
Behavior The largest of all the rodents, the capybara is active throughout the day in areas where it is not hunted much. It gathers in small groups which go in search of food together. The diet consists mainly of aquatic plants. Capybaras are very good swimmers and when they are not diving below the surface their nostrils are held out of the water, as are their eyes and ears. Gestation lasts for 4–5 months. The single annual litter has 2–8 young, which are independent after a few weeks, but do not reach sexual maturity for a year or more.
Note This animal is hunted by man for its flesh and hide. Its natural enemies are jaguars and crocodilians.

211 DINOMYS BRANICKII
Pacarana

Classification   Order Rodentia, Family Dinomyidae.

Description   The coat is dark brown and black with 2 fairly continuous white stripes running lengthwise along the back and other scattered white markings. On the belly the coat is paler. The ears are short and round, the feet have 4 toes with long, powerful claws. The upper lip is divided by a deep cleft and the vibrissae are very long—almost the length of the whole head. Length of head and body 73–79 cm (29.2–31.6 in), tail about 20 cm (8 in); weight 10–15 kg (22–33 lb).

Distribution   The eastern slopes of the Andean chain from Colombia to Bolivia.

Habitat   Tropical forest.

Behavior   This is a docile and secretive creature about which very little is known. It was discovered for the first time in 1873, and has been thought to be nearing extinction at various times since then. Several have been caught and sent to zoos and, although some have been successfully reared on a diet of fruit, leaves, and plant stems, few have reproduced in captivity—so little is known about their reproductive behavior. Only 1 or 2 young are born in a litter.

212 AGOUTI PACA
Spotted paca

Classification   Order Rodentia, Family Agoutidae.

Description   The large, powerful body is covered with a hispid coat that is dark brown and black with white markings and stripes on the back. The legs are stocky, the front feet are 4-toed, and the hind feet are 5-toed. The head is large and has conspicuous eyes; the ears are of average size. The female has 4 nipples. Length of head and body 60–79 cm (24–31.6 in), tail 2–3 cm (about 1 in).

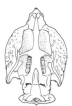

Distribution   From southern Mexico to Brazil.

Habitat   Forest, near waterways.

Behavior   The spotted paca is nocturnal and spends the daylight hours resting in its den, which is dug out among the roots of trees or among rocks, along riverbanks or on mountainsides. The den has several exits which are often concealed among foliage. It feeds on leaves, roots, and fruit. It is a very able swimmer and takes refuge in water if threatened by some danger. It is mostly solitary. The female gives birth twice a year to a single young—rarely 2. The spotted paca is hunted for its fat and tasty flesh.

213 DASYPROCTA LEPORINA
Agouti

Classification Order Rodentia, Family Dasyproctidae.
Description The body is covered with a dense, soft, yellowish, brown, or sometimes white fur. The legs are long; the front feet have 4 toes, and the hind 3. The ears are quite large, and the eyes are of average size. The female has 8 nipples. Length of head and body 42–62 cm (16.8–24.8), tail 1–3 cm (0.4–1.2 in); weight 1.5–4 kg (3.3–8.8 lb).
Distribution Northeastern South America.

Habitat Cultivated land, damp woodlands, and savanna.
Behavior This solitary, entirely herbivorous rodent feeds on roots, tender stems, grass, and fruit. It is active by night, and spends the daylight hours hiding in lairs made in hollows in trees or in cracks and crannies in the ground. If, however, it finds itself in an area where man poses a threat it adapts to a completely nocturnal way of life. The lair consists of various chambers and long passages which lead directly to areas where there is an abundance of food. This agouti frequently causes serious damage to sugar cane plantations. Gestation lasts 3 months and the female usually bears 2 young, twice a year. The offspring are completely independent after a few months.

---

214 LAGOSTOMUS MAXIMUS
Plains viscacha

Classification Order Rodentia, Family Chinchillidae.
Description This animal is entirely covered with a hispid coat. The head is quite large, and the ears are of average size. The front legs are short, with small, 4-toed feet; the hind feet have 3 toes with powerful claws. Facial markings are distinctive. The female has 4 nipples. Length of head and body 47–66 cm (18.8–26.4 in), tail 15–20 cm (6–8 in); weight about 7 kg (15.4 lb), but up to 9 kg (20 lb).
Distribution Argentina and southeastern Bolivia.
Habitat Pampas.

Behavior This viscacha lives in groups which can number up to 50 individuals. Underground burrows house the entire colony and have various entrances and chambers. It emerges from its burrow at night to forage for food—grass, roots, and other plant matter. It has been much hunted because of its burrowing and digging activities, which cause a great deal of damage because horses may trip in the holes or even break their legs. The most unlikely objects crop up in their burrows, because the viscacha hordes anything and everything it comes across. Other animals also take up residence in the viscacha's burrow—lizards, snakes, and burrowing owls. The gestation period lasts for 154 days, after which 1–4 young are born. One litter per year is born in the southern part of its range, and two in the north.

215 LAGIDIUM VISCACCIA
Mountain viscacha

Classification   Order Rodentia, Family Chinchillidae.

Description   The coat is dense, soft, and woolly, and is tawny all over except for the paws and belly, which are paler. The ears are large and the vibrissae are quite long. Both the hind and front feet have 4 toes, and the legs are somewhat frail. The soles of the feet are hairless. The female has 4 nipples. Length of head and body 32.8–40 cm (12.8–16 in), tail 23–32 cm (9.2–12.8 in); weight 1–1.5 kg (2.2–3.3 lb).

Distribution   The Andes.

Habitat   Mountainous regions with many rocks and little vegetation.

Behavior   The mountain viscacha lives in large colonies on rocky mountainsides, finding hideaways in the clefts in rocks. It is very agile, and moves with ease in inaccessible terrain. It is diurnal and feeds on grass and plants. Should some threat or danger approach while it is feeding or playing near its burrow, males acting as sentries make a distinctive call to alert their group members. Mating takes place in October–November and after a period of about 3 months, the female gives birth to a single young.

Note   One of the largest of the chinchillids, the mountain viscacha has been extensively hunted for its fur, even though it is not so highly prized as that of its "cousin," *Chinchilla lanigera* (**216**).

---

216 CHINCHILLA LANIGERA
Chinchilla

Classification   Order Rodentia, Family Chinchillidae.

Description   The soft, dense coat is a distinctive silver-gray. In appearance the chinchilla closely resembles a squirrel, with a bushy, plumelike tail. The ears are quite long and the eyes are large. The female has 6 nipples. Length of head and body about 25 cm (10 in), tail about 17.5 cm (7 in); weight about 500 g (1.1 lb).

Distribution   Originally from the southern Andes in Chile; now bred on ranches worldwide.

Habitat   In the wild state it prefers semidesert terrain and rocky mountainsides.

Behavior   The chinchilla has now almost completely disappeared from the wild because of the merciless hunting for its highly prized fur. It is active at night, but it can also be observed during the day at the entrance to its burrow. It feeds on roots, tubers, bulbs, and mosses, which it holds tightly in its front feet and moves up to its mouth for a nibble. It is fairly easy to rear in captivity. In a year, it can have three litters, with 1–6 young in each (but usually 2). Unfortunately, the coat of the ranch-bred chinchilla is not as beautiful and uniform as that of the chinchilla living in the natural state.

Note   The map shows the original distribution of the species.

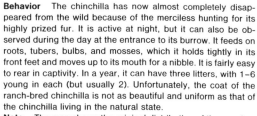

217 GEOCAPROMYS BROWNII
Jamaican hutia

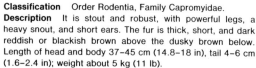

Classification   Order Rodentia, Family Capromyidae.
Description   It is stout and robust, with powerful legs, a heavy snout, and short ears. The fur is thick, short, and dark reddish or blackish brown above the dusky brown below. Length of head and body 37–45 cm (14.8–18 in), tail 4–6 cm (1.6–2.4 in); weight about 5 kg (11 lb).
Distribution   The island of Jamaica in the Caribbean.
Habitat   Forests and rocky areas.
Behavior   This nocturnal hutia feeds on roots, bark, shoots, fruit, and foliage of many different plants. Its gait is usually waddling but it can run fast when startled. It can jump and climb well, but spends most of its time on the ground. It is basically solitary but sometimes is found in small family groups up to 5 or 6 (rarely, 8–10). It bears 1 or 2 (rarely 3) young after about 123 days of gestation. Most females bear 2 litters a year. The young are quite precocial; they are able to move about and eat solid food within 2 days of birth. Because of its secretive habits and its habitat in areas of exposed limestone with an abundance of natural crevices, it is still relatively widely distributed in remote hills despite intensive hunting in earlier years and some hunting today.
Note   The Capromyidae occur only on islands in the Caribbean region, and are rather diverse. There are 12 living species in this family; another 28 species recently became extinct, largely because of hunting by humans.

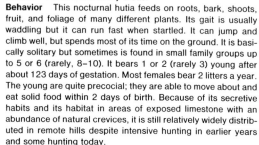

218 MYOCASTOR COYPUS
Coypu, nutria

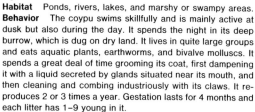

Classification   Order Rodentia, Family Myocastoridae.
Description   The body is covered with a soft, dense, slate-colored coat with long bristles. The tail is covered with scales and is round. The eyes and ears are small, and the snout has long vibrissae. The hind feet are partly webbed and, like the front feet, hairless. The incisors are large, conspicuous, and yellow. Length of head and body 40–65 cm (16–26 in), tail 30–45 cm (12–17.7 in); weight 7–9 kg (15.4–19.8 lb).
Distribution   Originally from southern South America, introduced into Europe and the United States (for farming and rearing).
Habitat   Ponds, rivers, lakes, and marshy or swampy areas.
Behavior   The coypu swims skillfully and is mainly active at dusk but also during the day. It spends the night in its deep burrow, which is dug on dry land. It lives in quite large groups and eats aquatic plants, earthworms, and bivalve molluscs. It spends a great deal of time grooming its coat, first dampening it with a liquid secreted by glands situated near its mouth, and then cleaning and combing industriously with its claws. It reproduces 2 or 3 times a year. Gestation lasts for 4 months and each litter has 1–9 young in it.
Note   This animal is reared for its highly prized coat, from which the coarser bristles are removed to leave the fine underfur. The map shows its original distribution.

219 CTENOMYS PERUANUS
Peruvian tuco-tuco

Classification   Order Rodentia, Family Ctenomyidae.
Description   The genus *Ctenomys* includes more than 30 species, with the coat varying in color from dark brown or pale brown to tawny-gray or tawny-white. The head is somewhat thickset and has small eyes and ears. The incisors are large and prominent. The front legs are slightly shorter than the hind legs and all the toes (5 on each foot) have powerful claws designed for digging. The female has 6 nipples. Length of head and body 17–25 cm (6.8–10 in), tail 6–11 cm (2.4–4.4 in); weight 300–500 g (0.7–1.1 lb).

Distribution   Southern Peru. The map shows the combined range of several species of Andean tuco-tucos.
Habitat   In arid, sandy terrain in steppes, grasslands, and upland plateaus.

Behavior   This is mainly a solitary animal, which spends much of its life under the surface of the land, digging long tunnels to a depth of up to 10 feet. This tunnel system, the entrances to which are easily detectable by the small mounds of earth nearby, consists of a main corridor from which various blind alleys and secondary tunnels branch off. There is a nesting chamber, lined with grass, and various storage rooms. In addition to their rightful owners these burrows often house lizards, mice, and other creatures. Gestation lasts for about 105 days and there is usually 1 litter a year with 1–5 young in it.
Note   The cry emitted by this creature is a distinctive "tuco-tuco-tuco."

220 OCTODON DEGUS
Degu

Classification   Order Rodentia, Family Octodontidae.
Description   The soft coat is yellow-brown dorsally and cream-colored underneath; the distal half of the tail is black, with a black tuft. The ears are quite large, dark and sparsely furred. The legs are pale grey and have 4 well-developed toes; the fifth toe is much smaller. The hind feet have long bristles projecting over the claws. The female has 8 nipples. Length of head and body 25–31 cm (10–12.2 in), tail 7–13 cm (2.8–5 in); weight about 250 g (8.8 oz).
Distribution   Chile.
Habitat   Open areas, thickets, and stone walls.

Behavior   The degu feeds on grass, bark, leaves, and seeds. Although it does not hibernate, it puts aside a food reserve for the winter months. It lives in colonies and may reach a population density of 75 per hectare. It can best be seen in early morning or late afternoon, running with its tail in the air or climbing in bushes and trees in search of food. The burrow is a complex network of underground chambers and tunnels, the entrances to which are often covered with twigs or cow dung. It reproduces twice a year. After the gestation period of 90 days the female gives birth to 4–6 young which are born hairless and blind. After 4–6 weeks the young are weaned and the adults bring grass and leaves to the nest for them. The young may reach sexual maturity as early as 45 days, but usually later.

221 THRYONOMYS SWINDERIANUS
Great cane rat

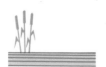

Classification   Order Rodentia, Family Thryonomyidae.

Description   This large rodent has a stocky, powerful body and short legs. Typically, this rat's tail is covered with short, sparse hairs which are almost spiny. The coat is brown with a variety of shading ranging from beige and gray to off-white in the lower parts of the body. The female has 6 nipples. Length of head and body up to 60 cm (23.6 in), tail 7–25 cm (2.8–10 in); weight to 8 kg (17.6 lb).

Distribution   From Senegal to Somalia, and south to South Africa, except Madagascar.

Habitat   Damp or humid areas near lakes and marshes, but also in arid regions.

Behavior   This rat generally leads a solitary existence or lives in pairs, but only rarely in larger groups. It is nocturnal, and spends the day in its burrows (which are sometimes the abandoned burrows of aardvarks). It can swim well. It is a vegetarian and has a liking for roots, fruit, the bark of trees, and tender shrubs. It can easily cause considerable damage to crops. The litter is dropped among vegetation or in the burrow after a gestation of 155 days; the 2–4 young are born with fur and can quickly follow their mother. They are weaned after a few weeks, and are sexually mature in about a year. There are 2 litters a year.

222 HETEROCEPHALUS GLABER
Naked mole rat, naked sand rat

Classification   Order Rodentia, Family Bathyergidae.

Description   This is the only member of the order Rodentia that is basically hairless (except for scattered tactile hairs near its mouth). The skin is reddish or yellowish. The head is thick-set, the eyes are very small, and there are no external parts of the ear. The feet are wide, each with 5 toes with short claws. On the feet are stiff hairs that project to the sides and beyond the toes and effectively broaden the foot when it is used to move soil. Length of head and body 8–9 cm (3.2–3.6 in), tail 3.5–4 cm (1.4–1.6 in); weight 40–80 g (1.4–2.8 oz).

Distribution   Northern Kenya, Somalia, and eastern Ethiopia.

Habitat   Sandy terrain in arid regions.

Behavior   Mole rats live in quite large colonies of up to 100 individuals and spend their whole lives underground; not surprisingly, their diet consists of roots, tubers, and bulbs. They are most active in the morning and afternoon. They dig intricate tunnel systems in the ground at a depth varying from 1–40 inches. Loose earth is pushed out of the burrow by the hind feet, up to a distance of 10–12 inches. It has been reported that most or all reproduction in a colony is by one female only; she will produce a number of large litters in the course of the year.

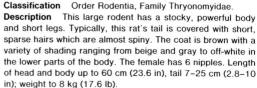

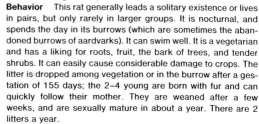

WHALES AND DOLPHINS,

CARNIVORES INCLUDING SEALS

223 INIA GEOFFRENSIS
Boutu or Amazon porpoise

Classification   Order Cetacea, Family Iniidae.
Description   It is gray on the back and paler on the under-side. It often has a pinkish hue. There are a few hairs on the nose. The eyes are very small. It has 25–33 teeth in each half-jaw; the teeth are small and in general conical in shape, but the posterior teeth tend to have a lower second cusp or ledge at the inner edge. Total length can exceed 3 m (10 ft); weight up to 110 kg (242 lb).

Distribution   The upper Amazon basin as far as 1500 miles from the mouth of the river. Also found in the upper Orinoco.
Habitat   Freshwater rivers and lakes.
Behavior   This porpoise usually swims in pairs or in small groups, sometimes in association with another species of freshwater cetacean of the genus *Sotalia*. When swimming, the long snout is kept under the water so that only the back breaks the water surface. It rarely jumps out of the water, and will only do so when at play. It feeds on fishes which it rouses from the muddy riverbed and catches when they are closer to the sur-face. It also feeds on piranha. It breathes every 30–40 sec-onds, with a maximum interval of 110 seconds. A single calf is born, already about 32 inches long.

224 BERARDIUS BAIRDII
Baird's beaked whale

Classification   Order Cetacea, Family Ziphiidae.
Description   The body is cylindrical with a distinctive pointed snout and a rounded forehead. The tail fin can be as wide as 3.5 m (11.5 ft). The body is bluish dark-gray with paler areas of varied size on the underside. Scars on the body are often clearly visible. The first and second cervical vertebrae are sometimes fused. On each side of the mandible, or lower jaw, there are 2 pair of large teeth set about 20 cm (8 in) apart. Total length up to 12.8 m (42 ft), weight to 11,380 kg (12 t); female usually slightly longer than the male.

Distribution . Northwestern Pacific Ocean as far as the Sea of Japan. Never found north of the Bering Strait.
Habitat   Offshore waters at least 1000 meters deep in the northern Pacific.
Behavior   This whale moves about in small groups, or pods, of 10–30 individuals of both sexes. When swimming it makes several short dives, and then a longer dive which may last as much as 20–30 minutes. If threatened it can remain sub-merged for more than an hour. Mating occurs in February and the single young, about 14.7 feet in length, is born in Decem-ber. Gestation lasts 519 days, the longest known for any ceta-cean.

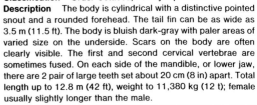

225 PHYSETER MACROCEPHALUS
Sperm whale

Classification   Order Cetacea, Family Physeteridae.

Description   The enormous head makes up at least a third of the entire body; the lower jaw is narrow and pointed. The head is filled for the most part with the reserve of sperm oil. The dorsal fin is little more than a curved hump on the back. The first cervical vertebra is free, while the others are fused together. Only the lower jaw is equipped with teeth (20–30 on each side). The layer of fat (blubber) reaches a thickness of 30 cm (12 in) and accounts for a third of the animal's total weight. Total length up to 18 m (60 ft), weight about 36,000 kg (40 t); females about 80% of length of male, 50–60% of weight.

Distribution   Oceans throughout the world between latitude 70° N and latitude 70° S.

Habitat   Coastal and deep waters, rarely found farther than 300 miles from the coast.

Behavior   The sperm whale travels in small pods consisting of one or two large males and several females; males migrate from warmer to colder waters in accordance with the time of year. It feeds on molluscs. It is often possible to see on the head the traces of wounds incurred during skirmishes as with giant octopus or squid. Mating takes place around April, and one calf is born after a gestation period of 16 months. The female reaches sexual maturity at about 9 years; the male, at about 25.

226 DELPHINAPTERUS LEUCAS
Beluga, or white, whale

Classification   Order Cetacea, Family Monodontidae.

Description   The body is cream-white in adults and a darker bluish gray in the young. There are 8–10 teeth on each side of each jaw, each tooth about 2 cm (0.8 in) in diameter. There is a low ridge on the back but no dorsal fin and the lateral fins are rounded. The cranium is asymmetrical and the blowhole is situated to the left. Total length up to 5.5 m (18 ft), weight 1575 kg (3500 lb); females somewhat smaller.

Distribution   Arctic coasts of Europe, Asia, and North America.

Habitat   Coastal waters, estuaries, and some larger rivers.

Behavior   This whale moves about in pods often of 20–200 individuals. It swims slowly and barely exposes its body to the air when it comes to the surface to breathe. The gestation period lasts for a year after which one young is born in April–June. It feeds on bottom fish and molluscs. It migrates regularly from north to south in the fall and returns in the spring. It will often swim up the large rivers in its distribution area such as the Yukon and the St. Lawrence, and has even been sighted in the Rhine.

Note   Today the total world population is estimated at more than 40,000 individuals.

227 MONODON MONOCEROS
Narwhal

Classification Order Cetacea, Family Monodontidae.
Description The color of the body varies with age; the new-born narwhal is blue-gray, and after it is weaned it becomes black or blue-black. As an individual matures, it develops white stripes and markings in the anal region; the genital region, and the umbilical region, until the entire underside and the sides of the body are so covered. The adult is cream-white on the underside and mottled dark-gray to black on the back. The distinctive feature of the narwhal is the tusk, a specialized tooth which is found in males and sometimes in females, and which can reach a length of 3 m (10 ft). It is straight, slender, and spiraled, and issues from the upper lip (there are no functional teeth). The mouth is small, narrow, and turned upward at the corners. The lateral fins are of moderate size; there is no dorsal fin. Length (excluding tusk) up to 4.6 m (15 ft); weight up to 1350 kg (3000 lb) in males and 900 kg (2000 lb) in females.
Distribution Arctic Seas between latitude 70° N and latitude 80° N.

Habitat Very cold seas.
Behavior It feeds on fishes, cephalopods (octopus, squid), and crustaceans. It lives in pods of 6–20 individuals of the same sex; or of both sexes. Gestation lasts 14–15 months and the single newborn calf is 5 feet long. The sounds made by the narwhal, which resemble gargling, roaring, mooing, and whistling are probably associated with respiration.

228 CEPHALORHYNCHUS COMMERSONII
Commerson's dolphin

Classification Order Cetacea, Family Delphinidae.
Description The forehead is less pronounced than that of many other dolphins. The distinctive coloring makes it easy to identify; the head and dorsal part from the fin up to and including the tail are black; the rest of the body is white. It has 30 small pointed teeth, on each side of each jaw, above and below. Total length about 1.5 m (5 ft); weight about 50 kg (112 lb).
Distribution Southern waters off Patagonia and Tierra del Fuego, and as far east as South Georgia.

Habitat Coastal waters, bays, and fjords.
Behavior Little is known about this dolphin, and sightings are rare. It lives in small groups of 3–5 individuals and feeds on krill and small fishes; the shape of the mouth suggests that it does not eat large prey. It does not seem to have a migratory pattern and the species is rarely found north of latitude 40° S. It readily enters the mouths of rivers even if the water there is cloudy and muddy, unlike the other dolphins which carefully avoid such environments.
Note The distribution of this species may extend to the Kerguelen Islands, where the genus has been definitely sighted, but the species has not been identified for certain.

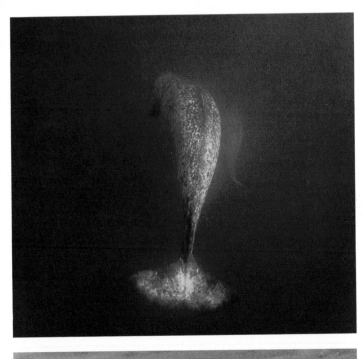

229 STENELLA ATTENUATA
Spotted dolphin

Classification   Order Cetacea, Family Delphinidae.

Description   The upper parts of the body are blackish; the sides are grayish gradually fading on the underside to almost white. The fins are black and there is a black stripe running from the corner of the mouth to the lateral fins. The rostrum, or beak, is relatively short and very dark; the eyes are surrounded by a black ring. The dorsal parts are covered with paler markings and the lower parts have darker spots, although these are not always easy to see. There are 37–39 teeth on each side of both the upper and lower jaw. Total length up to 2.4 m (8 ft), weight to 115 kg (253 lb).

Distribution   Tropical parts of the Atlantic, Pacific, and Indian Oceans.

Habitat   Deep ocean waters.

Behavior   This dolphin lives in pods of 20–50 individuals which hunt fish together. It can swim rapidly, reaching a speed of about 20 mph. Its distribution seems to be associated with the water temperature, which must range from 26–30° C (79–86° F.) After a gestation of 11–12 months, a single calf, 3.3–4 feet in length is born.

Note   In recent years, thousands of spotted dolphins, trapped in nets set for tuna in the Pacific Ocean, have drowned because they are unable to break free and reach the surface to breathe.

---

230 DELPHINUS DELPHIS
Common dolphin

Classification   Order Cetacea, Family Delphinidae.

Description   This species has been divided into subspecies occurring in different seas or oceans and details of local populations need further study. The color, size, and length of snout vary from place to place as well as from one individual to another. There are 40–50 teeth on each side of each jaw; the first two cervical vertebrae are fused. The fins are all markedly pointed and triangular. Total length up to 2.6 m (8.5 ft), weight to 140 kg (308 lb); female slightly smaller.

Distribution   All the seas and oceans in the world except the polar seas; frequent in the Mediterranean and the Black Sea.

Habitat   Coastal and open waters, but rarely near shore or in shallow water.

Behavior   This dolphin swims in pods of 10–100 individuals, but has been sighted in groups of more than 1000. It migrates continuously throughout the year; in the Atlantic its migratory route takes it from the Mediterranean to the coasts of America, following a circular itinerary. It can swim up to speeds of 25 knots, and is often seen playing near ships. It feeds on fish. Mating takes place in summer and autumn and gestation lasts for about 11 months, after which a single calf 3.3–4 feet long, is born. Dolphins become sexually mature after 3 or 4 years and can live as long as 25–30 years.

231 TURSIOPS TRUNCATUS
Bottle-nosed dolphin

Classification   Order Cetacea, Family Delphinidae.
Description   The basic color is a silvery gray. In the southern parts of its range the color tends to be darker. The ''beak'' is short and the mouth seems to be permanently smiling. The lower jaw protrudes farther than the upper. There are 23–25 teeth on each side of each jaw, each tooth about 1 cm (0.4'') across. The dorsal fin has a distinctive triangular shape, angled backwards. Total length up to 3.9 m (12 ft); average weight about 227 kg (500 lb) but may reach 650 kg (1430 lb).
Distribution   In all temperate seas.
Habitat   Coastal waters on the continental shelf primarily, but also the open sea.
Behavior   This is the dolphin best known to the general public. Its exploits and intelligence have received much attention. These dolphins live in pods usually numbering about a dozen individuals but sometimes as many as several hundred will be in one area. They enjoy approaching ships and following them at the same speed for some time. They also like playing, jumping out of the water, and splashing. This dolphin can swim at a speed of at least 14 knots and dive for more than 6–7 minutes. They feed on all types of fish. Gestation lasts about 12 months; the single calf is about 3.5 feet long at birth and nurses for over a year.
Note   There have been some experiments in training this and other dolphins to perform tasks that might be of practical value to human beings.

232 LAGENORHYNCHUS OBLIQUIDENS
Pacific white-sided dolphin

Classification   Order Cetacea, Family Delphinidae.
Description   The back is black, merging into gray on the sides. The underside is white and separated clearly from the gray sides by a black line which runs from the corners of the mouth along the lateral fins to the anus. The fins are pointed, and the dorsal fin is tall, hooked, and bicolored. There are 29 teeth on each side of the upper jaw, and 32 on each side of the lower jaw. Total length up to 2.5 m (8.3 ft), weight to 140 kg (308 lb).
Distribution   ·The northern Pacific Ocean.
Habitat   Coastal waters, up to 125 miles from the shore.
Behavior   This dolphin lives in large pods sometimes numbering several thousand individuals, although the average is usually about 100. It feeds on small ocean fish, but seems to have a special preference for cuttlefish. The mating season extends through the summer, and gestation lasts for about 1 year. The single young, at birth, is 4 feet long and has a large number of tactile hairs on the snout which disappear with growth. Migration from northern to warmer waters occurrs in the autumn and it appears that migration reaches lower latitudes along the coasts of America than along Asian coasts.

233 GRAMPUS GRISEUS
Risso's dolphin

Classification   Order Cetacea, Family Delphinidae.
Description   The color is quite variable but is usually gray and paler forward of the dorsal fin, but, particularly in younger individuals, the back is bluish. The belly has two whitish areas. The coloring fades with age. There are no teeth in the upper jaw, but in the lower jaw there are 2–7 teeth on each side which are about 3.5 cm (1.4 in) long. The first 6 cervical vertebrae are fused and form a single structure with the seventh, very slender vertebra. Total length up to 4 m (13.2 ft), weight to 700 kg (1540 lb).
Distribution   Almost all temperate and tropical seas.

Habitat   Deep waters immediately off the coast.
Behavior   This dolphin usually lives in small groups of 2–5 individuals, but groups can sometimes number 40–50. It does not swim very fast but shows considerable endurance. It can remain underwater for up to half an hour if necessary, but normally surfaces in a few minutes. It can be found in all seas at all times of year, although it is most frequent in more temperate seas in the winter months. It feeds primarily on cuttlefish. In the Northern Hemisphere the single young is born in December and is about half the length of its mother.

234 ORCINUS ORCA
Orca, killer whale

Classification   Order Cetacea, Family Delphinidae.
Description   The black and white color is distinctive. An easy way to identify this species is by the great length of the dorsal fin, which can reach 1.7 m (68 in) in adult males. The first 3 or 4 cervical vertebrae are fused; there are 10–12 conical teeth on each side of each jaw. Total length up to 9 m (30 ft), weight up to 8100 kg (9 t); females somewhat smaller.
Distribution   All seas, but most abundant in sub-Arctic and sub-Antarctic areas.
Habitat   Coastal waters over the continental shelf; more rarely in open seas.

Behavior   This whale usually lives in pods of 2–8 individuals, sometimes increasing to as many as 30–40; isolated individuals are always males. It attacks any animal which might be considered prey, including penguins, seals, fishes, whales, and other species of dolphins; it is never threatened by predators and is quite unafraid of approaching ships. It can swim at speeds of up to 35 mph and makes huge leaps out of the water. Sometimes it will stay motionless in the water with its head above the surface to see what is going on. It is an intelligent creature and is easy to train. The young are born in winter after a gestation believed to be about 16 months long.

235 GLOBICEPHALA MELAENA
Long-finned pilot whale

Classification   Order Cetacea, Family Delphinidae.

Description   The color is coal-gray, but the underside is paler. The dorsal fin is not very high and is situated on the forward half of the body. The lateral fins are long and pointed. The forehead is markedly bulging and increases in size with age. There are usually 10 (9–12) teeth on each side of each jaw, about 40 in all. Total length up to 6.4 m (21 ft), weight about 2900 kg (3.2 t); females somewhat shorter and only half the weight of males.

Distribution   The Atlantic Ocean in the northern temperate region.

Habitat   Coastal waters, but not close to the shore; rarely oceanic.

Behavior   It lives in pods of 5–20 animals, but in northern waters this number can increase to more than 100. It swims to great depths, more than 3300 feet, and can stay submerged for up to 2 hours. It feeds on fish, especially cuttlefish. There is a migratory movement, but the routes and destinations are not well known. After a 15–16-month gestation a single calf about 6 feet long is born in July–October. It is not fully weaned until about 2 years old, although teeth erupt and feeding on squid begins at about 6–9 months.

Note   These whales occasionally beach themselves, thus virtually committing suicide. Efforts to return them to the sea are frustrated by the fact that as soon as they are back in the water they head straight back to shore.

236 BALAENOPTERA PHYSALUS
Fin whale

Classification   Order Cetacea, Family Balaenopteridae.

Description   Like other rorquals, the fin whale is sleek and fast and has grooves on the throat and belly. The brown-black of the back fades on the sides of the body to pure white on the belly. The upper jaw is completely brown but the lower jaw is black on the left and white on the right. In the mouth there are 350–450 whalebones (plates of baleen) on each side of the upper jaw. Baleen is unique to the suborder Mysticeti and serves as a strainer to capture food (see photograph on page 50). The dorsal fin is set well toward the rear of the body. Length up to 25 m (82 ft), weight to 45,000 kg (50 t).

Distribution   In all the world's oceans.

Habitat   Deep offshore waters, rarely near the coast, never in areas with pack ice.

Behavior   The fin whale is thought to be monogamous and is generally only seen in small groups. It migrates to colder waters in the summer to feed on the abundant krill and fishes there, and then returns in winter to warmer waters in order to reproduce. Gestation lasts for 11 months. At birth the single young whale measures about 22 feet; it nurses for 6 months. It can swim at speeds of more than 23 mph and can stay submerged under normal circumstances for about 30 minutes.

237 BALAENOPTERA MUSCULUS
Blue whale

Classification   Order Cetacea, Family Balaenopteridae.
Description   This is probably the largest animal that ever lived. It is grayish blue with some paler spots and the tips and undersides of the fins are often white. The dorsal fin is very small. The ventral grooves extend to the belly. In the mouth there are 270–400 baleen plates on each side. The enormous stomach can contain up to a ton of food. Average total length about 24 m (80 ft) but can reach 30.5 m (100 ft); average weight 130,000 kg (143 t).

Distribution   Worldwide, but especially in the Southern Hemisphere.
Habitat   Oceanic, as far as the coasts of Antarctica.
Behavior   Data relating to the life history of this species are from fragmentary observations gathered in all the world's seas at various times. In addition the species is now virtually extinct because of overhunting in earlier years and this hampers further study. These whales used to travel in groups of 30–50 animals in a vague formation spread over several miles; it would migrate to the polar regions in the spring and then moved to the open sea in the autumn to spend the winter. It feeds mainly on krill. Mating takes place in summer and the gestation period lasts 11 months. The single calf is 24 feet long at birth.

Note   There are possibly no more than a few thousand of these whales left, or less than 10% of the population probably present before whaling began on a large scale.

---

238 MEGAPTERA NOVAEANGLIAE
Humpback whale

Classification   Order Cetacea, Family Balaenopteridae.
Description   It is gray-black on the back and dark on the underside of the body; the fins are partly white. The entire body is covered unevenly with bumps. The huge pectoral fins are up to 4 m (13.5 ft) long. A good half of the body is covered with about 28 ventral grooves. The mouth contains about 250–350 pair of baleen plates. Average total length 13 m (42 ft) but may reach more than 15 m (50 ft); average weight 26,500 kg (29 t).
Distribution   All oceans.
Habitat   Deep waters near coasts.

Behavior   This whale is unafraid of ships and is easy to approach especially when it spends long periods of time playing, with spectacular leaps out of the water. It travels between cold and warm waters in the summer and winter seasons. This is the famous "singing" whale, whose long vocalizations are more elaborate than in any other known whale song. It feeds on krill and fishes. Gestation lasts 12 months and the young whale, 12–14 feet long at birth, is weaned after 11 months.

Note   This species is one of those most threatened with extinction (there may be fewer than 10,000 now living). It is now protected, but illegal hunting continues, precisely because these whales are so easy to catch.

239 BALAENA GLACIALIS
Right whale

Classification Order Cetacea, Family Balaenidae.
Description The right whale is black and the underside has a few white markings. On the tip of the snout there is a large wart-like growth or "bonnet"; the blubber can be more than 40 cm (16 in) thick. The rear fins are up to 6 m (20 ft) across. There is no dorsal fin. Total length up to 17.5 m (58 ft); average weight 40,000 kg (44 t) but may reach 65,000 kg (71.5 t).
Distribution The Southern Hemisphere between latitudes 20° S and 50° S, and the Northern Hemisphere between latitudes 20° N and 70° N.
Habitat Coastal waters.

Behavior This whale leads a solitary life, or lives as a pair and moves with the seasons from cold to warm waters, but it never enters the polar seas. It feeds exclusively on plankton which it gathers with its long baleen. It swims slowly and punctuates 3 or 4 short breaths with a dive that lasts 15–20 minutes. There are 2 blowholes as in other mysticetes, and the 2 jets of water and exhaled air, up to 27 feet high, can be seen from afar. Mating takes place between February and April and the single calf is born 1 year later, already 16 feet long.
Note This species has been reduced nearly to extinction. Despite the fact that now it is protected no more than 2000–4000 are left throughout the world.

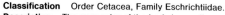

240 ESCHRICHTIUS ROBUSTUS
(California) Gray whale

Classification Order Cetacea, Family Eschrichtiidae.
Description The gray color of the body is usually marked by a profusion of spots, scratches, and other blotches, some caused by the numerous external parasites found on this species. The fins are often damaged. It has no dorsal fin, but the back has 6–14 humps on it. There are 2, or sometimes 4, grooves on the throat. There are about 150 pair of yellowish white baleen plates. The blubber can reach a thickness of 25 cm (10 in). The 7 cervical vertebrae are separate. There are a lot of tactile hairs on the snout and lower jaw. Total length up to 14 m (47 ft), weight to 32,700 kg (36 t).
Distribution Northern Pacific Ocean.
Habitat Coastal waters, often in the lee of beaches in bays and estuaries with very shallow water.

Behavior In the 19th century it was possible to see groups of more than 1000 of these whales, but today it is rare to sight more than 40–70 together at the same time. They migrate southward in separate groups of pregnant females, adult males, and young males, reaching their winter quarters (California and Mexico) in January–February. They then return north again in March–April. It feeds on plankton, and only feeds in the summer months, living off its stored fat for the rest of the year. Mating occurs in February, and the single young, about 15.5 feet long, is born in the same month a year later.

241 CANIS LATRANS
Coyote

Classification   Order Carnivora, Family Canidae.
Description   Similar in appearance to the gray wolf, *Canis lupus* (**242**), the color and texture of the coat varies geographically. Northern coyotes have thicker fur. Black patches may be found on the front of the forelimbs and near the base and tip of the tail. The ears are longer than those of the wolf. Length of head and body 100–135 cm (40–54 in), tail about 40 cm (16 in); weight 15–20 kg (33–44 lb).

Distribution   Central America to Alaska.
Habitat   Plains and open country.
Behavior   The diet is varied and includes small rodents, rabbits, carrion, and small domestic animals. Coyotes are normally observed as lone individuals or as pairs. On occasion large groups are present, but there are no data as to whether or not they hunt in packs. Communication between coyotes employs visual, auditory, olfactory and possibly tactile signals. Like the other members of the family Canidae, (dogs and jackals), it uses feces and urine as olfactory signals to mark its territory. It is a very active creature, and is most active in the early evening, especially in winter. Mating occurs in January–March, and after a gestation period of 60–64 days an average of 6 young are born in a den usually dug by the female. The young are blind and defenseless at birth, and only emerge from the burrow after 2–3 weeks; they nurse for 5–7 weeks, are completely independent at after 6–9 months, and reach sexual maturity in their second year of life.

242 CANIS LUPUS
Gray wolf

Classification   Order Carnivora, Family Canidae.
Description   This is the largest member of the Canidae family; it is a powerful animal and has great endurance. It varies in color from white in Arctic regions to black in parts of North America, but is usually grayish. Color and size vary greatly in the different regions of its range. Length of head and body reaches 120 cm (48 in), tail 30–45 cm (12–18 in); weight 18–80 kg (40–167 lb).

Distribution   Originally throughout the Palaearctic and Nearctic regions; now restricted to northern North America and Asia, and residual populations in Mexico, Europe, and Scandinavia.
Habitat   All habitats and topography except deserts and high mountain tops. It also adapts to environments altered by man.
Behavior   It lives in packs of 5–15 individuals based around a dominant pair and governed by strict domestic hierarchies for both sexes. It hunts in this pack, the preferred prey being large herbivores such as elk, deer, bison, and mountain sheep, but it will also take smaller game, most commonly beaver and domestic animals. Usually only 1 female per pack reproduces. Mating usually occurs once a year in January or February. Gestation lasts for 63 days, after which 4–7 cubs are born. The den is usually in a hole in the ground or in a crevice and is often used year after year.

243 CANIS DINGO
Dingo

Classification   Order Carnivora, Family Canidae.
Description   It resembles a large yellow dog: the color is more or less uniform, sometimes with reddish or beige highlights. The coat is relatively short and hispid; the tail is held fairly high and is curved 25–40 cm at the tip. Length of head and body up to 110 cm (44 in), tail 25–40 cm (10–16 in); weight up to 35 kg (77 lb).
Distribution   Australia, may have arrived along with aboriginal humans.

Habitat   Scrub and semidesert environments.
Behavior   The dingo generally leads a solitary life or lives in pairs. Sometimes, but not regularly, large packs are formed. This was perhaps a useful characteristic when hunting large kangaroos, a difficult task requiring considerable effort and strength. Once the rabbit was introduced into Australia, this species became the dingo's primary prey, followed by the smaller marsupials. Because of man's persecution of the dingo it is now threatened with extinction in large areas of its range. The dingo reproduces once a year, and not twice like the domestic dog. Gestation lasts for 2 months and the female gives birth to 5–7 pups in early spring. The pups are reared by both their parents, and if within a pack, all adult members participate in their care. It is sometimes regarded as a feral population of the domestic dog species.

244 CANIS AUREUS
Golden jackal

Classification   Order Carnivora, Family Canidae.
Description   It is a uniform color between dirty yellow and reddish, with some black on the back. The back of the ear is darker and the tail is reddish with a black tip. Length of head and body 60–75 cm (24–30 in), tail 23–35 cm (9.2–14 in); weight 7–14 kg (15–31 lb).
Distribution   North Africa and throughout the whole of the Sahel; southern Europe and Asia as far east as Thailand.
Habitat   Savanna, grasslands, and arid and open woodlands.

Behavior   This jackal adjusts quickly to environmental changes. It is nocturnal but is also commonly sighted during the daylight hours, especially when the climate is harsh or the weather bad. It feeds on anything that is edible, but prefers rodents, insects, and lizards. A scavenger of larger carcasses as well, the golden jackal has learned to wait until its larger competitors—hyena, lion, African hunting dog—have eaten their fill. It usually lives alone or in pairs, but occasionally forms groups. After about 62 days of gestation 3–8 young are born. They are weaned in 4–6 weeks. The females are sexually mature after 10–11 months, the males after 21–22 months.

245 CANIS SIMENSIS
Simian jackal

Classification   Order Carnivora, Family Canidae.
Description   In size it is between a fox and a wolf, but looks more like the fox, with a pointed face and large ears. The body is lightly built with long legs. It is reddish with a white throat and 2 brick-red collars around its neck. The lower part of the legs is white or whitish. The tail is bushy and has a black tip. Length of head and body up to 100 cm (40 in), tail 30 cm (12 in); weight 10 kg (22 lb).

Distribution   The upland plateau of Ethiopia
Habitat   High montane grassland.
Behavior   Of all the Canidae, this is probably the least known because of the difficulty of studying it in its environment. It lives alone or in pairs, and is active both day and night. It feeds on rodents and other small prey. It is probably territorial. Nothing is known about its reproductive biology.

Note   It is often blamed for destroying sheep, goats, and poultry, and consequently it is hunted ferociously. In addition the destruction of its habitat has reduced the numbers of this species to no more than 400 individuals. A World Wildlife Fund/IUCN international protection project was interrupted recently by the political situation in Ethiopia.

246 ALOPEX LAGOPUS
Arctic fox, blue fox

Classification   Order Carnivora, Family Canidae.
Description   This fox has short legs and a snub face. The soles of its feet are covered with long hairs in the winter, enabling it to walk more easily in fresh snow. The coat is white (except for a few black hairs on the tip of the tail) in winter, but in the summer there are 2 phases: in the first it turns cream-colored with darker color on the back; in the second, the "blue" phase, it takes on various grayish, dark bluish hues. Only some Arctic foxes exhibit both summer phases. Length of head and body 50–70 cm (20–28 in), tail 30–40 cm (12–16 in); weight 3–5 kg (6.6–11 lb) but up to 9 kg (20 lb) has been reported.

Distribution   Arctic and tundra regions of North America and Eurasia; south to the mountainous regions of Scandinavia.
Habitat   Tundra and ice.

Behavior   It lives in burrows, and is mostly nocturnal. It is a monogamous species; pairs remain together throughout the breeding season and perhaps longer. Mating takes place in May–June. After a 49–57-day gestation, an average of 3 or 4 cubs are born (up to 10 have been reported). There is a high mortality rate because of the harsh climatic conditions. It feeds on anything edible: garbage, reindeer droppings, carrion, rodents, birds, eggs, hares, and even berries. Migratory movements may take the Arctic fox several hundred miles from the lair where the young are born.

247 VULPES MACROTIS
Kit fox

Classification Order Carnivora, Family Canidae.
Description It is typically foxlike in appearance with a lean body, large ears, and a long, plume-shaped tail. The legs are long and slender. The color of the coat varies geographically; but is usually gray on the back, paler on the sides, and light buff to white on the underside. The tail is darker toward the tip. The female has 8 nipples. Length of head and body up to 52 cm (20.8 in), tail 26–32 cm (10.4–12.8 in); weight 1.5–2.8 kg (3.3–6 lb).
Distribution Western United States.
Habitat Desert and semiarid regions.
Behavior The diet consists mainly of nocturnal rodents and lagomorphs (pikas, rabbits, and hares), but it eats ground-nesting birds and reptiles. It hunts at night. The den has between 2 and 24 entrances. Although the dens are individual, they are grouped together in a particular spot, and this is where the kits spend the day. The young are born in February–March after a gestation period of 49–56 days. The 4 or 5 cubs are born blind and furred. After a month they venture outside the den to play. The family usually separates in October, but one or two of the cubs sometimes remain in the den with the adults.
Note This fox is threatened with extinction.

---

248 VULPES VULPES
Red, silver, or cross, fox

Classification Order Carnivora, Family Canidae.
Description The size and color both vary considerably in relation to the environmental conditions. The head and body are reddish, and the underside gray and white; there are whitish markings on the throat and chest as well. The tail is long, blackish toward the tip, which is white. Length of head and body 60–90 cm (24–36 in), tail 35–40 cm (14–16 in); weight 2–7 kg (4.4–15.4 lb).
Distribution Palaearctic and Nearctic regions as far south as North Africa, Egypt, and northern Sudan.
Habitat All types of habitat, even large cities.
Behavior In its ability to adapt, this species is a close rival to man and the rat. It is active both during the day and at night, and invariably returns to its den in the ground. The social structure varies from the isolated animal to family groups with strict hierarchic organization. Territoriality is based on the availability of food and a territory may range in size from a few acres to more than 3750 acres. The red fox is omnivorous, eating fruit and vegetables as well as whatever small animals it catches. Reproduction is adjusted to the prevailing conditions. There are 2–10 (usually 4–6) young per litter and usually only one litter per year. Gestation lasts about 52 days. The cubs nurse for 7–8 weeks; at the age of 1 year, the young fox leaves to find its own territory, sometimes at a great distance.

249 UROCYON CINEREOARGENTEUS
Gray fox

Classification   Order Carnivora, Family Canidae.
Description   The coat is dark gray on the back, reddish brown on the sides of the body, the neck, and legs, and white on the underside. There are distinctive black, white, and rufous markings on the face. Length of head and body 53–73 cm (21.2–29.2 in), tail 28–44 cm (11.2–17.6 in); weight 4–7 kg (8.8–15.5 lb).
Distribution   Southern Canada to the northern part of South America, in suitable habitat.
Habitat   Broadleaf woodlands and rocky and bushy areas.
Behavior   This fox climbs trees with great ease. Once in a tree it will raid nests and feed on berries and fruit. It also eats small mammals, birds, and insects. It is nocturnal and only moves about during the day in exceptional circumstances. Home range size varies with sex and geography, ranging from 185–1600 acres. This territory is patrolled nightly. The dens may be underground, in hollow logs or in rocky crevices. It prefers to use underground dens already made by another species. During the breeding season, January–May, the den is lined with soft, dry material. After a gestation period of about 50 to 60 days (exact time is unknown) an average litter of 4 cubs is produced. By the age of 4–5 months, at the start of their first winter, the cubs are completely independent.

---

250 VULPES ZERDA
Fennec

Classification   Order Carnivora, Family Canidae.
Description   One of the smallest of the foxes, the fennec has adapted to life in the desert. It has huge, triangular ears. Its tiny body is pale beige with a very soft coat. The soles of the feet are completely covered with long hair to enable it to walk on sand. The lower part and base of the tail are almost white, but the tip of the tail is dark brown. Length of head and body about 40 cm (16 in), tail about 30 cm (12 in); weight usually less than 1.5 kg (3.3 lb).
Distribution   Africa north of the Sahara, in the Sahara, Arabia, and the Sinai peninsula.
Habitat   Desert, especially in sandy areas and where there are dunes.
Behavior   This sociable fox lives in small groups of 10–15 individuals. It is a nocturnal animal and spends the day in the den it has dug in the sand, which often consists of several chambers. It feeds on insects and small vertebrates (locusts, lizards, and nestlings), and sometimes eats plants. It can go for a long time without drinking. It can dig at great speed to capture prey or to escape from an enemy. After a gestation period of about 50 days the female gives birth to 2–5 cubs in March or April.

251 NYCTEREUCTES PROCYONOIDES
Raccoon-dog

Classification   Order Carnivora, Family Canidae.
Description   The legs are short and covered with a coat which is almost black. The tail is short and bushy. The body is dark brown and yellowish (because of the yellow tips of the hairs). Among the Canidae this species has the least bladelike teeth, and there is often an extra upper molar, bringing the total number of teeth to 44. Length of head and body up to 60 cm (24 in), tail 18 cm (7.2 in); weight to 7.5 kg (16.5 lb).
Distribution   Originally only in Siberia, Japan, Manchuria, China, and northern Indochina; introduced to western Russia and now spreading rapidly into central and northern Europe.
Habitat   Deciduous forests.

Behavior   This is a solitary and nocturnal creature which moves with great caution in dense woodlands and forests; it is especially cautious in the presence of humans. It lives on the ground and digs a deep burrow. In winter it enters a state of lethargy, the length of which depends on the harshness of the climate. It is omnivorous. Breeding begins in February or March, and there is a variable gestation period. There are usually 6 young per litter, but sometimes 9–12. The young reach adult size by fall.
Note   In its original distribution area it has been hunted almost to extinction; in Japan at this time it is considered an endangered species and is protected.

252 DUSICYON GYMNOCERCUS
Paraguayan fox

Classification   Order Carnivora, Family Canidae.
Description   The back and flanks are gray, with a black stripe running along the center of the body. It sometimes resembles a small coyote. The coat is dense and the undercoat is very thick. The tail is long and bushy. Length of head and body up to 80 cm (32 in), tail to 35 cm (14 in); weight 8 kg (17.6 lb).
Distribution   From Paraguay and southern Brazil, south to the Strait of Magellan.
Habitat   Grasslands, plains, steppe, but also in mountains up to an altitude of more than 13,500 feet.

Behavior   This fox lives alone or in pairs, and is essentially nocturnal. It hides in burrows dug by itself or by other animals among bushes and at the bases of trees. Near the end of the southern spring, October–November, the female gives birth to 3–5 young. Nothing else is known about its reproductive and "child-rearing" patterns. It is omnivorous and will sometimes make successful attacks on small domestic animals in pens. It is thought to be capable of killing lambs and sheep, and as a result has been actively hunted. In many regions this has led to its complete extinction. It has been reported that when this fox finds itself facing an enemy with no escape at hand, it may throw itself on the ground and feign death.

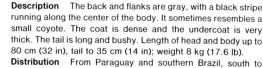

253   CUON ALPINUS
Dhole, red dog

Classification   Order Carnivora, Family Canidae.
Description   The coat is a distinctive rust-red color on the back, and paler underneath. The tail usually has a black tip. The female has 16 nipples. This species has 40 teeth. Length of head and body 88–113 cm (35–45 in), tail 40–50 cm (16–20 in); weight 14–21 kg (31–46 lb).
Distribution   Remnant populations in India, Malaysia, Thailand, and Java.
Habitat   Almost every habitat from mountainous regions to open country in Tibet. In India it lives almost exclusively in dense forest.

Behavior   Its main prey is large mammals (deer, wild sheep and goats, even the water buffalo) but it also eats small rodents and domestic animals. It hunts in packs usually of 5–12 individuals. It is a highly social animal however, little is known of the social organization of the pack in the wild state. It is most active in the early morning and evening. Mating occurs between September and January, and after a gestation period of 60–63 days the female gives birth to 4–6 cubs in a den, either in the ground or in a rocky cavern.
Note   Man's encroachment on nature threatens this species.

---

254   CHRYSOCYON BRACHYURUS
Maned wolf, aguara guazu

Classification   Order Carnivora, Family Canidae.
Description   The coat is long and soft, reddish yellow in color with distinctive black markings on the legs and often on the face and tail. The long, dark hair on the back forms an erectile mane. The tail occasionally has a white tuft at the tip. Length of head and body about 110 cm (44 in), tail 39 cm (15.6 in); weight up to 25 kg (55 lb).
Distribution   From northeastern Brazil to northern Argentina.
Habitat   Grasslands and steppes.

Behavior   This is an elusive species which lives in remote areas. It lives alone or in pairs, and is generally nocturnal. It hunts by lying in wait for, and then ambushing small prey which are caught in one bound, and immediately swallowed. It will eat eggs and plants also, and only rarely kills livestock, although local farmers believe that it does regularly. Because of this, the species has been virtually wiped out; small populations exist in only a few remaining undisturbed areas. After about a 2-month gestation, 1–5 young are born. It is believed they nurse for at least 2–3 months and that they reach sexual maturity in the year following their birth, but little is known.
Note   Since 1978 the World Wildlife Fund has given special attention to this species in an attempt to study and protect it more effectively.

255   LYCAON PICTUS
African, or Cape, hunting dog

Classification   Order Carnivora, Family Canidae.
Description   It is the same size and shape as a large dog, but its mottled coloring and large ears make it unmistakable. The head is large and resembles that of a hyena; the muzzle is black and the forehead has a black line in the middle of it. The legs are long and slender, and the feet have only 4 toes. The coat pattern is never the same in any two African hunting dogs. The tail has a white plume at the tip. Length of head and body up to 100 cm (40 in), tail 30–40 cm (12–16 in); weight to 30 kg (66 lb).

Distribution   Sub-Saharan Africa, except forested areas.
Habitat   Savanna.
Behavior   This dog lives in large packs of 5–20 individuals; rarely as many as 50. It plays the ecological role of the wolf in Africa. It is one of the most efficient of all predators, and will attack victims of all sizes, from large elands to small hares. Its organized method of hunting enables it to bring down its prey quickly, sometimes in a few seconds. The prey is fed upon, sometimes while still alive, and may be entirely consumed within a few minutes. After a 72-day gestation as many as 12 pups may be born in a litter, but usually only a few survive. The pack contributes to the feeding of the young by regurgitating food for them. Those that do survive achieve a very gradual independence, and remain with the pack as adults. The den is made in the ground.

256   SPEOTHOS VENATICUS
Bush dog

Classification   Order Carnivora, Family Canidae.
Description   The back and the sides of the body are reddish brown; the hind legs and tail are darker, and the forelegs and head are paler. The ears are small compared to its fairly large head. In overall appearance it resembles a badger, with its stocky body and short legs. Its black tail is the shortest among the canids. This dog has the fewest teeth in the dog family, only 38. Length of head and body 58–75 cm (23–30 in), tail 12–15 cm (4.8–6 in); weight up to 7 kg (15.4 lb).

Distribution   From Panama to northeastern Peru, Paraguay, and central Brazil.
Habitat   Grasslands and open forests.
Behavior   Little is known about this species; what is known, has come from studies of captive individuals. It is nocturnal and hunts in packs of adults and young. It is territorial. It swims well and will pursue prey into the water. It often spends the day in deserted armadillo dens. It is aggressive and will prey on species larger than itself, although it feeds mainly on different species of rodents. After a gestation period of 65 days, 4–6 young are born in a den usually taken by force from some other species that dug it.

257   OTOCYON MEGALOTIS
African bat-eared fox

Classification   Order Carnivora, Family Canidae.

Description   It is mostly yellow-brown with the feet and tips of the ears black. The face is also blackish. The legs are relatively short and the tail is bushy and blackish toward the tip. This species has 48 teeth which are somewhat weak. Length of head and body 58 cm (23 in), tail 24–34 cm (9.6–13.6 in); weight 3.5–4.5 kg (7.7–10 lb).

Distribution   East and southern Africa.

Habitat   All types of savanna and open plains.

Behavior   This animal lives alone, in pairs, or in small groups of up to 6 or 7 individuals. Generally it is nocturnal, but it is often seen moving about during the day. It will often approach houses, and is inquisitive. It hides among tall grasses, in thick bushes, or in holes in the ground. It feeds mostly on insects, preferably termites, as its teeth indicate, but will eat small rodents, eggs, lizards, and other animals. It never preys on livestock. Gestation lasts for 60–70 days and 3–5 young are born in December–February in a burrow. It is preyed on by large raptors such as eagles.

---

258   TREMARCTOS ORNATUS
Spectacled bear

Classification   Order Carnivora, Family Ursidae.

Description   The head is relatively small, the snout is short, and the legs are long. The rather tousled coat is black with two conspicuous white rings around the eyes. In some cases these "spectacles" are joined to a white patch on the chest. Its teeth and jaws are adapted to a vegetarian diet. Length of head and body up to 1.8 m (6 ft); shoulder height about 75 cm (30 in); weight to 140 kg (308 lb).

Distribution   The northern Andes from western Venezuela to northern Bolivia.

Habitat   Mountainous regions in woodland and forest.

Behavior   Only 5% of its diet consists of insects or animal matter; the rest consists of fruit, leaves, shoots, and bulbs. It is nocturnal and spends the day in ravines or in dense vegetation close to water. It is cautious in areas inhabited by man, but in uninhabited areas it is frequently seen in open places. It climbs well on trees and lianas. It is usually solitary but will occasionally form small family groups which feed in the branches of the same tree. Gestation lasts 8–8.5 months. As is the case with all the other bears, the 1–3 young are very small at birth, and defenseless.

Note   The numbers of this species have decreased considerably, but it is not seriously endangered.

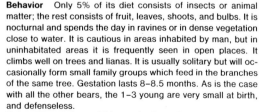

259 URSUS THIBETANUS
Asiatic black bear

Classification   Order Carnivora, Family Ursidae.

Description   The short coat is a glossy black with a distinctive V or Y design on the chest formed by long white hairs which fan out from its shoulders. The 5 claws on each foot are short and curved. The head tapers to a pointed snout, and the ears are large and conspicuous. Its teeth are weak. Length of head and body up to 170 cm (68 in); shoulder height to 90 cm (36 in); weight to 150 kg (330 lb).

Distribution   From Pakistan to northern India, to China and the Indochinese peninsula, then north as far as Mongolia and Amur region of the Soviet Union.

Habitat   Tropical and temperate broadleaf woodlands.

Behavior   It is generally solitary except for the female and her young who remain together during the first year. It feeds mainly on plant matter, and its diet only includes animals and insects in the autumn, when it forms its fat reserve for the winter and following spring. It is inactive for 4–5 months, depending on the ambient climate. During this period, the black bear withdraws to a hollow in some large, half-destroyed tree. It can climb well and is a good swimmer. It is believed to be both diurnal and nocturnal. This is not a threatened species, except in local areas.

Note   Although many species of Ursidae enter an inactive phase during the colder months, no ursid is a "true" hibernator.

---

260 URSUS ARCTOS
Brown bear

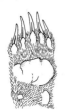

Classification   Order Carnivora, Family Ursidae.

Description   This species is divided into several subspecies; among these are the grizzly, the Kodiak and the European brown. The dimensions tend to increase from west to east and from south to north. The color varies from brown and silver-gray or blue, to black and pale beige. Females often are only half the size of males. The weight of the bears varies between spring, after the winter fast, and autumn, when they can weigh as much as double their normal weight because of the reserves of fat accumulated for the winter months. Length of head and body 2–3 m (6.5–10 ft); shoulder height 70–120 cm (30–48 in); weight 150–780 kg (330–1716 lb).

Distribution   Much of Eurasia and western North America.

Habitat   Woodlands; sometimes as far north as the tundra.

Behavior   The brown bear is essentially vegetarian, although it may prefer flesh when available. It is capable of killing animals the size of an ox, or fishing for salmon with great skill. It is mostly solitary or found in small family groups consisting of a female and her cubs. It winters in hollows which it lines with soft earth and leaves. The females have a longer period of inactivity than the males, and give birth in mid-winter after a 7–8-month gestation. The 1–3 young live with their mother in the cave until spring, and then remain with her for another year. They are sexually mature at 3 years, possibly earlier.

261 URUS AMERICANUS
American black bear

Classification   Order Carnivora, Family Ursidae.
Description   Most individuals are black but it is quite common to see brown, gray, or pale beige members of this species. In the northwestern Pacific region there are also individuals that are almost white (they are not albino). Unlike most other bears, which have at most vestigial stumps at the base of the spine, it has a true, albeit very short (about 12 cm/4.8 in long) tail. American black bear in eastern America are larger than those farther west where the species competes with the larger *Ursus arctos* (**260**). Length of head and body up to 180 cm (6 ft); shoulder height 60–90 cm (2–3 ft); weight 102–227 kg (225–500 lb).

Distribution   Canada and central and eastern United States.
Habitat   All types of woodland.
Behavior   This is the best known bear in America. In autumn it enters a state of lethargy, but not true hibernation, which varies in length depending on the climatic conditions outside, but individuals living in warmer regions still have a period of lethargy. The winter is spent in a cave or beneath a large fallen tree. The American black bear eats anything and everything, but is basically vegetarian. It is a solitary animal, and is active during the day and at night. Mating takes place in June–July and after a gestation period of 225 days, 2 or 3 cubs are born; these stay with their mother until they are a year and a half old.

262 HELARCTOS MALAYANUS
Malayan sun bear

Classification   Order Carnivora, Family Ursidae.
Description   The smallest member of the family Ursidae, this bear is black with a paler face, which sometimes is dirty white. On the chest there is a yellowish ringlike or horseshoe-shaped design. The head is large and the muzzle is flexible. The tongue is long and extensible. There are fewer premolar teeth than in other bears, the total number of teeth is only 38. Length of head and body is 1.1–1.4 m (3.6–4.6 ft); shoulder height up to 70 cm (28 in); weight to 60 kg (132 lb).

Distribution   The Indochinese Peninsula, southern China, Sumatra, and Borneo.
Habitat   Mostly tropical forests and woodland.
Behavior   Of all the bears this is the most agile climber, and it spends a great deal of its time in trees, where it often builds a nest with branches and foliage. It feeds on fruit and leaves gathered directly from the branches. It will eat insects, especially termites, which it gets by digging the nest. It is solitary, and is mainly active at night, and spends the day basking in the sun and sleeping. The duration of the gestation period in the wild is not known, but in captivity it is said to have ranged from 95–240 days.

Note   All ursids have relatively massive, blunt teeth suitable for crushing food. Their diets are quite varied, from place to place and season to season.

263 URSUS MARITIMUS
Polar bear

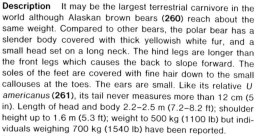

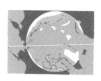

Classification   Order Carnivora, Family Ursidae.

Description   It may be the largest terrestrial carnivore in the world although Alaskan brown bears (**260**) reach about the same weight. Compared to other bears, the polar bear has a slender body covered with thick yellowish white fur, and a small head set on a long neck. The hind legs are longer than the front legs which causes the back to slope forward. The soles of the feet are covered with fine hair down to the small calluses at the toes. The ears are small. Like its relative *U americanus* (**261**), its tail never measures more than 12 cm (5 in). Length of head and body 2.2–2.5 m (7.2–8.2 ft); shoulder height up to 1.6 m (5.3 ft); weight to 500 kg (1100 lb) but individuals weighing 700 kg (1540 lb) have been reported.

Distribution   Circumpolar; occasionally seen further south.

Habitat   Ice floes and coastal waters.

Behavior   The diurnal polar bear is solitary. Pairs are only formed for a few days while mating takes place (April–May). In October, the female leaves the floes and hides in a den dug out of ice on land. The young are born in December, but the mother and her cubs do not emerge from the den until April. The mother nurses her cubs (1–3 but usually 2) for 18 months. Adult polar bears wander from ice floe to ice floe, but do seem to have a favorite hunting ground. It is truly carnivorous, feeding on seals and fish. A good swimmer, it paddles with its front legs only.

264 MELURSUS URSINUS
Sloth bear

Classification   Order Carnivora, Family Ursidae.

Description   Sloth bears are black, with a V-shaped design on the chest, and an off-white face; their fur is very shaggy, and their ears strikingly hairy. They are the most specialized of the bears in certain ways. The long lower lips are mobile and extensible, as is the tongue; there are no upper incisors and the mouth can be fashioned into a tube with which it sucks up insects. The claws are long and sickle-shaped; they are used for flipping stones and breaking tree stumps. Length of head and body 1.4–1.8 m (4.6–6 ft); shoulder height 61–92 cm (2–3 ft); weight up to 140 kg (308 lb).

Distribution   India and Sri Lanka.

Habitat   Tropical forests and woodland.

Behavior   The diet largely composed of insects, specifically termites, has a major influence on the life of this bear; it must constantly search for food. It also climbs slowly through trees looking for fruit and blossoms. It moves about at night, making a lot of noise with its digging, sucking, and blowing, all part of its feeding behavior. Its senses of sight and smell are poor. It lives in shallow caves, alone or in small family groups. After about a 7-month gestation, 1 or 2 (occasionally 3) cubs are born, which may remain with their mother for 2–3 years.

Note   This species has been reduced by encroachment on its habitat and hunting to about 10,000 individuals.

265 BASSARISCUS ASTUTUS
North American ring-tailed cat, cacomistle

Classification   Order Carnivora, Family Procyonidae.
Description   Its back is pale brown with some darker areas on the neck and legs; the underside of the body is whitish. The tail is often longer than the body and has black and white rings; the hair on the tail is long and bushy. Claws are semiretractile. Length of head and body up to 37 cm (15 in), tail about the same; weight about 1 kg (2.2 lb).
Distribution   From Oregon and Texas to southern Mexico.
Habitat   Forests and rocky terrain.
Behavior   Using its claws, it climbs nimbly through trees and branches. Catlike in build, it is nocturnal, and hunts small rodents and insects. It also eats plant matter. It builds a den among rocks, in hollows in trees, in ruined houses, or in the ruins of old Indian settlements. The 3 or 4 young are born in May–June after a gestation period of about 70 days. In the first fortnight of their life, only the mother looks after them, but later on she is helped by the father. They become completely independent after a few months. The ring-tailed cat often gathers in groups, but not for long. This species is easy to tame and it adapts well to living in gardens or city parks.

---

266 PROCYON LOTOR
North American raccoon

Classification   Order Carnivora, Family Procyonidae.
Description   The coat is long, dense, and gray-black. There is a distinctive mask around the eyes. The tail has 5–7 black rings. The feet have 5 toes with curved, nonretractile claws; the soles are hairless. The front feet are adapted to seizing, feeling, and handling objects while the hind feet support the weight of the body. Its size varies geographically; northern raccoons are larger. Length of head and body 60–95 cm (24–38 in), tail 20–40 cm (8–16 in); weight 7–20 kg (15–44 lb).
Distribution   From southern Canada to Panama; introduced into France and the USSR.
Habitat   Virtually anywhere.
Behavior   This mostly nocturnal, solitary raccoon feeds on plant and animal matter, eggs, berries, grapes, acorns, the seeds of various plants, and arthropods (crustaceans and insects). It rarely preys on other vertebrates. It does not hibernate, but in the summer and autumn it accumulates a fat reserve to see it through the winter. It is known for its habit of washing food, and if there is no water at hand it rubs the food with its hands. Only the male has a territory; he displays territorial behavior only when confronted by other males. The mating season in spring and summer varies from place to place. The gestation period lasts for 63 days. There are 2–5 young per litter.

267 NASUA NASUA
Northern, or white-nosed, coati

Classification   Order Carnivora, Family Procyonidae.
Description   This coati is reddish to gray in color, with white lips and a pale stripe that runs along the nose from the eyes. The nose is long, tapered, and mobile. The coat, which is short on the head and the legs, becomes longer and hispid on the body itself. The tail usually has rings more marked in some individuals than in others, and is held upright at a right angle to the body. Length of head and body to 65 cm (26 in), tail to 68 cm (27.2 in); weight 3–6 kg (6.6–13.2 lb).
Distribution   From southwestern United States as far south as Argentina.
Habitat   Tropical forest.
Behavior   The coati is omnivorous and active by day. Older males are usually solitary, but the females and young sometimes form large wandering groups. During the mating season, the strongest males keep weaker rivals at a respectful distance. The structural unit on which the social behavior of the coatis is based is nevertheless the single female with her young, which stay with her until they are 2 years old. Mating takes place in March, and after a gestation period of 74 days 3–7 young are born.

268 POTOS FLAVUS
Kinkajou

Classification   Order Carnivora, Family Procyonidae.
Description   The coat is short and velvety and olive-brown to reddish in color. The long tail is prehensile. (This feature is shared with only one other member of the order Carnivora, *Arctictis binturong*, **293**.) The head is round with relatively small, square ears and prominent eyes. The toes are joined by a membrane that extends a third of the way down each toe. The soles of the feet are covered with hair. It has scent glands on the face, throat, and belly. Length of head and body 41–57 cm (16–22 in), tail about the same; weight 1.8–4.6 kg (4–10 lb).
Distribution   Southern Mexico to the Mato Grosso in Brazil.
Habitat   Tropical forests.
Behavior   Kinkajous form small groups without a well-defined hierarchy. It feeds primarily on fruits such as wild figs, guavas, mangos, and avocados, but also eats insects and sometimes birds' eggs or young birds. Its long tongue enables it to catch insects and to suck the nectar from flowers. It is nocturnal and is permanently arboreal. It moves agilely through the tree tops like a monkey. In autumn, after a gestation period of 112–118 days, 1 or 2 young are born in a tree hollow or other protected place. The mother carries these about with her for almost 4 months, after which the young are almost independent.

269 AILURUS FULGENS
Lesser, or red, panda

Classification   Order carnivora, Family Procyonidae.
Description   The coat is long and soft; unlike most it is darker underneath: its underside is black while the head is white and the back rust-brown. The tail is rust-brown with black and paler rings. The head is unusually large and the snout is pointed. The legs are short and bearlike, and the feet have sharp and semiretractile claws. Length of head and body 51–64 cm (20–25.6 in), tail about the same; weight 3–4.5 kg (6.6–10 lb).
Distribution   Southern edge of the Himalayan range, from Nepal to the Chinese provinces of Yunnan and Sichuan.
Habitat   Forests, especially of bamboo.

Behavior   The red panda typically lives alone or in pairs. Because of its sharp claws, it can climb rapidly through trees, where it rests with its legs dangling in mid-air and its belly lying flat on top of a branch. It is mostly active from dusk to dawn. It feeds on bamboo shoots, succulent plants, roots, and sometimes on eggs and small vertebrates. It frequently washes itself with its tongue like a cat, licking the sole of the foot and then using the moistened sole to clean the fur. When it drinks it may plunge its paw into the water and then lick the paw. In the spring after a gestation period of about 130 days, 1–4 young are born. They nurse for a few months, are completely self-sufficient after several months, but may remain with their mother for more than a year.

270 AILUROPODA MELANOLEUCA
Giant panda

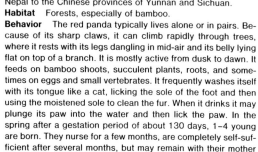

Classification   Order Carnivora, Family Ailuropodidae
Description   The outward appearance is like that of a bear, but the most distinctive coat makes the panda unmistakable; it is white with black markings around the eyes; the ears are also black, as are the front and hind legs, a stripe on the shoulders, and in some cases, the tip of the tail. The giant panda is near-sighted and has a highly developed sense of hearing. The front feet have a small pad or cushion which acts as a thumb for holding bamboo stalks. Length of head and body 1.2–1.5 m (4–5 ft), tail about 13 cm (5.2 in); shoulder height 60–80 (24–32 in); weight 80–160 kg (176–352 lb).
Distribution   South central China.
Habitat   Bamboo forests, at an altitude of 7590–12,870 feet.

Behavior   Its diet is based on bamboo shoots and other plant matter, but it also eats small mammals as well as birds and fish. When feeding, it sits so as to have its forefeet free to wrench off shoots and carry them to its mouth. Usually it is solitary, except for females and their young; and in the mating season (March–May), small groups of 2 or 3 may be formed. Gestation lasts about 5 months (it has ranged from 112–163 days in zoos). Of the 1 or 2 (sometimes 3) young born, only 1 is raised. It matures in about 6 years. The giant panda does not have a permanent den, but takes shelter in hollow trees or in fissures among rocks. It is active from twilight to dawn.

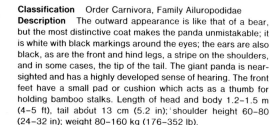

271 MARTES PENNANTI
Fisher

Classification   Order Carnivora, Family Mustelidae.
Description   The dense, soft coat is glossy dark brown, with the front parts grayish and the legs and tail darker in color. The body is slender, but more bulky than that of *Martes martes* (**272**). There are 38 teeth, including 4 premolars on each side. Length of head and body 60–80 cm (24–32 in), tail 35–40 cm (14–16 in), weight 3.5–5.5 kg (7.7–12 lb); female somewhat smaller and considerably lighter.
Distribution   Canada and the northern United States.
Habitat   Coniferous forest.
Behavior   Like the other martens the fisher is aggressive. It is solitary, principally nocturnal, and shelters in tree hollows. Its diet is totally carnivorous and consists mainly of rodents. One of its preferred prey items is the Canadian porcupine (*Erethizon dorsatum* **206**) which it kills using an elaborate technique; first the porcupine is flipped over on its back, then swiftly attacked in the belly where there are no protective quills. The fisher has also been known to kill small deer, especially in deep snow. It is arboreal, but is equally agile on the ground. Fishers exhibit delayed implantation of 10–11 months; 1–5 (usually 2 or 3) young are born in the spring, and may nurse until the fourth month. They become completely independent shortly thereafter.
Note   Because of the value of its fur, this species has been more or less wiped out in many parts of its range.

272 MARTES MARTES
Pine marten

Classification   Order Carnivora, Family Mustelidae.
Description   The coat is long, dense, and glossy brown with a honey-colored patch on the throat; the tail is also glossy brown, and the fur is even longer. The face is pointed, the eyes are large, and the ears are round. The pads on the feet are covered with thick hair. The 5 toes on each foot have long claws. Length of head and body 42–52 cm (16.5–20.5 in), tail 22–28 cm (8.7–11 in); weight 1.2–1.8 kg (2.6–4 lb).
Distribution   Europe.
Habitat   Coniferous woodland; rarely in deciduous woods.
Behavior   The pine marten is mostly solitary. It hunts mainly in the evening or early morning, but may be seen at midday, also. Its preferred prey includes birds, squirrels, rats, mice, and hares. It will also eat insects and fruits. During the day it sleeps in hollows in trees or in abandoned nests. It has highly developed senses of sight and hearing. Largely aboreal, it is quite agile and climbs and jumps with ease. Mating takes place in July–August. The gestation period is prolonged, and may last up to 9 months, at the end of which the female gives birth to 4 to 6 young; these are blind and sparsely haired. They nurse for 6–7 weeks, and become independent at 2–3 months.
Note   This species has been eliminated in many areas due to overhunting. The fur is very valuable.

273 MUSTELA ERMINEA
Ermine

Classification   Order Carnivora, Family Mustelidae.

Description   Like all of the other members of this genus, its legs are short. Size varies geographically. Males are usually larger than females. The coat on the back is brown, and yellow or yellowish white on the underside. The facial part of the head is short. In the winter, in many parts of the world, the coat becomes snow-white, with only the tip of the tail remaining black. Length of head and body 20–24 cm (7.9–9.4 in), tail 4–10 cm (1.6–4 in); weight 50–200 g (1.8–7 oz).

Distribution   Northern Europe, northern and central Asia as far east as Japan, and North America; introduced in New Zealand.

Habitat   Woodlands, cultivated land, mountains and hilly areas.

Behavior   The solitary ermine is mainly nocturnal but sometimes can be seen during the day. It is a skillful climber and an excellent swimmer. It hunts mice, rats, and birds. It can also catch small fish. Sometimes it will steal the eggs from birds nests. If in danger it emits an unpleasant odor from glands situated at the base of the tail. Mating takes place in July and August, but there is a delay in implantation. As a result the female (which may breed as early as 3–4 months of age) gives birth in April–May, after a gestation period of about 255 days. Each litter has 4 or 5 young in it. The nest is usually made in cracks among rocks, in old buildings, or in underground burrows.

---

274 MUSTELA FRENATA
Long-tailed weasel

Classification   Order Carnivora, Family Mustelidae.

Description   In summer the coat is brown on the back and paler on the underside. Some localized subspecies have white markings on the face. In winter members of the species living in northern areas become white all over, while in southern areas they merely become paler. The tip of the tail always remains black. Length of head and body up to 25 cm (10 in), tail to 12.5 cm (5 in); weight to 250 g (8.8 oz).

Distribution   From southern Canada to Bolivia.

Habitat   Forests.

Behavior   Like other species of *Mustela*, *M. frenata* is a highly carnivorous creature, feeding on small birds, eggs, and rodents and any other small mammals it might come upon. Its extremely effective hunting technique includes rapid movements and the fatal bite it inflicts on the nape of its victim's neck. It makes its den in a hole in the ground or under rocks or logs. Mating takes place in July–August, but implantation is delayed until 4 weeks before the birth occurs in April–May. The offspring nurse for 6–8 weeks, and become independent at about 3 months. Females are sexually mature at 4 months, but the male takes a year to reach the same stage. This weasel is a nocturnal, solitary animal. It often causes severe damage in chicken coops, but is a welcome antidote to mice.

275 MUSTELA NIVALIS
Common, or least, weasel

Classification Order Carnivora, Family Mustelidae.
Description Similar in appearance to the ermine (**273**), this weasel is just slightly smaller. The coat is reddish brown on the back and white on the underside. The tail never has a black tip, as does the ermine's. It has short legs. Length of head and body 17–25 cm (7–10 in), tail 1–8 cm (0.5–3.2 in), weight 80–190 g (2.8–6.7 oz); females considerably smaller than males.

Distribution Europe, northern Asia, North Africa, and North America south to Wyoming and North Carolina.
Habitat It adapts to a variety of habitats, but prefers rolling or flat countryside.

Behavior The mostly solitary common weasel is probably active both day and night, alternating periods of activity with periods of rest. It is a ruthless hunter of mice, rats, and moles. Because of the slenderness and suppleness of its body it can enter the burrows of these animals. It also hunts frogs and small birds. Its agile movements and ability to climb enable it to reach birds' nests, where it consumes both eggs and nestlings. Gestation lasts 35 days; there may be delayed implantation. The female gives birth, possibly twice a year, to 4–6 young which she looks after in a nest lined with grass and dry leaves in the hollow in a tree. It is possible that the male plays a part in rearing the young. The young become independent in about 6–8 weeks.

---

276 EIRA BARBARA
Tayra

Classification Order Carnivora, Family Mustelidae.
Description The body is slender with legs of moderate length, much like the marten (**272**). The long neck supports a head that is quite large in relation to the body; the ears are round and short. The dense, short, very soft coat is brown with yellowish areas in some individuals; the head is usually slightly paler than the body. Length of head and body 60–68 cm (23.6–26.8 in), tail up to 46 cm (18.2 in); weight 4–5 kg (8.8–11 lb).

Distribution Southern Mexico, south to Argentina.
Habitat Woodlands and areas rich in vegetation.
Behavior This animal lives alone or in a pair for a temporary period around the mating season. It eats guinea pigs, mice, squirrels, and agoutis, and often preys on poultry; it will also eat fruits and insects. It is active both day and night, and rarely rests. It climbs nimbly up and down trees, and hides in hollows in branches or in the underground burrows of other animals, particularly rodents, which it first kills. The female probably reproduces at different times of the year, and gives birth to 2–4 young in each litter; little else is known about the reproductive cycle and "infancy" of the tayra.

Note This species is sometimes kept by local people to help control rodents in their homes and gardens.

277 GALICTIS VITTATA
Greater grison

Classification   Order Carnivora, Family Mustelidae.
Description   The coat consists of long, soft hairs. A white stripe runs from the forehead, over the ears as far as the shoulders, and separates the black face, throat, and chest from the grizzled gray back. The general appearance is ferretlike with a long body and short legs, but the color pattern is distinct. Length of head and body 47–55 cm (18.8–22 in), tail about 16 cm (6.4 in); weight 1.4–3.2 kg (3–7 lb).
Distribution   Southern Mexico to Peru and Brazil.
Habitat   Woodlands and grasslands, also found near inhabited buildings, at an altitude up to about 4000 feet.
Behavior   It hunts both night and day, and is often seen in small groups. They live in crevices in rocky areas and beneath tree roots. It feeds on chinchillas, viscachas, and other rodents which it kills with a swift bite on the back of the neck. It can cause damage to domestic animals. It is easily tamed, and is used to combat rodent infestations or to hunt chinchillas as ferrets are used in Europe to hunt rabbits. The female gives birth in October to 2–4 young.

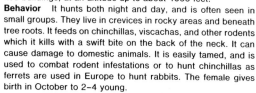

---

278 GULO GULO
Wolverine

Classification   Order Carnivora, Family Mustelidae.
Description   This is the largest of the Mustelidae. The long, soft, dense coat is dark brown; on the forehead there is a white mark, and on the sides of the body from the shoulders to the tail, there are two broad yellowish white stripes. Length of head and body 72–107 cm (29–43 in), tail 17–22 cm (6.8–8.8 in); weight up to 19 kg (42 lb).
Distribution   Scandinavia, northern Asia, and North America.
Habitat   Woodland with rocky hillsides.
Behavior   This is a solitary créature, active both day and night. Despite its seemingly rather awkward physical build and strange bounding or galloping gait it is quite agile, can run at considerable speed, and is a good swimmer and climber. It hunts small rodents living in the same habitat, but also feeds on birds, frogs, and plant matter. It sometimes manages to catch larger prey such as reindeer. Its favorite hunting method is the ambush. Mating takes place in July–August; after 8–9 months the female gives birth to 1–4 young in a nest scantily lined with bits of fur and vegetation and hidden among rocks. The young reach independence at about 5 months, but take 3 years to reach sexual maturity.
Note   Wolverine fur has an unusual ability to shed ice crystals and was especially favored by Eskimo peoples as a trim or lining for the hoods of fur parkas.

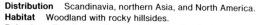

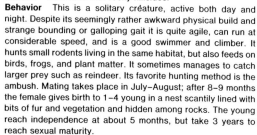

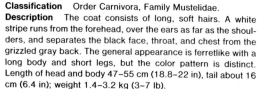

279 ICTONYX STRIATUS
Zorilla, striped polecat

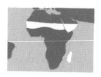

Classification   Order Carnivora, Family Mustelidae.
Description   On the back there are four large white stripes on a black background. There are also three conspicuous white marks on the face. The tail is densely furred and mostly white, with a blackish base. The coat is long and soft. Length of head and body 28–38 cm (11–15 in), tail up to 30 cm (12 in); weight about 1.5 kg (3.3 lb).
Distribution   From Senegal to the Sudan, and south to the tip of Africa.
Habitat   Savanna and open grasslands.
Behavior   This solitary creature is strictly nocturnal. It can only be spotted at sundown, or dawn before it scuttles off to its burrow (which is usually found among rocks or roots). Sometimes it will use a burrow previously dug by some other animal. It feeds on rodents, birds, snakes, and hares. When necessary it will eat insects and carrion instead. It has 2 highly developed perianal glands which emit a substance that smells strongly; it can propel this scent a considerable distance, like all American skunks. There are 2 or 3 young in each litter; they are born with short fur and with the striped pattern already apparent.

---

280 MELLIVORA CAPENSIS
Ratel, honey badger

Classification   Order Carnivora, Family Mustelidae.
Description   The ratel is similar to the European badger; its body is thickset and compact, its head is large, and its feet are powerful with strong claws. The upper back varies from gray to whitish and contrasts sharply with the black underparts. The color pattern varies geographically. The tail is short and often held upright; it is black on the underside. Length of head and body 25–30 cm (10–12 in), tail 20–30 cm (8–12 in); weight up to 12 kg (26.4 lb).
Distribution   Africa south of the Sahara, and in southwestern Asia to Nepal and western India.
Habitat   All types of habitat, from savanna to forest.
Behavior   This is a brave creature, which will not hesitate to attack animals much larger than itself. It lives alone or in pairs, and is nocturnal. It digs large burrows in the ground. It is omnivorous, feeding on insects, plant matter, and small vertebrates. It seems to prefer honey and bee larvae, often climbing into trees to find suspended hives. It is impervious to bee stings, because of a thick layer of subcutaneous fat. The gestation period lasts about 180 days and usually 2 young are born in each litter.
Note   It will often use the calls of the honeyeater (a bird, *Indicator indicator*)—whose presence indicates that bees are nearby—to find hives.

281 MELES MELES
Eurasian, or Old World, badger

Classification   Order Carnivora, Family Mustelidae.
Description   The legs are short and powerful, and the soles of the feet rest flat on the ground. This gives the thickset Eurasian badger a rather swaying gait. On the sides of the white head there are black stripes which run over the eyes as far as the ears; the back is gray and the belly is black. It has powerful claws. Length of head and body 61–85 cm (24–33.5 in), tail up to 30 cm (12 in); weight 10–20 kg (22–44 lb).
Distribution   Throughout Eurasia except the northernmost regions of Asia and areas bordering on India.
Habitat   Woodlands, sometimes to high altitudes.
Behavior   This is a nocturnal and gregarious animal and often lives in large family groups. It spends the day and the winter months in its burrow system which is called a "set"; it consists of a maze of passages, chambers, and entrances, with a large central chamber. It emerges from the set at night to hunt. It feeds on a variety of things, from plants to living and dead animals. About three-fourths of its diet is plant material. During the mating season, in summer, it emits loud shrill cries. The fertilized egg is not implanted in the uterus for 4–5 months; after implantation, gestation lasts for 6–8 weeks and 3–5 young are born in February–March.
Note   This species is protected in many countries.

282 ARCTONYX COLLARIS
Hog badger

Classification   Order Carnivora, Family Mustelidae.
Description   It has the same coloring as the Eurasian badger (281) but the face, ears, and throat are all white, as is the tail. The snout is elongated and forms a sort of mobile, hairless proboscis that ends in a disk about the nostrils, like a pig's snout. The claws are powerful, fairly straight, and white. Length of head and body 55–70 cm (22–28 in), tail 12–17 cm (4.8–6.8 in); weight 7–14 kg (15.4–31 lb).
Distribution   China, northeastern India, the Indochinese Peninsula, and Sumatra.
Habitat   Woodland and forest in lowlands and mountains.
Behavior   Little is known about this species. No data exist for it from observations in the wild, and there is little information from captive individuals. It is nocturnal and is probably partly aboreal, as it climbs trees easily. It feeds mostly on plants, but it can easily become a scavenger if little food is available. Nothing is known about its reproductive or social behavior.

283 TAXIDEA TAXUS
North American badger

Classification   Order Carnivora, Family Mustelidae.
Description   The shaggy coat is grayish or brownish with a white stripe on the head often extending down the back. The body is stout with short legs; the front feet are partially webbed and have long, curved claws, and the hind feet have shovel-like claws. There are 2 white-ringed black markings on the face. Length of head and body 60–73 cm (24–29 in), tail 10–14 cm (4–5.6 in); weight 6.4–11.8 kg (14–26 lb).
Distribution   Western and central North America.
Habitat   Plains, grasslands, and tundra.

Behavior   The diet is varied and includes squirrels and other rodents, lizards, insects, birds' eggs, and nestlings. When frightened it can be quite aggressive, snarling and growling. It is normally solitary except during the reproductive season when pairs may form. It is a good swimmer, and is active both by day and by night. It lives in dens in burrows. Mating occurs in late summer or early autumn, and 1–5 young are born in March–April. The young are born furred, but blind. They are independent by August. The fur has little commercial value. The main predators of the American badger are coyotes and eagles, but the main enemy of this species is the automobile; traps, guns, and poisoned bait have also played a large part in greatly reducing its numbers.

284 MEPHITIS MEPHITIS
Striped skunk

Classification   Order Carnivora, Family Mustelidae.
Description   The body is stocky; the head is small and elongated, with small round ears. The legs are short with 5-toed feet with powerful claws. The coat is long, black and shiny with a white stripe on the forehead, two other white stripes fan out from the nape and run down each side. Also has some white hairs, especially at the tip. The anal glands are highly developed. Length of head and body up to 45 cm (18 in), tail 18–40 cm (7–16 in); weight 1.2–5.3 kg (2.6–11.7 lb).
Distribution   Canada to northern Mexico.
Habitat   Open woodland and grassland.

Behavior   The striped skunk is a docile animal and is to some extent gregarious. The females often share territories or even dens. The striped skunk lives in underground burrows consisting of various chambers and entrances. Mating takes place in the burrow in February–March, and after a gestation period of 59–77 days, an average of 5–8 young are born (up to 10 in rare cases). The young nurse for 2 months. In winter, the striped skunk does not hibernate, but enters a period of inactivity during which several individuals gather together in a den and stay there sleeping and drowsing. The skunk is omnivorous and nocturnal. One notable defensive behavior is the discharge from its anal glands of noxious scent when in danger.

285 SPILOGALE PUTORIUS
Spotted skunk

Classification   Order Carnivora, Family Mustelidae.
Description   The spotted skunk weighs much less than the striped skunk (**284**). The ordinary coat is identifiable by a striking pattern of irregular white stripes all over the body. The tail is long and bushy but less so than in the striped skunk. Length of head and body 35–40 cm (14–16 in), tail 17–22 cm (6.8–8.8 in); weight up to 1.1 kg (2.4 lb).
Distribution   From British Columbia to Costa Rica, including most of the United States.
Habitat   Woodland and grassland, but also in stony and desert terrain.
Behavior   This nocturnal, solitary species is definitely more active than the striped skunk, and has no trouble climbing up and down trees and bushes. It often builds a sort of shelter or refuge in hollows in trees, or it may either dig out a burrow in the ground or take over the burrow of another species. The spotted skunk threatens aggressors by raising the hind part of its body. This intimidates most enemies. If the enemy persists, it receives, in the eyes, a malodorous secretion which is squirted from the anal glands; this secretion can be sprayed accurately up to a distance of 20 feet. It has an omnivorous diet. After perhaps about 120 days of gestation the female gives birth to 1–6 young; she may have 1 or 2 (2 is more common in the southern part of its range) litters per year. The offspring are weaned at about 8 weeks and reach adult size by about 4 months.

286 LUTRA LUTRA
Eurasian otter

Classification   Order Carnivora, Family Mustelidae.
Description   The long, streamlined body of this otter is well adapted to aquatic life. The coat is dense, glossy brown, and waterproof. In adults there is often a white patch on the throat. The head is broad and flattened, and the ears, which close off when the otter dives underwater, are almost completely concealed by the coat. The legs are short, the feet are webbed and have 5 toes with small claws. Length of head and body 65–85 cm (26–33 in), tail 36–52 cm (14.4–20.8 in); weight 5–15 kg (11–33 lb).
Distribution   Europe; Asia east to Java; Morocco and Algeria.
Habitat   Streams, lakes, and rivers.
Behavior   This otter is generally solitary except during the mating season, and is active mainly at night. It preys on fish, waterfowl and other birds and freshwater crayfish and other invertebrates. It digs a den, which has an underwater entrance, among the vegetation on the riverbank. It reproduces throughout the year and gestation lasts for about 61 days. The litter has 2 or 3 young, which nurse for 2–3 months. They may remain in a family group for as long as a year and reach adult size at about 2 years of age.
Note   In many areas, river otters have disappeared because of overhunting by man for the fur or because it is considered to be a pest, and because of pollution in rivers and lakes.

287 PTERONURA BRASILIENSIS
Giant otter

Classification   Order Carnivora, Family Mustelidae.
Description   In general appearance it resembles other otters but is larger and more powerful. The tail is flattened vertically and has a ridge on either side. The toes are long and bear short, strong claws; the toes are joined together by a membrane. Length of head and body 1–1.5 m (3.3–5 ft), tail about 70 cm (28 in); weight about 24 kg (53 lb).
Distribution   The Amazon basin; also in rivers in Venezuela and Guyana, and in the Uruguay and Parana rivers.
Habitat   Tropical rivers and lagoons.

Behavior   Little is known about this species because of the difficulty of observing it. It is active during the day and often gathers in noisy groups. It generally prefers slow-flowing rivers where it hunts, emitting long whistles and shrill cries. It feeds on small mammals, fish, and birds, and any creatures living near the bank. Not much is known concerning reproductive behavior, except that the female gives birth to 1 or 2 young a year. It builds a shelter in the vegetation or among rocks along the riverbank, where it rests and eats.
Note   In many parts of its distribution area this species is endangered, and strict conservation measures are being imposed.

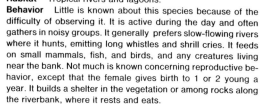

288 AONYX CAPENSIS
African clawless otter

Classification   Order Carnivora, Family Mustelidae.
Description   The distinguishing features of this otter are that the feet are only partly webbed, and are clawless. The upper coat is a uniform brown; the underside is paler. The neck, throat, upper lip, and edges of the ears are white. Length of head and body 95–100 cm (37.4–39.4 in), tail up to 55 cm (21.2 in); weight 14–23 kg (31–51 lb).
Distribution   Locally in central and southern Africa.
Habitat   Rivers in savanna and lowland forested areas where the current is slow-moving, and in pools formed by loops in rivers.

Behavior   Like all the otters, this species lives in close association with water, but it is sometimes found at a distance from water. It lives either alone or in pairs, and sometimes forms small groups. It feeds on anything it can find in the water, from fishes to waterfowl, and from succulent plants to molluscs. It is mainly active at night, but in wilder areas is active during the day as well. It is fond of sunning on rocks along riverbanks. The female gives birth to 2–5 young in the spring, after a gestation period of about 2 months. For shelter or refuge it often uses burrows dug by other animals, in vegetation or along sandy riverbanks.

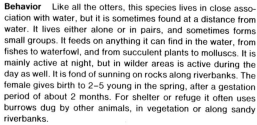

289 GENETTA GENETTA
Common, or small-spotted, genet

Classification   Order Carnivora, Family Viverridae.

Description   The coat is long and coarse, pale gray or brownish with a prominent black crest on the back formed by longer hairs. There are brownish or black markings on the upper parts and flanks that are arranged in lines. The long tail, which is generally held in an extended horizontal position, has 9 or 10 dark rings and a whitish tip. This genet has relatively long legs and a short face for a viverrid. The 5 claws on each foot are retractile. Length of head and body 40–51 cm (16–21 in), tail 40–48 cm (16–19.2 in); weight about 2.3 kg (5 lb).

Distribution   Throughout Africa, deserts and tropical forests; east to Jordan; in Spain; and in southern Arabia.

Habitat   Savanna, arid areas, and scrub.

Behavior   This nocturnal creature spends the day in its burrow, or among rocks. It is terrestrial and arboreal and moves easily in both environments; it can readily negotiate narrow and tricky paths. It preys on many species of mammals that are smaller than hares, and will often create havoc among poultry. It also eats snakes, lizards, and some fruits. It often eats only the head and breast of its victims, and discards the rest. It lives alone or in a pair. After a gestation period of 10–11 weeks, 3–4 young are produced in a litter (there are 2 litters per year). The young are probably weaned at about 2 months of age.

290 CIVETTICTIS
African civet

Classification   Order Carnivora, Family Viverridae.

Description   This is the largest of the civets and one of the largest members of the family Viverridae. The coat is a contrasting mixture of black stripes and markings on a pale background. The snout is white and separated from the gray forehead by a broad black band which extends across the eyes. Along the back a strip of long, black, erectile hairs forms a crest. The tail is broad at the base and tapers towards the tip. The claws are partly retractile. Length of head and body about 70 cm (28 in), tail about 50 cm (20 in); weight about 20 kg (44 lb).

Distribution   Africa south of the Sahara except the tip of South Africa.

Habitat   Savanna; forests that are not too humid.

Behavior   This civet is solitary and completely nocturnal. It is retiring and difficult to observe. It feeds on anything edible, including insects, plants, and carrion. It uses the burrows of aardvarks (*Orycteropus afer*, **130**), caves, or tree hollows, to hide in during the day. It is territorial and has a habit of depositing its droppings in the same spot, as a territorial marking signal. The anal glands emit a substance with a very penetrating smell. This musk is used in the manufacture of perfumes. 2–4 young are born. There are normally 2 litters per year.

291 VIVERRA ZIBETHA
Large Indian civet

Classification   Order Carnivora, Family Viverridae.

Description   The large Indian civet is yellow-gray with dark brown to black markings arranged in incomplete stripes. The facial mask, throat, legs, and end of tail are also dark. The perianal glands produce the substance called civet, which has a strong odor. The claws are semiretractile. Length of head and body up to 80 cm (32 in), tail to 46 cm (18.4 in); weight about 25 kg (55 lb).

Distribution   Southeast Asia.

Habitat   Tropical and subtropical forests.

Behavior   Nocturnal and solitary by nature, this is one of the most fearsome of small predators, as it can easily kill prey larger than itself. The hunting technique consists of repeatedly biting the prey in the hindquarters while it is running, then shaking it until dead. Young are usually born in May–June and each litter has 3 or 4 young. This species is easy to domesticate and is sometimes penned so the civet substance can be gathered more conveniently.

Note   In the islands of southeast Asia this civit is replaced by a similar species, *Viverra tangalunga*, known as the Malay civet.

---

292 PRIONODON LINSANG
Banded linsang

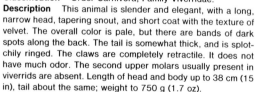

Classification   Order Carnivora, Family Viverridae.

Description   This animal is slender and elegant, with a long, narrow head, tapering snout, and short coat with the texture of velvet. The overall color is pale, but there are bands of dark spots along the back. The tail is somewhat thick, and is splotchily ringed. The claws are completely retractile. It does not have much odor. The second upper molars usually present in viverrids are absent. Length of head and body up to 38 cm (15 in), tail about the same; weight to 750 g (1.7 oz).

Distribution   Malaysia, Sumatra, Java, and Borneo.

Habitat   Tropical forest.

Behavior   This is a solitary, basically nocturnal species, which lives almost exclusively in trees, moving with great agility. It can move swiftly on the ground and is an efficient predator of small vertebrates and insects. Its diet includes eggs, which are crushed between the front paws. It can reproduce twice a year, in February and August, when the female gives birth to 2 or 3 young in a burrow in the ground or in a hollow tree. The young open their eyes after 20 days and become independent after 4 months.

293 PARADOXURUS HERMAPHRODITUS
Common palm civet

Classification   Order Carnivora, Family Viverridae.

Description   The coat is pale brown or gray and the stripes and markings on the back are sometimes hard to see. The forehead has a pale band running across it. The claws are not retractile. The secretion from the anal glands is strong and distinctive. Length of head and body up to 65 cm (26 in), tail to 66 cm (26 in); weight to 4.5 kg (10 lb).

Distribution   India, Sri Lanka, southern China, southeast Asia, the Philippines, and the East Indies.

Habitat   Forest and woodland, including areas inhabited by man.

Behavior   This civet is nocturnal and arboreal and is often found in palm trees in villages and towns, but also in many other types of tree. Its name derives from its liking for palm wine. It feeds on rats and mice (which it catches in homes and cellars), fruit, insects, and small vertebrates. The palm civet often makes its own home in the roofs of houses. Little is known about its reproductive habits, but it is thought that the female gives birth to 3 or 4 young per litter, possibly several times a year.

---

294 ARCTICTIS BINTURONG
Binturong

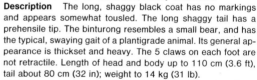

Classification   Order Carnivora, Family Viverridae.

Description   The long, shaggy black coat has no markings and appears somewhat tousled. The long shaggy tail has a prehensile tip. The binturong resembles a small bear, and has the typical, swaying gait of a plantigrade animal. Its general appearance is thickset and heavy. The 5 claws on each foot are not retractile. Length of head and body up to 110 cm (3.6 ft), tail about 80 cm (32 in); weight to 14 kg (31 lb).

Distribution   Burma, Malaysia, Indochina, Sumatra, Java, Borneo, and Palawan Island.

Habitat   Tropical and subtropical forest.

Behavior   This viverrid is well adapted for life in the trees. On the ground it seems slightly awkward. It moves slowly through the trees, and it will not let go with its tail until it is quite sure it has a firm grip with its feet. In captivity, however, it has also been observed swinging and skipping about quite acrobatically. When moving it emits grunts or hissing noises. Its diet consists of fruit, as indicated by small teeth; and it has flat molars for crushing plant and animal matter, which it eats as well. It is solitary and nocturnal. There seem to be 2 reproductive periods, in March–April and in October–November. The gestation period lasts for 90 days and there are 1 or 2 young in each litter.

295 CRYPTOPROCTA FEROX
Fossa

Classification   Order Carnivora, Family Viverridae.
Description   The coat is smooth, thick, and reddish brown. This unusual species has survived on the island of Madagascar, where it is the largest native carnivore. It incorporates features found in the cat family, such as relatively short face, reduction in posterior teeth, and retractile claws, and its systematic position is still somewhat blurred. Unlike other viverrids, which typically have 36 teeth, the fossa only has 32. The female has a double uterus. It is plantigrade, and has 5 powerful and completely retractile claws on each foot. There are small anal glands in an anal pouch. Length of head and body 61–76 cm (24–30 in), tail almost as long; weight 5–6 kg (11–13 lb).
Distribution   Madagascar.
Habitat   Tropical and subtropical forest.
Behavior   The fossa is nocturnal and solitary. It lives in the thickest parts of the forest, where it moves nimbly among the branches and easily scales tall tree trunks. It feeds mostly on animals, and because it often attacks and kills domestic animals it is hunted by local people, who also eat it. Mating has only been observed in captivity; it takes place in late April and lasts 1–3 hours. After about 10 weeks, 2 or 3 young are produced. The fossa reaches sexual maturity at about 5 years of age.

---

296 FOSSA FOSSA
Fanaloka

Classification   Order Carnivora, Family Viverridae.
Description   The basic color of its relatively short, fine coat is pale beige, against which there is a series of darker markings or stripes running lengthwise from head to tail. The underside of the body is lighter. There is a conspicuous white patch on the head near the rearmost corner of the ear. The legs are short and slender. The claws are not retractile. The fanaloka resembles the true civets but lacks anal glands. Length of head and body about 40 cm (16 in), tail about 20 cm (5 in); weight 2.5 kg (5.5 lb).
Distribution   Madagascar.
Habitat   Tropical forests.
Behavior   This rare carnivore preys on small vertebrates and insects, and steals eggs from nests. Little is known about this species: there have been few chances to study it in captivity, and it is seldom seen because it is solitary, nocturnal, and lives in the heart of tropical forests. Rarity may be its normal population density, or it could have been caused by human interference with its habitat, which can be particularly dangerous in the case of a species that is uncommon to begin with.

297 SURICATA SURICATTA
Suricate, meerkat

Classification   Order Carnivora, Family Herpestidae.
Description   It is a small mongoose with a narrow, pointed muzzle, and a striking pattern. On the back, the shoulder and the tail, there is a series of dark stripes running crosswise. On the face, black rings surround the eyes. The ears are black and barely visible. The lower parts of the head and body are usually white. The tail is brown, but darker toward the tip and has a conspicuous black tuft of hairs. Length of head and body 25–35 cm (10–14 in), tail about 24 cm (9.6 in); weight about 2.5 kg (5.5 lb).
Distribution   South Africa.
Habitat   Arid, open plains.
Behavior   The meerkat is highly sociable and lives in large colonies, often in association with other mongoose species, or with ground squirrels and small rodents. It chatters continually. It is active during the day and it is commonly seen basking in the sun near the entrance of the burrow. Although it is quite capable of digging its own burrow, the meerkat prefers to use burrows dug by other animals. It feeds mainly on insects, millipedes, and spiders, which it digs out of the ground. It habitually deposits its droppings in shared places. Gestation lasts for about 11 weeks, after which 2–4 young are born. They nurse for about 8–12 weeks and reach sexual maturity at about 1 year.
Note   The meerkat is easy to tame and is often kept as a pet.

298 HERPESTES ICHNEUMON
Egyptian mongoose

Classification   Order Carnivora, Family Herpestidae.
Description   Largest of the African mongooses, its coat is long, especially on the sides of the body, and coarse. It has a uniformly grizzled appearance. The coat appears to be brownish-gray due to contrasting fur colors. The flanks and underparts are buffy-colored. The tail is long, bushy at the base, and tapers down to a dark tuft at the tip. It has 5 reasonably strong, slightly curved, nonretractile claws on each foot. Length of head and body 53–66 cm (21–26 in), tail 50 cm (19.7 in); weight 2–3.5 kg (4.4–7.7 lb).
Distribution   Africa, except deserts and equatorial forest; Spain; Israel.
Habitat   Wooded savanna and scrub; never very far from water.
Behavior   This terrestrial mongoose is active by day and at night. It is terrestrial and digs holes in the ground to serve as burrows and temporary resting places. Generally it is solitary, but small family groups may be formed. When in a group, they travel in single file, with each individual almost holding on to the tail of the one in front. It feeds on all kinds of small animals, and can cause damage to domestic poultry. It will also eat fish and crabs. After a gestation period of about 8–9 weeks, 2–4 young are born; the young are nursed for about 2 weeks.

299 HELOGALE PARVULA
Dwarf mongoose

Classification   Order Carnivora, Family Herpestidae.
Description   This is the smallest of all the African mongooses. The general color is speckled reddish brown. There is much variation in coloration, which has resulted in the definition of various races. The short legs are brown, with darker feet. The claws are nonretractile. The tail is short and does not have a dark tip. Length of head and body 17–23.5 cm (6.8–9.4 in), tail about 20 cm (7.9 in); weight about 680 g (1.5 lb).
Distribution   Much of eastern southern Africa.
Habitat   Savanna and scrub.
Behavior   This is a gregarious mongoose which lives in large groups of 20 or more individuals. These colonies occupy old termite nests or the burrows of other animals, which the dwarf mongoose adapts to its requirements. It is noisy, and constantly busy throughout the day. It is not shy and can be frequently seen. It issues a wide range of sounds and cries. It will sometimes attack prey as a group. It sometimes preys on small rodents, birds, and reptiles. Moreover, the diet consists mainly of insects (locusts and termites). It is not territorial and will sometimes move considerable distances. After a gestation period of 50–54 days, 2–4 young are born in a hole in the ground or in a hollow in a tree. There are several litters a year. The offspring nurse for about 2 months and are independent about 1 month later.

300 CYNICTIS PENICILLATA
Yellow mongoose

Classification   Order Carnivora, Family Herpestidae.
Description   The long coat is yellowish orange, and is brighter on the hindquarters; the underparts and forelimbs are paler. The tail is rather bushy and is about the same color as the back, but the tip of the tail is marked by a conspicuous white tuft. The claws are nonretractile. Length of head and body 27–38 cm (11–15 in), tail 18–28 cm (7–11 in); weight 1.5–2 kg (3.3–4.4 lb).
Distribution   South Africa.
Habitat   Rolling plains.
Behavior   This mostly diurnal mongoose lives in large groups, sometimes with more than 50 individuals. It often associates with species that have similar behavior patterns, such as ground squirrels. It will move within a radius of 1–2 miles from its burrow to hunt for insects and small vertebrates. It hunts either alone or in pairs. It is an energetic burrower in loose soil. Its burrow system is very complicated, and designed so that the entire colony is connected underground. It is common to see it sitting upright on its hind legs so as to get a better view of its surroundings. At the slightest sign of danger an alarm is sounded and the whole colony retreats into the burrows. There are 2–4 young per litter.

301 PROTELES CRISTATUS
Aardwolf

Classification　Order Carnivora, Family Protelidae.
Description　The aardwolf resembles the striped hyena, and is often mistaken for one, but it is smaller. The coat is yellow to dark brown, with several dark stripes running vertically down it. On the back, from the neck to the tail, there is a strip of long, dark hairs which form an erectile mane (which makes the aardwolf look larger than it is). The ears are narrow, pointed, and long. The legs also have dark stripes running across them. There are 5 clawed toes on each front foot and 4 on each hind foot. Length of head and body 55–80 cm (22–32 in), tail 20–30 cm (8–12 in); weight 3–4 kg (6.6–8.8 lb).
Distribution　Eastern and southern Africa.
Habitat　Savanna and arid, open plains.
Behavior　This animal is nocturnal; as a result not much is known about it. It is generally solitary, shy, and elusive. It is often seen in pairs or small groups. The females will form small groups in which the young are raised collectively. The female gives birth to 2–4 young in a burrow, often one that has been borrowed from an aardvark (*Orycteropus afer*, **130**). The aardwolf feeds on insects, mainly termites and larvae, but will eat rodents occasionally. When attacked, it instantly raises the crest on its back, takes up a sideways stance to the attacker and emits a strong, unpleasant odor from its anal glands.
Note　The aardwolf used to be considered a member of Hyaenidae, but has been placed in a family of its own because of major differences in dentition.

302 CROCUTA CROCUTA
Spotted, or laughing, hyena

Classification　Order Carnivora, Family Hyaenidae.
Description　It is the largest of all the hyenas, with a robust, powerful body, a large head, large eyes and rounded ears. The color of the coat is variable but tends to brown, yellow, and gray, with numerous dark spots. The short tail has a black tuft at the tip. The hind legs and the muzzle are sometimes black. Length of head and body 1.3–1.6 m (4.3–5.3 ft), tail 25–30 cm (10–12 in); weight 59–82 kg (130–180 lb).
Distribution　Sub-Saharan Africa except densely forested areas and the southern tip of the continent.
Habitat　Savanna and open grassland.
Behavior　This hyena is generally nocturnal, but does move around during the day. It lives alone or in pairs. It patrols a large territory and often follows large herbivores on their migratory routes. It feeds on carcasses, but can attack and tear apart animals the size of a gnu (**400**). It has learned to follow herbivores during the calving season and will kill the young almost as soon as they are born. It enlarges burrows abandoned by aardvarks (**130**), or it may dig its own. During the courtship and mating period it sometimes gathers in large packs which are quite noisy. The gestation period lasts for about 110 days, after which 1 or 2 young (rarely 3) are born. The offspring nurse for about 18 months.

303 HYAENA HYAENA
Striped hyena

Classification Order Carnivora, Family Hyaenidae.
Description The hind legs are heavier and shorter than the forelegs. The head is broad with pointed ears. The color of the coat varies from gray to light brown with vertical black stripes along the length of the body. On the back there is a conspicuous, darker erectile crest. The legs also have dark stripes on them. The coat is very long and tends to billow. Length of head and body 90–120 cm (3–4 ft), tail about 31 cm (12.4 in); weight 25–55 kg (55–121 lb).
Distribution Northern and eastern Africa through Arabia and Asia Minor to India.

Habitat Arid savanna, thorn bush, and stony desert within 6 miles of water.
Behavior It generally forages alone, or in pairs, and is almost completely nocturnal. It moves noiselessly, and may be unnoticed at close quarters. By day it stays hidden in vegetation or in dens in cracks among rocks. It feeds on refuse, carrion, and small animals (rodents, birds, reptiles). Some will also prey on domestic animals (sheep, goats, dogs, etc). It has a small territory around the den, but has a large home range (up to 28 square miles). Breeding occurs at any time of year. Litters of 1–5 cubs are born after a gestation period of 90–92 days.

Note This is a rare species due to hunting and habitat destruction. Populations in North Africa and Arabia are in danger of extinction.

---

304 LYNX LYNX
Lynx

Classification Order Carnivora, Family Felidae.
Description Similar in appearance to a large house cat, the coat is normally yellowish brown with dark spots and the underside is white and delicately speckled, but color varies geographically. The ears have terminal tufts of black hair. The tail is short and has a black tip. The feet are large and densely furred, even on the soles; like all felids except the cheetah, the claws are retractile. Length of head and body 80–130 cm (32–52 in), tail 11–24 cm (4.3–9.4 in); weight 18–45 kg (40–99 lb).
Distribution Eastern Europe and Asia.
Habitat Montane forests and woodlands at altitudes from sea level to high in the mountains.

Behavior The lynx is active mainly after sundown. It hunts rabbits, hares, birds, and small deer. It usually hunts by ambushing its prey, then leaping swiftly or by stalking its prey and then pouncing. It cannot run especially fast, but can climb trees, although not to any great height. It is solitary, except during the mating season, which occurs January–March. After a gestation period of about 63 days the female gives birth to 2–4 cubs which are born, blind and furred, in a den made in the hollow of a tree, among rocks, or in scrub. The young nurse for 4–5 months, but remain with their mother until the following spring.

305 LYNX CARACAL
Caracal

Classification   Order Carnivora, Family Felidae.
Description   The color of the coat is uniform reddish brown above and white underneath, but sometimes no darker than beige; pelage is short and very soft. As in *Lynx lynx* (**304**), there are long tufts of hair on the ears. The soles of the feet are hairless. The limbs are long in proportion to body size. Length of head and body 66–76 cm (26–30 in), tail 20–30 cm (8–12 in); weight 15–18 kg (33–40 lb).
Distribution   Africa, Arabia, the Middle East as far east as Pakistan.
Habitat   Savanna in Africa; desert areas in Asia.
Behavior   This animal is nocturnal, primarily to avoid the heat of the day (in the colder parts of its range, it also hunts by day). Despite its long legs it does not run a great deal. It jumps very well and often catches birds by jumping up. It feeds on many species of mammals and birds especially rodents and small antelopes, up to the size of francolins and guinea fowl. It is completely solitary in clearly defined hunting territories. The gestation period lasts 70 days and 2–4 kittens are born in each litter. The young nurse for about 10 weeks and are probably completely independent by the time they are 3–4 months old.

306 LYNX RUFUS
Bobcat

Classification   Order Carnivora, Family Felidae.
Description   The very soft coat is light brown with black markings, but the pattern varies considerably and individuals are found with a completely uniform beige coat. The underside of the body is white with black markings. The tail has a white tip. Length of head and body up to 100 cm (40 in), tail 13–18 cm (5.2–7.2 in), weight 6–16 kg (13.5–35 lb), females somewhat lighter.
Distribution   Southern Canada, the United States (except in the prairies), and parts of Mexico.
Habitat   Varied: most frequently found in forests.
Behavior   This is a solitary animal, living in well-marked territories where it makes tracks, burrows or dens, and places where it rests. It does not often travel outside this area, except when migrating to a new area. Only a few individuals actually migrate, and these are usually young male bobcats looking for food or a site for their territory. It feeds mainly on hares and cotton-tail rabbits, but also eats rodents and deer. Its den is always well tended, especially that of females, who give birth in it. After a gestation period of 62 days, 2–4 young are born. Mating occurs in late winter; the female reproduces every 2 years.

307 FELIS MANUL
Pallas cat, manul

Classification   Order Carnivora, Family Felidae.
Description   The coat is pale yellow; it is very long on the underside, probably an adaptation for snowy or icy environments. The ears are small and round and appear pushed backwards. There are a few black markings on the tail and face. The tip of the tail is invariably black and has 4 rings on it. Because of its short legs, the overall appearance is that of a thickset, bulky animal, which is unusual for a member of the cat family. The winter coat is less speckled than the summer coat; in addition there is considerable geographic variation. Length of head and body 50–65 cm (20–26 in), tail 21–30 cm (8.4–12 in); weight 2.5–3.5 kg (5.5–7.7 lb).
Distribution   From the Caspian Sea east to western and central China.
Habitat   Steppe and grassland, up to 13,000 feet.
Behavior   The Pallas cat feeds on rodents, pikas, rabbits, hares, and birds. It is solitary and keeps out of sight of man. It hunts at night and rests during the day among rocks, in caves, rock fissures, or dens of other animals. Little is known about its reproductive biology; the gestation period probably lasts for around 60 days, and the female gives birth to 5 or 6 kittens once a year.

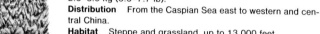

308 FELIS SERVAL
Serval

Classification   Order Carnivora, Family Felidae.
Description   Its legs are long and the head is small in proportion to the rest of the body. The ears are large, oval and vertical. The color of the coat and the distribution of the dark markings and stripes differ in different areas; in the eastern part of its range it often has stripes on the shoulders and back; and it has numerous small markings which give a speckled appearance. Length of head and body 70–95 cm (28–38 in), tail 36–45 cm (14–18 in); weight up to 18 kg (40 lb).
Distribution   Africa south of the Sahara, except forested areas and possibly in parts of northern Africa.
Habitat   Open savanna; common in wetlands on the edges of swamps and by the shores of lakes.
Behavior   This nocturnal felid hunts rodents, lizards, and amphibians on the ground, but it can also climb trees where it preys on birds. It is a solitary animal and only forms pairs during the courtship and mating period. After about 75 days of gestation, the female gives birth to 2–4 young in the old den or burrow of some other animal, which the female modifies to her needs. The serval also adapts well to living near places inhabited by humans and quickly learns how to make the most of farmyards and poultry runs. Because of this and also because of the value of the spotted coat, the serval is hunted a great deal and its numbers are dropping dramatically.

309 FELIS SILVESTRIS
European wild cat

Classification   Order Carnivora, Family Felidae.
Description   The European wild cat closely resembles the domestic cat, but is larger, has shorter legs, and has a rather cumbersome gait. The coat is very dense and thick, more so than in the domestic cat, and the coloring varies greatly: the ground color is gray or yellowish gray, with black stripes on the flanks and a black stripe which runs lengthwise down the back; the underparts are cream-colored. The black-striped tail is bushy and has a rounded tip. Length of head and body 36.5–75 cm (14.5–30 in), tail 21–37 cm (8.3–14.6 in); weight 6–13 kg (13.2–28.6 lb).
Distribution   Continental Europe (particularly in such mountainous regions as the Balkans), eastern Europe, and Asia Minor.
Habitat   Wooded and rocky regions.
Behavior   The European wild cat is solitary except during the mating season. It is mainly active in the early morning and at dusk, but will hunt at night. It preys on hares, rodents, small birds, and lizards. It also raids poultry runs, and as a result, has been persistently hunted and consequently wiped out in many areas. Once a year after a gestation period of 63–69 days, the female gives birth to 3 or 4 young in rocks or in hollow trees.
Note   It is believed that domestic cats were probably derived from this species, which may be conspecific with other wild cats from Africa and further east in Asia.

310 FELIS CONCOLOR
Puma, cougar, panther, mountain lion

Classification   Order Carnivora, Family Felidae.
Description   The size of the puma varies considerably over its large geographic range. The basic coloration is yellow-brown above and pale underneath. The young are born with a speckled coat and a ringed tail, but the markings disappear as the young grow. In the adult, the only traces remaining are black markings on the head. Length of head and body 1–1.6 cm (3.3–5.3 ft), tail up to 80 cm (32 in); weight to 100 kg (225 lb); females generally smaller.
Distribution   Western North America and the southeastern United States, Mexico, Central and South America.
Habitat   All types of habitat.
Behavior   This is a solitary and territorial animal; the male spends a lot of time marking his large territory, but rarely defends it convincingly. The female has a smaller territory, which may overlap slightly with one of a male. The puma preys on most species of mammals but seems to prefer deer. It is a powerful and expert hunter and can jump up to 20 feet in a single bound. By nature active both day and night, it has become strictly nocturnal in areas inhabited by man, its only enemy apart from wolves. After a gestation period of 90 days, usually 2 or 3, but sometimes as many as 6, young are born in protected dens in caves or under ledges or roots. The young pumas are independent after 2 years.

311 FELIS PARDALIS
Ocelot

Classification   Order Carnivora, Family Felidae.
Description   Ocelots that live in forested areas have a ground color between yellow-ochre and orange; those living in more arid areas are grayish. All ocelots are spotted on the head and limbs, and have stripes on the face and insides of the forelegs. The belly is whitish. Length of head and body 80–135 cm (32–54 in), tail 27–45 cm (11–18 in); weight 11–16 kg (24–35 lb).
Distribution   Southwestern United States south through much of South America.
Habitat   Forests, and any area with thick brush.
Behavior   The ocelot is a skilled climber and often hunts in trees, but it usually travels on the ground, lying in wait for small deer, rodents, monkeys, snakes, and other reptiles. Sometimes it will eat domestic animals up to the size of a calf. It lives in pairs, in a well-defined territory. Both partners hunt alone, but will work together when killing a large animal. It is nocturnal, and spends the day resting among branches. Gestation lasts 70 days, after which the female gives birth to 2–4 young.
Note   The fur of the ocelot is one of the most sought after commercially, and as a result the species has already been wiped out over much of its range. Urgent measures to restrict the market are necessary if the ocelot's numbers are to remain at a point where it can survive.

---

312 FELIS BENGALENSIS
Leopard cat

Classification   Order Carnivora, Family Felidae.
Description   The ground color is yellow-ochre or brown on the back, and the underside of the body and the insides of the legs are white. On the head and the nape of the neck there are 4 or 5 black stripes running lengthwise, which break up into 2–4 irregular rows of dark markings on the back. There are two conspicuous white and black markings above and in front of the eyes. The many geographical subspecies vary greatly in size: the length of head and body of the smallest, found in Java, only reaches 54 cm (21.6 in); that of the largest, found in north China, can exceed 60 cm (24 in). The animal pictured here is probably from one of the smaller, more southern subspecies, with a tail about 23 cm (9.2 in) long and weighing up to 2.5 kg (5.5 lb).
Distribution   Throughout eastern Asia, including Sumatra, Java, Borneo, and the Philippines.
Habitat   Forest and woodland, to an altitude of 10,000 feet.
Behavior   The leopard cat is solitary and hunts mainly in the twilight hours and at night. It is an agile climber, even on quite fragile branches, and it can swim very well. It is usually found in places where there is a permanent and abundant water supply. It preys on rodents, birds, hares, and also eats bats and fawns. The gestation period lasts 65–70 days, and litters usually consist of 3 or 4 young.

313 FELIS YAGOUAROUNDI
Jaguarundi

Classification Order Carnivora, Family Felidae.

Description There are three different color phases and all three can be present in the same litter; one is black, the second reddish brown, and the third gray. The young are born with a spotted coat. The jaguarundi is relatively small, has short legs, a small, flattened head, an elongated body, and a long tail. Length of head and body 55–77 cm (22–30.8 in), tail 33–60 cm (13.2–24 in); weight 4.5–9 kg (10–20 lb).

Distribution From Texas south throughout most of South America.

Habitat Forests and scrub, often near water.

Behavior This is a solitary cat which moves about with agility on the ground and in trees. It prefers to live in areas with scrub and bushes, and hides in low branches and brambles. It feeds on rodents, birds, frogs, rabbits, and occasionally domestic poultry. It is active both day and night, and tends to keep moving, unlike most other felids, which tend to be more sedentary. Reproduction possibly occurs twice a year, in summer and spring, during which time pairs form briefly. After a gestation period of 63–70 days, 2–4 kittens are born. They nurse for about 2 months and are independent about 4 weeks later. There are 2 litters a year.

---

314 PANTHERA ONCA
Jaguar

Classification Order Carnivora, Family Felidae.

Description The coat is bright yellow, almost reddish, on the back and has conspicuous circular markings, or rosettes, with a small black spot in the middle; the belly is white. The 8 subspecies are distinguished by minor features. The head is large and bulky; the body is robust and the short legs are powerfully built. Length of head and body 1.2–1.8 m (4–6 ft), tail 45–75 cm (18–30 in); weight 90–114 kg (200–251 lb).

Distribution From the southern United States to latitude 40° in South America.

Habitat Tropical forests.

Behavior The jaguar is most abundant around rivers or other bodies of water; it is a good swimmer. The jaguar hunts on the ground and in trees. Its prey varies from tapirs to monkeys, caimans to tortoises, and includes livestock. It is solitary and only forms pairs for the brief courtship and mating season, which occurs in the spring further north and at any time of the year in the tropics. Gestation lasts about 95 days after which 2–4 young are born. They nurse for 3–4 months and remain with the mother for about 2 years.

Note Because of man's interference—particularly hunting, and the destruction of its habitat—the number of jaguars has been drastically reduced, and the species is becoming seriously endangered.

315 PANTHERA LEO
Lion

Classification   Order Carnivora, Family Felidae.
Description   The normal color is tawny yellow but varies from gray to ochre and can be blackish; the female has paler coloring, especially on the throat and on the underside of the body. The length of the mane, found only in males, may be associated with the harshness of the local climate. Length of head and body in males 1.7–1.9 m (5.6–6.3 ft); tail about 1 m (3.3 ft), weight 150–250 kg (330–550 lb); females much smaller than males.

Distribution   Originally in suitable habitat throughout Africa and southern Asia to India; now sub-Saharan Africa and locally in India.
Habitat   Savanna and scrub; in India, Asia, it has adapted to forest life.
Behavior   Lions are social animals, living in prides usually made up of one or more adult males, 2 or more females, cubs, and adolescents. It hunts mainly at night, but is also active during the cooler part of the day. It hunts by ambushing prey (zebra, various bovids), and does not usually pursue it. The degree of cooperation has been exaggerated, but the resources of several lions are often combined: while the group stalks the prey, it may be ambushed by a lone lion, usually a lioness, which kills the prey with a single blow on the back, breaking the spinal column. Gestation lasts for 105 days, after which the female gives birth to 2–4 cubs which will remain with the group for at least 18 months.

316 PANTHERA TIGRIS
Tiger

Classification   Order Carnivora, Family Felidae.
Description   There is a large size difference between the different subspecies of tigers: the smallest subspecies is the Javan tiger; and the largest (see data below) is the Siberian, found in Manchuria and Siberia. Depending on climate, the length of the coat also varies, but the striped pattern is similar in all tigers. Length of head and body 1.4–2.8 m (4.6–9.2 ft), tail 60–90 cm (24–36 in); weight up to 300 kg (660 lb).

Distribution   India, Sumatra, Java, Malaysia, Soviet Far East, southern China, and in rare cases northern China.
Habitat   Variable, including most forest types.
Behavior   The tiger is essentially solitary. It has a clearly staked-out territory of up to 400 square miles, which it patrols at regular intervals, marking it with droppings and other signs. It hunts at night, lying in ambush for a wide variety of prey as deer, buffalo and goats, but also smaller mammals. It is an agile animal and swims well. In harsh climates it accumulates up to 2 inches of fat beneath its skin. Gestation lasts for about 104–106 days, after which the female bears 2–4 young, which nurse for 5–6 months and stay with their mother for a year or longer. Mating may occur at any time of year.

Note   The total number of tigers in the world is now reduced to a few thousand, and many local races are virtually extinct.

317 PANTHERA PARDUS
Leopard

Classification   Order Carnivora, Family Felidae.
Description   The beautiful and unmistakable coat of the leopard varies in the ground color from yellow to gray. The black spots are grouped in clusters or rosettes. The backs of the ears are black, with a white marking in the middle. Some individuals are completely black (black panthers); this is more common in parts of southern Asia than in Africa. Length of head and body 95–150 cm (38–60 in), tail 60–95 cm (24–38 in); weight 25–45 kg (55–100 lb).
Distribution   Africa, south of the Sahara and southern Asia.
Habitat   Wooded savanna and forests, at various altitudes; rocky semidesert areas with scrubby vegetation.
Behavior   The leopard is nearly always solitary except for a brief period of courtship and mating. It is completely nocturnal, and spends its days resting in branches of trees. It lies in ambush in trees for its prey, which is killed by either a throat bite or in large prey, by twisting the neck and breaking the cervical vertebrae. Its preferred prey is small antelopes, hares, warthogs, and ground birds, but it will eat most species of monkeys, especially baboons. It moves with agility in trees, where it often brings and devours its prey. The gestation period lasts for 90–105 days, after which 2 or 3 cubs are born. They nurse for several months and are independent at about 1 year of age. It adapts quite well to living near places inhabited by man, and will prey on livestock. It is hunted for its coat, and its continued survival is precarious.

318 NEOFELIS NEBULOSA
Clouded leopard

Classification   Order Carnivora, Family Felidae.
Description   Its body is elongated with short legs which are powerfully built; the soles of its feet are large. Its ground coloring is gray or brownish yellow with black, squarish markings, and oval and rosette-shaped spots. Its canine teeth are exceptionally long, almost three times as long as their diameter. Length of head and body 75–105 cm (30–42 in); tail 70–90 cm (28–36 in); weight 17–23 kg (37–51 lb).
Distribution   India, Indochina, Sumatra, Borneo, and Taiwan.
Habitat   Tropical forest.
Behavior   Little is known about this nocturnal creature in the wild, except that it tends to be solitary. It spends much of its life in trees, where it moves about with great agility. It lies in the branches of a tree where it waits for its prey to pass underneath; then it pounces. Its prey varies from rabbits to young buffalo. It is not known to have attacked man. In captivity it will play for hours and soon develops an affectionate relationship with its keeper. The gestation period is from 86 to 92 days and litter size is from 1–5 cubs. They nurse for 6–12 weeks and become independent at about 9 months.
Note   Although this species is commonly called the clouded leopard, it is not closely related to the true leopard. This species is very rare.

319 PANTHERA UNCIA
Snow leopard, ounce

Classification   Order Carnivora, Family Felidae.
Description   Fur is long and dense, pale gray on the back and white on the underside. A darker stripe runs along the back; the rest of the coat is spotted with solid circles on the head, neck, and lower limbs, and rosettes on the sides of the body and the tail. Length of head and body 100–130 cm (40–51 in), tail 80–100 cm (32–40 in); weight up to 70 kg (155 lb).
Distribution   Central Asia, from northwestern China to Tibet and the Himalayas.
Habitat   High mountains (to 19,700 feet); in winter it descends to lower altitudes.
Behavior   It feeds mainly on mountain goats and sheep, and also on marmots, deer, and other mammals, including domestic animals. Not much is known about the life history of the snow leopard; most of the information on them has been obtained from observing specimens in captivity. On the whole, however, the snow leopard behaves like the other members of the cat family. Its roar is not as loud as that of the leopard. It is most active in the early morning, and in the evening. The female usually gives birth to 2 or 3 young in April–June after a 98–103-day gesation period. The coat of the young has more evident markings than the adult. They are suckled for about 2 months; then they start to eat solid foods. At 3 months they follow their mother about, and remain together for a year or more.
Note   The snow leopard is sometimes classified in a genus of its own, *Uncia*.

320 ACINONYX JUBATUS
Cheetah

Classification   Order Carnivora, Family Felidae.
Description   It resembles an extremely streamlined leopard, and its head looks small in proportion to the rest of its body. Its legs are long and its back is concave. It has a distinctive black mark on each side of its face; the rest of its body is varying shades of yellow with numerous black spots. Length of head and body 1.4–1.5 m (4.6–5 ft), tail 60–70 cm (24–28 in); weight 55–60 kg (120–130 lb); female smaller than male.
Distribution   Africa south of the Sahara except in forests; Arabia, Iran as far as Turkestan.
Habitat   Savanna and arid, open grasslands.
Behavior   The somewhat gregarious cheetah hunts by day, preferably at dawn and sundown. It gets as close as possible to its prey, and then breaks into a short and very fast sprint in pursuit of its victim. It cannot run like this for very long, but it can reach speeds up to 70 mph, making it the fastest land mammal. It attacks many species of small gazelles and the young of other ungulates. It is not an aggressive animal and has often been tamed and used as a hunting aid. It is a quiet, shy animal, and does not tolerate environmental changes very well, nor does it like being near areas frequented by man. As a result, its numbers today have fallen drastically and its survival is in danger. After a 90–95-day gestation, 1–8 cubs are born; they nurse for about 6 weeks and become independent after a few months.

321 CALLORHINUS URSINUS
Northern fur seal

Classification Order Carnivora, Family Otariidae.
Description Adult males are dark brown, sometimes with grayish highlights on the back. The upper parts of females are grayer, the underparts are paler brown. The ears are small; the strong hind feet, which can be folded at an angle with the body, enable the northern fur seal to move rapidly on land. Total length 1.9–2.1m (6.2–6.9 ft), weight 136–280 kg (300–615 lb); female about 80% of length and 20% of weight of males.
Distribution Northern Pacific Ocean.
Habitat Coastal waters; island rookeries in summer.

Behavior This well-known seal spends most of the year at sea where it feeds principally on fish. Its breeding grounds are on the Pribilof and Commander islands where males arrive in spring to establish territories in which harems of females assemble later. Territorial males may remain for 3–4 months on the small territory with 10–20 females, which come and go while bearing and nursing young and breeding. A single young is born each year after about 12 months of gestation. Young are well developed at birth and grow rapidly, going to sea on their own in the autumn.

Note Indiscriminate hunting had decimated the northern fur seal population, but protective management over the past 70 years has enabled this species to make a spectacular comeback.

---

322 EUMETOPIAS JUBATUS
Steller sea lion

Classification Order Carnivora, Family Otariidae.
Description The male is the color of cork, with a darker chest and abdomen; the female is paler; and the pups are blackish. The neck is enlarged by the presence of a dense mane. There are 34 teeth. As in all pinnipeds, the teeth situated behind the canines are more or less the same and are called post-canines. Total length up to 3 m (10 ft), weight 1100 kg (2420 lb); females about 75% length and 25% weight of males.
Distribution Northern Pacific coasts of America and Asia.
Habitat Coastal waters and rocky coastlines.

Behavior This is the largest of all the eared seals. Like all the members of the family Otariidae, this sea lion lives in large groups during the breeding season. Preparation for breeding begins in May when the males arrive at the island rookeries. The males establish and defend their territories against one another. After a couple of weeks, the pregnant females arrive and form harems in the male territories. Soon the pups are born, and immediately following their birth, mating occurs. The fertilized egg does not become implanted in the uterus until the following October. Pups may remain with their mothers for up to a year.

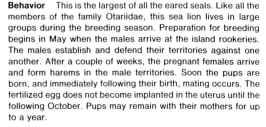

323 ZALOPHUS CALIFORNIANUS
Californian sea lion

Classification   Order Carnivora, Family Otariidae.
Description   The coat is chocolate brown with a few paler areas. Males have a large and impressive mane. The sagittal crest is pronounced and gives a conspicuous raised shape to the forehead. Total length about 2.4 m (7.8 ft), weight about 280 kg (616 lb); females about 75% of length and 33% of weight of males.
Distribution   The coast of California; the Galapagos Islands; coastal Japan.
Habitat   Coastal waters and rocky coastlines.
Behavior   This sea lion is the common one found in zoos and circuses, where it is easily tamed and trained. It lives in large groups in rocky areas. Between May and June, the males become territorial and guard harems of about 15 females each. Gestation lasts about 12 months, and the single pup is born the following year. It nurses for 2–3 months, but remains with its mother for several more months. These are cautious animals, and they dive into the water at any sign of danger. They feed on fishes and molluscs, but seem to avoid the larger deep-sea fish. They have a wide range of vocal sounds.

---

324 ODOBENUS ROSMARUS
Walrus

Classification   Order Carnivora, Family Odobenidae.
Description   The brown coat can be quite thin, and in older individuals the skin is completely bare. Insulation is provided by a layer of fat about 5–8 cm (2–3 in) thick. There are many stiff whiskers across the snout. There is no external ear. The upper canines form two tusks that can reach a length of 90 cm (35 in) and which cause the entire structure of the cranium to be altered. The other 18–24 teeth are similar to each other. Total length up to 3.8 m (12.5 ft), weight over 1200 kg (2600 lb); female 80% of length and 50% of weight of male.
Distribution   North circumpolar.
Habitat   Shallow coastal waters where there are ice floes.
Behavior   This gregarious species lives in large groups. It spends much of the day sleeping on the ice. It usually flees if attacked, but there have been cases of walruses attacking the boats of Eskimos. A cow, in particular, will vigorously defend her young. It feeds largely on molluscs which it may wrench from the seabed with its tusks. Females breed every other year, and after an 11–12-month gestation, 1 or 2 young are born in April–June. The females become sexually mature at 4–5 years and the males at about 7 years.

325 PHOCA VITULINA
Harbor seal

Classification   Order Carnivora, Family Phocidae.

Description   The coat is light gray with scattered black and white markings, which are more numerous on the back. The front flippers have sharp but weak claws. There are no external ears, the eyes are large, and the hind flippers do not bend forward. Total length up to 2 m (6.6 ft), weight to 150 kg (330 lb); female only slightly smaller than male.

Distribution   Along all coasts in the Northern Hemisphere.

Habitat   Coastal waters, especially where there are sandbanks.

Behavior   The harbor seal feeds mainly on fish and shellfish, usually the most plentiful species in a given area; as a result it is often hunted by fishermen. Special hunts are organized to protect migrating salmon. A single pup is born on dry land in April–May in southern part of range or later farther north, and mating may take place immediately after birth, in the sea. Gestation lasts for about 10 months and includes 2–3 months of delayed implantation. At birth the single pup is about 40 inches long and weighs about 33 pounds. It nurses for about 2 months, but stays with its mother beyond that time. The 5 subspecies of harbor seal have different reproductive periods and the pups' coats are of different color. Their greatest enemies, apart from man, are killer whales and polar bears.

---

326 PHOCA GROENLANDICA
Harp seal

Classification   Order Carnivora, Family Phocidae.

Description   The coat is basically gray with a distinctive pattern; the face is black, and a V-shaped black stripe runs along the back from behind the neck and spreads out over the sides of the body. In the female, which is darker, this stripe is less visible; it is absent in young harp seals, which are entirely white at birth. Total length 1.4–2 m (4.6–6.6 ft), weight up to 180 kg (396 lb); female slightly smaller.

Distribution   The Arctic waters of the Atlantic Ocean.

Habitat   Arctic waters and ice floes.

Behavior   The species is divided into three main populations, in the Arctic Ocean, in Greenland, and in Newfoundland. It is migratory, moving north in the summer and returning south in the winter to reproduce. Birth takes place on the pack ice, at some distance from the water, to offer better protection for the pups. The single pup is born in February–March. It nurses for 3–4 weeks and becomes independent shortly after it is weaned.

Note   The fluffy white fur of the pups is highly valued, but taking it means that young must be killed within the first 2 weeks of their life. An agreement among the various countries concerned governs the times and the number of pups which can be slaughtered. Many people oppose the slaughter, however.

327 HALICHOERUS GRYPUS
Gray seal

Classification   Order Carnivora, Family Phocidae.
Description   Coat color is silvery to dusky gray and varies from individual to individual. When the gray seal is wet it looks black; when dry, it is gray-brown. The neck is bulky and fat, and has three conspicuous folds of skin. The claws on the front flippers are long, narrow, and curved. Total length up to 3 m (10 ft), weight to 300 kg (660 lb); females about 75% of length and 80% of weight of males.
Distribution   The North Atlantic, south as far as Nova Scotia and France.
Habitat   Coastal waters among reefs and rocky shores.
Behavior   This is a gregarious species, living and feeding in groups. After the females climb ashore to give birth, the males battle for the best territory and the largest harems. Generally there are 6 or 7 females in a harem. The reproductive period varies widely from one population to another, but gestation is usually somewhat less than 12 months. The single pup nurses for 1–2 months and becomes independent shortly thereafter. There is no migratory pattern, but young males disperse and it is thought that they stay at sea for the first 2 years of their life. They feed on fish.

328 ERIGNATHUS BARBATUS
Bearded seal

Classification   Order Carnivora, Family Phocidae.
Description   The pelt is light brown with a well-marked gradation from the dark back to the lighter underside, where there are no markings. The face is broad, with distinctive long, thick whiskers. Unlike other phocids, which have 2, the bearded seal has 4 nipples, a feature shared only with the genus *Monachus* (monk seals, **329**). Total length 3–3.8 m (9.8–12 ft), weight to 400 kg (880 lb); females slightly smaller.
Distribution   Arctic waters, around the North Pole.
Habitat   Preferably shallow Arctic waters.
Behavior   This species is not gregarious, nor does it migrate; it travels passively, allowing itself to be carried by floating pack ice, drifting with the currents during the spring. The young are born on the ice in April–May after 6–11-month gestation. The female produces one pup every other year, another unusual feature for a phocid. The pup nurses for about 2 months, but stays with its mother for a long time. Sexual maturity is not achieved until the late age of 7 years for males and 6 for females. It feeds exclusively on animals living on the seabed, using a technique like that of the walrus (**324**). Because it is easy to get close to these seals, they are easily hunted, but their hide is of little commercial value.

329　MONACHUS MONACHUS
Mediterranean monk seal

Classification　Order Carnivora, Family Phocidae.
Description　It is gray-brown on the back and lighter on the underside, sometimes with large white patches on the belly. The tips of the brown hairs are often yellowish. There is practically no underfur. The female has 4 nipples. Total length up to 3 m (10 ft), weight to 300 kg (660 lb); female about the same.
Distribution　The Mediterranean sea; in a few isolated colonies in the Aegean Sea; and a colony off the coast of Mauritania.

Habitat　Warm coastal waters of the Mediterranean and inaccessible rocky coasts; often found in submarine caves and grottoes.
Behavior　Little is known about this rare species. The remaining small, isolated colonies probably total no more than 500–1000 individuals. It is extremely difficult to observe these seals, because they hide in caves and grottoes which often have underwater access only; perhaps the decades of hunting by fishermen (who blame the monk seal for destroying their nets) has caused this behavior. It probably reproduces in summer, and feeds on fish and molluscs.
Note　This seal is currently the subject of a major conservation campaign by the governments of Mediterranean countries, particularly Greece.

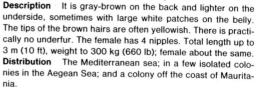

330　CYSTOPHORA CRISTATA
Hooded seal

Classification　Order Carnivora, Family Phocidae.
Description　The adult coat is gray with brown speckling on the back, and white spots on the underside. The young, when born, have a very beautiful coat which is bluish on the back. The name of the species is associated with the inflatable sac on the nose of the male; when fully extended this may be 30 cm (12 in) long and may have a circumference of 16–18 cm (6.3–7 in). The exact function of this structure, perhaps in social behavior, is not known. Total length 2–2.5 m (6.6–8.2 ft), weight 300–400 kg (660–880 lb); female slightly smaller.
Distribution　North Atlantic from the Spitzbergen Islands to Greenland and south to Nova Scotia.

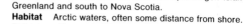

Habitat　Arctic waters, often some distance from shore.
Behavior　For most of the year this species is solitary. It forms small family groups during the reproductive period (March–April) and large colonies in the area of the Skagerrak and Kattegat during the molting period (June–July). The hooded seal does not feed during these periods. Since they are most frequently studied then, little is known of their feeding habits. They breed shortly after giving birth to a single pup, which nurses 2–4 weeks. Gestation lasts about 12 months.
Note　The pup is hunted for its hide; the adult is hunted commercially for its flesh and fat, which are used for animal feed.

331 MIROUNGA LEONINA
Southern elephant seal

Classification   Order Carnivora, Family Phocidae.
Description   This is the largest of the pinniped carnivores.
The male is dark gray, the female is browner. The proboscis,
which functions in social and sexual display, is formed by muscular sacs which can be erected either by blood pressure or by
air. In adult males the proboscis increases in size during the
breeding season. Total length up to 6.5 m (21.3 ft), weight over
3500 kg (7700 lb); female about 50% of length and 25% of
weight of male.
Distribution   Islands and archipelagoes in Antarctic waters
and on the shores of Tierra del Fuego.
Habitat   Rocky coasts of islands and the mainland in the Antarctic.

Behavior   The reproductive period begins in September when
the male comes ashore; the females follow. Harems of 40–50
females are formed, and larger harems of up to 100 have been
observed. The young are born in October and the females mate
after about 18 days. They remain on land for about 25 days to
nurse their pups. During this period they do not eat and may
lose up to 660 pounds as a result. The pup may quadruple its
weight in 3–4 weeks. The males do not eat either, because
they are constantly defending their harem against rival males.
This defense may involve only threatening postures, but there
may be bloody duels, fought with their large upper canines.
When they do eat, squid is the primary item in their diet.

332 LOBODON CARCINOPHAGUS
Crabeater seal

Classification   Order Carnivora, Family Phocidae.
Description   The pelt is light brown and the whole body is
covered with white spots. The front fins are dark. In summer
the color is paler, tending to cream. In January, when molting
takes place, the brown coat reappears. The cheekteeth are unusual in possessing elaborate cusps. Total length up to 2.8 m
(9.2 ft), weight up to 250 kg (550 lb); males slightly smaller.
Distribution   Coasts of Antarctica and of the major islands of
the southern seas.
Habitat   Coastal and open waters in the Antarctic Ocean.

Behavior   Although this is the most common seal in the
southern seas, little is known about its habits. It is gregarious,
and spends much of the year in water. The single young are
born in September–November, and presumably, mating takes
place at this time also, although it has never been observed. It
feeds on krill, which it gathers by swimming at great speed with
its mouth wide open, and then ejecting the water, through the
spaces in its teeth. These seals move with drifting ice occasionally reaching the coasts of South America, New Zealand,
and Australia.

333 HYDRURGA LEPTONYX
Leopard seal

Classification Order Carnivora, Family Phocidae.
Description The coat is either dark gray above and paler underneath or light gray above and below with conspicuous dark spots. The head is relatively narrow and elongated, and the body is long and supple. The teeth are specifically adapted to holding on to prey, and tearing it to pieces; they have three sharp cusps. Total length up to 4 m (13.1 ft), weight to 380 kg (840 lb); males slightly smaller.
Distribution Antarctic shores, and occasionally on the coasts of Australia, New Zealand, South Africa, and South America.
Habitat Open and coastal waters.
Behavior This is a solitary seal, and not very common. In winter, it undertakes long migratory journeys toward the shores of various Antarctic islands. It is not known when the reproduction (as with most pinnipeds, breeding follows parturition very closely) occurs, but it is presumed to be between November and January. The adults molt in February. It feeds on a large variety of food, but it prefers penguins. It pursues and kills these birds under the water; the victim's body is then carried to the surface where it is slammed against the surface of the water and shaken with such violence that it may be dismembered.

334 LEPTONYCHOTES WEDDELLI
Weddell seal

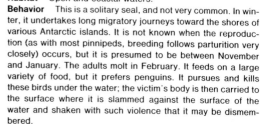

Classification Order Carnivora, Family Phocidae.
Description The pelage is dark brown with numerous lighter markings on the back and head, but there is considerable color variation from individual to individual. Molting may occur any time during the summer months between December and March. The upper incisors and canines project forward. Total length up to 3.3 m (10.8 ft), weight to 350 kg (770 lb); males slightly smaller.
Distribution Coasts of Antarctica.
Habitat Waters close to the shore and pack ice.

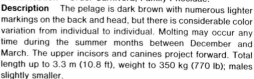

Behavior Although this seal gathers in large groups during the pupping season, it tends to be solitary for the rest of the year. In September and October, after a gestation period of 9–10 months, the pregnant females gather together to give birth. The single pup is weaned at 6 weeks but remains with the mother until it is capable of feeding itself. While nursing, the females do not eat. They protect their young vigorously; if a pup dies the mother will stay by the body for several days. They feed on fishes and squid. In winter these seals spend most of their time in the water, breathing through holes in the ice made by their large canine teeth, which frequently break because of this activity.

ELEPHANTS, HYRAXES,

DUGONG AND MANATEE, UNGULATES

335 ELEPHAS MAXIMUS
Indian elephant

Classification   Order Proboscidea, Family Elephantidae.
Description   They are usually gray and may have light blotches over the body. There are only a few long, stiff hairs present on the body; the tip of the tail, however, has a tuft of hairs. The forehead is flat. Its long trunk, formed of upper lip and nose, has a single process at the tip. Compared with the African elephant, the Indian elephant has much smaller ears, 4 nails on each hind foot instead of 3, and 19 pair of ribs instead of 21; the tusks, present only in some males, are generally shorter. Length of head and body including trunk up to 6.5 m (21.3 ft), shoulder height 2.5–3.2 m (8.2–10.5 ft), weight up to 5400 kg (5.9 t); females somewhat smaller.
Distribution   India, the Indochinese peninsula, Sumatra, and Sri Lanka.
Habitat   Varied; from forests to plains.
Behavior   The Indian elephant lives in groups of 10–30, although groups of this size are becoming increasingly rare. The group is made up of individuals which are closely related, and is led by an elderly female. It rests during the hottest hours of the day and frequently sprays dirt over itself to keep away insects. When the herd travels, it usually does so in single file. Gestation lasts for 18–22 months and a single young is born (although twins are not unknown), which weighs about 220 pounds at birth. Females reach sexual maturity at 9–15 years of age, males at about 15 years. The life span is 70–80 years.

336 LOXODONTA AFRICANA
African elephant

Classification   Order Proboscidea, Family Elephantidae.
Description   This is the largest living terrestrial mammal. Its enormous ears serve to dissipate body heat and brush away insects from its eyes. The upper incisors form tusks, which average about 1.5 m (5 ft) long and weigh about 16 kg (35 lb). The trunk has two fingerlike processes at the tip. The forest subspecies of this elephant is smaller than the savanna race. Length of head and body including trunk up to 7.5 m (24.8 ft); shoulder height to 4 m (13 ft); weight may exceed 6000 kg (6.6 t).
Distribution   Sub-Saharan African except southern Africa.
Habitat   From semidesert to forest at different altitudes.
Behavior   This elephant is a social creature living in family groups which have a matriarchal structure. The head of the group is an elderly female; she makes decisions about when and where to move, and keeps the peace. Groups of African elephants can number more than 100 individuals in periods of drought. The groups are constantly moving when the animals are feeding. The elephant must drink daily, and enjoys bathing in waterholes. Breeding occurs all year, but a female will only give birth once every 4 years. Gestation lasts for 22–24 months, at the end of which a single offspring is born, weighing about 220 pounds. It nurses for 2–3 years.

337 DENDROHYRAX DORSALIS
Beecroft's tree hyrax

Classification   Order Hyracoidea, Family Procaviidae.

Description   The coat is short and dense. The nose is hairless. On the back there is a yellow-white patch of fur surrounding the dorsal gland. The female has a pair of nipples in the inguinal region. The soles of the feet are black and have numerous ridges. The front feet have 4 toes, the hind feet only 3. Length of head and body 42–59 cm (17–24 in), tail 1–3 cm (0.4–1.2 in); weight 1.9–4.5 kg (4.2–9.9 lb).

Distribution   West and Central Africa to Zaire and northern Uganda.

Habitat   Tropical forest.

Behavior   This is a herbivorous, arboreal animal, which spends the daytime in tree hollows. It descends from the trees to forage at night. It is usually solitary, but small groups of 2 or 3 individuals are often seen. The main predators of this hyrax are leopards, genets, pythons, and birds of prey. Gestation lasts for about 8 months, and the young are born in March–April in Gabon and the Cameroons, and in May–August in western and southern Zaire. In most cases just 1 young is born, rarely 2. This hyrax is also hunted by man for food and pelts.

Note   The hyraxes have molar teeth that look like miniature rhinoceros teeth; large, persistently growing, upper incisors; hooplike nails on most toes, and many other anatomical details that are distinctive. Immunological data suggest relationship with aardvarks, elephants, and sirenians.

338 PROCAVIA CAPENSIS
Cape, or large-toothed rock, hyrax

Classification   Order Hyracoidea, Family Procaviidae.

Description   The usual color is brownish gray on the back and cream underneath. There are often two distinct color forms: one yellowish, and the other dark. The coat is dense with thick underfur. On the back, there is a hairless area corresponding to the position of a dorsal gland which produces the characteristic odor of the species. The gland is surrounded by longer, erectile hairs which are yellow, orange, brown, or black. The upper incisors are triangular in cross section and evergrowing, as in rodents. Length of head and body 30–55 cm (12–22 in), tail 1–2 cm (0.4–0.8 in); weight up to 4.3 kg (9.5 lb).

Distribution   Africa south of the Sahara except the Congo Basin; Arabia and the Middle East.

Habitat   Rocky terrain in savanna and semiarid regions.

Behavior   This is the only species of hyrax found outside of Africa. It lives in colonies composed of family units; these may number more than 50 individuals. It usually remains close to the rocky crevices where it lives. It is diurnal and spends much time sunning itself. It is completely vegetarian, and will travel as far as 55 yards from the hiding place in seach of food. It drinks very little water. Gestation lasts for 6–7 months. The female gives birth to 2–4 young, which have open eyes and a fully developed pelage. They include solid food in their diet after 3 or 4 days and are weaned by 10 weeks.

339 DUGONG DUGONG
Dugong

Classification   Order Sirenia, Family Dugongidae.
Description   The back and sides of the body are slate-gray and the underside is paler. The body is covered with scattered hairs, with denser whiskers on the face. The eyes are small, round and black. The ears are tiny openings with no external parts. The nostrils are large and crescent-shaped and are closed by muscular valves. The female has 2 nipples. Total length 2.4–4.1 m (8–13.3 ft), weight 230–908 kg (506–2000 lb).
Distribution   Indian and Pacific oceans.

Habitat   Coastal waters in tropical and subtropical latitudes.
Behavior   The main activity of the dugong is searching for and consuming food. It moves about in herds which once numbered up to several hundred individuals, but now usually have only 6 individuals. It swims by propelling itself along with tail movements, while the forelimbs are held close to the sides of the body. It feeds at night, but its activities are probably governed less by light than by tidal movements. The forelimbs are used to dig out roots and tubers of sea grasses, which are then torn off by the mouth. Breeding occurs throughout the year. To give birth, the female leaves the water for a place just above water level in a sandy spot. Here she gives birth to a single young, which then follows its mother back into the water. At first, the young only uses its forelimbs to swim with, but soon learns to use its tail. The young remain with their mothers for about 1 year.

340 TRICHECHUS MANATUS
West Indian manatee

Classification   Order Sirenia, Family Trichechidae.
Description   It is gray with pink patches. The front feet have claws. The tail is flattened horizontally and spatula-shaped. The body is covered with scattered hairs and there are thick whiskers on the face. The eyes are small and can be closed by means of a sphincter muscle. The ear openings are also small. As the teeth wear out in the front, they are replaced from the rear. Total length 2.5–4.5 m (8–15 ft), weight up to about 500 kg (1100 lb).
Distribution   Tropical and subtropical regions of the New World Atlantic Ocean.

Habitat   Rivers, estuaries, and coastal waters.
Behavior   This is a herbivorous mammal. In saltwater, it feeds on sea grasses, and in the rivers, on various aquatic plants. Generally, this manatee is solitary, but small groups of 2–6 individuals are often seen. It spends most of its time eating and sleeping. It breathes through its nose, and is incapable of breathing through its mouth. When breathing, only the tip of the snout is above the surface. Breeding appears to occur throughout the year. Mating takes place at a depth of about 2.5 m (8 ft), or in shallower water. The gestation period is probably 385–400 days. The female usually gives birth to a single young, but sometimes 2. She suckles the pup while in a horizontal position; the young manatee will stay with its mother for 1–2 years.

341 EQUUS PRZEWALSKI
Wild horse

Classification   Order Perissodactyla, Family Equidae.
Description   The coat is reddish brown on the flanks, becoming gradually paler towards the underside. In summer the coat is considerably shorter than in winter. The mane is dark brown and permanently erect. It has long, slender limbs with 1 large hoof on each foot. Length of head and body up to 2.8 m (9.2 ft), shoulder height to 1.2 m (4 ft); weight to 350 kg (790 lb); females slightly smaller.
Distribution   On both sides of the Altai Mountains in Mongolia.
Habitat   Grassland and steppe.
Behavior   This is the only wild horse remaining in the world and may belong to the same species as the domestic horse, *Equus caballus*. Przewalski horses have been nearly wiped out and it is no longer possible to come across the large herds in which this horse used to gather. Today the wild horse is still being interbred with domestic horses in Mongolia, and before long the species may die out altogether in the wild, and only be found in zoos. In nature this is a very "wild" species, constantly on the alert for enemies (man and wolves); it can defend itself quite vigorously. It lives to an age of 30 years. After an 11–12-month gestation, the foal is born usually in April–May. It can go a long time without water. It feeds exclusively on grass.

342 EQUUS BURCHELLI
Common, or Burchell's, zebra

Classification   Order Perissodactyla, Family Equidae.
Description   The black-and-white striped coat is unmistakable and shows great variation among the 5 different subspecies—and from individual to individual as well. In fact, no two zebras look the same. The white background may be cream-colored in some cases. The mane is short and erect, and the tail has a long black or whitish tuft. Length of head and body 2–2.2 m (6.6–7.3 ft); shoulder height 1.1–1.5 m (3.6–5 ft); male weight 248–357 kg (546–785 lb), female slightly less.
Distribution   Eastern Africa.
Habitat   Savanna and open forests.
Behavior   This is an adaptable animal which can fully utilize the scarce food resources in its semiarid environment. It grazes on short grass, and eats leaves and shoots. It is always found near a water supply. It gathers in large herds numbering several hundred individuals, especially in the dry season, and will often associate with other species such as the gnu, the single other 2 species of zebra, and many species of antelope. They are fast runners and when fleeing predators will remain in a close-knit group. Gestation lasts about a year, after which a single foal is born. Its life expectancy is 25–30 years. Its main enemies are lions, hyenas, cheetahs, and wild dogs. All attempts to domesticate the zebra have failed.

343 EQUUS HEMIONUS
Asiatic wild ass, onager

Classification   Order Perissodactyla, Family Equidae.
Description   The color is pale, especially on the flanks, the face, and the underside. The coat is dense in winter. The mane is often incomplete and hispid. The legs are short and the feet are small. The tail is short and has a tuft of very long hairs at the tip. Length of head and body up to 2 m (6.6 ft), shoulder height to 1.4 m (4.6 ft); weight about 250 kg (550 lb).
Distribution   Mongolia, northern Iran, Tibet, India, and Pakistan.
Habitat   Steppe and desert.
Behavior   The onager lives in groups of varying sizes which are led either by a male or by an elderly female. It is always on the alert for possible encounters with enemies, wolves and humans; its primary defense is speed. It feeds on grass, but can also survive on straw and other plant matter which is of little nutritive value. It can go for a long period without drinking. This ability to endure periods of drought has enabled the onager to survive in the deserts of Asia where its only other competitor is the gazelle. After an 11-month gestation, a single foal is born; it nurses for 9–12 months.
Note   The onager has been domesticated and used for heavy labor since earliest times.

344 TAPIRUS INDICUS
Malayan tapir

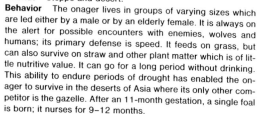

Classification   Order Perissodactyla, Family Tapiridae.
Description   The color of the adult is unmistakable: the forward part of the body and the hind legs are black, and the rest of the body white. The young have quite a different color, brown with white longitudinal markings. The hide is not thick and is covered by just a few scattered hairs. The tail is no more than a large stump. The nose is extended as a short proboscis. In the front feet the first toe has been lost in evolution and the fifth toe is small and is used only on soft ground. Length of head and body up to 2 m (6.6 ft); shoulder height about 1 m (3.3 ft); weight up to 270 kg (600 lb).
Distribution   Burma, Thailand, the Indochinese peninsula, and Sumatra.
Habitat   Tropical forest.
Behavior   It is mainly solitary, but sometimes lives in pairs. It lives only in the thickest parts of the forest, where it moves about at considerable speed and without any difficulty. It is mostly nocturnal. It will often follow the same tracks for years, and it makes well-worn thoroughfares in the dense undergrowth. It feeds on tender plants, preferably where there is water. Nearby water is a necessity for this species, which likes to remain submerged for hours on end. Gestation lasts for about 400 days, after which 1 young is born, or rarely, 2. There does not seem to be a clearly defined breeding season.

345 TAPIRUS TERRESTRIS
Brazilian tapir

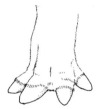

Classification   Order Perissodactyla, Family Tapiridae.
Description   The adults have a uniform pinkish brown colora-tion while the young are brownish and have whitish stripes and spots until 6–8 months of age. The adults also possess a kind of sparse mane; otherwise the hair is short. A rather long pro-boscis is formed by the upper lip and the nose. The small tail is inconspicuous. The female has only a single pair of mammary glands. Length of head and body up to 2 m (6.6 ft); shoulder height to 1 m (3.3 ft); weight about 225 kg (500 lb).
Distribution   South America.
Habitat   Dense forest.
Behavior   This solitary species lives in forests and near water. It swims well. It is timid, fleeing at the first sign of dan-ger, but is capable of defending itself by biting. The greatest enemy is the jaguar. Tapirs are particularly vulnerable at night when they emerge from the water to sleep on the river bank. It feeds mainly on plants and sometimes makes forays into culti-vated fields. It has always been a favorite prey of Indian hunt-ers, who will sometimes capture the young and keep them in captivity until they mature. A single young is born after about 400 days of gestation.
Note   The total number of tapirs—of all species—is declin-ing. The major reason for this is the destruction of the forest which is their sole habitat.

346 RHINOCEROS UNICORNIS
Great Indian rhinoceros

Classification   Order Perissodactyla, Family Rhinocerotidae.
Description   It can be distinguished from the African rhinoc-eros not only because it has just a single horn, but because the hide is covered with bumps and has many folds. The coloring of these folds may be pink. There are no hairs on the hide, apart from a tuft on the tail and at the base of the ears. The feet are all 3-toed; the legs are short and powerful, although they ap-pear less bulky than those of the African rhinoceros. Length of head and body up to 4 m (13.3 ft); shoulder height to 1.8 m (6 ft); weight to 4000 kg (8800 lb).
Distribution   Nepal and northeastern India.
Habitat   Grassland and open areas in forests.
Behavior   The Indian rhino is generally solitary in its feeding areas but it may share wallows or bathing places. The mother is accompanied by a single offspring for several years. It rarely attacks and usually flees from danger. It likes to be near water, and bathes frequently. It is both nocturnal and diurnal. It feeds on grass, shoots, and tender plants. Gestation lasts for 15–16 months, after which the female delivers a single young between late February and April. It nurses for about 2 years and reaches sexual maturity in 3–5 years.
Note   For centuries people in the Orient have believed that many parts of the rhinoceros have magical properties. As a re-sult the species has been hunted almost to extermination.

347 DICEROS BICORNIS
Black rhinoceros

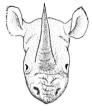

Classification Order Perissodactyla, Family Rhinocerotidae.
Description It differs from the white rhinoceros (*Ceratotherium simum*, **348**) in having a proportionately smaller head, smaller ears set more to the side, no hump at the base of the neck, and an upper lip that is triangular in shape, very flexible, and prehensile. There are 2 horns, the front one being longer and measuring up to 135 cm (53 in). In some individuals the front horn points forward rather than upward. Length of head and body about 3.7 m (12.2 ft); shoulder height about 1.5 m (5 ft); weight 900–1360 kg (1–1.5 t).
Distribution Locally in East Africa and as far south as South Africa.
Habitat Scrub and savanna, open forested areas, up to 11,500 feet.

Behavior Males are usually solitary and females are often accompanied by their offspring. The black rhino travels along regular paths over its home range, which encompasses 1 or 2 watering places. The rhino drinks daily and likes to wallow. It feeds on leaves, acacia bark, and shoots, by wrenching off vegetation with its prehensile lip. It rarely grazes on the ground. Highly aggressive, it charges (sometimes for no apparent reason) at a considerable speed. It generally deposits its droppings in the same place, and then scatters them about with its hind feet. It has weak vision, but highly developed senses of smell and hearing. Gestation lasts for 18 months and the female reproduces every 3 years.

348 CERATOTHERIUM SIMUM
White rhinoceros

Classification Order Perissodactyla, Family Rhinocerotidae.
Description It is larger and heavier than the black rhinoceros and can be readily identified by the hump on the nape of its neck. The head is carried low. The horns are longer and thinner—up to 166 cm (65 in). The ears are broad and have hairs on the edges. The upper lip is square-shaped. Length of head and body up to 3.8 m (12.5 ft); shoulder height 170–185 cm (5.6–6.1 ft); weight about 3200–3600 kg (3.5–4 t).
Distribution Southern Sudan and South Africa.
Habitat Grasslands, savanna; also near swamps and rivers.

Behavior This is the largest land mammal other than the elephants. It is less aggressive than the black rhinoceros. It rarely charges and males only engage in combat during the mating season. The males are usually solitary, but females with calves may be seen in groups. It feeds on grass, grazing with its broad, square lip. It, too, needs water daily, and often wallows at length. It moves slowly and always uses the same tracks and paths. It is active both during the day and at night. It has poor sight, but has acute hearing. The female has one calf every 3–4 years after an estimated 17–18-month gestation.
Note This is one of the most endangered species in the world; about 4000 still survive. In only a few game reserves in South Africa are its numbers remaining steady. The major threat to the white rhino is poaching for the horns.

349 POTAMOCHAERUS PORCUS
Bush, or red river, pig

Classification   Order Artiodactyla, Family Suidae.
Description   On the back there is a long whitish crest of hairs which can be erected when the animal is excited or alarmed. The coat is long and bristly and varies geographically in color, from black in the southern and eastern forms to reddish in the western forms. The tusks are short but sharp; and there are two warts on the snout in old males. The tail is long (about 30 cm/12 in) and is held low. Length of head and body up to 1.5 m (5 ft); shoulder height 64–75 cm (25–30 in); weight 54.5–82 kg (120–180 lb).
Distribution   Africa south of the Sahara.
Habitat   Dense forest and underbrush.
Behavior   This gregarious animal lives in groups of up to 40, although the average number is nearer 20. The group moves together over large territories searching for food. This pig feeds on almost anything, including vegetable matter, insects, eggs, and carrion. In its search for roots and tubers it ploughs up large tracts of land and can cause serious damage to crops. It is nocturnal and spends the day in dense forest. The average litter has 3–6 young. The numbers of this pig are increasing sharply, partly because their principal predators, leopards, are becoming rarer and rarer.

350 SUS SCROFA
Wild boar

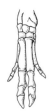

Classification   Order Artiodactyla, Family Suidae.
Description   The coat is coarse, bristly, and brownish, and tends to turn gray with age. The young have a series of longitudinal yellowish stripes on a brown background. The upper canines form distinctive tusks which curve outward and upward; the lower canines are extremely sharp from rubbing against the uppers. The head is relatively long and pointed compared to other artiodactyles, and is without warts. Length of head and body up to 1.5 m (5 ft); shoulder height about 79 cm (31 in); weight about 91 kg (200 lb).
Distribution   Southern Europe, Asia, and northern Africa and the Sudan.
Habitat   Scrub and forests, including arid environments.
Behavior   This hardy, powerful animal adapts easily to different habitats and to a scarcity of food supplies. It often lives in herds of 20–30 individuals, but not much is known concerning the social structure. Old boars tend to be solitary, though. It is mainly nocturnal and will travel quite far each night searching for food. It is basically vegetarian, but easily adapts to an omnivorous diet. It is very aggressive, especially females with young. Litters may have up to 10 or more young.
Note   The wild boar is the ancestor or the domestic pig, and produce fertile young when they interbreed.

351 PHACOCHOERUS AETHIOPICUS
Wart hog

Classification   Order Artiodactyla, Family Suidae.
Description   The adult color is blackish, brownish, or grayish; the young are pinkish. The hide is almost hairless, with only a few hairs present on the cheeks and on the back where they form a mane. The tail is long, has a tuft of hair at the end, and is carried in a distinctive vertical position when the animal is moving. The head is disproportionately large and has two pair of large warts. The tusks form a semicircle between them, pointing forward and upward. The lower canines are extremely sharp. Length of head and body about 100 cm (40 in); shoulder height 64–75 cm (25–30 in); weight 75–100 (165–220 lb); females somewhat smaller.

Distribution   Sub-Saharan Africa, except forests.
Habitat   Savanna and grassland.

Behavior   The wart hog usually lives in small family groups, but several families will often band together temporarily to form larger herds. It is diurnal, but spends the hottest part of the day sheltered by vegetation or in its den. The dens are usually adapted from old aardvark burrows. It is vegetarian and can often be seen grazing in a characteristic kneeling position. It feeds mostly on short grasses and herbs. It does not damage crops, and prefers to remain away from areas where there is human activity. Its main enemies are lions and leopards. After about 175 days of gestation 2–4 young are born which nurse for a few months and become independent about 1 year after birth.

352 BABYROUSA BABYRUSSA
Babirusa

Classification   Order Artiodactyla, Family Suidae.
Description   The color of the hairless hide ranges from gray to brown, the underside paler. The body has only a few scattered yellowish hairs on it. The skin often has large folds on the neck and belly. The legs are relatively long. The upper tusks stick upward through the skin of the snout. They curve sharply backward, as do the lower tusks. Their function is possibly one of sexual decoration, and the male has larger tusks than the female. Length of head and body up to 100 cm (40 in); shoulder height to 80 cm (32 in); weight to 90 kg (200 lb).

Distribution   Sulawesi (Celebes), and Togia and Sula.
Habitat   Forests and canebrakes, always near rivers.
Behavior   It lives in small groups which move around at night. The male digs up the ground and the females and young follow to feed on whatever is uncovered, usually tubers and roots. While the males plough up the ground they emit a succession of brief grunts. It can run fast and swim well. Gestation lasts approximately 140 days, after which 2 young are born in the early part of the year.

Note   This species is completely protected, but it is still threatened with extinction because local people still hunt it for its flesh.

353 TAYASSU TAJACU
Collared peccary

Classification Order Artiodactyla, Family Tayassuidae.
Description Its general appearance is similar to that of the Suidae family, but its tail is vestigial and the hind feet are 3-toed rather than 4-toed. The coat is bristly, blackish, and has a yellowish white band, or collar, on the shoulders. On the back there is a glandular area secreting an oily substance with a strong smell of musk. Length of head and body 75–100 cm (30–40 in); shoulder height up to 55 cm (22 in); weight 20–30 kg (44–66 lb).
Distribution From the southern United States to southern Brazil.
Habitat Plains with bushes and cacti.
Behavior This peccary's diet includes animal and plant matter, but consists mainly of roots, fruit, and tubers. It gathers in groups of 10–20 (but up to 3 dozen) individuals of different ages and both sexes. In summer the group is active only in the cooler parts of the day, but in winter it is busy all day long. If it is alarmed or frightened it can flee rapidly. Its natural enemies are jaguars and pumas. The mating season is not restricted to a certain season. Gestation lasts about 150 days and the female usually gives birth to 2 young.
Note This family, Tayassuidae, comprises 3 species, all located in the Americas, and is the New World counterpart to Suidae. All members of both families have a dislike nasal cartilage. The tayassuids have only 3 toes on the hind feet, however, unlike the suids, which have 4.

354 CHEOROPSIS LIBERIENSIS
Pygmy hippopotamus

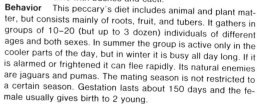

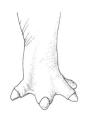

Classification Order Artiodactyla, Family Hippopotamidae.
Description The back is blackish, and the sides and underparts are more grayish; the hide is almost hairless with only a few scattered hairs. The legs are proportionately longer, the head is rounder and not so broad, and the toes are slightly broader and have sharper nails than in the larger hippopotamus (**355**). Also the eyes are set more to the side of the head and are not so prominent. Length of head and body 1.5–1.75 m (5–5.8 ft); shoulder height 75–100 cm (30–40 in); weight 160–240 kg (350–530 lb).
Distribution Guinea and Liberia.
Habitat Rivers and swamps in dense forests.
Behavior This hippo is nocturnal, and is usually seen alone. Its aquatic habits are less evident than those of its larger relative. In fact, in the event of danger, it prefers to take refuge in dense forest rather than in water. However, it is a good swimmer. It feeds on various land plants and has a more varied diet than the common hippopotamus (**355**). The female gives birth to 1 young after a gestation period of about 210 days.
Note This is a rare species whose numbers have dropped alarmingly. Its restricted distribution accentuates the precariousness of its situation.

355 HIPPOPOTAMUS AMPHIBIUS
Hippopotamus

Classification   Order Artiodactyla, Family Hippopotamidae.
Description   The body is a uniform brownish gray dorsally, paler beneath, with pinkish areas on the face. The eyes, nostrils, and ears can all remain above the surface of the water when the rest of the hippo is submerged. The hide is hairless. The canine teeth are long and curved; the long incisors point forward in the lower jaw, and downward in the upper jaw. This is a huge, fat animal with short legs, a massive body, and a large head. Length of head and body up to 4.5 m (14.8 ft); shoulder height about 1.5 m (5 ft); weight about 1200 kg (2650 lb) but up to 2500 kg (5525 lb).
Distribution   Sub-Saharan Africa, except the southernmost part.
Habitat   Rivers and lakes, surrounded by grassland.
Behavior   The hippopotamus is well adapted to an amphibious life. It spends most of its time submerged in water. It emerges at sundown to feed on the grassy plains along the riverbank. It swims well, but usually walks on the riverbottoms. It usually lives in groups of 10–15 individuals. Little is known about the social structure. Hippos often fight violently with each other, frequently opening their mouths widely as a threat signal. At irregular intervals, after a gestation period of 227–240 days, the female produces a single calf which she nurses for 4–6 months. The calf is born and is nursed underwater.

356 CAMELUS DROMEDARIUS
Dromedary, Arabian camel

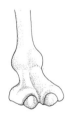

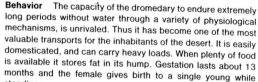

Classification   Order Artiodactyla, Family Camelidae.
Description   The coat is beige or a uniform pale brown, with the underside just slightly lighter. In adult camels, there are horny areas where the limbs touch the ground when the animal is sitting down. It has a single hump on its back where fat is stored. The upper lip is deeply cleft and highly flexible. Length of head and body up to 3 m (10 ft); shoulder height to 2 m (6.7 ft); weight to 600 kg (1350 lb).
Distribution   North Africa, Arabia, and the Middle East.
Habitat   Desert.
Behavior   The capacity of the dromedary to endure extremely long periods without water through a variety of physiological mechanisms, is unrivaled. Thus it has become one of the most valuable transports for the inhabitants of the desert. It is easily domesticated, and can carry heavy loads. When plenty of food is available it stores fat in its hump. Gestation lasts about 13 months and the female gives birth to a single young while standing.
Note   Today this species is either domesticated or has become feral. There are no true wild dromedaries left. The large population of wild dromedaries in Australia all originate from domesticated stock introduced there.

357 CAMELUS BACTRIANUS
Bactrian camel

Classification   Order Artiodactyla, Family Camelidae.

Description   It has two humps. The long, woolly coat varies from dark brown to beige; it hasv a mane, and beardlike hair on the throat. The stomachs of camels have 4 chambers but these do not coincide anatomically with those of the ruminants. The feet are broad and adapted to walking in sandy terrain. Length of head and body may exceed 3 m (10 ft); shoulder height up to 2 m (6.6 ft); weight may exceed 700 kg (1575 lb).

Distribution   In its wild state, only in the Gobi Desert.

Habitat   Desert.

Behavior   The Bactrian camel has a remarkable capacity to endure extreme temperatures, both high and low. It lives in small groups of 6–20 individuals, led by an adult male. After a 13-month gestation, 1 calf (rarely, 2) is born, which matures in 3–5 years. It can be crossbred with the dromedary and produce fertile offspring.

Note   This species is in danger of extinction; perhaps no more than 500 Bactrian camels survive in the wild.

---

358 LAMA GUANICOE
Guanaco

Classification   Order Artiodactyla, Family Camelidae.

Description   Except for the head and the legs, the body is covered with long, soft, hair: it is red-brown on the back; paler, almost white, on the underside. Its tail is aboutt 25 cm (10 in) long. The neck is long and slender; the head is long, ending in a somewhat drooping upper lip which is cleft in the middle. The ears are long, upright and mobile. The sole of the foot is divided into two by a deep cleft; the feet are long and narrow. Length of head and body 1.8–2.3 cm (6–7.5 ft); shoulder height 90–120 cm (36–48 in); weight about 70 kg (160 lb).

Distribution   In the Andean range and south to Patagonia and Tierra del Fuego where it occurs at sea level.

Habitat   Arid, usually mountainous areas.

Behavior   The guanaco lives in small herds made up of a male, several females, and young of various ages. If danger is imminent the male warns the group with a sort of bleating noise, and all the members immediately flee, with the male bringing up the rear. It has an ambling gait, created by moving both legs on the same side of the body at the same time. During the courtship period, males become aggressive and fight violently. The mating season occurs November–February and after 11 months of gestation the female delivers a single calf which is born completely covered with hair and with its eyes fully open. It becomes independent at several months.

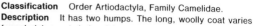

359 VICUGNA VICUGNA
Vicuña

Classification   Order Artiodactyla, Family Camelidae.
Description   The vicuña is more delicate and graceful than the guanaco, and smaller. The long, woolly coat is tawny-brown on the back while the hair on the throat and chest is white and quite long. The head is slightly shorter than the guanaco's and the ears are slightly longer. Length of head and body 1.45–1.6 m (4.8–5.3 ft); shoulder height 75–85 cm (30–36 in); weight 35–65 kg (77–143 lb).
Distribution   South America, in the central Andes.
Habitat   Grasslands and plains in mountainous regions at an altitude of 12,500–16,500 feet.

Behavior   The behavior of the vicuña is similar to that of the guanaco (**358**). Like the latter, it will frequently lick calcareous stones and rocks, which are rich in salt, and it will also drink salt water. Its diet consists mainly of low grasses which grow in clumps on the ground. It lives in family-based groups made up of a male, and 5–15 females and their young; each group has its own territory, the size of which depends on the availability of food. Mating usually occurs in March–April, and after a gestation period of about 11 months the female gives birth to a single young which nurses for about 10 months and becomes independent at about 1–1.5 years.

Note   Because of its magnificent coat the vicuña has been indiscriminately hunted, with a subsequent decrease in its numbers. It now survives only in areas where it is protected.

---

360 LAMA GLAMA
Llama

Classification   Order Artiodactyla, Family Camelidae.
Description   The long shaggy coat varies in color from white all over through spotted or speckled, to brown, black, or reddish brown all over. It is somewhat like the guanaco in appearance but stockier, with long and more varied coat texture and color. Length of head and body up to 2 m (6.6 ft); shoulder height to 1.2 m (4 ft); weight over 130 kg (290 lb).
Distribution   South America, in the Andes.
Habitat   Mountains and upland plateaus at an altitude of more than 10,000 feet.

Behavior   The llama tends to live in small groups made up of a dominant male with a harem of about 5–10 females and their young. Young males are kept away from the group and lead a bachelor existence. Breeding occurs in the spring, and after 10 months of gestation, the female gives birth to a single young. There are no true wild llamas; all are domesticated and are used to transport goods at high altitudes.

Note   As far as zoological systematics is concerned, this species still poses a problem. Some authors consider it to be a domesticated form of the guanaco (**358**), even though domestication may have happened a long time ago; others consider it a separate species. Similarly, the alpaca (*Lama pacos*) is considered by some to be a race of llama, while others consider it a separate species.

361 HYEMOSCHUS AQUATICUS
Water chevrotain

Classification   Order Artiodactyla, Family Tragulidae.

Description   The coat pattern is unmistakable: the basic color is reddish brown, and there are 6 or 7 vertical rows of white spots on the back. In addition, a white line runs horizontally along each side from shoulder to rump. On the face, the black and white bands form a distinctive mask. Its head is small; the snout is pointed, and in adult males, the upper canines are long and slightly curved. Its tail is short, and its high body is set on long, thin legs. Length of head and body about 100 cm (40 in); shoulder height 30–35 cm (12–14 in); weight about 14 kg (31 lb).

Distribution   West and central Africa.

Habitat   Dense tropical forest, near waterways.

Behavior   It is a very able swimmer, and will plunge into the water when disturbed. It lives alone except during a brief social period when mating occurs. It rarely strays far from its small home range. It is nocturnal, which added to its preference for dense forests, makes it difficult to observe. It is, nevertheless, quite common. It is vegetarian, but may, when necessary, become omnivorous. Gestation lasts for about 120 days. Its major enemy is man, who hunts it with dogs, snakes, and long nets.

362 TRAGULUS MEMINNA
Indian spotted chevrotain, mouse deer

Classification   Order Artiodactyla, Family Tragulidae.

Description   The brown coat is speckled with white markings. The body is stocky, with rounded hindquarters; the legs are slender and the feet are 4-toed, but the outer toes are small. It has 34 teeth. The upper canines in the male are longer and more pointed than those of the female. Length of head and body 45–55 cm (18–22 in); shoulder height 20–33 cm (8–13 in); weight about 2.5 kg (5.5 lb).

Distribution   Southern India and Sri Lanka.

Habitat   Equatorial forest.

Behavior   This nocturnal animal is very timid and disappears in dense vegetation at the least hint of danger. It is thus very difficult to observe in the wild. It is solitary, except for the mating period. Its diet is quite varied, and includes both plants and small animals. Gestation lasts for about 6 months, after which the female generally gives birth to 2 young.

Note   The living tragulids include 4 species of small, somewhat deerlike herbivores with large upper canines, at least in adult males. The foot structure of the tragulids is less advanced in degree of bone fusion than in more advanced artiodactyles as deer and bovids.

367 CERVUS ELEPHAS
Red deer, wapiti

Classification   Order Artiodactyla, Family Cervidae.
Description   The 23 geographical subspecies of this deer differ greatly in size: the North American races are largest; the European races, smallest. The coarse coat is reddish brown in summer and grayish brown in winter; around the tail there is a tawny area. The branched antlers, present only in males, are deciduous; when they grow back the following year, there is usually an additional branch. Length of head and body 1.8–2.5 m (6–8.2 ft), tail 12–22 cm (4.8–8.8 in); shoulder height 1.0–1.7 m (3.3–5.7 ft); weight 100–260 kg (225–650 lb).

Distribution   North Africa, Europe, Asia, and North America.
Habitat   Varied; Mediterranean woodland, broadleaf and coniferous forests, and high montane regions.

Behavior   The adult males form herds separate from those of the females, which also include fawns and adolescents of both sexes. During the mating season, each stag establishes a territory into which he lures as many females as possible for his harem. In this period the stags become extremely aggressive against any intruder, and violent fights often take place. About 34 weeks after mating, the female gives birth to a single fawn.

368 ELAPHURUS DAVIDIANUS
Père David's deer

Classification   Order Artiodactyla, Family Cervidae.
Description   The coat is a reddish tawny color. The long tail ends with a tuft. The deciduous antlers, which are found only in the male, are branched, with the longest branches near the base and the other branches decreasing in length toward the tips. The eyes are large, the ears short and pointed. The legs are long; and the hooves are relatively long and spread apart, providing support on soft soil. Length of head and body about 1.5 m (5 ft), tail about 50 cm (20 in); shoulder height 1.2–1.3 m (4–4.3 ft); weight 150–200 kg (330–440 lb).
Distribution   Originally native to central and northern China; now only about 200 individuals in zoos and game parks.
Habitat   Probably marshy lowlands.
Behavior   This species was discovered in 1865 by Père David, a French Jesuit missionary and naturalist. He managed to catch a glimpse of the deer over the wall which surrounded the Imperial Park near Peking, where the several hundred remaining individuals were kept. Nothing is known about their life in the wild.
Note   Fortunately, this deer has been successfully bred and reared in captivity. In an English sanctuary, rutting takes place in June–August and after about a 250-day gestation, 1 or 2 young are born in April–May.

363 MUNTIACUS MUNTJAK
Indian muntjac, barking deer

Classification   Order Artiodactyla, Family Cervidae.
Description   The coat is short, shiny, and reddish. Antlers, present only in the male, are twin-pronged, with a maximum length of 10–12 cm (4–5 in), and grow on a high pedicel or base of skin-covered bone. Distinctive canine teeth protrude from the upper jaw in males and can reach a length of 3 cm (1.2 in). Length of head and body 90–100 cm (36–40 in), tail 13–23 cm (5.2–9.2 in); shoulder height 45–65 cm (18–26 in); weight 14–16 kg (31–35 lb).
Distribution   The 20 subspecies are distributed throughout India, and eastward into Indonesia to Java, and through China to Taiwan.
Habitat   Tropical forest up to an altitude of 10,000 feet.
Behavior   The muntjac usually is solitary and is active mainly at twilight and at night. It feeds on grass, leaves, and fruit. When annoyed or alarmed by the unexpected appearance of an enemy (tigers and other members of the cat family), it emits a distinctive noise like the baying of a dog. When mating occurs, at any time of year, there are often violent duels between males, with the rivals inflicting deep wounds on one another with their horns and canine teeth. Gestation lasts for about 6 months, after which the female delivers 1 or 2 young.

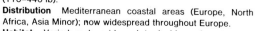

364 CERVUS DAMA
Fallow deer

Classification   Order Artiodactyla, Family Cervidae.
Description   It is an elegant creature, with a coat that is reddish speckled with white in summer and gray-brown in winter. The antlers, which are grown only by stags, are deciduous, or shed annually; the tips are palmate, or flattened. Length of head and body 1.3–2.3 m (4.3–7.5 ft), tail 15–20 cm (6–8 in); shoulder height about 1 m (3.3 ft); weight 50–200 kg (110–440 lb).
Distribution   Mediterranean coastal areas (Europe, North Africa, Asia Minor); now widespread throughout Europe.
Habitat   Varied; rocky arid scrub to deciduous forest.
Behavior   The females and their young live in large herds, and the males gather in smaller groups. During the mating, or rutting, season each male seeks females for his harem. At this time there are violent duels between males. Mating takes place in September and gestation lasts for 7.5 months. The female gives birth to 1 or 2 fawns, which she nurses for a few months. The diet is similar to that of other deer.

365 CERVUS AXIS
Axis deer, chital

Classification   Order Artiodactyla, Family Cervidae.
Description   The coat is a distinctive pinkish brown, with rows of white markings that are retained throughout life. The inside of the legs and the throat are also white. The branched antlers, present only in males, are shed annually. Length of head and body 1.1–1.4 m (3.6–4.5 ft), tail 20–30 cm (8–12 in); shoulder height about 80 cm (32 in); weight about 50 kg (110 lb).
Distribution   India and Sri Lanka.
Habitat   Woodland, forests, and clearings near waterways.
Behavior   This deer often lives in large herds, with many females and 2 or often 3 stags. It grazes in the early morning and evening, and rests in cool places during the heat of the day. If an enemy (tiger, leopard, or dhole) approaches, the axis deer flees and often takes refuge in streams or rivers where it can swim to safety. Gestation lasts 7–7.5 months. She gives birth to 1–3 fawns.

366 CERVUS UNICOLOR
Indian sambar

Classification   Order Artiodactyla, Family Cervidae.
Description   There are 6 distinct subspecies which vary in size and color. The coat is hispid and long. Only the stags have antlers, which usually have three tines each and can reach a length of 1 m (3.3 ft). Length of head and body 1.7–2.7 m (5.7–9 ft), tail 22–35 cm (9–14 in); shoulder height 1.2–1.5 m (4–5 ft); weight 150–315 kg (340–710 lb).
Distribution   India and Indonesia.
Habitat   Humid tropical and subtropical forests, up to an altitude of 10,000 feet.
Behavior   The diet consists mainly of grass, leaves, and wild fruit. It is not easy to catch a glimpse of the sambar, even where it is numerous because at the slightest sound it darts off into the depths of the forest. If attacked by a tiger, leopard, or wild dogs, it often takes to streams and swims away. Except for the mating season, it is solitary. During the mating season the stags acquire harems which they defend vigorously from rivals. In central and southern India the females give birth during May and early June, but reproduction occurs at different times in other parts of its range. After an 8-month gestation, 1 or rarely 2 fawns are born; they are nursed for a few months.

369 HYDROPOTES INERMIS
Chinese water deer

Classification Order Artiodactyla, Family Cervidae.

Description The coat is short, thin, and red-brown in summer; in winter it is dark, dense, and woolly. A special feature of this species is the presence of long upper canine teeth, up to 6 cm (2.4 in) in length, which protrude from the upper jaw like the canines of chevrotains (**361**) and musk deer (**362**). Another unusual feature is the absence of antlers. The front legs are slightly shorter than the hind legs. Length of head and body 75–97 cm (30–39 in), tail about 8 cm (3.2 in); shoulder height 45–55 cm (18–22 in); weight around 15 kg (33 lb).

Distribution Eastern China and Korea.

Habitat Swamps, marshlands, and plains near rivers and streams.

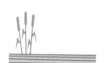

Behavior It lives alone or in pairs in dense vegetation. If disturbed it remains motionless and silent, but if the danger persists, it runs away rapidly. In the mating season the stags engage in violent clashes in which the long canine teeth are used as weapons. Gestation lasts for about 6 months. The female gives birth to 1–6 fawns, whose coats are speckled with white. They nurse for a few months, and leave their mother when they are about 6 months old.

370 ODOCOILEUS VIRGINIANUS
White-tailed deer

Classification Order Artiodactyla, Family Cervidae.

Description In summer the coat is reddish-brown, and in winter gray-brown. The underside of the tail is completely white. Only the males have antlers; its branches point upward at regular intervals from the gracefully curving main stem. The 39 subspecies vary widely in size: length of head and body 85–205 cm (2.8–6.6 ft), tail 10–35 cm (4–14 in); shoulder height up to 92 cm (36.8 in); weight 50–200 kg (110–450 lb).

Distribution Southern Canada, south to northern South America.

Habitat Temperate to tropical deciduous forest.

Behavior This deer gathers in small herds, usually of not more than a dozen animals of the same sex. It feeds during the day and at night on branches and leaves of bushes in winter, but prefers to eat tender grass and herbs in summer. If alarmed, it bounds swiftly away into dense vegetation with its tail raised. This "white flag" signals danger and perhaps assists the group to re-form. Pairs may form briefly at mating. The female gives birth to 1 or 2 fawns, whose coats are speckled with white, after about 7 months of gestation. The young can walk a few hours after they are born, but remain quietly hidden in scrub waiting for their mother to return to feed them.

371 MAZAMA AMERICANA
Red brocket

Classification Order Artiodactyla, Family Cervidae.

Description The coat is yellowish red, and darker on the back. The short, spikelike antlers, present in the male only, are not branched. They may not be shed each year as in most deer. The front legs are much shorter than the hind legs. Length of head and body 95–135 cm (38–54 in), tail 10–15 cm (4–6 in); shoulder height 43–65 cm (17–26 in); weight 16–20 kg (35–44 lb).

Distribution Central and South America.

Habitat Woodland with undergrowth and bushes.

Behavior The small size of this solitary deer enables it to hide easily in the thick vegetation. It emerges at night to graze or find melon plantations or vegetable gardens. At dawn it returns to its resting place, sleeping in hollows among tree roots or beneath fallen tree trunks. The males have territories which they mark with glands situated at the base of the antlers; these secrete a strong-smelling substance when rubbed against tree trunks. The female enters the male's territory only to mate. There is no precise breeding season. Gestation lasts about 7.5 months. The female gives birth to a single fawn with a white-speckled coat, which she nurses for several weeks. It goes off on its own after a few months.

---

372 ALCES ALCES
Moose, elk

Classification Order Artiodactyla, Family Cervidae.

Description The coat is gray-brown or dark gray, but paler on the legs. The head is large and elongated with a flattened mouth. The male has impressive palmate antlers (the largest in the deer family), with points of varying lengths. The hooves are large and can be spread apart. The back is lower at the rump; the neck is powerful and has a dewlap of skin in males which hangs down. Length of head and body about 3 m (10 ft), tail about 17 cm (6.8 in); shoulder height about 1.9 m (6.3 ft); weight about 595 kg (1315 lb); females usually slightly smaller than males.

Distribution There are 7 subspecies, distributed in northern parts of Europe, North America, and Asia.

Habitat Boreal forest including taiga, bogs, and marshlands.

Behavior The moose feeds mainly on aquatic plants and young shoots. It spends much of its time feeding with its feet immersed in water or mud. It is active mainly in the morning and evening. Males are usually solitary, while females are accompanied by that year's calf. Mating occurs in the autumn; the males emit loud calls, and engage in violent battles over the females. A single calf (whose coat is red-brown) is born in April–June after a 250-day gestation. It nurses for several months, but stays with its mother for a year or two. Their main predators are bears, wolves, and man.

373 RANGIFER TARANDUS
Reindeer, caribou

Classification Order Artiodactyla, Family Cervidae.
Description The coat is dense, warm, and waterproof. In summer, it is dark-brown; in winter, it is gray, tending toward white. Both sexes have antlers; the female's are thinner and less branched than the male's, which are very large and asymmetrical, with the first branch or brow line fanning out in the shape of a shovel. The hooves are very broad and enable the reindeer to walk easily in deep snow. Length of head and body 1.8–2 m (6–6.6 ft), tail 10–20 cm (4–8 in); shoulder height 1.1–1.4 m (3.6–4.7 ft); weight up to 320 kg (705 lb); females usually smaller than males.
Distribution Scandinavia, Asia, and northern North America.
Habitat Arctic tundra.

Behavior Reindeer, or caribou, live in large herds which migrate twice a year as the seasons change. In summer they graze in the northernmost parts of their range on aromatic plants; in winter they head south to feed on mosses and lichens. Mating begins in late September or early October. At this time the mane around the male's neck becomes denser and longer. The males do not gather females in harems, instead, they pursue females in heat. Duels between males are rare. In April–May, after a gestation period of about 8 months, the female gives birth to a single calf, which can start following its mother within minutes.

Note The reindeer has been domesticated by the Lapps, who travel with them across the northern regions of Norway.

374 CAPREOLUS CAPREOLUS
Roe deer

Classification Order Artiodactyla, Family Cervidae.
Description The smooth summer coat is reddish; the winter coat is denser gray-brown. Only the stag has antlers, and these are shed annually. They usually have 6 branches, although as many as 10 branches have been observed. The head is slender and the legs are long; the tail is more or less nonexistent. Length of head and body 95–140 cm (3.1–4.6 ft); shoulder height 65–75 cm (26–30 in); weight 15–50 kg (33–110 lb); females smaller than males.
Distribution Europe, Asia Minor, and northern Asia.
Habitat Thick woodland in mountainous regions and in lowlands.

Behavior The roe deer is generally solitary but sometimes lives in small family groups (a male, a female, and that year's young). The stag marks his territory with secretions from glands on the forehead, from anal and metacarpal glands, and with urine. Males and females may mate in summer and again in autumn, but the 1–3 young are always born in the spring because the embryo, no matter when fertilized, will not begin to develop until autumn. Gestation then proceeds normally for 5 months. The fawns, whose coats are speckled at birth, remain concealed for the first 3–5 days, then begin to follow their mother. They nurse for 2–3 months, and go off on their own a few months later.

375 GIRAFFA CAMELOPARDALIS
Giraffe

Classification   Order Artiodactyla, Family Giraffidae.
Description   This is the tallest living animal. The coat pattern is made up of brown spots of varying sizes, separated by a network of light-colored lines. This pattern varies a great deal between the different geographical subspecies. The giraffe has two small horns and a medium bulge on its forehead, which are covered with skin and hair. Shoulder height about 3.5 m (11.5 ft), height to the head up to 6 m (20 ft); weight up to 1200 kg (1.3 t).

Distribution   Irregular range in sub-Saharan Africa.
Habitat   Savanna; rarely in sparse scrub.
Behavior   This gregarious creature lives in herds which can number up to 30–40 individuals; the group is dominated by an old bull giraffe, but is led by a female when on the move. Sometimes exclusively male groups are formed. The giraffe is vegetarian, and will feed on spiny or thorny plants which it handles easily with its prehensile upper lip and very long tongue. When it walks it has an ambling gait, but when it runs or canters it moves its front legs together and its back legs together, in sequence. Giraffes breed year round and give birth after a 15 month gestation to a single young. The offspring nurses for about a year, but begins to eat leaves after a few weeks. The female reaches sexual maturity at 3.5 years of age, the male at 4.5 years. The range of the giraffe today has been drastically reduced by hunting, farming, and epidemics of rinderpest.

376 OKAPIA JOHNSTONI
Okapi

Classification   Order Artiodactyla, Family Giraffidae.
Description   The coat pattern is distinctive; the sides of the buttocks and upper limbs are barred with black and white stripes varying in width. The shape of the body is reminiscent of that of the giraffe because the hindquarters are fairly low, but the neck is much shorter. Also like the giraffe, it has a very long tongue. The legs are noticeably long in proportion to the torso. In males, there are two small horns on the forehead which point backward and are covered with hair. Length of head and body about 2 m (6.6 ft); shoulder height about 1.6 m (5.3 ft); weight up to 228 kg (500 lb).

Distribution   The Ituri forest in northeastern Zaire.
Habitat   Equatorial forest near waterways.
Behavior   This is an extremely timid and elusive animal. It is mainly nocturnal and lives alone or in pairs in the densest parts of the forest. It feeds on plants, fruit, shoots, and leaves, foraging with its long tongue. Little is known about the reproductive biology of the okapi, but it is believed to have a gestation of about 440 days. A calf is born in August–October.
Note   The only other living member of the family Giraffidae, this species was not discovered until the beginning of this century because of its retiring nature and the inaccessibility of its habitat. Its distribution is more or less limited to the Ituri forest.

377 ANTILOCAPRA AMERICANA
Pronghorn

Classification   Order Artiodactyla, Family Antilocapridae.

Description   Both male and female have horns which grow above the eye sockets. The males' horns are dark, with a white and a short process at the front. The outer sheath of the horn is shed once a year, about a month after the rut. The horns are quite distinctive, usually branched, and range from 33–50 cm (13–20 in) in males and up to 12 cm (5 in) in females. The legs are relatively long and slender. Length of head and body about 1.4 m (4.6 ft); tail 7–10 cm (2.8–4 in); shoulder height 80–100 cm (2.6–3.3 ft); weight 35–70 kg (77–155 lb).

Distribution   Canada, United States, and western Mexico.

Habitat   Grasslands.

Behavior   In a family by itself, the mostly diurnal proghorn is a dainty eater and feeds on a wide variety of plants. It usually lives in herds, but solitary animals are sometimes seen. During the mating season the adult males become territorial and mark their territory with droppings and urine. If another male encroaches on the territory, the owner adopts various specific defensive postures, and if the intruder does not retreat, the males may engage in a full-scale duel. The mating call of the rutting male is a guttural cry. If the female accepts the male's advances she raises her tail, and the male approaches with very short steps. Usually 2 young are born after a gestation period of about 250 days.

378 TRAGELAPHUS SCRIPTUS
Bushbuck

Classification   Order Artiodactyla, Family Bovidae.

Description   It is dark-brown to hazel in ground color, with a pattern of white stripes and spots which varies a great deal over its geographic range. The female is smaller, paler, and lacks horns. In the male, the horns are slightly bent, have a longitudinal ridge in cross section, and make a single twist of a spiral. Length of head and body 1–1.5 m (3.3–5 ft); shoulder height 69–94 cm (27–37 in); weight 32–77 kg (70–170 lb).

Distribution   Africa south of the Sahara except Somalia and the southwestern region. '

Habitat   Open forest and densely wooded savanna.

Behavior   This nocturnal animal rarely leaves its very small territory. It feeds on leaves, shoots, and sometimes on roots (it eats more grass when it is young). It is usually solitary, in pairs, or in a group composed of a mother and that year's offspring. After a gestation of about 220 days, a single young is born. It is a preferred prey of leopards and pythons.

Note   The bushbuck and the following four entries (379–382) are all members of the subfamily Tragelaphinae, which has 9 living species in all.

379 TRAGELAPHUS STREPSICEROS
Greater kudu

Classification   Order Artiodactyla, Family Bovidae.
Description   The general color is bluish gray to grayish brown; its flanks have a conspicuous series of 7–10 vertical white stripes. There is a long erectile fringe of hair from the chin down the length of the neck, and another along the back as far as the tail. The long horns, found only in the male, average 1.3 m (51 in) long, make 2 or 3 complete twists of a spiral and diverge slightly. Length of head and body about 2.5 m (8.2 ft); shoulder height about 1.6 m (5.2 ft); weight up to 327 kg (720 lb); female somewhat smaller.
Distribution   Eastern and Southern Africa.
Habitat   Scrub and open forest; rarely in plains.
Behavior   The kudu lives in small family groups of 4 or 5 individuals, often without males. The males sometimes form their own herds, but are frequently solitary. It is largely nocturnal, resting in the shade during the heat of the day. It feeds on leaves and shoots of a large variety of plants, including many usually rejected by other herbivores because of an unpleasant taste. The greater kudu runs heavily and very clumsily, but is an accomplished jumper. After a 7–8-month gestation, a single offspring is born.
Note   Hunting of these creatures for trophies, their horns are particularly beautiful, has endangered the last surviving pockets of this species.

---

380 TRAGELAPHUS ORYX
Eland

Classification   Order Artiodactyla, Family Bovidae.
Description   The appearance is similar to that of an ox, both in terms of size and proportions. The basic color is pale beige-brown, which tends to turn gray with age. On the shoulders there are a few inconspicuous white stripes. On the throat there is a dewlap which runs down to the chest and has a tuft of black hairs on the lower part. On the back, there is a line of black hair which follows the outline of the body. The large horns are slightly divergent, and curve slightly backward. They average 76 cm (30 in) long, and make two complete spirals in the lower half. The female is smaller, and has lighter, but often longer horns. Length of head and body 2–3.5 m (6.6–11.5 ft); shoulder height 1.4–1.8 m (4.6–5.9 ft); weight usually 591–682 kg (1300–1500 lb) but up to 909 kg (2000 lb).
Distribution   Eastern and southern Africa.
Habitat   Savanna, plains; only rarely in open forests.
Behavior   The eland lives in large groups, usually of 25–70 individuals, but occasionally up to 200. These herds live in association with other herbivores including zebras and gemsbok. Old males tend to be solitary. It is diurnal, and feeds on leaves and tender branches, and will dig in the ground to unearth tubers and roots. After a 250–270-day gestation, a single young is born. The females become sexually mature at 5 years, the males at 4.

381 BOSELAPHUS TRAGOCAMELUS
Nilgai

Classification Order Artiodactyla, Family Bovidae.

Description The coat is relatively short; the male's is gray with blue highlights, and the female's is brown. There is an erectile mane. The horns, present only in the male, are 20–25 cm (8–10 in) long and curve slightly forward. The head is long and slender, the neck is short and stocky; the body is bulky; and the legs are slender. Length of head and body 1.8–2 m (5.9–6.6 ft); shoulder height 1.2–1.5 m (3.9–4.9 ft); weight up to 200 kg (440 lb).

Distribution India.

Habitat Grassy steppe and woodland.

Behavior The diurnal nilgai lives in groups of 8–10 individuals of both sexes. Each group has its own territory, in which paths are followed to resting places, watering holes, and areas where the dropping are deposited. The mating season occurs at the end of March and the young are usually born in December. The female usually gives birth to twins after a gestation.

Note Although the nilgai doesn't clearly resemble other tragelaphines, it shares with the rest of the subfamily the spiraling horn and certain behavioral traits, such as dropping to the knees when bulls fight.

---

382 TETRACERUS QUADRICORNIS
Four-horned antelope

Classification Order Artiodactyla, Family Bovidae.

Description The body is covered with a short dark brown coat. Only the males have horns; these are curved and point upward. A second, shorter pair of horns is often present on the foremost part of the forehead. The legs are slender, and the body is higher in the area of the rump. Length of head and body 90–110 cm (36–44 in); shoulder height about 60 cm (24 in); weight 17–21 kg (37–46 lb).

Distribution India.

Habitat Wooded areas rich in vegetation, near streams and rivers.

Behavior This diurnal animal is usually solitary and has a retiring disposition. If alarmed by the presence of strangers it flattens itself in the scrub, or dashes away with impressive leaps and bounds. It must drink at regular intervals and so must not go too far from a source of water. In the mating season, which occurs during the monsoons (June–September), the males become quite aggressive toward other stags. After a gestation of 7–8 months the female gives birth to 1–3 young.

383 BUBALUS BUBALIS
Water buffalo

Classification   Order Artiodactyla, Family Bovidae.
Description   The coat is slate-gray or black. The lower legs and throat are white. The horns, present in both sexes, are large and triangular in cross section. The hooves are broad and can be widely spread. Length of head and body 2.6–2.8 m (8.5–9.2 ft); shoulder height 1.5–1.8 m (5–5.9 ft); weight up to about 1000 kg (2200 lb).
Distribution   Southeast Asia; Indochina and the Philippine Islands.
Habitat   Marshlands and wetlands.

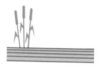

Behavior   In the wild this creature lives in small herds of 10–20 individuals, and in the mating season the males gather harems of females. It spends most of its time wallowing in water or swimming in marshes and swamps, eating grass. The natural enemy of the buffalo is the tiger, but it rarely succeeds in killing a buffalo because the herd bunches together with the powerful horns outward for defense. The gestation period lasts 300–340 days; then the female, or cow, delivers a single calf which attains complete maturity in about 2 years.
Note   The number of wild water buffalo has been reduced to about 2000 individuals because of the extensive reclamation and development schemes which have drastically reduced its natural habitat. This species is not endangered, however, because it has been domesticated. It is used as a draft animal and as a source of milk.

384 SYNCERUS CAFFER
African buffalo

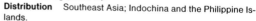

Classification   Order Artiodactyla, Family Bovidae.
Description   There are 3 subspecies of African buffalo: a smaller one lives in the forested areas of western and central Africa; a medium one in grassy areas of the Sahara and east to the Sudan; and a larger one in the savanna of eastern and southern Africa. The body is sparsely haired in adults, but is furred in young animals. It is heavily built with stout legs, a short neck, a broad muzzle and large ears. The horns are heavy with a broad base and are present in both sexes; the set of horns may span more than 1 m (3.3 ft). The tail has a terminal tuft. Length of head and body 2–3 m (6.6–10 ft); shoulder height 1–1.7 m (3.3–5.6 ft); weight 318–818 kg (700–1800 lb).
Distribution   Africa, south of the Sahara, except the southernmost region.
Habitat   From forest to savanna, always near water.

Behavior   This animal gathers in groups that can reach up to 2000 individuals. The herd is dominated by an old bull, but is led by a cow. Often, the older bulls will go off on their own or wander in small groups. It feeds mainly on grass, but also eats leaves, twigs and shoots, and must drink at least once a day. It likes to wallow in water, and retreats into vegetation to rest during the hottest time of the day. Gestation lasts 330–345 days, after which a single calf is born; it will nurse for 6–8 months and reach sexual maturity in 1.5–2.5 years.

385 BOS GRUNNIENS
Yak

Classification   Order Artiodactyla, Family Bovidae.
Description   The coat is dense, long, and woolly, and dark brown in wild yaks; in domesticated yaks it varies in color. The head is broad and bulky, with curved horns which grow from the sides of the head; they are slender and point upward, and may reach up to 95 cm (38 in) in length. Length of head and body about 3 m (10 ft); shoulder height up to 2 m (6.6 ft); weight to 550 kg (1215 lb); female smaller than male.
Distribution   Tibet.
Habitat   Montane, at an altitude of 13,500–20,000 feet.
Behavior   The yak is extremely nimble in its mountainous terrain, despite its impressive size, and so well adapted to cold climates that it would not survive in milder conditions. It feeds on various types of grass, lichens, and tubers, and must have water daily to survive—it rarely manages with snow. It grazes in the morning and evening. The females and young live in herds of 10–12 individuals, while adult males are usually solitary, except during the mating season (Sepember) when they join the herds of females; during this time there are often violent duels between rival males. After a gestation period of about 9 months the female gives birth to a single calf, which remains with the mother for about a year.

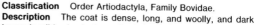

386 BOS FRONTALIS
Gaur

Classification   Order Artiodactyla, Family Bovidae.
Description   The coat is short, coarse, and fairly dense; in the male it is very dark brown, while in the female it is rust-colored. Both sexes have horns, but the male's are more impressive: they start at the sides of the cranium and curve upward, reaching a length of 70 cm (28 in). Length of head and body 2.6–3.3 m (8.7–11 ft); shoulder height about 2.2 m (7.2 ft); weight 700–100 kg (1540–2200 lb).
Distribution   India, Indochina, and the Malay Peninsula.
Habitat   Tropical forest and woodland interspersed with clearings.
Behavior   The guar, largest of the Asiatic bovids, lives in small herds of 4–8 individuals. In the heat of the day it rests, chewing the cud in the densest parts of the forests; in the morning and evening it goes to clearings to graze. It feeds on tender grasses, bamboo shoots, and the young shoots of other trees and bushes. The older males usually are solitary, but during mating season (November–April) they join the herd and there are often fights with younger males. When rutting, the male gaur emits a distinctive mating call, which attracts both females and other males; it can be heard for almost a mile. Gestation lasts for 270–280 days. The single young gaur (rarely, twins) is suckled by its mother for about 9 months and reaches sexual maturity in its third year of life.

387 BISON BISON
American bison

Classification   Order Artiodactyla, Family Bovidae.
Description   The coat is dark brown; it is long and shaggy on the shoulders, head, neck, and front legs, which emphasizes the powerful forequarters of the bison's body. On the forehead the hair is thick and curly, and under the chin it forms a beard. The horns are present in both sexes and are short and curve upward. Length of head and body up to 3.8 m (12.5 ft); shoulder height to 1.8 m (6 ft); weight to 1000 kg (2210 lb); females much smaller.
Distribution   United States and Canada.
Habitat   Prairie.

Behavior   In the winter, males and females gather in separate herds. Some herds move south, in search of a milder climate, while others remain in their territory and search for food by digging down into the snow on the ground to uncover small grazing areas. During the mating season, which occurs in summer, the herds unite, and it is possible to witness violent fights between males over a female. The gestation period lasts for 270–280 days, after which the female produces a single calf, which becomes completely mature in 3 years.
Note   As a result of wholesale slaughter in the last century, the enormous herds of bison that roamed the plains nearly became extinct. Now it is protected, and its number has grown to about 35,000.

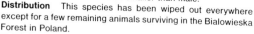

388 BISON BONASUS
European bison

Classification   Order Artiodactyla, Family Bovidae.
Description   The coat is dense, long, and either dark brown or black; it is longer on the neck and head, where it almost forms a mane. The lower section of the horn projects outward, and the tip then curves upward; they are present in both male and female. Length of head and body 2.5–3 m (8.2–10 ft); shoulder height up to 2 m (6.6 ft); weight 800–1000 kg (1800–2210 lb); female much smaller than male.
Distribution   This species has been wiped out everywhere except for a few remaining animals surviving in the Bialowieska Forest in Poland.
Habitat   Forests of central and northern Europe.

Behavior   In the wild the European bison lives in herds which are led by a mature male. Older individuals of both sexes lead a solitary existence. The bison is active during the night and also to some extent during the day; it rests in the afternoon. The mating season is in September, when there are wild fights between adult bulls. The gestation period lasts for about 9 months, when the female gives birth to a single calf. At the present time there are no more than 300 European bison in the wild.
Note   There are 15 species in the subfamily Bovinae, of which 383–388 are members.

389 CEPHALOPHUS DORSALIS
Bay duiker

Classification   Order Artiodactyla, Family Bovidae.
Description   This medium-sized duiker has a characteristic wide black band running from the head to the tail and fanning out over the hindquarters. The general color is reddish brown with the lower part of the legs darkening almost to black. The horns, present in both sexes, are parallel, nearly straight, and rather long for duikers in general. Length of head and body up to 80 cm (32 in); shoulder height about 56 cm (22 in); weight about 20 kg (44 lb).
Distribution   West Africa, and central equatorial Africa.
Habitat   Dense forest.
Behavior   This nocturnal creature lives in the heart of tropical forests. It is usually solitary or in pairs and, spends the day hidden in dense vegetation found beneath old tree trunks or in tangled bushes. It moves easily through the dense undergrowth along paths, which resemble tunnels through the undergrowth. The head is generally held low; an adaptation to life in dense vegetation. Because of the bay duiker's habits it is difficult to observe, and as a result, little is known about its behavior. The gestation period is about 120 days and the usual number of offspring is 1.
Note   The duikers (**389–391**) are members of the subfamily Cephalophinae.

390 CEPHALOPHUS ZEBRA
Banded duiker

Classification   Order Artiodactyla, Family Bovidae.
Description   Among the 14 species of duiker this is the most easily identifiable. The coat pattern is unmistakable. It has about 12 vertical black bands alternating with white ones on a pale brown background across the back and rump. The legs are reddish with broad black markings. The horns, present in both sexes, are very small and almost hidden by the crest of hair on the forehead. The tail is whitish and long. Length of head and body up to 70 cm (28 in); shoulder height about 40 cm (16 in); weight 9–16 kg (20–35 lb).
Distribution   Guinea and Liberia.
Habitat   Dense forest in mountainous regions.
Behavior   This rare species lives in a fairly inaccessible region. Data about its behavior are therefore few. It is solitary and nocturnal, and feeds mainly on plant matter such as leaves and fruit; it rarely eats grass. Gestation is probably about 120 days. When threatened it emits a sound that is like a whistle or a shrill hiss. It is preyed upon by leopards, pythons, and other predators inhabiting primary forests.
Note   This species is in danger of extinction because of the destruction of its habitat.

391 SYLVICAPRA GRIMMIA
Common, or gray, duiker

Classification   Order Artiodactyla, Family Bovidae.

Description   The color is generally uniform, ranging from ochre to pale brown mixed with gray, especially on the hindquarters. There is considerable geographical variation in the color and length of the coat. Horns are present in males (sometimes in females) and are sharply pointed and straight. There is often a black strip down the face, but this is sometimes confined to the area just around the nose. The tail is short, black on top and white on the underside. Length of head and body 85–115 cm (34–46 in); shoulder height 57–67 cm (22–26 in); weight 14–17 kg (31–37 lb).

Distribution   Africa, south of the Sahara.

Habitat   Open terrain, variable, but never in densely forested areas; also found in areas inhabited by humans.

Behavior   This adaptable species has managed to survive where other species have been eliminated. It is nocturnal, and travels singly or in pairs. During the mating season, it sometimes gathers in small groups. It feeds mainly on plants, but will eat animal matter, such as insects. It often wanders into cultivated land and can cause considerable damage to drops. It drinks normally when water is available but can go without for long periods. It has great speed and stamina and can normally outdistance dogs. Duration of gestation is about 4 months.

---

392 KOBUS ELLIPSIPRYMNUS
Defassa waterbuck

Classification   Order Artiodactyla, Family Bovidae.

Description   This species includes two races that once were considered separate species: the form west of the Rift Valley to Senegal has a completely white rump patch; the form east of the Rift Valley and south has a rump patch that is a white semicircle on a gray background. In both forms the coat is otherwise gray to grayish brown, with darker legs. The outward and upward-curving horns are present in the male only, and are about 76 cm (30 in) long. Length of head and body 1.8–2.2 m (5.9–7.3 ft); shoulder height 1.2–1.4 m (3.9–4.4 ft); weight up to 273 kg (600 lb).

Distribution   Sub-Saharan Africa.

Habitat   Scrub and savanna; never far from water.

Behavior   Both nocturnal and diurnal, this gregarious creature lives in herds of 5–30 individuals. Each herd is led by an elderly bull. Often, young adult males form separate, independent groups of about the same size. The waterbuck is usually found near water, but it is not so closely associated with water as other reduncines such as sitatungas or lechwes (**393**). It feeds on grass and other fresh vegetation, and drinks large amounts of water. It is territorial, but often changes its territory. The coat is impregnated with strong-smelling, oily secretions from skin glands. After a 7–8-month gestation, one young is born. The main predator is the lion.

393 KOBUS LECHE
Lechwe

Classification   Order Artiodactyla, Family Bovidae.
Description   The coat is rather long and rough; the male's is dark, almost black, while the female's is reddish. The horns are long, slender, and lyre-shaped. They are found only in the male. The hooves are long and narrow. The hindquarters are noticeably higher than the shoulders. Length of head and body 1.3–1.8 m (4.3–5.9 ft); shoulder height 85–105 cm (34–42 in); weight 64–123 kg (140–270 lb).
Distribution   Southern Africa.
Habitat   Marshy terrain near rivers and lakes.

Behavior   The lechwe feeds on grass and marsh and aquatic plants. It spends much of the day in shallow water. If disturbed it runs at great speed, with impressive leaps, and takes refuge in water; it is a good swimmer. It gathers in large herds which can number thousands. During the mating season (October–January), the sexes mix in the herd. After that period they form separate herds. The gestation period lasts for 7–8 months, after which the female gives birth to a single young. The lechwe is preyed on by cheetahs, lions, leopards, wild dogs, and large birds.

Note   Once numerous, this species has had its numbers reduced to just a few thousand, living mainly in national parks.

---

394 REDUNCA REDUNCA
Bohor reedbuck

Classification   Order Artiodactyla, Family Bovidae.
Description   The color is a uniform reddish or deep yellow above and white underneath. Beneath each ear there is a gray patch of bare skin. The tail is short, bushy, and white underneath; this is conspicuous when it holds its tail erect when running. The horns, present only in the male, are broad at the base, and grow backward and then forward again to form a hook. There are several different geographical races, which differ in the size and shape of the horns. Length of head and body 1.1–1.4 m (3.6–4.6 ft); shoulder height 69–89 cm (27–35 in); weight up to 52 kg (115 lb).
Distribution   Africa, from Senegal to the Sudan and Tanzania.
Habitat   Grassland.

Behavior   The reedbuck is often seen in small family groups or alone. Sometimes young males will band together in groups of 3 or 4 individuals. It lives in grassland, never far from water. It is active during the day, but spends the hottest part of the day resting in thick vegetation. Gestation lasts about 232 days.

Note   Entries **392–394** all belong to the subfamily Reduncinae.

395 HIPPOTRAGUS NIGER
Sable antelope

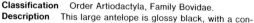

Classification   Order Artiodactyla, Family Bovidae.
Description   This large antelope is glossy black, with a conspicuous white pattern on the face, and contrasting white underside. On the neck there is a mane of long, stiff hair. The female is slightly paler. The horns are very long—up to 100 cm (40 in) in males—almost parallel and curved backward. They are shorter in the female. Length of head and body 1.9–2.4 m (6.3–7.9 ft); shoulder height 109–137 cm (43–54 in); weight up to 257 kg (565 lb).
Distribution   Eastern Africa, from Kenya south to Mozambique and Angola.
Habitat   Wooded savanna.
Behavior   Sable antelopes form herds of 10–20 females and young, dominated by a large bull. Often, the other males gather in separate herds. Gestation lasts 270–280 days. As parturition approaches, the female leaves the male and enters a group with other females. Most young are born in August–February. They feed on grass and move as necessary for food. If seasonal conditions are favorable, the sable antelope may remain in a small area indefinitely. Sable antelopes are prone to fighting among themselves and are able to defend themselves against most predators, including lions.
Note   The subfamily Hippotraginae, to which **395** and **396** belong, comprises 7 species.

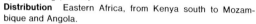

396 ORYX GAZELLA
African oryx, gemsbok, beisa

Classification   Order Artiodactyla, Family Bovidae.
Description   This is a powerful-looking antelope with a well-defined pattern on the head and body. On the face, there are three black stripes alternating with three white ones. There is a black stripe running down the center of the back. The white underside is separated from the gray flanks by a black line. The tail is long and has a black tuft. The horns are nearly straight and almost parallel, and average about 76 cm (30 in) long. The female's horns are usually longer and slimmer. There are two distinct races of gemsbok, a northern form which often has its ears fringed in black, and a southern form with longer horns, rounder ears, and a darker rump. Length of head and body to 1.9 m (6.2 ft); shoulder height about 122 cm (4 ft); weight up to 205 kg (450 lb).
Distribution   From Eritrea to Kenya and Tanzania in East Africa, and in southwestern Africa.
Habitat   Savanna.
Behavior   Gemsbok generally live in herds of 10–40 individuals, often in association with other species of antelope, or with zebras. The males are often solitary. Active from dawn through nightfall, it feeds on grass and leaves, and can survive long periods without drinking any water. The horns are effective weapons; in fighting, the head is lowered between the forelegs in order to impale the enemy. Gestation lasts 260–300 days.

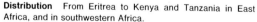

397 ADDAX NASOMACULATUS
Addax

Classification   Order Artiodactyla, Family Bovidae.

Description   The coat varies from pure white to pale gray; a white pattern running across the face from the cheeks to the nose is evident in dark individuals. On the forehead, there is an area covered with dense black hair. The tail is long and has a black tuft at the tip. The horns are long and thin, and make 2 or 3 twists. They average 89 cm (35 in) long; females have thinner horns than males. The hooves have a wide base, which is an adaptation to sand and soft ground. Length of head and body 1.5–1.7 m (5–5.6 ft); shoulder height 1–1.1 m (39–43 in); weight up to 134 kg (295 lb).

Distribution   The Sahara.

Habitat   Desert.

Behavior   The addax is well adapted to life in the desert, even in the most arid parts, where there is virtually no vegetation. It survives on the sparse growth that occurs in the desert after the rare, meager rain falls. It can survive for long periods without drinking water. It must travel great distances to find adequate food supplies. The body temperature of the addax varies during the day and this lessens the need for evaporative thermo-regulation and thus conserves water. It is active from dusk through sunrise, and lives in groups of 5–15 (these groups were formerly much larger). It is believed that gestation lasts 10–12 months; one offspring is produced.

398 DAMALISCUS LUNATUS
Topi, sassaby, korrigum

Classification   Order Artiodactyla, Family Bovidae.

Description   The ground color is brick-red with broad black markings on the face, shoulders, and flanks. The coat has an iridescent sheen in sunlight. The slope of the back is typical of the alcelaphine antelopes, with the rump considerably lower than the withers. The horns, present in both male and female, have conspicuous rings and are broad. Many different races have been defined based on the coat color and size and shape of the horns. Length of head and body 1.5–2.0 m (5–6.6 ft); shoulder height 99–130 cm (39–51 in); weight 91–159 kg (200–300 lb); female usually slightly smaller than the male.

Distribution   Africa in the Sahel region, east to Tanzania, and in southeastern Africa.

Habitat   Savanna.

Behavior   This species of antelope may gather into huge herds (up to 12,000) at particular times of the year when migrating in search of new grazing areas. Usually, however, the korrigum lives in small groups of 15–20 individuals, which graze side by side with other animals. They often eat dry grasses not eaten by other species. They can run very fast when alarmed. During the brief mating season (December–March in the Serengeti), the males become territorial and mate with females which wander into their territory. After a 7–8-month gestation, a single young is born.

399 ALCELAPHUS BUSELAPHUS
Hartebeest

Classification Order Artiodactyla, Family Bovidae.
Description The coloring is almost uniform, ranging from light brown to a pale sandy color. There can be dark markings on the legs. The shoulder is considerably higher than the rump. The head is long and narrow, and the legs are slender. The horns vary in shape, but always sprout from the top of the head; they are present in both sexes. There are several different subspecies of hartebeest, differing in the size and shape of the horns, coloration, and also in the proportions of the body. Length of head and body 1.8–2.5 m (5.9–8.3 ft); shoulder height 120–145 cm (48–58 in); weight may exceed 205 kg (450 lb).

Distribution From Senegal eastward throughout East Africa.
Habitat Savanna and sparse scrub.
Behavior This is a diurnal, gregarious antelope which often congregates in large herds that include other antelopes and zebras. The young males may form separate groups. The males are territorial during the mating season, and mate with females who wander into their territory. This hartebeest feeds on grass, including the driest types, and does not need water daily. It is a favorite prey of lions. Normally 1 young is born after a gestation period of 214–242 days.

Note The subfamily Acelaphinae comprises 7 species of which three (**398–400**) are discussed in this book.

400 CONNOCHAETES TAURINUS
Gnu, wildebeest

Classification Order Artiodactyla, Family Bovidae.
Description This antelope looks markedly bovine, heavily built and of clumsy appearance. The head is massive with a broad muzzle and a median tuft of hairs. Under the throat, there is a beard of stiff black or white hairs. The forequarters are disproportionately heavy in relation to the hindquarters. This imbalance is accentuated by the long mane. The tail is long and black, and ends in long, course hair. The horns, which occur in both sexes, have a distinctive curved shape. Length of head and body 1.8–2.4 m (5.9–7.9 ft); shoulder height 1–1.3 m (3.3–4.3 ft); weight 230–275 kg (506–605 lb).

Distribution Kenya, south throughout southern Africa.
Habitat Savanna and plains.
Behavior The gnu is active both day and night, constantly moving. It generally lives in herds numbering several thousand. In periods of drought the herd moves toward watering holes; when the rains arrive, the herds tend to scatter. It feeds mainly on grass, showing distinct preferences for certain species. In the breeding period, males strive to isolate harems of females temporarily; they rejoin the main herd after a few hours or days. The single calf is born in February–March after about a 9–10 month gestation, and is up and running within 30 minutes of birth. The gnu is a major prey species for many of the large predators, including lions, cheetahs, and wild dogs.

401 OREOTRAGUS OREOTRAGUS
Klipspringer

Classification   Order Artiodactyla, Family Bovidae.

Description   Its color ranges from olive green to yellow, becoming brown on the muzzle. The underside of the body is always white. The ears are large, round, and have a conspicuous black border. The horns average 10 cm (4 in) long, and curve slightly forward. The body is compact, and its long-legged appearance is enhanced because it walks on the blunt tips of its hooves. Length of head and body 75–110 cm (30–44 in); shoulder height 45–60 cm (18–24 in); weight 11–16 kg (24–35 lb).

Distribution   Eastern Africa from Ethiopia south to southern Africa.

Habitat   Isolated rocky areas in the veld (kopjes or koppies) or sweeping terrain like the upland plateau of Ethiopia.

Behavior   This semigregarious creature is often seen in small groups. It is diurnal, but spends the hottest part of the day resting among rocks. It moves about on bare rock, where there is no apparent foothold, without difficulty. The texture of the foot beneath the hoof is rather like hard rubber. It can make impressive leaps and bounds, during which its legs remain stiff. It feeds on grass and can go for a long time without water; it makes do with the liquids contained in the succulent plants on which it feeds. Gestation lasts for about 214 days, after which a single young is born. Most births take place between September and January.

402 OUREBIA OUREBI
Oribi

Classification   Order Artiodactyla, Family Bovidae.

Description   The slender shape of this small neotragine is accentuated by its long neck and tall, oval-shaped ears. Beneath each ear there is a blackish patch of hairless skin. The upper coat is uniform pale brown to reddish; the coat is pure white underneath. The tail is short and bushy, with a conspicuous black tip. Only the males grow horns. There are several geographical races, which differ in the size and shape of the horns. Length of head and body 93–110 cm (37–44 in); shoulder height 50–70 cm (20–28 in); weight 14–21 kg (31–46 lb).

Distribution   In the Sahel region and in southern Africa.

Habitat   Lowland areas and savanna, never far from water.

Behavior   The oribi is active both day and night, but it remains concealed in vegetation during the hottest hours of the day. It lives singly, in pairs, or in small groups of up to 6 individuals of both sexes, and moves swiftly, with leaps and quick sprints. It feeds on grass and must drink water regularly. When in flight it makes a specific movement called "stotting," which consists of jumping into the air with all four legs held stiff. After a gestation of about 210 days, a single young is born.

403 RAPHICERUS CAMPESTRIS
Steenbok, steinbok

Classification   Order Artiodactyla, Family Bovidae.
Description   The coat is a uniform reddish color, sometimes turning grayish with a light silvery sheen. The delicate appearance of this slightly built neotragine is accentuated by the long legs and thin neck. The ears are long and broad, and the tail only a short stump. The horns, present only in the male, curve slightly forward and average 13 cm (5 in). Length of head and body 70–85 cm (28–34 in); shoulder height about 56 cm (22 in); weight up to 16 kg (35 lb); male sometimes lighter than female.
Distribution   Southern Africa and part of East Africa.
Habitat   Open plains and lightly wooded savanna.

Behavior   The steenbok is active both day and night, constantly moving in search of food. It feeds on many plant species, eating grass, tubers, leaves, and fruit. It can go for long periods without drinking. It is found in lowland habitats, and never ventures into hilly areas. It is said sometimes to take refuge in the old burrows of aardvarks. It is generally solitary and is seen only briefly in pairs during the short mating season. Gestation lasts about 7 months, and 1 young is born.
Note   The subfamily Neotraginae (**401–406**) comprises 14 species of small African antelope.

404 NEOTRAGUS PYGMAEUS
Royal antelope

Classification   Order Artiodactyla, Family Bovidae.
Description   This is one of the smallest of the African ungulates, no larger than a rabbit. The upper body is pale brown, becoming darker on the head and flanks; the underparts are white. On the neck there is a red collar which interrupts the white color of the throat. The longish tail is white on the lower half and at the tip, and the upper half is reddish. The horns are very small, no more than 2.5 cm (1 in) long, and grown only by the male. Length of head and body 50–62 cm (20–24.8 in); shoulder height 25–30 cm (10–12 in); weight 3–4 kg (7–9 lb).
Distribution   Western Africa, from Guinea to the Ivory Coast.
Habitat   Dense forest.

Behavior   This extremely shy, nocturnal animal is very difficult to observe because of its diminutive size and habitat. Little is known about its life history. It lives either alone or in pairs, and feeds on leaves and fruit; it frequently finds its way into peanut plantations. It moves very swiftly, and can jump up to 9 feet.

405 MADOQUA SALTIANA
Salt's dik-dik

Classification   Order Artiodactyla, Family Bovidae.

Description   One distinctive feature of this neotragine is that the hind legs are considerably longer than the front legs. The neck and back are usually gray and the flanks tend to reddish (the extent of this reddish color varies considerably over the geographic range of the species). On the forehead a tuft of erectile hairs forms a crest which partly covers the small horns, about 5 cm (2 in) long. Each eye is surrounded by a conspicuous white ring and in front of this there is a hairless glandular area. Length of head and body 50–70 cm (20–28 in); shoulder height 36–41 cm (14–16 in); weight 2.7–3.6 kg (6–8 lb).

Distribution   Ethiopia, Somalia, and northern Kenya.

Habitat   Scrub and wooded savanna.

Behavior   This dik-dik is active at night or at dusk and is very shy, fleeing at the slightest sign of danger. It is solitary and lives in well-defined, small territories. It feeds on leaves and shoots, particularly those of acacia trees. It is named after the sound it emits, which resembles that of a bird. It is difficult to observe, even where numerous.

406 MADOQUA KIRKI
Kirk's dik-dik

Classification   Order Artiodactyla, Family Bovidae.

Description   The coat is gray on the back, changing to pale beige underneath. As in other dik-diks, the snout is elongated to form a small proboscis. The eyes are surrounded by white. Small horns about 6 cm (2.4 in) long, grow on the forehead of the male and are surrounded by a tuft of erectile hairs. Length of head and body 52–65 cm (20.8–26 in); shoulder height 36–41 cm (14.4–16.4 in); weight 4.5–5.5 kg (10 lb).

Distribution   Kenya and Tanzania; southwest Africa and Angola.

Habitat   Savanna and scrub.

Behavior   This dik-dik shows considerable differences in size and coloration between the northern and southern parts of its geographic range. Like other dik-diks, this species is able to survive for long periods without water. It feeds on tubers and roots, which it digs out of the ground. When startled, it runs in a zigzag pattern, with frequent leaps and bounds. Another distinctive characteristic of dik-diks is that they deposit their droppings in certain selected places, forming large piles of feces. It lives in pairs, and is active both at night and during the day. After about a 6-month gestation, 1 young is born, which matures rapidly.

407 ANTILOPE CERVICAPRA
Blackbuck

Classification   Order Artiodactyla, Family Bovidae.

Description   The young and the females have a tawny coat, while adult males are much darker on the back and halfway down the flanks, and are white on the underside. The rings around the eyes, and the front part of the face, are also white. Only the males have horns, which are 50–60 cm (20–24 in) long and twisted in tight spirals. Length of head and body 100–150 cm (40–60 in); shoulder height 70–80 cm (28–32 in); weight about 38 kg (84 lb).

Distribution   India.

Habitat   Dry woodland and arid clearings.

Behavior   The diurnal blackbuck lives in herds of 15–50. Each herd is led by an adult male. When the younger males in the herd become adult, they are driven away, and have to win their own harems of females, after bitter duels. In the mating season (February–March) the male marks its territory by rubbing its facial glands against tree trunks and branches. The courtship procedures are distinctive; the male approaches the female with his nose stretched upward and forward. After a gestation of about 180 days, 1 or 2 young are born.

Note   This antelope has been the victim of ruthless hunting, and its numbers have been drastically reduced as a result. It is very rare outside game reserves.

---

408 AEPYCEROS MELAMPUS
Impala

Classification   Order Artiodactyla, Family Bovidae.

Description   This graceful antelope has a glossy, reddish brown coat which varies geographically. The chin, throat, rump, and underside of the body are white. There is a conspicuous black line on the hind part of the thighs and black tufts on the heels of the hind legs. The tail is fairly long and has a white tuft at the end. The slender horns, present only in the male, are 50–75 cm (20–30 in) long and form an S-shaped curve. Length of head and body 1.1–1.5 m (3.6–5 ft); shoulder height 77–100 cm (33–39 in); weight up to 80 kg (176 lb); female somewhat smaller.

Distribution   Africa south of the Equator, except forests.

Habitat   Wooded savanna.

Behavior   Impalas live in herds of about 15–25 females and young with a dominant adult male. Young males form herds by themselves. During the dry months, males and females gather into large herds of up to several hunded individuals. When in flight, it makes remarkable leaps, up to 30 feet, often for no apparent reason. It feeds mainly on leaves and twigs of acacia trees, bushes, fruits, and short grass. Generally dependent on water, it can survive several days on dew. It is active both night and day. The main predators of impalas are leopards, cheetahs, and wild dogs. Gestation lasts about 171 days, after which 1 young (rarely 2) is born.

409 LITOCRANIUS WALLERI
Gerenuk

Classification   Order Artiodactyla, Family Bovidae.

Description   The most obvious feature of the gerenuk is its very long, slender neck; it also has long, slender legs. The general color is reddish brown; darker on the back and lighter on the flank. There is a line separating the color of the flanks from the white underside. The eyes have a white rim around them. The tail is short, broad at the base, and ends in a black tuft. The horns, present only in the male, are stout and noticeably ringed; they average 35 cm (14 in) long. Length of head and body about 1.5 m (5 ft); shoulder height about 1 m (3.3 ft); weight up to 50 kg (110 lb).

Distribution   Ethiopia, Somalia, and Kenya.

Habitat   Scrub, and sometimes desert.

Behavior   The diurnal gerenuk travels singly, in pairs, or in small groups of 5 or 6 individuals. It is well adapted to arid environments and rarely needs to drink; instead, it extracts water from the vegetation it eats, mainly the leaves and tender shoots of bushes and small trees. It can stand upright on its hind legs, with its forelegs resting on the tree trunk, and using its long neck, reach high branches. When in flight, it runs with its head held forward and at the same level as its body.

Note   Entries **407–413** are all members of the subfamily Antilopinae, which comprises 21 species.

410 GAZELLA THOMSONI
Thomson's gazelle

Classification   Order Artiodactyla, Family Bovidae.

Description   The yellow-ochre of the back is interrupted on the flanks by a black band, below which begins the white of the underside. The eyes are rimmed with a white line which then extends to the nose. The rear of the hindquarters is white, edged by a vertical black line. The tail is completely black. The horns are strongly ridged, curved backward, slightly divergent, and about 30 cm (12 in) long. The female's horns are very small. Length of head and body about 110 cm (44 in); shoulder height about 66 cm (26 in); weight 18–27 kg (40–60 lb).

Distribution   Sudan, Kenya, and Tanzania.

Habitat   Open plains and grasslands.

Behavior   This gazelle is the most common gazelle in East Africa. It is most active at dawn and sundown, preferring to rest in the hottest part of the day. It lives in herds of 5–60 females and young, with a single adult male, but the structure of these herds is loose and varies from hour to hour. It feeds on grass, and to a lesser extent, on leaves and shoots. When alarmed, it has a characteristic leap called "stotting," in which it keeps all four legs and head stiff and it springs up and down in a wooden manner. Thomson's gazelle is relatively silent, and has well-developed senses of sight and smell. It is preyed on by most of the large carnivores. Once or twice a year, after a 5–6 month gestation, a single young is born.

411 GAZELLA DAMA
Addra, or dama, gazelle

Classification Order Artiodactyla, Family Bovidae.

Description The head is white, and the neck and most of the back and flanks are uniform reddish or chestnut. The hindquarters and underside of the body are white. There is considerable variation in color both from individual to individual, and among the various geographical races. The tail is short and white, with a black tip. The horns are about 35 cm (14 in) in length; the female has very small horns. Length of head and body 90–170 cm (36–68 in); shoulder height 90–100 cm (35–43 in); weight up to 73 kg (160 lb).

Distribution Saharan Africa.

Habitat Desert, to the edge of the Sahel.

Behavior There was a time when this diurnal gazelle could be seen in herds numbering as many as 500. Presently, the average number per herd is 15–20 animals. This reduction in numbers resulted from poaching. The addra gazelle makes long journeys from desert areas to the Sahel region after the light rainfalls which allow the vegetation to grow. It feeds on dry, bushy plants and grasses and needs more water than some of its desert relatives, although it can withstand fairly long periods of drought. It is often found in association with other species of gazelle.

412 ANTIDORCAS MARSUPIALIS
Springbok, springbuck

Classification Order Artiodactyla, Family Bovidae.

Description The head is white with a brown band through the eyes which runs from the cheeks to the tip of the nose. The overall coloring is reddish brown with a darker strip which separates the back from the white underside. On the top of the hindquarters there is a fold of skin which is evident when the springbok is excited or alarmed; in such moments a conspicuous crest of long, bristly, white hairs appears. The horns are relatively short, powerful, markedly ringed, and average 36 cm (14 in) long. The female's horns are lighter and shorter. Length of head and body 1.2–1.5 m (4–5 ft); shoulder height 73–87 cm (29–34 in); weight 32–36 kg (70–80 lb).

Distribution Southern Africa.

Habitat Open dry plains.

Behavior This gregarious antelope lives in mixed groups which split, during the breeding season, into separate herds of females and young males; many adult males remain alone. Huge herds of springboks used to make impressive migratory journeys, following the seasonal food supply, and damaging the country as they passed through, before their numbers were drastically reduced. In some parts of the range, these migrations still occur. It feeds on grass, leaves and shoots, and can go for long periods without water. They mate in May; about 6 months later a single young is born.

413 SAIGA TATARICA
Saiga antelope

Classification Order Artiodactyla, Family Bovidae.
Description The dense coat is much shorter in summer than in winter. The head is large and the nose forms a short, soft, supple proboscis hanging above the mouth. The body is robust and the legs relatively short and slender. The horns of the male are 28–30 cm (11–12 in) long, lyre-shaped, and light-colored. Length of head and body 95–135 cm (37.4–53 in); shoulder height 75–80 cm (30–32 in); weight 40–70 kg (88–154 lb).
Distribution Russia and Kazakhstan.

Habitat Saline, muddy steppe.
Behavior The saiga feeds on grasses. In summer, during the hottest part of the day, it rests, and does not become active until dusk. In winter, it is active all day as well. It lives in herds of up to 30–40 individuals, in which there is no hierarchic structure. It is only in the mating season that the males lead harems of 5–15 females. After mating, the adult males form small groups of 5–10 individuals, while the others return to the larger herds. Females in heat, pregnant females, and females that have given birth join together in separate groups. Gestation lasts 5 months, after which (around May) the female gives birth to 2 young. These nurse for about 4 months. The young females become sexually mature at 7–8 months, the young males at about 2 years of age.

---

414 NEMORHAEDUS GORAL
Common goral

Classification Order Artiodactyla, Family Bovidae.
Description The gray-brown coat develops a thick shaggy wool in winter. Both sexes have short, pointed horns about 15 cm (6 in) long. The legs are slender. Length of head and body 95–130 cm (38–52 in); shoulder height 55–75 cm (22–30 in); weight 25–35 kg (55–80 lb).
Distribution The Himalayas, China, and Korea.
Habitat Mountainous regions at an altitude of 3300–13,500 feet.

Behavior This extremely nimble creature can move at high speed in inaccessible terrain. It lives in family groups made up of about half a dozen individuals. The males are solitary, except in the mating season (September–October). During the day the goral hides among rocks; it grazes on plants, grass, leaves, small branches, and acorns, early in the morning and in the evening. If faced with danger it "freezes" and then suddenly runs if the danger gets too close. Gestation lasts about 6 months, after which the female delivers a single calf.
Note The last 13 entries (**414–426**) are all members of the subfamily Caprinae, which comprises 27 species worldwide.

415 CAPRICORNIS SUMATRAENSIS
Mainland serow

Classification   Order Artiodactyla, Family Bovidae.
Description   The guard hairs of the coat are hispid and cover the underfur to varying degrees. A mane runs from the horns to the withers. The horns, present only in males, are light-colored, short (about 15 cm/6 in), and curve slightly backward. The serow has large preorbital glands which produce a strong-smelling substance which is used for marking territory. Length of head and body up to 1.8 m (5.9 ft); shoulder height to 1 m (3.3 ft); weight to 140 kg (315 lb).
Distribution   From northern India to southern China, and throughout the Indochinese peninsula and Sumatra.
Habitat   Forest and scrub, including tropical and montane environments.
Behavior   The serow lives alone or in small groups. It is attached to its territory, which usually covers just a few miles square, and does not move far when feeding. It grazes on grass and also eats shoots and leaves. It is most active at dawn and dusk, and spends the rest of the day in thick vegetation. It has paths along which it moves, and traditional spots where it marks its territory and deposits its droppings. The gestation period lasts about 8 months and the single young is born in September–October.

416 OREAMNOS AMERICANUS
Mountain goat

Classification   Order Artiodactyla, Family Bovidae.
Description   The mountain goat has a white, woolly coat which turns yellowish in winter. The males start to shed their coat in June and continue shedding until mid-July; the females do not complete their molt until mid-August. The slightly curved horns, present in both sexes, are black. It is possible to tell the age of the mountain goat by counting the rings on the horns. The first ring forms at the age of 22–24 months, and an additional ring is then added each spring. Length of head and body 124–178 cm (50–70 in); shoulder height up to 100 cm (40 in); weight 80–140 kg (176–308 lb).
Distribution   Western Canada and western United States.
Habitat   Montane.
Behavior   The mountain goat grazes in meadows above the timberline; in winter it descends to lower altitudes. It is active from dawn to mid-morning, and then starts grazing again in the late afternoon; it is frequently active throughout the night. It lives in small flocks, but tends to be solitary in summer and autumn. In the mating season (October–December), the males rub the glands that are behind their horns against trees; they also use urine to mark their territory. The gestation period lasts for 147 days, after which the female gives birth to 1 or 2 kids. They nurse for 3–4 months, and may remain with their mother until the following year when the succeeding kids are born.

417 RUPICAPRA RUPICAPRA
Chamois

Classification Order Artiodactyla, Family Bovidae.

Description The summer coat is short and smooth; the winter coat long and dense, with soft underfur. A distinctive feature of this species is the slender, hook-shaped horns which can reach a length of 27 cm (11 in) and are present in both sexes. The ability of this animal to move about with ease among rocks in relatively inaccessible terrain is due mainly to the structure of the hooves, which have an elastic base and a hard, thin edge. Length of head and body about 1 m (40 in); shoulder height 70–80 cm (28–32 in); weight 30–60 kg (65–130 lb).

Distribution The Alps, Apennines, Pyrenees, Carpathians, and in Asia Minor.

Habitat Rocky areas, alpine pastures.

Behavior The females and young males live in usually small flocks of 5–15, while the adult males lead a solitary existence and engage in combat only to acquire a harem during the mating period. In this period the males probably become territorial, marking tree trunks and branches with the smelly secretion of the gland at the base of the horns. The duels between males are often violent clashes with resounding blows of the horns. After a gestation period of about 6 months, the female gives birth to a single kid in April–June.

---

418 BUDORCAS TAXICOLOR
Takin

Classification Order Artiodactyla, Family Bovidae.

Description The bulky-looking body is covered by a long, dense coat ranging from yellowish to grayish in different areas. The legs are short and strongly built. Both sexes have strong horns 25–30 cm (10–12 in) long which grow outward before curving backward and then upward. Length of head and body 1.7–2.2 m (5.7–7.3 ft); shoulder height 1–1.3 m (3.3–4.3 ft); weight up to 350 kg (790 lb).

Distribution The Himalayas and western China.

Habitat Montane, at an altitude of 6500–15,000 feet.

Behavior The takin lives in groups. In summer these groups become very large, numbering several hundred. In winter they split up and move to lower altitudes. It spends much time hidden in vegetation; it grazes early in the morning and in the evening. The female gives birth to a single young every other year. The young takin is nursed for about 9 months, although it joins the herd soon after it is born.

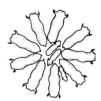

419 OVIBOS MOSCHATUS
Musk ox

Classification   Order Artiodactyla, Family Bovidae.
Description   The body is covered with a long, dense coat of dark brown guard hairs over paler underfur. It protects the musk ox from the dry, cold conditions of the Arctic regions. Both sexes have horns about 60–70 cm (24–28 in) long; the base of the horns is flat, covering the forehead and running down the sides of the head. The tips of the horns curve upward. The legs are short and strongly built, with large hooves. Length of head and body 1.8–2.5 m (6–8.2 ft); shoulder height 1.4–1.5 m (4.6–5 ft); weight 200–300 kg (450–675 lb).
Distribution   From northern Canada to western Greenland.
Habitat   Arctic tundra.

Behavior   The diurnal musk ox lives in herds led by one or more dominant males. During the mating season (which peaks in August) the males fight furiously to acquire and keep a harem. During this period, the males emit a distinctive smell of musk (hence its name). In summer, it feeds on birch and dwarf willow leaves; in winter, it digs with its hooves into the snow mantle in search of mosses, lichens, and roots. The gestation period lasts 8–9 months, after which a single calf is born (twins rarely). Females become sexually mature at about 3.5 years, males at about 5 years. The main enemy of the musk ox is the Arctic wolf. In defense, a circle is formed with the females and young in the center and the males on the outside facing outward. When the wolf approaches, the musk oxen drive it away with blows of their horns.

420 HEMITRAGUS JEMLAHICUS
Himalayan tahr

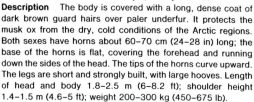

Classification   Order Artiodactyla, Family Bovidae.
Description   It is covered with a dense, woolly coat with soft underfur. The horns grow in a curve upward and backward and may reach 45 cm (18 in) in the male; less in the female. The eyes are large; the ears small and pointed. There are no facial or inguinal glands, but the tail contains a large number of glands which secrete a very strong-smelling substance. Length of head and body 1.3–1.7 m (4.2–5.6 ft); shoulder height 60–100 cm (24–40 in); weight 85–105 kg (187–231 lb).
Distribution   The Himalayas, southern India and southeastern Arabia.
Habitat   Varied: the Arabian subspecies lives in rocky, desert areas; the other three subspecies live in montane woodland.

Behavior   Males, and females with their young, live in separate groups which join in the mating season. It grazes in the evening and in the early morning. The rest of the day it lies hidden in vegetation. The gestation period lasts 180–242 days and the females generally give birth to a single kid, which is suckled for about 6 months. Sexual maturity is reached at an age of about 18 months.

421 CAPRA IBEX
Ibex

Classification   Order Artiodactyla, Family Bovidae.

Description   The coat is short but not shaggy; males have a beard at the chin. The ram has long, scimitar-shaped horns with knotty protuberances on the front. The horns may reach 90 cm (36 in). The ewe's horns are thinner and curve slightly backward; they reach a maximum length of 38 cm (15 in). Length of head and body up to 1.5 m (5 ft); shoulder height 65–105 cm (26–42 in); weight 75–120 kg (170–270 lb); females smaller.

Distribution   The Alps and the Iberian peninsula, central Asia, the Caucasus, Arabia, and North Africa.

Habitat   Montane pastures, at an altitude of 7500–11,500 feet.

Behavior   The diurnal ibex lives in separate groups, males in one, females and young in another. In the mating season (December–January), there are bitter combats between males for supremacy of the flock. After a gestation period of 150–180 days, a single young is born.

Note   The ibex was formerly subjected to intensive hunting because of the therapeutic properties attributed to various parts of its body. Its number has diminished in most of the range, but over 3000 now live in the Gran Paradiso National Park, established in the Italian Alps in 1922 for its protection. About 5000 others now live in other parts of the Alps as well.

---

422 CAPRA FALCONERI
Markhor

Classification   Order Artiodactyla, Family Bovidae.

Description   The coat is short and smooth in summer and longer in winter; it is heavier in the northern part of its range. The males have a long beard on the chin and long hair on the throat, chest, and shanks; females have smaller fringes of long hair. The horns, which are present in both sexes, are spiral shaped, and are much smaller in the female. Length of head and body 161–168 cm (64–67 in), tail 8–14 cm (3.2–5.6 in); weight 80–110 kg (176–242 lb); females smaller than males.

Distribution   Afghanistan and the western Himalayas.

Habitat   Montane regions at medium and high altitudes.

Behavior   Although one of the largest of the Caprinae, or wild goat, this usually solitary, nimble creature climbs and jumps over rocky terrain with ease. In the winter months it descends to lower altitudes to avoid extreme cold. Mating occurs in the winter. In summer the females gather in small groups which include the newborn young. Gestation lasts for 5.5 months; then the female delivers 1 or 2 kids. The numbers of this diurnal species have been considerably reduced because of hunting, and because of epidemics transmitted to them by domestic animals.

423 PSEUDOIS NAYAUR
Bharal, blue sheep

Classification   Order Artiodactyla, Family Bovidae.
Description   The coat is dense, short, and slate gray; the underparts, backs of legs, and underside of tail are white. The horns, which are present in both males and females, are set quite close together at the base, then turn sideways and curve backward. In the ram they may reach 80 cm (32 in); the ewe's horns never exceed 20 cm (8 in). The eyes are large; the ears small and pointed. Length of head and body 1.1–1.7 cm (3.6–5.6 ft); shoulder height 70–80 cm (28–32 in); weight 25–80 kg (55–180 lb).

Distribution   The three subspecies are distributed in the Himalayas and in China in the region of Sichuan.
Habitat   Montane regions at an altitude of 10,000–18,500 feet.
Behavior   The bharal lives in small groups and is active in the morning and evening. It feeds on grass, tubers, and lichens. It moves nimbly in rocky terrain and if in danger, stands motionless, camouflaged by its color, which blends with that of the rock. Mating occurs in October–November and the young are born in May–June. The ewe gives birth to a single lamb, which nurses for about 6 months.

---

424 AMMOTRAGUS LERVIA
Barbary sheep, aoudad

Classification   Order Artiodactyla, Family Bovidae.
Description   The color is generally uniform pale brown, sometimes lighter and tending to beige. The coat is dense and of average length, with a long fringe of soft and very light-colored hairs on the throat, chest, and front legs. This fringe seems to completely envelop the front legs. The tail is long and also fringed. The horns are thick and up to 84 cm (33 in) long in males. The females have a smaller fringe and smaller horns. Length of head and body up to 1.6 m (5.3 ft); shoulder height to 196 cm (77 in); weight to 145 kg (319 lb); females much smaller.

Distribution   Isolated pockets in northern Africa.
Habitat   Montane regions of the Sahara.
Behavior   The color of the Barbary sheep blends perfectly with the rocks where it lives. In the evening, it climbs down to the sparsely vegetated valley floor to feed. It lives in family groups led by a large male; other adult males are excluded. Old males and pregnant females are solitary. It moves among rocks and overhangs with great agility, leaping impressive lengths. Mating usually occurs in the autumn, but may occur at other times. Gestation lasts 22–23 weeks, after which 1 or 2 young are born. Twins are fairly common. The young are extremely agile at birth. They nurse for about 6 months and reach sexual maturity at about 1.5 years of age.

425 OVIS CANADENSIS
American bighorn, mountain sheep

Classification   Order Artiodactyla, Family Bovidae.
Description   The pelage is relatively smooth, consisting of brittle guard hairs and gray, crimped fleece (underfur) beneath; it is tawny, darker on the flanks and yellowish white on the underside. It has a distinctive white marking on the hindquarters. The horns, which both sexes have, form a spiral at the sides of the head, and in the ram, can reach a length of 50 cm (20 in). Length of head and body about 1.8 m (5.9 ft); shoulder height about 1 m (3.3 ft); weight 130–150 kg (286–330 lb).
Distribution   Rocky Mountains.
Habitat   Montane pastures.
Behavior   The bighorn feeds on alpine grasses. It lives in large flocks in which the superiority of one male over another is decided by long, exhausting duels. Clashes between males usually occur between individuals with the same sized horns; individuals with smaller horns are considered to be of lower rank. The natural enemies of the bighorn are wolves, pumas, and coyotes. Gestation lasts 180 days; then the female gives birth to 1 or 2 young which she nurses for 5–6 months. The females reach sexual maturity in 2–3 years; the males, around 3 years.

---

426 OVIS DALLI
Dall, or white, sheep

Classification   Order Artiodactyla, Family Bovidae.
Description   The color of its smooth coat varies with the latitude at which the animal is living; it is white in the north and almost black in the southern parts of its range. The yellowish horns are larger in the ram than the ewe. The ewe has 2 teats. Length of head and body up to 1.6 m (5.3 ft); shoulder height 91–102 cm (36–41 in); weight 60–90 kg (150–205 lb).
Distribution   Alaska and northwestern Canada.
Habitat   Coastal parts of mountain ranges, always in harsh, craggy habitats.
Behavior   The behavior of this species closely resembles that of the bighorn. It normally lives in small groups of about 10 animals. In summer the sexes are separated, and it is only in the autumn that the males join the females and lambs. The males engage in fierce duels which decide the hierarchy of the flock. The rivals are often dazed by the force of the blows they receive and deliver with their horns. They breed in November–December. After a gestation of about 6 months, a single young is born; it may nurse as long as 9 months. Dall sheep feed on a large variety of plants and survive the winter by eating lichens.

GLOSSARY

Albino an animal with a hereditary anomaly, resulting in an absence of pigment in the hair, eyes and skin.

Amnios the membrane that envelops the embryo of reptiles, birds and mammals; it is filled with a fluid that immerses the embryo.

Arboreal living in trees.

Bilateral (symmetry) refers to an animal organism that can be divided by a plane into two identical parts.

Brain the part of the nervous system, well-developed in vertebrates, that is the organ of thought and neural coordination.

Browsing refers to vegetarian animals that feed on the leaves of trees and bushes, and not on grass.

Canine (teeth) the sharp teeth situated between the incisors and the premolars in carnivores.

Carnivore an animal that feeds on flesh.

Carrion a scavenging animal that feeds on the remains of the prey of other animals.

Cerebral (hemispheres) the two halves of the brain.

Cerebellum the part of the head situated in the lower rear section of the skull of vertebrates.

Cervical (vertebra) neck vertebra.

Cloaca the end of the alimentary canal where the ducts of the urinary system and the gonads meet.

Cranium the part of the skeleton that encloses the encephalon.

Cusp the sharp conical point on the cutting edge of a tooth.

Digitigrade refers to an animal that walks with only its fingers and/or toes on the ground.

Dimorphism (sexual) the presence of different features in the males and females of the same species.

Embryo an organism in the initial period of development, within the egg or the mother's womb.

Endemic typical of and exclusive to a given place.

Endocrine (gland) a ductless gland that secretes hormones.

Enzyme a catalyst that accelerates specific chemical reactions in living organisms.

Epidermis the outermost layer or layers of the body.

Evolution (convergent) a process that occurs when two systematically separate animals adapt in the same way to similar environments.

Fallopian tube the duct that links the uterus to the ovary.

Food chain (or trophic chain)   the way in which animals and plants are associated as far as food is concerned: for example, carnivorous animals feed on herbivorous animals that, in turn, feed on plants.

Fossil   the preserved evidence of creatures that lived in the past; petrified or mineralized bones, parts of plants, and even animal tracks may be conserved as fossils.

Frugivorous   feeding on fruit.

Gamete   a germinal cell that, by merging with another, gives rise to a new organism. The egg or ovum (egg cell) is the female gamete; the spermatozoon is the male gamete.

Gene   the theoretical unit that governs the transmission of hereditary characteristics in all living organisms. The genes are aligned in the chromosomes, inside the cell's nucleus.

Gonad   the gland in the reproductive apparatus in which the gametes are formed (and, in some cases, the sex hormones).

Gonadotropins   hormones that stimulate the activity of the gonads.

Grazing   feeding (of a vegetarian animal) on grasses.

Habitat   where an animal lives, i.e., its environment.

Herbivore   an animal that feeds on plants; this term embraces both browsing and grazing (cf.) animals.

Hermaphrodite   an animal (or plant) having both male and female sex organs.

Heterothermic (or poikilothermic)   an animal—also mistakenly called "cold-blooded"—whose body temperature depends on the ambient temperature.

Homoiothermic   an animal—also mistakenly known as "warm-blooded"—that controls its own body temperature by means of mechanisms within its own body.

Incisors (teeth)   the front teeth, ranging in number from none to three on each half-jaw.

Insectivore   an animal that feeds on insects.

Ischiatic (callosity)   leathery swelling found on the buttocks of many of the more evolved Old World primates.

Mandible   the lower jaw.

Maxilla   the upper jaw.

Metabolism (metabolic intensity or rate)   the speed at which the various chemical changes take place in an organism. It has to do both with the formation and degradation of the protoplasmic compounds.

Molar   the tooth situated at the rear of the upper jaw in mammals.

Natural selection   the process whereby animals most adapted to their particular environment survive the longest and thus reproduce most easily, handing down their specific features to their offspring: the survival of the fittest.

Niche (ecological)   the specific place taken up by an animal in the wild; refers to its habitat, its feeding habits, when it is active, and so on.

Omnivorous   feeding on both plants and flesh.

Opposable (thumb)   the type of thumb that is opposable to the other fingers on the same limb and is essential for all types of handhold.

Oviduct   the duct through which the eggs produced by the ovary travel outward.

Oviparous   egg-laying.

Ovoviviparous   reproducing by means of eggs, which nevertheless develop within the mother's body.

Patagium   a fold of skin which, in certain species of flying or arboreal mammals, extends between the neck, the front limbs, the hind limbs, and the tail.

Placenta   the fetal appendage typical of most of the mammals (the *eutheria* or placental mammals) which regulates the conveyance via maternal and fetal blood of all the substances necessary to the metabolic processes.

Plantigrade   refers to an animal that walks with the whole sole of the foot (or palm of the hand) on the ground.

Polymorphism   the presence of individuals that belong to the same species but have different characteristics.

Predator   an animal that feeds on other animals.

Premolar   a tooth situated immediately in front of the molars in mammals.

Retina   the nerve membrane that receives the images formed by the eye's crystalline lens.

Saprophagous   feeding on decomposing substances.

Sebaceous (gland)   a skin gland that secretes an oily substance.

Specialized   having undergone changes in the course of evolution in order to adapt to a special function or to a specific environment.

Species   a distinct group of animals that can mate and procreate fertile offspring.

Symbiosis   the association between two different species that derive mutual benefit therefrom.

Systematics   the placing of an organism in the classification of living things.

Taxonomy   branch of the natural sciences that deals with the classification of living things.

Territorial (behavior)   the defense of an area by an individual or a group of individuals against members of the same species.

Tetrapods   vertebrates with four limbs.

Tragus   a cartilaginous protuberance situated in front of the aural duct of certain mammals.

Ureter   the duct that carries urine from the kidneys to the bladder or cloaca.

Uterus   the organ in mammals that carries the fertilized egg.

Vertebrate   an animal with a backbone or spine.

Viviparous   giving birth to young that are in a state of complete development.

BIBLIOGRAPHY

Anderson, S., and J. K. Jones, Jr. (eds.). 1967. *Recent mammals of the world, a synopsis of families.* New York: Ronald Press, 453 pp.

Colbert, E. H. 1955. *Evolution of the vertebrates.* New York: John Wiley & Sons, 479 pp.

Corbet, G. B., and J. E. Hill. 1980. *A world list of mammalian species.* London: British Museum (Natural History), viii+226 pp.

Darlington, P. J. 1957. *Zoogeography: the geographical distribution of animals.* New York: John Wiley & Sons, 675 pp.

Grassé, P.-P. (ed.). 1955. *Traité de zoologie.* Paris: Masson et Cie, 17 vols.

Grzimek, B. (ed.). 1972–1975. *Grzimek's animal life encyclopedia.* New York: Van Nostrand Reinhold (English ed.), vols. 10–13, 1485 pp.

Honacki, J. H., et al. 1982. *Mammalian species of the world.* Lawrence, Kansas: Assoc. Syst. Collections, ix+694 pp.

Mammalian species. 1969–1983, nos. 1–200. American Society of mammalogists.

Murie, O. J. 1954. *A field guide to animal tracks.* Boston: Houghton Mifflin Co., 374 pp.

Romer, A. S. 1976. *Vertebrate paleontology.* 2nd ed. Chicago: Univ. Chicago Press, 687 pp.

Simpson, G. G. 1945. *The principles of classification and a classification of mammals.* Bull. Amer. Mus. Nat. Hist. 85:1–350.

Walker, E. P., et al. 1975. *Mammals of the world.* 3rd ed. (J. L. Paradiso, ed.). Baltimore: Johns Hopkins Press, 1500 pp.

Young, J. Z. 1957. *The life of mammals.* London: Oxford Univ. Press, 820 pp.

INDEX OF ENTRIES

PICTURE CREDITS